PONTIAC'S
WAR

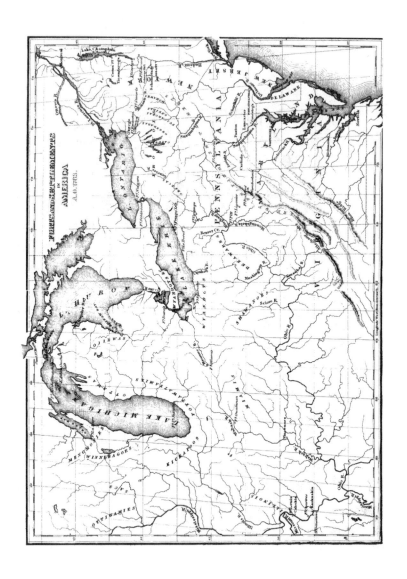

PONTIAC'S
WAR

ITS CAUSES, COURSE
AND CONSEQUENCES

RICHARD MIDDLETON

Routledge
Taylor & Francis Group
New York   London

Routledge
Taylor & Francis Group
270 Madison Avenue
New York, NY 10016

Routledge
Taylor & Francis Group
2 Park Square
Milton Park, Abingdon
Oxon OX14 4RN

© 2007 by Taylor & Francis Group, LLC
Routledge is an imprint of Taylor & Francis Group, an Informa business

Printed in the United States of America on acid-free paper
10 9 8 7 6 5 4 3 2 1

International Standard Book Number-13: 978-0-415-97913-9 (Softcover) 978-0-415-97914-6 (Hardcover)

Library of Congress Cataloging-in-Publication Data

Middleton, Richard, 1941-
  Pontiac's War : its causes, course and consequences / Richard Middleton.
    p. cm.
  Includes bibliographical references and index.
  ISBN 0-415-97913-7 (hardback : alk. paper) -- ISBN 0-415-97914-5 (pbk. : alk. paper)
    1. Pontiac's Conspiracy, 1763-1765. 2. Pontiac, Ottawa Chief, d. 1769. 3. Ottawa Indians--Wars. 4. United States--History--Colonial period, ca. 1600-1775. I. Title.

E83.76.M54 2007
973.2'7--dc22   2006036676

Visit the Taylor & Francis Web site at
http://www.taylorandfrancis.com

and the Routledge Web site at
http://www.routledge.com

War is the Continuation of Policy by other Means.

Karl von Clausewitz

We know them now to be a very jealous people, and to have the highest notions of liberty.

George Croghan to the Board of Trade

Brothers, I am glad to hear what you have said ... as peace is much better than war.

Henry Bouquet to the Delaware

Contents

Preface

Pontiac's War was one of the most successful campaigns fought by the Indian peoples of eastern North America in three centuries of European contact. In the first few weeks of the conflict, every British fort west of the Allegheny Mountains was captured with the exception of Detroit, Fort Pitt, and Niagara. As a result the British had to mount two major offensives in 1764 to regain the initiative. Even then Pontiac and a number of his allies remained in arms, determined to oppose the occupation of the Illinois, Wabash, and western Great Lakes. The British, stretched by their imperial commitments, had to resort to diplomacy to assert even nominal authority over these territories. The result was a restoration of the Covenant Chain of Friendship in a spirit of mutual forgiveness. Such an outcome was almost unique in the annals of Indian and European American conflict.

Although there have been several books on the subject in recent years, none provides a balanced account of the conflict itself. William R. Nester, *Haughty Conquerors: Amherst and the Great Indian Uprising of 1763* (2000), is mainly concerned with the responsibility of British Commander-in-Chief Jeffery Amherst for provoking an unnecessary conflict. Gregory Evans Dowd, *War under Heaven: Pontiac, the Indian Nations and the British Empire* (2002), offers a study of Indian culture rather than an account of the war itself while David Dixon, in his book *Never Come to Peace Again: Pontiac's Uprising and the Fate of the British Empire in North America* (2005), concentrates on western Pennsylvania and the Ohio Valley; he is also more concerned with the impact of the war on the frontier and its importance for an understanding of the American Revolution. Finally, Colin G. Calloway, *The Scratch of a Pen: 1763 and the Transformation of North America* (2006) deals with the frontier peoples throughout eastern North America, many of whom were not affected by Pontiac's War.

This book accordingly sets out to identify more precisely the contributions of the various combatants with a view to establishing "who did what, when, where, and why." Although the British and American colonial sides of the story have been relatively well covered, those of the Native American participants and the French inhabitants have not, in part because of a lack of source material. Hence this book is an attempt (where possible) to reevaluate the role of the different Indian nations, many of whom have been inadequately assessed, notably the Seneca and northern Ojibwa.

Since Francis Parkman's magisterial *The Conspiracy of Pontiac and the Indian War after the Conquest of Canada* (1851), historians have ascribed the success of the Indians mainly to chance, asserting that each nation acted in copycat fashion, responding to events rather than dictating them. But, as this book suggests, the Indians operated in a more coordinated fashion than is commonly supposed, despite the fragmented nature of their political and social structures. Most importantly the conflict with the British Empire produced a leader in Pontiac, who orchestrated a successful resistance for almost three campaigns. Of course, other chiefs played important roles, as did sections of the French community. Nevertheless the contribution of Pontiac seemed sufficiently important to keep his name in the title of this book.

Writing Native American history about events long ago poses certain problems of evidence. The native peoples had only an oral culture for recording events. Hence, all the material for this study has had to come from European and European American documents. Postmodernists argue that these are irredeemably biased and therefore worthless. However, no account would be possible without them, since archeological evidence is of little use for this kind of study. The same is true of the technique of "upstreaming." Present-day tribal members may help interpret the customs and language of their eighteenth-century ancestors. But no individual can remember (or ever have known) the details of events two hundred and fifty years ago. The problem of tainted evidence, in any case, is not as bad as it is often portrayed. European Americans in general were too convinced of their own moral and material superiority to falsify the records of their dealings with the native peoples, except in land matters where fraud was a powerful motive.

For clarity I refer to the inhabitants of Canada as Canadians or French Canadians to distinguish them from the officials and officers of metropolitan France. Similarly I use the term "British" for imperial officials and the personnel of the regular army to avoid the ambiguous term "English," which strictly speaking should be reserved for the inhabitants of England. However, since that term often appears in contemporary documents, I have necessarily had to retain it in passages of quoted text. Otherwise the English-speaking inhabitants are referred to as European Americans, colonists, or provincials. For simplicity I also use the term "Algonquian" when referring collectively to those nations that spoke an Algonquian language. Finally I include the Miami (sometimes referred to as the Twightwee) when mentioning the Wabash peoples, since their location near the head of the Maumee River made them close neighbors of the Kickapoo, Wea, and Piankashaw, to whom they were also related.

Wherever possible I have cited printed copies of documents rather than manuscript versions for reader accessibility. I have also attempted to keep one reference to each point, unless more than one source is involved, in which case they have been grouped together. Finally, for readability, I have partially modernized the spellings and punctuation of the quoted material.

Extracts from this book have already appeared in an article entitled "Pontiac: Local Warrior or Pan Indian Leader?", *Michigan Historical Review*, volume 32, number 2, Fall 2006, 1–32. I am accordingly indebted to the editors and publishers of that journal for permission to reproduce this material.

Acknowledgments

This project began while I was on study leave from Queen's University, Belfast. Normally one would acknowledge the value of this privilege. However, British universities are so obsessed with research and publication as to make this a somewhat dubious benefit. Like the servant in the parable of the talents, woe to the scholar who returns from leave without his work in publishable form. Fortunately, early retirement has enabled me to complete this book in more congenial circumstances.

Inevitably I have incurred obligations to numerous persons while doing my research. I should especially like to thank Simon Davies of Queen's University French Department for help in the translation of several important documents relating to Louisiana and the Illinois. I am also indebted to Shirley Reid for reading various drafts and making pertinent comment. In addition, I owe a special thanks to the staff of the William L. Clements Library at the University of Michigan, notably the director John Dann, and curators Brian Dunnigan and Barbara DeWolfe, for their assistance and hospitality while I researched this book.

Other institutions that gave me valuable help include the American Antiquarian Society, the Bodleian Library Oxford, the British Library, the Burton Collection in the Detroit Public Library, the University of London's Institute of Historical Research, the Kentish Record Office, the Library Company of Philadelphia, the Library of Congress, the National Archives of Great Britain (formerly known as the Public Record Office), the Newberry Library, Nottingham University Library, the Pennsylvania Historical Society, the National Library of Wales, and the Library of Queen's University Belfast. Finally, I should like to thank the publisher, Routledge, for accepting this work, Kimberly Guinta for directing it, and the project editor, Sylvia Wood, for making it presentable.

Richard Middleton

Institute of Historical Research, London

List of Abbreviations

AP: Amherst Papers in the William L. Clements Library, Ann Arbor, Michigan

BHC: Burton Historical Collection, Detroit Public Library

BP: *The Papers of Henry Bouquet*, edited by Donald H. Kent, Louis Waddell, and Autumn L. Leonard, 6 vols. (Harrisburg, Pa., 1951–1994).

CAN: Canadian National Archives

CO: Colonial Office records in the National Archives of Great Britain, London

GP: Gage Papers in the William L. Clements Library, Ann Arbor, Michigan

JP: *The Papers of Sir William Johnson*, edited by James Sullivan et al., 14 vols. (Albany, N.Y., 1921–1965)

MVHR: *Mississippi Valley Historical Review* [from 1964 the *Journal of American History*]

NA: National Archives of Great Britain (formerly the Public Records Office [PRO]), London

NL: Newberry Library, Chicago

NYCD: New York, *Documents relating to the Colonial History of the State of New York*, edited by Edmund B. O'Callaghan, 15 vols. (Albany, N.Y., 1853–1887)

PA: Pennsylvania Archives, Harrisburg

PCR: Pennsylvania Colonial Records (council minutes), Philadelphia

PHS: Pennsylvania Historical Society, Philadelphia

PMHB: *Pennsylvania Magazine of History and Biography*

WCL: William L. Clements Library, Ann Arbor, Michigan

WMQ: *William and Mary Quarterly*

WO/34: War Office Records in the National Archives of Great Britain (formerly the Public Records Office [PRO]), London, Class 34, Amherst Papers

Introduction
The Middle Ground of Onontio

An Entente Cordiale, 1700–1755

Early on the morning of 7 September 1760, Colonel Louis-Antoine de Bougainville, a French army officer, left Montreal for the camp of General Sir Jeffery Amherst, the British commander-in-chief, who had arrived the previous afternoon to the west of the city with his invading army. Bougainville's mission was to seek a ceasefire pending news of peace in Europe, of which there were rumors. Even at this late stage, the Marquis de Vaudreuil, the French governor of Canada, still hoped to prevent the total loss of his beloved colony. Amherst, however, rejected the suggestion, replying adamantly, "I have come to take Canada and I will take nothing less."[1] He made just one concession: Vaudreuil might submit his thoughts about a surrender in writing, providing he presented his ideas by midday. Confronted by overwhelming odds, Vaudreuil had little choice but to comply, which he did in the form of fifty-one articles. Most concerned the welfare of the Canadian population, the rights of the Catholic Church, and the treatment of the French army and militia. But among them were several provisions regarding the native inhabitants of Canada, the most prominent being Article 40 guaranteeing the Indians their lands, freedom of religion, and right to missionaries.[2]

The concern of Vaudreuil for the native inhabitants reflected the role which many of them had played in the defense of Canada. Some of those nations present in the vicinity of Montreal had been allied to the French since Samuel de Champlain's arrival and the founding of Quebec in 1608, when they had sought his help against the Iroquois Confederacy, who were attempting to conquer much of eastern North America. The French had readily responded, seeing an alliance with the Huron peoples of the St. Lawrence Valley as the best means of establishing their own presence. As the seventeenth century progressed, alliances were also made with the Algonquian-speaking peoples of the Great Lakes region, notably the Ottawa, Ojibwa (often called the Chippewa), and Potawatomi. They were wise to do so since the Iroquois Confederacy, comprising the five nations of the Mohawk, Oneida, Onondaga, Cayuga, and Seneca, had by no means given up their grand design. Indeed, such was their onslaught after 1650 that most of the Algonquian nations were driven to the periphery of the Great Lakes, while the Huron-Erie and Neutral peoples effectively disappeared. Not until the last years of the century were the French and their allies able to gain the upper hand, following several bloody invasions of the Iroquois homeland. Although the Iroquois Five Nations finally made peace with their neighbors in 1701, the remaining Huron and the Algonquian-speaking Great Lakes nations remained closely allied to the French.

However, the relationship between the French and their Indian allies was not just a military one. Economic ties were also strong, based on a shared interest in the fur trade. The upper St. Lawrence Valley and Great Lakes region had been rich in furs, especially beaver, which were highly valued in European markets. During the seventeenth century, the Algonquian and Huron peoples brought their furs to the French at Montreal, exchanging them for European manufactures. The most popular items were firearms and ammunition, though all kinds of metal goods from iron pots to knives and axes were eagerly taken. European textiles were also popular, being more fashionable and comfortable than clothing made from animal skins. All these items became necessities for the native peoples as traditional craft skills were discarded.

Peace with the Iroquois in 1701 allowed a considerable expansion of French influence in the region. That same year, Detroit was established between Lake Huron and Lake Erie while Fort Chartres was built on the Mississippi in the Illinois country. This was followed in 1715 by Michilimackinac at the northern end of Lakes Huron and Michigan, where previously there had only been a mission settlement. Then in 1719, the desirability of a link between Canada and Fort Chartres led to the construction of Forts Miami and Ouiatanon to guard the communication between the Maumee and Wabash Rivers. But most important was the establishment in 1721 of Niagara. Prior to this, communication between Canada and the Great Lakes had been via the Ottawa River to avoid Iroquois attack. Its construction effectively completed French domination of the region and the valuable trade that went with it.[3]

These posts served a variety of purposes. They gave the French a pretended sovereignty against the claims of other European powers. Secondly, they were a place where the Indians could bring their furs and purchase French goods. In addition, some of them provided centers for missionary activity; indeed, posts like Sault Ste. Marie near the entrance to Lake Superior had been established for that purpose. Lastly, the posts offered some protection to the French and their Indian allies, though the protection was often more symbolic than real. Before 1755 almost all the western posts were trade centers rather than forts in a European sense, though this was partly to avoid antagonizing the natives. Hence Niagara comprised a large stone house surrounded by a wooden picket fence, being effective only against small arms. It rarely had more than twenty or thirty defenders. Similarly, Detroit never had a garrison of more than twenty, while Miami, St. Joseph, and Ouiatanon usually had no more than an officer and six men. The only exception was Fort Chartres on the Mississippi, where two companies were usually stationed. This fort was also unique in being built of stone according to the best European designs.[4]

The French usually provided a smith and an interpreter at each post, both of whom were vital for maintaining Indian friendship. The smith could repair weapons and tools while the interpreters helped prevent misunderstandings. The latter were usually chosen from persons of mixed descent. The lack of Frenchwomen on the frontier meant that many traders and even soldiers took Indian wives, resulting in offspring who were comfortable with the language and culture of both races. Such was the case of Charles Langlade, whose father was a prominent trader at Michilimackinac and whose mother was the daughter of an Ottawa chief.[5] Another notable Indian French dynasty was that of Thomas Joncaire, whose two sons, Philip and Daniel, lived with the Seneca as youngsters, developing both familial and economic ties.[6]

Though the trade was organized around the posts, it was by no means uniformly administered, since the French had three kinds of establishment. The first category was the so-called posts of trade, which were sold to the highest bidder for a fixed number of years. There were eleven such monopolies, among them Sault Ste. Marie, La Baye, and St. Joseph. The second was the so-called free posts of Michilimackinac, Detroit, Miami, and Ouiatanon, which were open to anyone who bought a license. Finally, there were the five royal posts of Niagara, Cadaraqui, Toronto, Presque Isle, and Fort Duquesne, where the king's own officials conducted the business, allegedly for the benefit of the Crown.[7] Since much of the trade was conducted under the watchful eye of French officialdom, it seemingly provided a well-regulated structure that protected the Indians from extortion while bringing profit to the Crown. In reality the system never worked that well, since the traders and officials often colluded against the Indians. Even more importantly, a considerable number of freelance operators, known as the *coureurs de bois*, constantly roamed the forests in defiance of the rules. As the governor of Louisiana, Louis Kerlérec, commented in December 1754, the *coureurs* not only undermined the legitimate trade, but often cheated their Indian customers as well, creating disputes which led to conflict. Over the years numerous ordinances had been passed against such trafficking, but not even the threat of death had curbed these intrepid entrepreneurs.[8]

Nevertheless the system worked sufficiently well for the Indians of the Great Lakes and St. Lawrence Valley to continue their attachment to the French. Indeed, many of those who had fought against the Iroquois during the seventeenth century continued living near their French allies. This was especially true at Detroit, where the Algonquian Ottawa and Potawatomi, and the Huron-Wyandot (Huron who had migrated to what is now the United States), had important settlements after the founding of that post. A similar situation existed at Michilimackinac, where the Ojibwa and Ottawa lived at the nearby missions of St. Ignace and L'Arbre Croche. Other Franco-Indian communities included the Potawatomi at St. Joseph, the Miami at Fort Miami, and the Kickapoo, Wea, and Piankashaw near Ouiatanon. But as the threat from the Iroquois declined, some nations moved away from physical proximity to the French. The Ojibwa in particular established themselves at new locations at Saginaw Bay, the Grand River, and Mississauga near Toronto. Some Detroit Huron (i.e., the Wyandot) also founded a settlement at Sandusky on the southern shore of Lake Erie. But even these more dispersed nations still looked to the French for trade and security.

After 1701 there were only two significant breakdowns in relations between the French and their Indian allies. The first occurred when the Great Lakes and Illinois nations insisted on going to war with the Fox, with whom they had long been at odds. The French would have preferred a diplomatic solution that kept the Fox within their orbit. Their Algonquian allies thought otherwise. The result was a series of wars in which the Fox were heavily defeated.[9] Then a challenge of a different kind developed in the late 1740s, when a breakaway group of Miami sought to open trade with the British colony of Pennsylvania at a new settlement called Pickawillany on the headwaters of the Great Miami River. This threatened French control of the fur trade. Accordingly, in June 1752 Langlade led a force of Great Lakes Algonquians against the dissident Miami, resulting in the death of their principal chief, La Demoiselle, and the destruction of his settlement. The dissidents were then forcibly reincorporated into the French system.[10]

The French, however, did not rely solely on the benefits of trade to maintain good relations. They also presented gifts on a regular basis. They were wise to do so. Gift giving was an essential part of Indian culture, since it was an indication of a chief's wealth and power. The more he received, the more he could give his followers, reflecting the esteem in which he was held. The most popular items were brandy, clothing, vermilion, guns, and ammunition. The system was expensive but necessary for consolidating that mutually beneficial relationship which the historian Richard White has called the "middle ground."[11] When the French attempted to reduce their distribution of gifts in 1744, following shortages on the outbreak of King George's War, angry protests occurred and a number of traders were killed. Eventually the system had to be reinstituted.[12]

In the seventeenth century, the French had relied heavily on the Catholic Church to sustain their cause. By the middle of the eighteenth century the Church's missionary zeal had faded, though a small number of Jesuits remained active. The majority of native people, therefore, were not Christian, though there were important exceptions, notably the Wyandot at Detroit and the Ottawa at L'Arbre Croche.[13] The St. Lawrence Valley also contained several mission settlements, though these were populated by refugees from the Iroquois and eastern Abenaki rather than the original seventeenth-century Huron inhabitants. The lack of apostolic zeal was probably an advantage to the French, since it meant that the native spiritual leaders did not feel threatened. The French never attempted to copy the Spanish example of forcing the

Indians to convert to Christianity. As a result, Christian and pagan lived in close proximity and relative harmony.

There was one other vital ingredient that made the "middle ground" a viable concept in the era of French predominance. This was the absence of widespread settlement. The French Crown operated tight controls on emigration to its overseas colonies in North America. Only persons of rank could apply for the privilege of organizing a seigniory, while the Catholic Church ensured that no heretics settled therein. The French peasantry, in any case, could only emigrate with the permission of their landlords. The harsh climate and poor economic prospects meant that few nobles were interested in organizing such feudal estates. The merchant bourgeoisie were equally unenthusiastic, except for those involved in the fur trade. Even after 150 years, the population along the St. Lawrence Valley between Montreal and Quebec did not contain more than fifty thousand inhabitants. This was in stark contrast to the British colonies, which by the mid-eighteenth century had over one and a half million people. The absence of settlers was a point made by a French officer in 1753. He told the Indians on the upper Ohio, "They [the English] plant all your country and drive you back so that in a little time you will have no land. It is not so with us; though we build trading houses on your land, we do not plant it."[14] This was the crucial difference between the two European powers. The Indians should take note.

THE FRENCH KING CALLS FOR HELP

Until the late 1740s, the French had shown little interest in the Ohio Valley. The tribes were scattered and the area was not especially productive in furs. However, the rapid growth of the English-speaking colonies led to a new appreciation of the strategic value of the region. If the British established themselves across the mountains on the upper Ohio, a vital link between Canada and Louisiana would be broken. British control of the Ohio would also open the floodgates to their merchants, as the Pickawillany episode demonstrated. The governor of Canada, accordingly, ordered the construction of a chain of forts in 1753 between Lake Erie and the River Ohio, comprising Presque Isle, Le Boeuf, and Venango.

These moves did not go unnoticed by the British. Initially, they hoped to check the French through the Covenant Chain of Friendship with the Iroquois, which Governor of New York Edmund Andros had first negotiated in 1677. It was accordingly decided to hold a special congress at Albany in the summer of 1754, attended by representatives from the main English-speaking provinces.[15] However, while the British talked, the French took action, expelling a party of Virginians from the Forks of the Ohio, where they had been building a fort. The French then defeated a relief force under George Washington, compelling him to make a humiliating surrender. Clearly more decisive action was required. The colonies were too important for the ministry in London to overlook the French design. Plans were accordingly made for a four-pronged attack to recover the territories claimed by the British Crown. Not only was the post at the Forks of the Ohio to be retaken, but Niagara, Crown Point on Lake Champlain, and the French fort of Beausejour on the Nova Scotia isthmus were also to be seized. To achieve these objectives, two regular regiments were to be sent from the British garrison in Ireland under the command of General Edward Braddock.[16]

The French government responded by organizing an expedition under the Marquis de Montcalm. However, his force would not arrive until several months after Braddock's. In this crisis, Governor Vaudreuil turned to France's Indian allies, just as he had done three years earlier at Pickawillany. Those solicited had little hesitation in answering the call of their "Father," "Onontio," as they called the French governor. The Wabash Kickapoo, Piankashaw, and Mascouten enlisted under Captain François-Marie de Lignery, while the Great Lakes Ottawa, Ojibwa, Potawatomi, Wyandot, and Menominee joined Langlade. Both groups then set off for the newly constructed post of Fort Duquesne at the forks of the Ohio.[17] There, to the surprise of most Europeans, they scored a decisive victory, routing a force more than twice their size. The battle appeared a triumph for Indian warfare. As the Virginian, Adam Stephen, graphically observed, the enemy crept up "hunting us as they would do a herd of buffaloes or deer." "The British troops were thunderstruck to feel the effects of a heavy fire and see no enemy. They threw away their fire in the most indiscreet manner, and shamefully turned their backs on a few savages and Canadians." After the battle Stephen concluded, "You might as well send a cow in pursuit of a hare as an English soldier loaded in his way." What was required was a method of warfare similar to that of the Canadians, who were lightly dressed, could shoot accurately, and ran swiftly like the Indians.[18]

Most of the Ottawa, Ojibwa, Potawatomi, and Wyandot returned home after the battle to enjoy the spoils of war, as was their custom. Fortunately, victory brought new allies to the French cause, especially in the Ohio Valley. Among the most important nations in upper Ohio at this time was the Delaware, who had moved there after being displaced by the advancing tide of white settlement in Pennsylvania. The Delaware had originally lived on the river of that name, where they welcomed the English under William Penn, or "Miquon,"* as they called him. Penn and his Quaker co-religionists were almost unique among English-speaking peoples in believing that the Indians were their equals in the sight of God. Equitable treaties had accordingly been signed for the purchase of land in what was effectively an English version of the "middle ground." Unfortunately, Penn's sons, Thomas and John, subsequently preferred profit to harmony with their Indian neighbors. They

---

* The Iroquois word for William Penn was "Onas." Both terms meant a quill or quill pen, a reference to their use by Penn when signing treaties.

produced a series of dubious patents, allegedly negotiated with Penn, the most notorious being the Walking Purchase Treaty of 1737, which ceded such land as could be traversed in one and a half days. The Delaware assumed this would be performed by one person walking at a normal pace. The Penn brothers instead used a team of runners, which hugely increased the size of the patent. To aid them in this fraud, they sought the assistance of the Iroquois, who claimed suzerainty over the Delaware by virtue of their conquest in the seventeenth century, though there is no evidence to support such a claim. Nevertheless, in Iroquois parlance, the Delaware had been reduced to the status of women. Women did not make decisions about land. The Delaware, therefore, should accept the Walking Purchase grant and live elsewhere as directed by their masters.[19]

Many Delaware, faced by such sharp practices, moved westward to new settlements on the Susquehanna River. However, as the tide of white settlement advanced, others went further to the upper reaches of the Ohio.[20] Initially, both the eastern and western Delaware remained neutral in the enveloping Anglo-French rivalry, since they still looked to the Quakers for justice. They were also fearful of antagonizing the Iroquois.[21] However, the defeat of Braddock and disruption of the trade meant that the Delaware now had a real incentive to join the French, especially when the latter promised to restore them to their lands and free them from Iroquois domination.[22] They were joined in their new alliance by the Shawnee, another refugee nation, who had moved into central Pennsylvania early in the eighteenth century. The Shawnee too felt the pressure of white settlement and began moving down the Ohio Valley in the 1730s to new locations on the Scioto and Muskingum Rivers.[23]

The decision of the Delaware and Shawnee to support the French meant that the Iroquois were now the sole friends of the British among the native peoples of the Great Lakes and northeastern North America. Their goodwill was especially important because they occupied the strategic corridor from Albany to Lake Ontario. Unfortunately for the British and their colonists, the Covenant Chain had become "rusty" after years of neglect, which the recent Congress of Albany had done nothing to change. Most of the confederacy, now called the Six Nations following the accession of the Tuscarora, determined to remain neutral when confronted by the rivalry of Britain and France. The advantage of doing so meant that they could play one European power off against the other, holding the balance of power, which they had intermittently done since the Treaty of 1701. Consequently, they told Vaudreuil in the summer of 1756 that as the French and British were "the common disturbers of this country," they were "resolved to keep friends on both sides as long as possible."[24] Only the Mohawk, the easternmost member of the confederacy, remained supportive of the British, because of their friendship with Sir William Johnson, the superintendent for Indian affairs.

Few Six Nations warriors consequently supported the British when Montcalm attacked the strategic post of Oswego in August 1756. The situation was no better a year later when Montcalm attacked Fort William Henry at the foot of Lake George, where he once again enjoyed wide support from the St. Lawrence Valley and Great Lakes nations. The British in contrast were almost friendless except for the presence of a few Mohawk. The result was another defeat, culminating in the surrender of Fort William Henry and the "massacre" of three hundred of the garrison as they made their way back to the British lines.[25] Cultivation of the "middle ground" had produced a rich dividend for the French.

THE CHANGING FORTUNES OF WAR

Despite the successes at Fort Duquesne, Oswego, and Fort William Henry, the relationship between the French and their allies was not without friction. On the capture of Fort William Henry, Montcalm tried to prevent his allies from seizing and scalping British prisoners, since this contravened European convention regarding the surrender of an enemy. But to the Indians there was little point in going to war if they were denied such booty, especially as the French had fewer gifts to offer due to the British naval blockade of Canada. As one Abenaki warrior told his priest, "I make war for plunder, scalps and prisoners. You content yourself with a fort."[26] To Indian thinking, the white man's way of war was stupid. Their anger resurfaced the following year when Montcalm confronted the army of General Abercromby as it advanced on Montreal. When his Indian allies failed to arrive in time for the battle at Ticonderoga, Montcalm asked them contemptuously, "Are you come only to behold dead bodies?" Relations were eventually patched up by Vaudreuil, but Indian respect for the French had been undermined.[27]

Indian discontent with the French was also apparent on the Ohio, where another British army under Brigadier James Forbes was advancing on Fort Duquesne. The alliance between the French and the Ohio peoples was recent, and its benefits were already proving doubtful. The French were short of supplies and barely able to feed themselves, let alone their Indian allies. Moreover, many Delaware continued to cherish their former harmony with Pennsylvania's Quaker population. They also sensed that the military balance was tilting against the French. It was time to seek an accommodation with the British if they were to be on the winning side. The eastern Delaware sachem, Teedyuscung, had already made peace with Pennsylvania the previous August, whereby his people were to be resettled on the east branch of the Susquehanna River. In return, Teedyuscung would use his good offices to secure an accommodation with the western Delaware and other nations beyond the mountains.[28]

Proof that the British were winning the hearts and minds of the Indians was seemingly confirmed in July 1758, when Teedyuscung announced that ten nations along the Ohio and Wabash Rivers had accepted articles of peace similar to those negotiated for himself.[29] However, the Moravian missionary, Frederick Post, whom Governor William Denny of Pennsylvania had sent to the Ohio independently of Teedyuscung, found a very different situation when he met the leaders of the western Delaware near Fort Duquesne in mid-August 1758. Tamaqua the "Beaver," Shingas his brother, and Delaware George all denied having had "anything to do with Teedyuscung." However, they would welcome proposals from the governor of Pennsylvania, but made it clear that the British demand for the return of all "prisoners" would prove an obstacle, as would the insatiable desire of the European Americans for Indian land.[30] Peace would be a thing of time.

The western Delaware were reluctant to end hostilities in part because of the fluctuating military situation. By now the army under Forbes was approaching Fort Duquesne. The French, in response, had once more mustered the Ottawa, Ojibwa, Potawatomi, and Wyandot from the Great Lakes for its defense, confident of repeating their success of July 1755. Their opportunity seemingly arrived on 14 September 1758, when Forbes's advance guard of seven hundred men under Major James Grant foolishly approached Fort Duquesne in broad daylight. The Indians with help from the garrison attacked Grant from all sides, using the trees and terrain as cover. The result was another rout similar to that of Braddock, yielding a large number of scalps and prisoners.[31]

In this crisis, the British turned to diplomacy by calling a conference at the frontier town of Easton. The subsequent Treaty of Easton of October 1758 is usually presented as a triumph of Pennsylvania and Delaware diplomacy, because it led to the detaching of the Ohio nations from their alliance with the French. In reality, the conference achieved no such thing. Grant's defeat meant that no western nations were present at the talks, and the proceedings nearly stalled over the Six Nations' insistence that Teedyuscung and the Delaware reaffirm their status as "women." The only initiative regarding the western nations was the dispatch of Post with renewed pleas that the Ohio Indians abandon the French in favor of their old friendship with Pennsylvania. Otherwise, the main achievement at Easton was the winning over of the Six Nations to a more active role on the British side. Their price for doing so was the return of some lands that the Six Nations insisted had been sold surreptitiously to Pennsylvania at the Albany Congress without the consent of their grand council at Onondaga. Fortunately for the British, the Pennsylvanians agreed to make this concession, promising simultaneously to draw a boundary line to avoid future disputes.[32] The triumph, if any, belonged to the Six Nations.

Meanwhile, Post's journey was proving more successful this time. The hunting season was approaching and the Ottawa, Ojibwa, Potawatomi, and Wyandot had gone home, believing that Forbes would retreat after Grant's defeat.[33] As a result, only two hundred Ohio warriors accompanied the French when they attacked Forbes's advance guard at Loyal Hannon on 12 October

1758, and the assault was easily repulsed.[34] This setback made the Ohio nations even more inclined to heed Post's suggestion about an accommodation with the British. After one final plea to the western Delaware for help, the French accepted the inevitable and abandoned Fort Duquesne on 24 November 1758. However, the Delaware and Shawnee still had to make a formal peace with the British and resolve a number of issues. Most important were the return of white prisoners and the future of Fort Pitt, as Fort Duquesne was renamed by the British in what was now called Pittsburgh.[35]

The Ohio nations were not alone in reassessing their position with the Europeans. The Great Lakes nations also recognized the need to explore an understanding with the British in case the French were defeated. The Detroit Ottawa accordingly dispatched two envoys to Pittsburgh in February 1759 to find out if the reports of the Delaware making peace were true. Here they were informed that the British merely wanted the return of their captives and the ending of Indian support for France. However, they remained suspicious that the English-speaking peoples intended to rob them of their lands, a view that the French did everything to promote.[36] The Great Lakes Wyandot, Ottawa, Ojibwa, Miami, and Potawatomi accordingly agreed to join the French in an attack on Fort Pitt and its communication.[37]

Fortunately for the British, the Six Nations were now ready to play a more active role, following the restitution of their lands by Pennsylvania. But their change of heart also reflected a desire to be on the winning side, especially when Amherst decided to attack Niagara in the spring of 1759.[38] Six hundred and fifty Mohawk, Oneida, Tuscarora, Onondaga, Cayuga, and Seneca consequently joined Brigadier James Prideaux when he set off for Niagara with Johnson. However, the loyalty of Prideaux's allies was soon tested when thirty Seneca remained inside the fort with the French, which prompted the Six Nations to declare their neutrality.[39] This desertion coincided with the news that the Great Lakes nations were coming to relieve Niagara, after abandoning an attack on Fort Pitt.[40] In this crisis, Johnson, who had taken command on the death of Prideaux after being struck by a mortar shell, had to rely on the regular and provincial forces in his army. Nevertheless, he succeeded in putting his opponents to flight. The sight of their old seventeenth-century antagonists running away proved too much for many of the Iroquois, who joined in the pursuit, taking a considerable number of prisoners and scalps.[41] Among the latter were two western chiefs. Thirty Ottawa were also drowned while escaping across the Niagara River. These losses were to have important consequences shortly.[42] But for the moment the Six Nations at least were pleased, since Johnson allowed them to keep most of their prisoners and a considerable amount of plunder too.[43]

THE COLLAPSE OF NEW FRANCE

The loss of Niagara was to hemorrhage support for the French among the western Indians. As Charles Powers, a captive of the Detroit Wyandot, told George Croghan, Johnson's deputy, at the beginning of 1760, "Every spring [since 1755,] great numbers of Indians from over the Lakes" had gone "to war against the English, sometimes 700 men in one company." "The Indians were of opinion till last fall... that the French would conquer all the English in America. But since the fate of Niagara the Indians seem to be convinced that the English can beat them, for which reason the most sensible Indians are for standing neuter." If any further proof was needed about the decline of French power, it was provided by their evacuation of Presque Isle, Le Boeuf, and Venango.[44]

Most of the Great Lakes and Ohio nations accordingly sent fresh delegations to the British to discuss peace and the opening of trade. The diplomatic activity was most intense at Fort Pitt. Here Croghan met the Delaware, Shawnee, Ottawa, and Ojibwa in August 1759; the Six Nations, Ottawa, Miami, Delaware, and Shawnee in September; and various representatives of these nations during October and November.[45] Generally the tone of these exchanges was amicable, the main topics being the price of goods and the necessity for trade. As the Ottawa chief Mehennah commented at the September conference, the departure of the French meant that "we must now depend upon you for supplies and hope you will consider our necessities at this time." But he was quick to add, "When we get settled to our hunting and planting again, we will be able to purchase necessaries for our families and give you less trouble than we do at this time."[46] A Wyandot chief from Detroit expressed similar if less optimistic sentiments the following month. He explained that his people had been "obliged to come into French measures in order to get such necessities as we could not subsist without." The simple fact was that "no Indian nation" could "live now without being supported either by the English or the French ... as our Ancestors did before you came into our country." But providing these expectations were met, the English could count on their friendship.[47] Nevertheless Croghan noted that rumors were still circulating about the British intention to "cut off all the western Indian nations" once they had concluded matters with the French.[48] There was still much mistrust to overcome as the new campaign season approached.

It was for this reason that the British decided to dispatch Post on a further mission to the Ohio and Great Lakes peoples. The time was opportune since information had been received that these western Indians were planning a grand conference at Sandusky to discuss their future conduct. Before setting out, Post suggested that Amherst send a message reassuring the western Indians of his intentions respecting white settlement, for as he told the Pennsylvania provincial secretary, the Indians were "more afraid of losing their hunting grounds than their lives."[49] Amherst readily agreed, drafting a declaration that the British were not coming to take the Indians' lands but to defend them, for which reason forts were necessary.[50] Unfortunately the address contained as many threats as promises, and Post left it behind when he set out for Sandusky.[51] In the event, he got no farther than the west branch of the Susquehanna River, where he was stopped by the Seneca. The reason, Post believed, was their fear that he would discover the numerous captives being held by them.[52] But the Seneca were also motivated by the desire to prevent the British from extending their influence among nations whom they considered their dependents.

The British plan of campaign in 1760 was for three armies to move toward Montreal, one via Lake Ontario under Amherst, while the other two under Colonel William Haviland and Brigadier James Murray advanced via Lake Champlain and the St. Lawrence River.[53] Since Indians were still considered necessary for reconnaissance and the avoiding of ambushes, Amherst ordered Johnson to recruit the Six Nations once more, together with any others willing to serve.[54] Many in the confederacy were now fearful of any further extension of British power. Nevertheless, they were tempted by the spoils of war and the securing of valuable supplies. They also wanted to help their relatives in the St. Lawrence mission settlements, with whom they had been holding talks.[55] By the end of July 1760, some 1,500 had gathered at Oswego, though nearly half were women and children, much to Amherst's disgust. Among those present was the chief of the Swegatchie, who was rumored to have killed three hundred warriors in his long career.[56] His presence demonstrated that the St. Lawrence peoples were ready to desert their old alliance.

Amherst finally departed from Oswego on 10 August 1760. As the British advanced, the number of nations seeking peace rapidly increased. The Kickapoo, Miami, and Potawatomi came to Fort Pitt at the beginning of August, followed by the Delaware, Ottawa, Wyandot, and other western peoples a few days later.[57] The remaining Swegatchie also indicated that they would remain neutral.[58] At the same time, other nations ceremoniously returned the war hatchets they had received at the start of hostilities.[59] But few offered to fight for the British, though all were anxious to trade, many being on the verge of starvation. They acknowledged that they had been well treated recently by the British and heard that King George III was a good person whose "speeches always gave pleasure." They promised, in return, to send back the British captives, though one Delaware warrior chief begged not to be pressed on the matter, since it would be a thing of time.[60] Nevertheless, a new version of the "middle ground" appeared to be within reach.

By the third week of August, Amherst had entered the St. Lawrence River and reached the last obstacle to his advance on Montreal. Fort Levis on Isle Royale was a newly refurbished structure with a garrison of three hundred men. A frontal assault on a fortified position had no appeal for native peoples, since they had neither the technology nor the manpower for such operations. Nevertheless, the ending of the siege offered the warriors a chance for plunder and prisoners. It was just such a situation that had led to the disorder at Fort William Henry following its surrender in August 1757. Amherst was determined that no such episode would disgrace British arms. With eleven thousand redcoats and provincials, he was in a position to enforce his will. No Indians were allowed inside Fort Levis when it surrendered on 25 August 1760, and all the prisoners were put under guard into bateaux to be taken to New York via Oswego.[61]

To the Six Nations warriors, such treatment was a denial of their military code and a gross betrayal too, since it was clear that the same restraints would apply when they arrived at Montreal. Such humiliation was not what they had enlisted for. The majority, numbering five hundred warriors, accordingly returned home. The desertions were especially heavy among the Seneca, Cayuga, and Onondaga. As a result, less than two hundred Iroquois finished the campaign at Montreal.[62]

On the day of the surrender, Johnson and his remaining Six Nations allies were distant spectators. However, the Mohawk, Oneida, and Tuscarora had been instrumental in securing neutrality for their St. Lawrence compatriots before the army's arrival at Montreal.[63] Johnson now confirmed the terms agreed on between Amherst and Vaudreuil regarding their religion and the opening of trade. This he did at a separate gathering on 16 September 1760. The St. Lawrence Indians, in response, announced their pleasure at being allowed to keep their priests. They were also pleased that the road to Albany would be open for trade. In return they agreed to give up all their white captives, bury the hatchet, and send representatives to meet Johnson at Albany for a conference.[64]

The fall of Montreal on 8 September 1760 did not complete the overthrow of French Canada or the accommodation of its native peoples to the new order. Although the St. Lawrence Valley, Lake Ontario, and the upper Ohio were nominally under British control, the four upper lakes of Erie, Huron, Michigan, and Superior still had to be secured, and terms agreed on with its native inhabitants. Amherst accordingly ordered Major Robert Rogers with some rangers to proceed to Detroit, after first taking dispatches to Brigadier Robert Monckton, the southern area commander, at Fort Pitt. Here, he was to be joined by Croghan and such additional men as Monckton saw fit to allocate. On arrival at Detroit, the two men were to administer an oath of loyalty to the French inhabitants, negotiate treaties with the Indians, and send detachments to occupy the French western posts of Michilimackinac, La Baye, St. Joseph, Ouiatanon, Miami, and Vincennes.[65]

The two men set off for Detroit at the end of October 1760. Contact with the western peoples was initially made on 5 November near Presque Isle, when thirty Ottawa appeared carrying a British flag. Here they smoked tobacco with the Indians' council pipe, which the latter had brought to demonstrate their sincerity.[66] At a second meeting that day, Croghan told them that the British would allow a free trade at the posts, meaning a competitive market rather than a monopolistic one as under the French system. The advantage of such a system was that it would produce lower prices. He also promised the Indians the peaceable protection of their hunting country.[67] The Ottawa in response expressed their satisfaction at Croghan's words and trusted that all previous disputes would be forgotten. The Detroit Indians had supported the French because of their need for European goods. They hoped, therefore, that the British would take pity on them, especially their wives and children. They then begged for a little ammunition so that they could hunt for the support of their families, to which Croghan consented. During this exchange, the principal Ottawa chief commented that he was old and would soon die. He then introduced Croghan and Rogers to two younger men who had gone to Fort Pitt the previous year to hear details of the peace being offered by the British. He hoped that proper notice would be taken of them.[68]

On 22 November, near their journey's end, Rogers and Croghan met a further party from the Detroit Ottawa, Potawatomi, and Wyandot. After a joint council, they all affected to welcome the departure of the French and their replacement by the British.[69] However, the French commander, Captain François-Marie Bellestre, refused to surrender until he had received formal notification from Vaudreuil that Detroit was included in the surrender terms. Rogers in response produced a copy of the surrender terms. The flotilla then proceeded up the Detroit River accompanied by the chiefs of the three nations to signal their welcome. Detroit itself was occupied on 29 November 1760, and the surrender completed on 2 December 1760 when the French garrison departed under escort. However, Bellestre addressed the several nations before leaving, advising them that the departure of the French would only be temporary. They should watch and wait for their "father's" return.[70]

Croghan and Rogers then held their own conference with the Indians. First the Ottawa, Wyandot, and Potawatomi chiefs acknowledged that the arrival of the British signaled a new era. Nevertheless, they expected some aspects of the old order to continue, notably a smith to repair their guns and tools as well as a doctor to tend their sick. They also asked if Amherst or Johnson had a message for them before they departed on their winter hunt. Throughout the speech they used the term "brethren" rather than "father," indicating that they were the equal of the British, not vanquished peoples. [71]

Croghan in response told the chiefs that the French inhabitants had become British subjects. The two peoples were now one. However, the Indians could depend on a "free" trade and the protection of the king, providing they behaved. Croghan then raised the matter of prisoners, pointing out disingenuously that the nations at Pittsburgh had recently agreed to give up all their white captives. The Detroit nations, he added, should do the same as this was "the only way you can convince us of your sincerity and future intentions of living in friendship with all his Majesty's subjects." As to the Indian custom of initiating young warriors in combat, he suggested that in future they attack their natural enemies, the Cherokee. Otherwise they should refrain from tribal wars as the northern nations had all become the allies of the British king. Finally, he promised his listeners that they should have the services of a smith and doctor until Amherst's pleasure was known.[72]

In reply the principal Wyandot chief, Achonnere, acknowledged the Detroit nations' lack of experience after losing so many leaders in the war. However, he could speak with authority since "all the Indians in this country are Allies to each other" and acted "as one people." On the point of the captives, he promised they would deliver them as soon as possible, "though we do not choose to force them that have a mind to live with us." The Indians were glad that the chain of friendship had been renewed and hoped that the promise of cheaper goods would be fulfilled. The speaker finished by alluding to the historic meeting between William Penn and the Algonquian Delaware in 1682, "when we first met under a Shade, as there were no houses in these Times." "It was then said that this Country was given by God to the Indians and that you would preserve it for our joint use." "We hope you remember your promises."[73] Prospectively, the "middle ground" had been restored to the Great Lakes peoples, albeit with new "brothers."

1
The New Order of Sir Jeffery Amherst, 1760–1761

Amherst and the British Establishment

If Indian hopes for a restoration of the "middle ground" were to be realized, much depended on the British commander-in-chief, General Sir Jeffery Amherst, and his senior officials. Canada and its dependencies were temporarily conquered provinces subject to military governance until a final peace with France. This gave Amherst enormous power. He had been generous in his treatment of the French inhabitants, ensuring protection for their religion and property according to European diplomatic protocol. His hope was that such leniency would assist the acculturation of the Canadians as subjects of the British Crown.

Unfortunately, such considerations did not apply to Canada's Indian inhabitants since they were considered beyond the normal conventions of European morality and diplomacy. Like most whites, Amherst suffered from the racial prejudice which had been endemic since the first contact between the European and Native American peoples at the end of the fifteenth century. The orthodox view was that the native peoples were savages and heathens who had to be first conquered and then civilized through the twin agencies of Christianity and European methods of production. Although the Indians were thought to be higher than Africans on the scale of human intelligence, it was not a significant concession. Africans at least appeared fit for work, whereas Indians were caricatured as incurably lazy, making them little better than vermin, to be driven from the land or exterminated.

This prejudice was reinforced by the perceived failings of the Indians' political and social structures. Amherst's first assignment in America had been the capture of Louisburg, the strategic fort guarding the entrance to the St. Lawrence. The Micmac population there comprised a few hundred hunter-gatherers. Their military resources did not go beyond attacking the occasional sentry or guard post. This "skulking warfare" was utterly despised by European soldiers and produced bafflement at how Braddock had been defeated in 1755. Nor did Amherst's views change when he took command in 1759 of the advance on Montreal by way of Lake George and Lake Champlain. When Brigadier General Thomas Gage advised against hiring two companies of

Stockbridge Indians, Amherst responded, "I know what a vile crew they are, and I have as bad an opinion of those lazy rum drinking scoundrels as any one can have." The advantage of taking them into the king's service was that it might "keep them from doing mischief elsewhere."[1]

Of course, the British military were not alone in their contempt for the Indians' martial qualities, since the French under Montcalm were equally prejudiced. Indeed, one senior officer attributed the loss of Canada in part to Vaudreuil's excessive reliance on the Indians.[2] But while the war continued, Amherst necessarily had to ameliorate his sentiments, though he privately told his officers "not to rely too much" on Indian promises, "for whatever they say to you today, they would say to the French tomorrow, had they any superiority over us." This did not mean that they should be gratuitously offended: "I would neither disgust them nor yet make them any promises that I did not intend to keep," telling "them very plainly that I mean not to take any thing from them." Amherst's guiding principle was that "when they deserve it they shall be rewarded according to their merit and if they give any just room of complaint I am determined to punish them."[3]

As the need for Indian help declined, so the disdain for the natives became more open. Croghan noticed by December 1759 that "the gentlemen" of the army were beginning to think that anything spent on the Indians was superfluous, since "they must from their necessities come into our measures."[4] Daniel Claus, a deputy agent and Johnson's future son-in-law, reported similarly from Montreal the following year that the Indians' constant importuning had made them "an eyesore to everyone about the General [Gage]."[5] Even those supposedly well disposed had a demeaning opinion of them. Frederick Post, the Moravian missionary, who was himself married to a Delaware, suggested that "the Indians were void of reason," while James Kenny, a Quaker merchant at Fort Pitt, commented that the Indians were "full of pride and ambition, but strangers to humility." Improvement could only be inculcated in the way that a dog learns obedience.[7]

Finally, the Indians had few genuine friends even among those responsible for liaising with them. Although Johnson and Croghan had a good rapport with the native peoples, each used his influence to advance his own interests rather than those of the indigenous peoples. Both men were obsessed with joining the ranks of the gentry by the acquisition of land.[8] As Johnson confessed to a political associate in June 1761, "my motive is the settling [of] the country which I have been promoting all the war."[9] Although Johnson was shortly to take an Indian partner, Molly Brant, he appears to have believed that the native peoples were a doomed race who would disappear as the tide of settlement advanced. Indeed, he subsequently advocated liberal quantities of alcohol "to let them shorten their days."[10] The Indian department's main task in the meantime was the management of that decline.

Gift Giving versus a Market Economy, 1760–1761

Until 1760, Amherst and Johnson were largely confined to dealing with the Iroquois Six Nations. The fall of Canada, however, brought more extensive responsibilities, involving the seven mission settlements in the St. Lawrence Valley; the Ottawa, Huron, Potawatomi, and Ojibwa of the Great Lakes; the Shawnee, Delaware, and Mingo in the Ohio Valley; and the Twightwee, Kickapoo, Mascouten, and Piankashaw along the Wabash and Maumee Rivers. All these nations had been allied to the French and were expecting a continuation of the "middle ground." In their view, they were undefeated. It was the French who had capitulated at Montreal. If the British wanted their friendship, then they would have to earn it.

The British perspective, of course, was very different. First, they did not consider the Indians a sovereign people. Second, the conquest of Canada had reduced the military value of the Indians since the war had now moved to the Caribbean and elsewhere. In addition, the fur trade, though still of some consequence, was far less important to the British than it had been to the French. Finally, the war in North America had been hugely expensive, contributing to a doubling of the British national debt. Now that military operations had ceased, it was assumed that the costs of the army in North America could be reduced. The Treasury in London was particularly of this view.

Amherst knew all about the latter. Any field officer serving overseas ultimately had to account to the Lords of the Treasury for all military expenditure. It was not a pleasant procedure, as Amherst knew, since he had already endured one audit after managing the commissariat in Germany prior to his departure for America in 1758. Consequently, any area of expenditure that was perceived to be peripheral, like the Indian department, was an immediate target for reduction. Amherst felt doubly justified economizing here since the Indians had played little part in the final stages of the war, following their desertion at Fort Levis. This meant they had unilaterally removed themselves from the military budget and had no further claim to aid.

The first area for cost cutting was the staff of the Indian department itself. This had been established in August 1755 to improve relations with the indigenous peoples. Two superintendents had been appointed: one for the region north of the Ohio under Johnson, and the other under Edmund Atkins for the area to the south of that river. The hope originally had been that the department would be financed from a "General Fund" raised by the colonies.[11] That had not happened, and Johnson and Atkins remained dependent on the military budget. The expenses of both departments had increased as the scope of the war widened, necessitating the appointment of additional personnel. Nevertheless, these officials had played an important role in winning native acceptance of the British. However, these considerations had little weight with Amherst once the conquest of Canada had been achieved. Accordingly, on 8 November 1760 he told Johnson to dismiss four officers from the Royal American regiment who were acting as aides, since in "the present circumstances of affairs, their services can be dispensed with."[12] Although Johnson was shortly afterwards given a new commission, he still had to obey directions from the commander-in-chief.[13] Not that Amherst was completely insensitive about the need for staff. After consulting Monckton, he agreed that some of Croghan's agents at Fort Pitt might temporarily remain on the payroll.[14]

The next target for a reduction in the Indian expenses was the practice of gift giving. Even before the fall of Canada, Amherst had called for a reduction in these when the Indians visited the forts and attended conferences. Gift giving might have been necessary during the war but was now indicative of what the late twentieth century would call the "dependency culture." In Amherst's view, the Indians must support themselves through their hunting and by market forces. Hunting would provide them with food for their families and skins to exchange for European clothing, ammunition, and other necessities. Accordingly, on 2 August 1760 Amherst informed his senior commanders that the Indians hereafter were only to be supplied with provisions at Niagara and Fort Pitt, and the greatest care taken in the distribution of other items.[15]

Soon the screw was being tightened further, as Monckton informed Colonel Henry Bouquet at Fort Pitt in October 1760. Presents in future should only be issued on special occasions.[16] When Johnson hinted that a more lenient policy might be advisable, Amherst acknowledged that "services must be rewarded … but as to purchasing the good behavior either of Indians or any others," this "is what I do not understand; when men of what race so ever behave ill, they must be punished but not bribed." Of course, "with regard to furnishing the latter with a little clothing, some arms and ammunition to hunt with, that is all very well in cases of necessity." But "when the intended trade is once established, they will be able to supply themselves with these from the traders for their furs." In other words, there was to be no adoption of the French system of subsidies disguised as gifts. Above all, there must be no regular issue of provisions. "When they find they can get it on asking for, they will grow remiss in their hunting, which should industriously be avoided; for so long as their minds are intent on business, they will not have leisure to hatch mischief."[17] The only exceptions to this rule were to be those Six Nations warriors who had completed the 1760 campaign. They were shortly to receive a silver medal commemorating that event with their name on one side and a view of Montreal on the other. On presenting their medals, they would be allowed "free egress and regress to any of his Majesty's forts, posts and garrisons," though only so long as they remained faithful to the British interest.[18]

One reason for Amherst's opposition to gift giving was his failure to appreciate the distressed state of the Indian economy. Europeans commonly assumed that the countryside was teeming with game, providing an endless supply of food and pelts. But as Henry Bouquet discovered while supervising the rebuilding of Presque Isle in the summer of 1760, the Ojibwa there had not killed a single deer in a fortnight's hunting.[19] Nature's bounty was rarely predictable. Equally parlous was the state of Indian agriculture. The war had prevented many nations from planting their corn. This was especially true along the St. Lawrence Valley, where Major Henry Gladwin felt moved to give the Swegatchie Indians corn to make up their losses.[20] The lack of food was inevitably accompanied by sickness. Nevertheless, Amherst was unmoved. He told Gage, "I am not sorry that the Indians are mostly destroyed at Swegatchie," adding approvingly how "the Sickness at Canadasaga," a Seneca settlement, "will decrease their number." Indeed, the Indians were seemingly "diminishing in all their settlements."[21] This could only be advantageous in the long term.

The denial of gifts was especially troubling to the chiefs, since a leader who could win no favors invariably lost the respect of his people. This was a point made by Delaware George, one of the few Ohio leaders to support the British during the entire war with France. In a speech at Fort Pitt in May 1761, he commented that the English were constantly complaining about the failure of the Indians to have fixed abodes. George had accordingly established a new town at Kuskuskies, confident that he would get British or colonial help in the building thereof. However, so far he had received little assistance, certainly not the doors and locks he had been promised for his new cabins. He was afraid that Indian visitors would "laugh" at his ramshackle dwellings and point out the folly of being allied to the British if this was how he was rewarded.[22] Indians believed in any case that gifts should be seen as reciprocity for allowing the Europeans to stay on Indian land.

Amherst's attempts to reduce Indian expenses did not go completely unchallenged. Captain Donald Campbell at Detroit admitted that he had given the natives "ammunition, as their support entirely depends upon it." But he argued that it was diplomatic to do so, for "there will probably be emissaries among them from the Illinois to endeavor to give us trouble."[23] It was a reminder that the French still had a foothold in North America and could rally the native inhabitants to their cause. Johnson gave a similar reply when Amherst queried the expenses of Croghan and Rogers following their visit to Detroit in November 1760. He pointed out that the dispatch of Croghan with gifts had been a necessary "safe guard to Major Rogers in an Indian country, where our troops were liable to be insulted." Johnson knew from past experience "that a little generosity and moderation will tend more to the good of his Majesty's Indian interest, than the reverse, which would raise their jealousy much more than it is now." Gift giving had been the policy of the French, "who certainly were very clever in extending their Indian Alliances." Admittedly it had been done at considerable expense, but the French had reaped great benefit thereby. "Should we, Sir, unexpectedly, or unhappily be obliged to give up Canada (which God forbid), it will in my opinion be (beyond all dispute) for the interest of Britain, to show these people a little generosity and friendship, and thereby show them it is their interest to keep well with us."[24]

Despite these arguments, Amherst refused to change his attitude, as Johnson discovered when he suggested a conference at Detroit in the summer of 1761 to confirm the peace with the Great Lakes nations. Amherst acknowledged that the superintendent was the best judge of handling the Indians. Nevertheless, Johnson was to confine his expenditure "to such only, as are absolutely necessary ... for it is not my intention to attempt to gain the Friendship of Indians by presents." Amherst in any case believed his policy was working, for by May 1761 even Campbell acknowledged that the Indians and French inhabitants were apparently becoming reconciled to the change of government.[25]

Trade and Ammunition

Although Amherst was against gift giving, he acknowledged that the Indians should have an equitable and plentiful trade based on market forces. The problem was that a free-for-all might result in abuse. Johnson accordingly wanted the trade to be regulated by his department. He had long been impressed by the French system, believing that it had prevented undesirable traders from cheating their Indian customers. Johnson accordingly proposed on 15 November 1760 that anyone wishing to trade with the Indians must first secure a passport from his officials.[26] Amherst, suspecting Johnson of empire building, refused his consent, arguing that the superintendent should await the views of the ministry of William Pitt and the Duke of Newcastle in London before taking on this responsibility.[27]

In the meantime, Amherst had a more limited proposal to make. He told Johnson in February 1761, "I propose so soon as the season will admit ... to appoint a person of knowledge and probity to be governor at the Detroit, with Directions to open a free and fair Trade." To speed up matters, Johnson was to provide him with "such hints as may enable me to establish this trade upon a lasting and good foundation." He wanted in particular to know "what commodities it will be most proper to send among those Indians, their value and the profit the Trader should have ... without imposing on the Indians."[28] Johnson quickly replied that a "free and open trade," under proper regulation and legal framework, would be best, since it would ensure both the right quality and quantity of goods. That in turn would keep the Indians firmly attached in the British interest. He accordingly forwarded a list of goods on which a profit of 50 percent would be reasonable, given the distances and dangers involved.[29]

However, if Amherst and Johnson believed the introduction of a market system would meet the natives' needs, they were badly misled. There had been numerous complaints during the war about the quality and quantity of British goods, though most of these had been dismissed as the result of wartime shortages. But by March 1761 little improvement had occurred, as the Six Nations pointed out on a visit to Johnson at his home near Schenectady. The

Onondaga speaker, Anaroongo, began by reminding the superintendent of the "many fair promises made to us since the commencement of the war, by all the Generals who have been here, as well as by yourself." Their promises were essentially three in number. "First, that we should have a free plentiful trade, carried on for our advantage, so soon as the French were subdued, or the war was ended." The second was "that the Covenant Chain of friendship should ever be kept bright and strong" by means of regular conferences. The third was "that we should not want for the necessaries of life if we joined his Majesty's arms, which we have done more or less every campaign." Unfortunately, "We are sorry to say these promises are not fulfilled, nay we are (by the dearness of goods sold to us in our country, and at the different posts) obliged to pay such exorbitant prices, that our hunting is not sufficient to purchase us as much clothing as is necessary to cover us and our families." Their distress was compounded because "our hunting is not so great as usual" due to "a want of ammunition which we can by no means procure."[30] The Indians needed help, not hindrance, in restoring their economy.

The constant rise in the price of European goods baffled the Indians, because to them one large white-tailed buckskin was as good as another, whatever the time or venue.[31] They could only explain these price fluctuations as the result of manipulation by unscrupulous traders. Nevertheless, Johnson was surprisingly unsympathetic to their plight. He suggested it was the Six Nations' own fault if the trade was not operating satisfactorily. They had not fulfilled their promises after being clothed, armed, and fed at great expense the previous year. Inevitably, their base desertion at Fort Levis "could not fail to exasperate the general." Even so, Amherst and Johnson were working to establish a free and fair trade by the summer of 1761, when "you may have goods reasonable and the more so whenever the war is entirely ended." As to the shortage of powder, this was something that the Indians had brought upon themselves. The British traders were discouraged from bringing powder "from the prejudice which you entertained always that French powder was better than the English." "When they find a demand for it, they will bring that article amongst you as well."[32]

Nevertheless, Johnson's optimism that the merchants would respond to market forces was not born out by experience. Campbell noted as late as June 1761 that the traders at Detroit were only bringing goods for the French inhabitants. "It would seem that they did not understand the Indian Trade, and have not proper assortments" of goods. This included ammunition. As a result, Campbell had been forced to dispense a great quantity himself.[33] The situation was no better at Fort Pitt, where the White Mingo, a sachem of Seneca descent, lamented that after losing several kegs on the river, "we must starve brethren unless you help us with a little powder and lead."[34] At Niagara, the Mississauga Ojibwa and other Great Lakes Indians were similarly desperate, begging "a little ammunition and provisions" from the commanding officer, Major William Walters. Without this, "they must die." Some of those present had traveled with their wampum belts and peace pipes "upwards of fifteen hundred miles to see their Brethren the English." They assured Walters that they would "always keep fast hold of their Brothers, the English." However, they could not speak for everyone, for "some rogues among the Seneca" were predicting that "the French will come and drive the English away."[35] The British should not take the Indians for granted.

The Indians found the shortage of powder especially alarming because it was seen as a ploy by the British to keep them in subjection. To some extent this was true, as Amherst revealed to Walters in November 1760: "They certainly should have a little [powder], but the less the better, for so long as they are deprived of it, they will do no mischief, for they cannot now get any ammunition elsewhere," meaning the French.[36] However, by early 1761 some Indians were putting an even worse construction on the scarcity. At a meeting with the Onondaga and Cayuga, Johnson observed that they had not visited him recently. The chiefs replied that they had heard a rumor among white Pennsylvanians that the British intended to destroy them by denying them powder. In consequence, they were using bows and arrows to conserve their diminishing supplies. Johnson in reply expressed surprise that they should listen "to such idle and wicked reports." "Have you not daily proofs of British humanity," he asked, even when the British were dealing with their enemies? They had no reason to mistrust their white "brethren."[37]

However, as the date for the Detroit conference approached, Johnson's attitude softened, if only to ensure the success of his forthcoming trip. He told Amherst that "unless all our old, as well as new Indian allies, are allowed ammunition for their livelihood or hunting, all treaties held with, or presents made to them, will never secure their friendship." Instead, the denial of powder would make them anxious, as was the case already. "I think it will be absolutely necessary to have it in my power to give them what I may see requisite."[38] Otherwise, it would give credence to the French argument that the British were withholding ammunition "with a design of falling upon them."[39] That could only spell disaster.

The Forts, and Law and Order

Another issue to bedevil relations between the British and Native Americans in the first year of Amherst's new order was the occupation of the former French forts. The Indians wanted French-style trading posts, not military bases, since these posed a threat to their lands. This point had been made by the western Delaware following the capture of Fort Duquesne. Kickyuscung, one of the Delaware leaders, told Post that if the British withdrew, all the Indians would be their friends. However, if they stayed at Fort Duquesne "and settled there," then "all the nations would be against them." Indeed, "he was afraid" there "would be a great war," and that the region would "never come to peace again." In response, Post focused on the need to prevent the French from returning to the area.[40] Not receiving any satisfaction, the Delaware and Shawnee repeated their views when they met the senior British commander, Colonel Henry Bouquet, at Fort Pitt on 4 December 1758. Bouquet reaffirmed that the British had not come to take the Indians' lands. Their main purpose was the opening of a cheap and extensive trade. However, that trade would need protecting, hence his determination to leave two hundred men at Pittsburgh. According to Croghan, who took minutes of the meeting, the Delaware chief Tamaqua seemingly accepted this argument.[41] In reality, the Delaware had told the garrison three times to go home. Since Bouquet appeared impervious to their pleas, they requested Post once more to "let the governor, general and all people know that our desire is that they should go back, till the other nations have joined in the peace, and then they may come and build a trading house."[42]

The British, of course, had no intention of evacuating a place they had spent so much effort in gaining. But while the war continued, they found it diplomatic to defuse such fears by emphasizing the benign nature of these installations. In his Declaration of April 1760, Amherst affirmed the now standard argument that some forts were necessary "to protect our trade with you, and prevent the enemy from taking possession of your lands." He continued, "I will even promise you some presents as a consideration for the land where such forts and trading houses are or may be built upon." But since provisioning the forts was an expensive business, Amherst requested the allocation of a little extra ground for growing crops to feed the garrisons and their Indian visitors. He suggested, "If you will lay out a space of ground adjoining every fort to raise corn … you will receive such a consideration for it as will be agreed between you and us to your satisfaction."[43]

In reality, Amherst was disingenuous in asserting that the forts were intended to protect the trade or provide the Indians with an income. As he made clear to Monckton two days after issuing his declaration, the posts between Fort Pitt and Presque Isle were to secure the communication, not least from Indian attack. However, to disarm Indian suspicions, Monckton was to suggest that the posts were necessary for an attack on Detroit. Implicitly, they would disappear once that objective had been achieved.[44] This provided the British with a convenient excuse for keeping them until a final peace was reached with the French. But inevitably, the suspicion grew that the forts were being retained as part of a scheme to enslave the native peoples.

The issue of the forts was additionally unsettling because two of them, Pittsburgh and Niagara, were being rebuilt in a much more formidable manner. Fort Duquesne under the French comprised nothing more than a wooden stockade, 154 by 160 feet, quite untenable against artillery.[45] But from September 1759, it began to be replaced by a pentagon-shaped stone structure, built according to the principles of Sébastien Le Prestre de Vauban, the doyen of European siege craft. The walls were to be twenty feet high and several feet thick, encompassing an area of 416 by 476 feet, or two acres of ground.[46] Croghan warned Johnson as early as December 1759 that the Delaware and Shawnee "are very jealous seeing a large fort building here."[47] Johnson forwarded the warning to Gage, now Amherst's second in command, commenting, "I am afraid that the building [of] so reputable a fort in their country as at Pittsburgh … will make them very lukewarm in our cause."[48] Indian anger was increased because attached to the new fort was a wooden stockade enclosing a further twelve acres of land, containing numerous houses for the merchants and their families. By April 1761, some 330 men, women, and children were living there. Nearby were fields of corn and hay, a saw mill, a brick kiln, a stone quarry, and an open coal mine.[49] This was more than the simple trading post expected by the Delaware and Shawnee.

The native peoples might have been less hostile to the retention of the forts if they had continued to be welcomed there after the fall of Canada. Early in 1761, Canaghquiesa, speaking on behalf of thirty Oneida and Tuscarora sachems, acknowledged that "the war is not yet ended" and that the forts along the Mohawk and Oswego Rivers would have to remain. But this did not excuse the conduct of "the Commanding Officers at the several posts," who "have used us very unfriendly and not as hereto." Accordingly, the sachems requested "that whilst you keep up these forts, you will post officers at them who may behave in a brother like manner towards us."[50] The Onondaga expressed a similar concern: "You recommended it to us about minding our hunting and trade, and to live on good terms with our Brethren at the several posts." The Onondaga chiefs affirmed that "nothing would be more agreeable to our inclinations, but we are sorry to observe that our Brethren don't seem desirous of living on any good terms with us," since they committed "frequent acts of violence" against both men and women. Equally aggravating was "their hindering us from fishing or hunting about the posts, although in our own Country." Adding insult to injury, the troops frequently stole "what we have killed or taken, contrary to promise and to the friendship subsisting between us and you." Unless the situation improved, "we shall be induced to believe what the French so often told us would be the consequences of your reducing them."[51] Despite this, Johnson still blamed the Indians for most incidents, suggesting they were "chiefly owing to their own behavior when in liquor." The solution was to drink less and not "idle your time about the posts, which you can so much better employ in hunting for the maintenance of your families.[52]

Relations were no better at Fort Pitt, especially after the killing of a Mingo warrior by a Lieutenant Piper of the Pennsylvania regiment. The Mingo were Seneca people who had moved to new settlements on the upper reaches of the Allegheny River. The dead warrior had been trying to steal some horses at Fort Ligonier. Piper not only killed the culprit but also brought the victim's scalp to Fort Pitt, an act of gross disrespect.[53] Bouquet was sufficiently aware of Indian anger to order Croghan to summon a meeting to explain that the army had to protect its horses.[54] The Mingo, however, were not appeased and demanded that Piper be delivered up to them in a spirit of reciprocity. Instead, he was allowed to leave Fort Pitt without redress to the dead man's family, as Indian custom required.[55] Hence, when news was received that several Mingo had been killed by the garrison at Venango, the rest of its inhabitants had gone "to [the] Chenussio very much discontented" to seek protection.[56] The "Chenussio," or Genesee Seneca, were the most powerful tribal group in this part of North America and dangerous enemies if provoked, as the British shortly discovered.

Such incidents angered the Indians because it appeared that there was one law for the whites and another for themselves. When a German settler was killed in the Mohawk Valley, Amherst insisted that the perpetrator be handed over to the nearest magistrate for punishment, adding superciliously that "had one of the Inhabitants committed a murder on one of the Indians, I should be for bringing that Inhabitant to justice in like manner." His proposal was disingenuous since it overlooked the partiality of white juries and Indian unfamiliarity with the European American judicial system.[57] Justice in consequence was all too often a one-sided affair.

The lack of respect for Indian lives and property was one reason for the widespread stealing of the army's horses, especially around Fort Pitt. One audacious theft involved a black mare belonging to Bouquet. Bouquet immediately dispatched one of Johnson's agents to Custaloga's town, the residence of a prominent western Delaware chief, where the suspected thief resided, but without success. The mare was eventually found six weeks later at Harris's Ferry (now Harrisburg, Pennsylvania) in the opposite direction, suggesting that the thieves were not Indian at all.[58] Nevertheless, the Shawnee at least could not deny the activities of their young men when their chiefs met Croghan at Fort Pitt at the beginning of March 1761. By way of conciliation, they promised to end such incidents, blaming the earlier thefts on the effects of liquor.[59] Bouquet was hopeful that the recent shooting at Fort Ligonier would make them more careful in the future.[60] In the meantime, he decided to place an embargo on traders visiting their settlements as a way of bringing them to their senses.[61]

Land and Settlement

Yet another contentious issue in the early days of Amherst's new order was that of land. During the war, British commanders like Amherst had given repeated assurances that Indian lands would be respected. In his Declaration of April 1760, he had promised that "no part whatever of your land joining the said forts shall be taken from you, nor any of our people be permitted to hunt or settle upon them." They would "remain your absolute property."[62] But even before the conflict was finished, numerous speculators were looking across the mountains and beyond. In Virginia, the Ohio Company resumed its plans for a colony of 500,000 acres near the Forks of the Ohio in accordance with its charter of 1753. To facilitate their scheme, the directors offered Bouquet a 25,000-acre share. Bouquet declined, believing it contravened the promises made at the Treaty of Easton.[63] However, his refusal was an honorable exception and did nothing to reduce the speculative fever. The area around Fort Pitt in consequence was increasingly infested by white hunters, many of them settlers looking for suitable sites.[64] Their activities inevitably disturbed the game, further disrupting the Indian economy.

A similar land fever prevailed in New York, as Alexander Colden, the provincial surveyor, reported in January 1761.[65] Three major claims now threatened the Mohawk. The first was the Kayaderosseras patent, which had originally been granted in 1704 as an Indian deed, though in dubious if not fraudulent circumstances. It had lain fallow for fifty years until the growing land hunger alerted the current patentees to its potential value.[66] The second threat came from the town of Albany, which claimed a substantial portion of the Mohawk Valley west of Schenectady, including the land on which the lower Mohawk castle of Caghnawaga was situated.[67] The third concerned the activities of Ury Klock, acting also on behalf of other "gentlemen," who had purchased lands previously patented by the Livingston family.[68] Their claims threatened the upper Mohawk castle of Canajoharie.

Klock's method, and that of other speculators for securing their patents, was to intoxicate small groups of Mohawk before producing a deed of sale for them to mark with their consent. After one such surreptitious deal, the Canajoharie chiefs not unnaturally denounced the "deceitfulness, and un-brotherly behavior of the white people towards them."[69] Such treatment merely confirmed "what the French have often told the Six Nations," namely, that the British were out to destroy them. If the British mistreated people who had risked everything "defending their and our country" during the recent war, "what must our friends the [other] Six Nations say or think?"[70]

Johnson was sufficiently concerned over the activities of Klock to write to the acting governor of New York, Cadwallader Colden, in March 1761 protesting these developments. Colden agreed about the need for fairness in the purchase of Indian lands. This had always been his policy, and Johnson should "assure the Indians of my firm resolution to that purpose." But Colden had no new proposals to make other than observance of the existing 1736 regulations. These stated that all purchases of Indian lands must have the consent of the Provincial Council. If the Indians had been injured, nothing would give Colden "greater pleasure" than to attend to them.[71] This reply hardly inspired confidence that anything effective would be done about their grievances. In reality, even Johnson was more interested in securing title to some 40,000 acres which the Mohawk had granted him for acting on their behalf. These were not the actions of a disinterested official.[72]

Finally, Indian concern was also raised at this time by the activities of the Susquehanna Company in Pennsylvania. The growth of population in Connecticut had led to the forming of a land company for the creation of a colony near the forks of the Susquehanna River. The project had first been hatched at the Congress of Albany in 1754, when some Six Nations chiefs sold a second large tract of land to a group of Connecticut speculators led by John Lydius.[73] Although the company was a private affair, the owners believed their purchase was legitimate, and they were determined to make good their claim now that the French had been removed. Only days after the surrender of Canada, the company had surveyors and workmen cutting roads and preparing townships. Among the sites was Wyoming, where Teedyuscung was endeavoring to settle.[74] The situation was fraught with danger, for as Governor James Hamilton had previously warned Connecticut Governor Thomas Fitch, a new Indian war was likely if the company proceeded with its plans. Teedyuscung was already threatening force against the settlers, and the Six Nations were ready to support him, since they claimed to be owners of the land.[75] The "middle ground" was in serious jeopardy.

Prisoners or Family?

One other issue to cloud relations in the first year of Amherst's new regime was the return of prisoners. Several hundred men, women, and children had been captured by the Indians during the war with Britain. The problem was that the two sides had irreconcilable views on the issue. European nations followed the convention that all prisoners should return to their own country on the conclusion of hostilities, since they were a by-product of the war, not a primary aim. But to the Native Americans, prisoners were valuable assets who served several purposes. Some might be ransomed, and others ritually tortured. However, the majority, especially women and children, were valued for adoption. The low fertility of Native Americans and the impact of European diseases meant that all the nations had declining numbers. Consequently, when a victorious war party returned home, those prisoners deemed suitable for adoption were distributed "in the room of deceased relatives."[76]

The native peoples had been remarkably successful in acculturating their captives, as the case of Eunice Williams demonstrated. For over fifty years, she had resisted all attempts by her family to redeem her following her capture at Deerfield, Massachusetts, in 1704 and integration into Caghnawaga society.[77] But however much the captives wished to remain with their adopted families, the British were similarly determined to see them returned. This included the children of white mothers and Indian fathers. To European Americans, the practice of replacing lost relatives through the adoption of prisoners was "a queer Indian custom" that was contradictory to their notions of family.[78] But there was another reason for the British stance. As the Reverend Stephen Williams, Eunice's brother, told Amherst after the fall of Quebec, his fervent hope was that "every Child, and descendent of New England," could now "be brought out of that land of darkness and slavery, into a land of light and liberty."[79] To whites, it was inconceivable that persons of European descent should want to live in a condition of savagery or irreligion. Their souls must be saved.

The need to save the captives' souls was a point made by Frederick Post at the start of the 1760 campaign. He wrote to Amherst that "should the Indians [at] any time or place be called to a public meeting or treaty ... it be insisted on that the Indians Deliver up all our People who are captives among them." Nearly all the nations had some captives. He continued, "To me it appears a scandal to Christianity to permit or suffer our flesh and blood to be made and used as heathen by the Indians, for they have already forced many to marry with them." As to the Indian argument that the captives did not want to return, Post urged that every such person be brought to a place where they could declare their true sentiments without fear of reprisal. Not to do so was to condemn "the poor women slaves to such Indians ... giving them a liberty to mock and revile at our holy Christian Religion."[80]

While the fighting continued, the British had to tread carefully to prevent potential allies from becoming enemies. Most nations in any case were disposed to meet the British halfway. Early in 1760 John Stanwix, the commanding officer of the southern military district, reported that the Ohio nations were honoring the recent treaty at Fort Pitt: "They all agree to give up their prisoners, many have been given up and they are daily giving up more," and "the whole will be delivered up in the spring." A similar attitude seemingly prevailed at Detroit, where Lieutenant McDonald of the 77th Highland regiment and a sergeant had been released. Others were on their way. But Stanwix confessed one unexpected obstacle: "What surprises me more is that a great many of our prisoners absolutely refuse to leave the Indians and a good many [have] gone back to them after [being] very formally delivered up here."[81] From a European perspective, it was most perplexing.

But the Indians were equally perplexed at the British demand for the surrender of every white captive, no matter what their wishes. By the end of 1760, the Indians had given up all those who had resisted adoption or were prisoners in a European sense. Any further surrender could only result in the break-up of families and made the nations increasingly insistent that the captives return of their own free will. This, of course, did nothing to abate the determination of European Americans to be reunited with their loved ones, as a petition of James McCullough to Bouquet made clear. In 1756 McCullough had lost two sons, John and James, aged thirteen and ten years. John had been adopted by a Delaware family near the Salt Licks, while James had been given to a French ensign. McCullough lamented that the loss of his two sons had made him and his wife truly wretched. They could only plead "their distressed case to all charitable and well disposed Christians."[82] Amherst himself was surprisingly indifferent about the captives, unless they were deserters. However, it was not an issue that either the British or the provincial authorities could ignore, given the numbers involved, for by July 1761 Bouquet calculated that the Delaware and Shawnee still had 250 captives between them.[83]

As the British pressure increased, the Indians found additional reasons to delay. Apart from family ties, the captives were now seen as an insurance against British attack. The British, however, believed the Indian reluctance to return the prisoners was because they wanted a ransom. Since gentle persuasion was not working, other methods would have to be used, Croghan warned the Shawnee, when explaining what the consequences of further refusal might be. "The English are very slow in entering into a war with the Indians, yet if they are forced to do it … their warriors will tread so heavy that they will crush their Enemies under their feet." Croghan affirmed that "we don't go to war as your fathers, the French, do in small parties to steal people. We go to conquer countries and subdue nations." The natives should take note.[84]

But it was time for the British to take note, too. Although diplomatic courtesies continued to be exchanged, the nations were increasingly disenchanted. The Six Nations were angry about the threat to their lands and lack of esteem; the Ohio peoples were anxious about the return of the prisoners, the retention of Fort Pitt, and the threat of settlement; while the Great Lakes and Wabash peoples were disillusioned about the lack of gifts and terms of trade, especially the want of ammunition. The middle ground had all but disappeared. In less than a year, Amherst had sufficiently antagonized some chiefs, notably the Seneca, for their leaders to contemplate a very different way of settling these issues.

2

The Seneca Plan: A War of Liberation

Tahaiadoris and Kiashuta: The French Connection

The Seneca were the most powerful member of the Iroquois Confederacy, able to deploy a thousand warriors, despite the general decline in the Indian population. Traditionally the Seneca had guarded the western gate to the Iroquois homeland, occupying nine "castles" or settlements south and east of Niagara. Among the more important were Canadasaga and Canandaigua near Lake Seneca, and Ganawagus and Geneseo, or "Chenussio" as it was known, further west on the Genesee River. Seneca migrants had also created the Mingo villages on the Allegheny River.

Like the rest of the Iroquois Confederacy, the Seneca had fought the French during the seventeenth century for control of the fur trade. However, after several bloody defeats, they too had made peace in 1701 in favor of neutrality. However, the proximity of the French at Niagara meant that the Seneca were effectively in their orbit, especially the Genesee villages. Johnson believed the storehouse at Niagara had been built specifically for bribing them.[1] The good understanding was strengthened by the Genesee relationship with the Joncaire family.[2] Nevertheless, the Seneca did not support the French on the outbreak of war in 1755. Indeed, by 1759 the changing fortunes of the war had led them to declare for the British with the rest of the Six Nations, thinking that the capture of Niagara would result in its becoming a trading post once more. Unfortunately, the British decided to keep the fort and strengthen its defenses. This breach of trust led the Seneca to warn Colonel William Eyre the commander at Niagara in May 1760 that "all the Indians to the westward and southward were determined to insist this place out of the hands of the English" and would "assemble very soon for that purpose, assisted by the French."[3]

Even so, 170 Seneca still accompanied Amherst in his advance on Montreal, spurred on by a desire for "revenge on the French for the former insults their ancestors had received on the first settlement of Canada." Consequently, when Amherst refused to allow them "to prosecute the war" at Fort Levis "agreeable to their own custom," the Seneca had little compunction in abandoning him. As one of their chiefs subsequently affirmed to Johnson, "They thought their turning back at a time when the General seemed not to want them, could not be a sufficient reason to refuse them a free and open trade and communications in their own country as they call it." The Seneca, like the rest of the Six Nations, could not understand why "no notice had been taken of them since the reduction of Canada," which "mystifies them greatly as they expected to be raised up above all nations." Instead they were being punished, not rewarded, despite their help in the capture of Niagara, without which "the place had not been taken." It seemed clear that "the English have some bad designs against them."[4]

The mood of the Seneca was not improved by the treatment of their Mingo relatives at Venango and Fort Ligonier. But soon they had an even more important grievance: that Amherst had "given away a part of the country," which the king had "long ago promised to keep for their use."[5] This latter was a reference to a treaty of 1726 with Governor William Burnet of New York, which they had negotiated as part of the Covenant Chain. The accusation was prompted by the discovery in April 1761 that Amherst had granted Captain Walter Rutherford the use of ten thousand acres at Niagara to facilitate the transportation of goods around the falls. Previously, the Seneca had worked the portage for the French. Now their services were being dispensed with and their lands occupied. This was a breach of the promises made by Amherst in his declaration of 27 April 1760. Amherst acknowledged privately that the scheme would ultimately need approval in London, but believed it would temporarily be beneficial "to the Trade, to Lake Erie and parts adjacent as well as to the garrisons beyond Niagara."[6] By the end of April 1761, the first workmen had arrived "to build houses, also horses and oxen," both "for farming" as well as "for the conveyance of boats and goods."[7] But this was not all, for the Seneca shortly discovered that the British were constructing two armed vessels for patrolling the upper lakes.[8] Seemingly, there was no limit to the intrusive presence of the British and their desire to "attempt enslaving them."[9]

The anger of the Genesee was especially strong, as a former soldier of the 44th regiment testified after staying with them over the winter of 1760. He affirmed they "were not well affected to the English, neither did they like our going beyond Niagara to garrison posts or even to trade." The Seneca insisted "that it was their country and they looked upon it that we were going to surround or hem them in." The informant believed that only a scarcity of powder prevented them from falling "upon some parties of our people going to Detroit."[10]

It is not clear who first raised the idea of a pan-Indian war against the British. The seeds may have been sown by the Detroit confederacy, who according to Croghan planned "a great meeting of all the Western Nations" in the spring of 1761 to which the Six Nations were invited.[11] However, the western peoples had shown no overt hostility to the British at this time, having recently allowed Rogers and Campbell to enter Detroit. In reality French influence was almost certainly the decisive factor at this point. Before surrendering Canada, Vaudreuil had instructed the officers at the western posts to tell the Indians that the British occupation would only be temporary. The king of France would not abandon his subjects or leave his Indian children to fend on their own.[12] But another reason for attributing French influence was the nature of the leadership behind the plan. The principal proponents were two disgruntled Seneca chiefs, the Genesee Tahaiadoris and the Mingo Kiashuta. Tahaiadoris was the son of Daniel Joncaire, the former interpreter, trader, and French colonial officer, who had retained his links with the Seneca until his capture at Niagara and deportation to France.[13] According to an Onondaga informant of Johnson, it was Joncaire "who before he was made prisoner recommended it to the Seneca that in case the French should be conquered, they were to propose to the other Nations to unite and fall upon the English."[14] The scheme now proposed certainly had the hallmark of someone thinking imperially, though such ambitions were not beyond the Iroquois themselves, since they had spent most of the seventeenth century seeking control of the beaver trade. Imperial vision was part of their culture.

The plan of Tahaiadoris and Kiashuta had six parts. Firstly, the nations about Detroit—namely, the Ottawa, Potawatomi, Wyandot, and Ojibwa—were to surprise its garrison, seizing the weapons and other goods of the British traders. Secondly, the Delaware, Shawnee, Miami, and "other nations settled between the Ohio and Lake Erie" were to attack Fort Bedford and Fort Ligonier, guarding the communication between Pennsylvania and Fort Pitt. This would then isolate that post, making the Allegheny Mountains a secure boundary. Thirdly, the Mingo and other Indians living on the Allegheny River were to capture the communication between Fort Pitt and Lake Erie, meaning the posts of Presque Isle, Le Boeuf, and Venango. Then the main body of the Six Nations and their dependents on the Susquehanna River were to seize the posts between Niagara and Fort Herkimer on the Mohawk River, where the line of settlement began. The expectation was that "by cutting off the communication everywhere, such posts as they could not take," like Fort Pitt and Niagara, they could "starve out and become masters of their country again."[15]

Perhaps the most ambitious part of the scheme was the proposal to involve the Cherokee. The idea probably originated with Joncaire and his colleagues since the French had held talks with that nation in an attempt to increase their influence.[16] Clearly the more enemies the British had, the greater the chance of success. Nevertheless, calling on the Cherokee was a radical step since the northern and southern nations had been in conflict for centuries. As Thomas King, an Oneida chief, subsequently commented, "We have been at war with them ever since we were created."[17] However, the maxim that one person's enemy was someone else's friend was still true, especially as the Cherokee were currently fighting the British in the defense of their homelands. Accordingly, Tahaiadoris and Kiashuta proposed that the Six Nations should send one hundred men to assist the Cherokee "to encourage them to continue the war against the English."[18] Indeed, two Cherokee deputies had already arrived "in the Seneca country waiting to see what part those Western Nations would act in the intended plot."[19]

Finally, the scheme not unreasonably assumed French help in view of the messages from Vaudreuil implying that an army and fleet would come to their rescue. The northern nations were accordingly "to join that army, while the western and southern nations" harassed "the frontiers." The "middle ground" would then be restored. "This" Tahaiadoris and Kiashuta "said was the Seneca Plan, which they had consorted since the reduction of Canada and the English refusing them ammunition."[20]

Prior to the departure of Tahaiadoris and Kiashuta, deputies with decorative belts of wampum were sent as far as Gaspé in the St. Lawrence Gulf and the Illinois to the west.[21] However, the Cayuga failed seemingly to forward the red-colored war belt to the eastern members of the confederacy, fearing they would betray the plan. Hence many were unaware of the mission's real design, as Sequarésere, a Tuscarora sachem, claimed when Johnson asked him for an explanation. Sequarésere believed that Tahaiadoris and Kiashuta had gone to offer condolences for the chiefs killed at Niagara in 1759. He also believed this was the reason why some Cayuga had visited the northern Indians at Cadaraqui, near the entrance to the St. Lawrence River. On being told by Johnson the true nature of the Detroit mission, Sequarésere declared "solemnly that no such design had ever been agreed to by the Six Nations, nor any such message sent by them to the Detroit, or Cadaraqui Meetings.... If any such thing was in Agitation it must come from the Seneca alone."[22]

Tahaiadoris and Kiashuta set off on their mission in early June 1761, accompanied by eight other "young men."[23] They first headed for the Ohio, where they were joined by Tamaqua and several Delaware and Shawnee chiefs. The two groups then proceeded to Sandusky, where the Delaware and Shawnee stopped, while the Seneca continued their journey to the Wyandot town opposite Detroit. Here they issued invitations to the Ottawa, Wyandot, Ojibwa, and Potawatomi to attend a conference to be held at Sandusky in company with the Delaware and Shawnee.[24]

Unfortunately for Tahaiadoris and Kiashuta, they met their first obstacle when the Detroit nations refused to travel to Sandusky. The latter insisted that the meeting be held at Detroit, expressing surprise that they should have been summoned to a council "in a land of brambles."[25] But from the start, it is clear that the nations around Detroit were equivocal about cooperating with the Iroquois. Memories of the seventeenth-century Beaver Wars and more recent events at Niagara remained strong. In addition, the Detroit nations had yet to feel the same sense of grievance as those nearer to the British settlements. For the moment, they preferred not to offend their new "brethren."

Tahaiadoris and Kiashuta accordingly returned to Sandusky to consult with the Delaware and Shawnee, since the latter refused to proceed without the support of the western nations.[26] This caution may have reflected the views of Tamaqua, who had theatrically gone home after first throwing the proffered war hatchet against a wall.[27] Despite this rebuff, the Seneca envoys determined to persevere with their scheme. With the consent of the remaining Delaware and Shawnee, they set off once more for a second meeting with the Detroit nations.

When the conference resumed on 3 July 1761, Tahaiadoris took the lead, indicating that the scheme was principally his. First he offered condolences for the affair at Niagara, suggesting that the episode be forgotten as many warriors had been slain on both sides. Next he urged the Detroit nations to keep their young men at home and "not to go to war against their ancient enemies the Cherokee," as they would have some other business for them.[28] Tahaiadoris then produced a large belt of red wampum, the color of war, which he claimed he had received from the chiefs of the Six Nations. In reality, it was the belt that his father had given him before the surrender of Niagara. Indeed, much of Tahaiadoris's address was delivered in the name of "Shabear Jean Coeur," who had once resided at Detroit and was known to the nations there.[29] Tahaiadoris continued, "The English treat us with much disrespect, and we have reason to believe by their behavior they intend to cut us off entirely," having "possessed themselves of our country." However, "It is now in our power to dispossess them and recover it, if we will embrace the opportunity before they have time to assemble together and fortify themselves there." Tahaiadoris particularly addressed himself to the Wyandot, a fellow Iroquoian-language people: "As you are the leading nation here, you have only to say the word and the others will follow your example." Accordingly, "We invite you by this belt to cut off the English at Fort Detroit" while the Six Nations simultaneously endeavored "to do the same with the garrisons at Niagara and Fort Pitt."[30]

The four nations present made no response other than to say that they first wanted a meeting with Captain Donald Campbell, the acting commander, to assess the British attitude. However, their real reason was that they had decided to tell Campbell about the plan. But unknown to them, the scheme had already been betrayed during the envoys' first visit to Detroit by "the Wiandot interpreter to whom the Seneca told their business in confidence." Tahaiadoris had made the fatal error of thinking that he could trust every Frenchman. Instead the interpreter, Jacques St. Martin, immediately informed Campbell "of the whole affair." Campbell quietly put the fort into a state of defense and dispatched fifty armed traders to secure weapons and ammunition at Sandusky.[31] St. Martin now played another key role, for he told Campbell that although there was support for the Seneca plan, he had persuaded most of the Wyandot to oppose it. This was crucial since the other nations wanted the decision to be unanimous. A grateful Campbell commented to Bouquet, "We can never too much reward" St. Martin "for his services in this affair."[32]

When the meeting was resumed on 4 July 1761, the red wampum belt was accordingly produced and given to the British commander, much to the astonishment of Tahaiadoris and Kiashuta. Tahaiadoris, seeing that the scheme was discovered, then proceeded to acknowledge his complicity, but justified his actions by telling the council that "the English had used them ill." He and Kiashuta had come to Detroit merely to seek assistance. However, since his audience had "refused to accept the hatchet, they had opened his heart and given him a new way of thinking." Accordingly, he would return home "with the sentiments of the Nations here which he believed would give them [the Six Nations] great joy." He then requested that Amherst and Johnson be informed of the affair in the hope that the British would treat the Six Nations better in future, "as they had dealt very badly with them lately."[33]

Since Campbell had only a hundred troops, he accepted Tahaiadoris's change of heart, though not before he had delivered a stern lecture, expressing his surprise "that the Six Nations, who had always been our allies, would endeavor to draw the other nations into war with us." He then desired the two envoys "to think better, and to go home and assure their chiefs that the nations here were well disposed to the English." To reinforce his message, he handed Tahaiadoris a white peace belt for the Six Nations, urging them to give up their bad designs. On route Tahaiadoris was to inform the Delaware and Shawnee at Sandusky of his change of heart, after which he was to carry some letters for Campbell to Bouquet at Fort Pitt. Campbell seems to have warmed to Tahaiadoris, since both men were able to converse in French. He told Bouquet, "I think him a very sensible fellow… If you use him well he will tell you the whole project, which was very great."[34]

Tahaiadoris and Kiashuta accordingly set off for Fort Pitt, where Croghan learned the details of the scheme with the help of some presents.[35] However, the two envoys were more circumspect in their meeting with Bouquet, where there was "dissembling on both sides." Nevertheless, after distributing further presents, they "parted very great friends."[36] But Bouquet, like Campbell, had quietly strengthened the fortifications of his post, organizing the male inhabitants into a militia for its better protection.[37]

Amherst, who was temporarily staying in Albany, affected to be unconcerned by these developments. He commended Walters at Niagara for putting his post on guard but agreed "you judge very rightly in thinking that it is not in the power of the Indians at present to hurt us." Although some troops had been sent to the West Indies, the army that had conquered America was still relatively intact on the North American mainland. Consequently, Amherst believed that even the plotters knew they that had no chance of success.[38] Not that Amherst was insensible to the part played by the Detroit Indians. He told Johnson, now on his way for the conference there, "to take proper notice of those that behave peaceably and quietly, and adhere to His Majesty's interest." In particular, he was to tell "the Ottawa, Wiandot, Chippewa and Potawatomie the sense I have of their prudence and good behavior at the Council to which they were called by the deputies of the Six Nations."[39] Amherst was not quite the heartless person often depicted by historians.[40]

Johnson Investigates: The Detroit Conference

The conference at Detroit had been agreed on by Amherst and Johnson prior to the news of the Seneca plan to confirm the chain of friendship with the Great Lakes nations which Croghan and Rogers had concluded in December 1760. Initially, Amherst toyed with the idea of joining Johnson on his trip.[41] But the tardiness of the provincial governments in raising troops and the need to organize the regulars for an expedition to Martinique made this impossible.[42] Johnson accordingly set out alone on 5 July 1761. Before starting, he spoke to the Caghnawaga Mohawk in an attempt to reassure them about their lands. They responded by expressing their unease at his journeying through "several nations of Indians, as yet much attached to the French."[43] Johnson, however, did not learn about the Seneca plot until 13 July, just as he was approaching Fort Stanwix on the Mohawk River. Here the Mohawk in his party urged him to turn back, fearing that their own castles would be attacked, since they were considered to be "entirely in the English interest."[44] But Johnson was not to be diverted, as Amherst wanted him to investigate in person.[45] Accordingly, he pressed on to Oswego for a meeting with the Onondaga, where he warned his audience to avoid all mischief with the western nations. He then distributed some of the campaign medals. The Onondaga in reply affirmed that they knew nothing of the Seneca plot, not having received any belt or war message. They had, however, plenty of complaints to make about the traders and soldiers at the forts. They also disliked Johnson's going to Detroit for a council which they believed should have been held at Onondaga, the traditional meeting place.[46]

Johnson then set sail for Niagara, where he first spoke to the Mississauga Ojibwa from Toronto, under their chief Wabbicommicot. He congratulated them on abstaining from the recent plot and invited their leaders to accompany him to Detroit, where they would receive details of the new trade prices. Wabbicommicot took advantage of this to relate the misery of his people caused by the want of ammunition and other goods. "Brother, I have tried several times with my hands to catch fish for my living but found it would not answer," not having a spear to kill them. "I am likewise prevented from hunting by reason of my guns being broke." If Johnson wanted the Mississauga Ojibwa to accompany him to Detroit, he must help them. Johnson in reply promised some clothing as well as a smith to repair their weapons at Niagara.[47] After this Johnson spoke to some visiting Sandusky Wyandot, advising them that Major Henry Gladwin would shortly appear with three hundred soldiers to occupy the remaining French posts. The Wyandot therefore should "not be alarmed at their approach." He then distributed some clothing and cash to buy bread for their journey home.[48]

However, the most important business at Niagara was to interview the Seneca, whom Johnson had summoned to explain their conduct. Instead, news arrived that most of the Seneca had returned home because one of their chiefs had fallen sick. This was undoubtedly a diplomatic illness to cover the embarrassment at the recent disclosures. As a result, Johnson was left to vent his anger on a small group led by the Genesee chief Sonajoana. Johnson began by expressing his surprise at the late arrival of the Seneca and the paucity of their delegation. Then he stressed his anger at learning of the plan to get the western nations "to take up the hatchet, and join with you against the English, — your Brethren, your Friends and your Allies." What must the other nations who had lately been in arms against the English think? But before condemning them, Johnson demanded to know whether the two messengers had been authorized to act on behalf of the Seneca nation.[49]

In his reply on 9 August, Sonajoana categorically stated that his nation was "not only innocent, but entirely ignorant of the whole charge against us … it having been always our intention to live in strict friendship with the English." He then repeated what others had been saying: that "as those messengers live near Fort Pitt, they must have been dispatched by some Indians from that quarter." In the meantime, he begged Johnson, on behalf of "the warriors and principal women," to "consider their poverty, and allow the former some ammunition to kill game for their support." Surely he would show "pity on our women who have scarcely clothing to cover their nakedness."[50] But this answer only angered Johnson. The "frivolous excuses that the messengers lived detached" from the Seneca were laughable. Johnson was certain that no "tribes of your nation (though ever so remote) would presume to undertake so dangerous an affair without your concurrence and approbation." The only way they could satisfy Amherst was by sending a deputation to the conference at Detroit to disavow the actions of their envoys. As to their want of ammunition, this "was entirely owing to their own ill behavior last year in abandoning his Majesty's troops after the surrender" of Fort Levis. The best Johnson could do was to give them a little powder and shot to see them home.[51]

Johnson finally set sail for Detroit on 19 August 1761, arriving on 3 September. Here he found Croghan with the "principal sachems and warriors of the Delaware, Shawnee," and other "nations residing over the Lakes or on the Ohio," whom Johnson had also invited to the conference.[52] After distributing a little tobacco and rum, Johnson received from Croghan the minutes of a conference which the Delaware had held before Johnson arrived. The Delaware had ostensibly organized this to express their desire for peace, though undoubtedly it was in reality to obscure their earlier support for Tahaiadoris and Kiashuta.[53] The diplomatic prelude continued on 6 September 1761, when Johnson met the local Ottawa, who informed him of their poverty and want of gunpowder. Johnson responded that he would consider their request for help, but hoped that "they would for the future by their hunting and by an industrious way of life, be enabled to support their families without any other assistance."[54] Finally Johnson attended a dinner and dance organized by Campbell, so that he could meet the ladies of the town. He opened the proceedings with "Mademoiselle Curie," Angelique Cuillerier, who he noted was "a fine girl." Johnson danced until five o'clock in the morning.[55]

The main conference itself opened on 9 September 1761. After the usual condolences for those who had recently died, Johnson began by affirming that Amherst was well pleased with the recent behavior of the Detroit nations, which had done much to strengthen the Covenant Chain. Their reward would be "an extensive plentiful commerce on the most equitable terms." He also delivered a message from Amherst assuring them that their lands were secure. Johnson confirmed, "It is not at present, neither hath it been his Majesty's intentions to deprive any nation of Indians of their just property by taking possession of any lands to which they have a lawful claim" other "than for the better promoting of an extensive commerce." However, if good relations were to continue, the Indians must end their habit of stealing horses.[56]

The next day, Anáiása, a Wyandot chief, replied, expressing his pleasure at what Johnson had said. He added that if Johnson wanted more information about the recent activities of the Seneca, he should question one of those attending, pointing at Kiashuta, who was representing the Mingo. He then raised the question of trade and the need for "plenty of goods and that at a cheaper rate than we have hitherto been able to procure," on which many promises had been made. Finally, Anáiása mentioned the matter of the white prisoners, saying that the Detroit nations had complied with the requests made two years earlier at Fort Duquesne. "But we must observe that they [the prisoners] are no slaves with us, being at their free liberty to go anywhere, or act as they please."[57]

Anáiása was followed by the Ottawa chief, Mackatepelecite. He affirmed that his nation now appreciated the British presence, which was not as the French had portrayed it would be. In future, they would pay no attention to "the people who sent the bad Bird lately amongst us to stir us up against our Brethren."[58] This second denunciation finally prompted Kiashuta to defend himself, saying that he knew nothing of the scheme attributed to him, having originally set out to visit Johnson at his home on the Mohawk River. At "Chenussio" he had accidentally met Tahaiadoris, who suggested going to Detroit instead, though without indicating his real intent. In consequence, he "was greatly astonished at hearing the proposals made by his companion to the Wiandot, of which he before had not received the least intimation."[59] However, Kiashuta's denials and those of his companion, the White Mingo, only added fuel to the fire, for their assertions of innocence were promptly contradicted by another Wyandot sachem, Adarighta, who "discovered everything which had passed." The White Mingo then confessed that Tahaiadoris and Kiashuta "had come several times to him at the Ohio, and pressed him and others living there to fall upon the English." At this point, Johnson asked "that they would not go to too great lengths," as they were "now joined in a stricter friendship and alliance than ever."[60] The last thing Johnson wanted was an outbreak of acrimony which might destroy his careful diplomacy.

The following day Johnson distributed presents to the attendees, after which an ox was roasted and a feast held. However, he decided to issue another warning to Kiashuta and the White Mingo about "the folly of undertaking any enterprise against so powerful a people as the English." As part of his investigation, he would call a conference of the Six Nations, at which time "the whole affair should be thoroughly canvassed."[61] In the event, Johnson had to wait another seven months before the Genesee publicly admitted their complicity. Even then, they blamed the Sandusky Wyandot for sending the initial invitations and proposing war.[62]

Before leaving, Johnson crossed the river for one final meeting with the Detroit nations. Here Anáiása again expressed his pleasure at the proceedings, but raised his concern that the trade was "not at present on the best terms." He continued in the now familiar refrain, "We were always told before the reduction of this country that whenever you became masters of it we should ... find the same treatment which we had met with from the French, and get from you such necessaries as we wanted, for which reason we now beg you will allow us a credit when the autumn comes in for what we shall want, as the French were used to do formerly." The Detroit nations also needed a smith to mend their guns and hatchets, together with help for the warriors sent to fight the Cherokee.[63] This was the minimum necessary to restore the "middle ground" even among the supposedly loyal Detroit Wyandot. Johnson replied that he had drawn up regulations for the trade, fixing prices so low that he was apprehensive the traders would stop visiting the posts. Credit was a matter for the merchants. However, he would get Croghan to send a smith from Fort Pitt to repair their guns and tools.[64]

Johnson set off for home well pleased with the outcome. He reported to Amherst, "It is with great satisfaction I now inform your Excellency that I have left the Western Indians extremely well disposed towards the English." "Matters are settled on so stable a foundation there, that unless greatly irritated thereto, they will never break the peace established with them." Johnson was oblivious that the acquiescence of the Detroit nations was conditional on their receiving better treatment from the British. Instead, he believed that the only remaining thing to be done was to arrange a meeting with the Six Nations.[65] The conquest of Canada had caused a revolution in their affairs: "Instead of being courted by two nations," Britain and France, "they now depended upon one power."[66] It was time to show them some appreciation, except for the Seneca.

The Detroit conference was notable for one other reason. The Shawnee, Delaware, Wyandot, and Miami believed that Johnson's invitation to attend meant that he had thrown "off the yoke of [the] Onondaga" from their shoulders. They were now "a separate power independent of the Six Nations," able to make an offensive and defensive alliance with the British. If true, this too was another unwelcome development for the Iroquois.[67]

The Occupation Completed: The Western Posts

While at Detroit, Johnson made arrangements with Gladwin for the occupation of Michilimackinac, La Baye, and St. Joseph. The initial attempt to take possession in December 1760 had been prevented by the onset of winter and a lack of troops.[68] The appearance of Gladwin now permitted the occupation to proceed, which the British believed was necessary for two reasons. The Illinois country was still under French control, the danger being that the garrison at Fort Chartres would continue the war by stirring up the native peoples. Secondly, it was essential to protect lives and property in areas nominally under British control.

Most pressing was the occupation of Michilimackinac, where a dangerous vacuum existed following the unilateral withdrawal of the French garrison under Captain Louis de Beaujeu to the Illinois, contrary to the surrender terms.[69] The place had been relatively quiet during the winter, but the return of the Ojibwa and Ottawa from their hunting made even the local priest anxious for the arrival of the British. He wrote to his superior in Montreal, "Our needs are too great for us to be able hereafter to dispense with the presence, or at least the assistance, of our conquerors." This was also the view of the inhabitants, the priest declared. Neither Langlade, the acting commandant, "nor any other Frenchman has any intention except the obedience due to that which has been arranged between the two generals," meaning Amherst and Vaudreuil.[70]

The delicate nature of the situation was confirmed by Alexander Henry, one of the first British traders to arrive at Michilimackinac. He found the local Ojibwa and Ottawa were both still at war, not having had an opportunity for making peace. These points were made to Henry by Minavavana, "the chief of the whole band of Chippewa from the island of Michilimackinac," so called because its shape resembled that of a turtle. Minavavana began by asserting that the king of France had merely fallen asleep, during which time the British had taken advantage of him and possessed Canada. However, he would surely wake up again. In any case, Minavavana asserted that "although you have conquered the French, you have not conquered us. We are not your slaves. These lakes, these woods and mountains were left to us by our ancestors. They are our inheritance and we will part with them to none." He then reminded Henry, "Our father, the King of France, employed our young men to make war upon your nation. In this warfare many of them have been killed; and it is our custom to retaliate until such time as the spirits of the slain are satisfied. But the spirits of the slain are to be satisfied in either of two ways; the first is by the spilling of the blood of the nation by which they fell dead; the other by covering the bodies of the dead, and thus allaying the resentment of their relations. This is done by the giving of presents." After consultation with the interpreter, Henry was able to pacify Minavavana with a present and his warriors with some rum.[71]

Shortly afterwards Henry received a similar visit from the Ottawa of L'Arbre Croche, the mission settlement twenty miles to the west of the fort. The main interest of the Ottawa, as for Minavavana, was the goods which Henry had brought with him, which they feared might be sent to the more distant Sioux. Their speaker accordingly suggested that Henry allow credit equivalent to fifty beaver skins so that they could make some purchases. The debt would then be repaid when the Indians returned from their next hunt. Henry, like other British merchants, was unaccustomed to granting credit. He only escaped his predicament on how to placate them by the news that British troops were about to land.[72]

The expedition to Michilimackinac comprised 120 men, commanded by Captain Henry Balfour, Gladwin being sick. Balfour's orders were to garrison the posts of Michilimackinac, La Baye, and St. Joseph, and relieve some rangers at Fort Miami near the head of the Maumee River. Before he departed, Johnson drew up guidelines on how the Indians were to be treated. The officers were to keep a good understanding by restricting contact between the ordinary soldiers and the natives, since this "often creates disputes and quarrels ... for want of understanding each other." Clearly, an interpreter would be necessary and each commander was to choose one of the most honest and best qualified from the French inhabitants, who would serve on a part-time basis. Equally importantly, each officer was "to see that all traders strictly adhere to the regulation made for that purpose, on pain of being banished," since abuses must be prevented. Johnson had decided that the Indian trade should be conducted at the posts, despite Amherst's objection. Accordingly, no trader was to be admitted who did not have a passport from Johnson or Croghan. Finally, the commanding officer at each post was to assist the Indians in the repair of their weapons, hiring a smith if practicable.[73]

Balfour left Detroit on 9 September 1761, arriving at Michilimackinac on 28 September. The fort appeared in reasonable order, though nothing of value was left inside. But the Indians still had to be reconciled to the British presence, especially when Balfour asserted that he had no ammunition to give them in the manner formerly practiced by the French. Balfour did not help relations by pompously telling his audience, "You cannot be ignorant that the arms of our Great King George" have "conquered and are become entirely masters of the dominions of the King of France in Canada." The British monarch's intention "in sending these garrisons here, is to preserve good order and to have the most strict justice done to his subjects as well as to protect all Indian nations who will render themselves worthy of his Royal Goodness." Earning the latter meant yielding any remaining prisoners and generally conducting themselves in a sober manner.[74]

Quinonchaming, the Ottawa chief, replied that he was glad to hear about the peace and prospects for trade but could give no answer until his people returned from their winter hunt.[75] The Ojibwa, courtesy of Kipimisaming, "a Delaware inhabiting amongst them", in contrast, decided to be more ingratiating with their new "brethren." Kipimisaming accordingly told Balfour that the Ojibwa had formerly been a happy nation with great chiefs and warriors. Now their circumstances were very different. "The chiefs who by their example inspired our Youth with fine sentiments are all dead, as are our Great Warriors, and there only remains the Children and Grand Children of those Chiefs, people without understanding and without authority." He hoped the commander would understand this and take it into account. He continued, "We are so poor that I have great fear our old people, our women and children will perish with hunger. We are destitute of everything, having neither powder, nor lead for hunting to support ourselves during the winter …. If you have not compassion for us, our ruin must be inevitable."[76]

This was not what Balfour wanted to hear, and he replied to the Ojibwa in a hectoring tone, "You had plenty of peltry last spring, what is become thereof?" The real reason for their poverty was that they had sold their "peltry for rum, without even buying powder, lead or any other things." They could not be considered men when they preferred rum to looking after their "old people, wives and children." This was the conduct of "beasts." However, Balfour had been able to negotiate some credit with the traders to help them over the winter. Thereafter, they must repay their debts and always treat the traders well.[77] Balfour then gave instructions to Lt. Leslie, the prospective commander, leaving him a sergeant and twenty-six privates with a suitable quantity of provisions.[78]

Balfour left Michilimackinac on the first of October for La Baye, which he reached on 10 October. Here he consigned the command to Lieutenant James Gorrell with one sergeant and sixteen rank and file, plus a suitable proportion of provisions. Gorrell, like Balfour, believed in laying down the law to the native inhabitants, though he had to wait until the spring for the warriors to return from their hunting. Most of Gorrell's audience at La Baye consisted of Menominee. He began equally bombastically about the triumph of British arms and the fact that "Canada with all its dependencies were ceded to the English King." He continued, "I am sent here to keep the best order and strictest justice amongst his subjects, as also to protect all the Indian nations that will by their good behavior deserve his royal bounty" Meanwhile, he had invited traders to come and sell at the cheapest prices possible, but if the Indians had any complaints they were to approach Gorrell. Most importantly, they were to observe the treaties recently made by their "neighboring brothers at Niagara, Detroit and Michilimackinac." These included the return of prisoners, which he knew they would understand the necessity for, "as you know it would grieve you to have your blood with any nation."[79]

The Menominee replied that they were a poor people who had lost not only three hundred warriors from smallpox but also most of their chiefs in the recent war. They were glad the British had pardoned them for supporting the French, but begged Gorrell to continue the former practice of providing a smith and also some rum. As to prisoners, they had sent all of them to Montreal during the war and had none remaining. Gorrell replied that he would ask for a smith but flatly refused the request for rum, as it might lead them to neglect their families and add to their poverty.[80]

Balfour meanwhile had long since left La Baye for St. Joseph, which he reached on 9 November 1761. Here he appointed Lieutenant Schlosser to the command with one sergeant and nine men. Finally he ordered Lieutenant Brehme to take fifteen men to relieve some rangers at Fort Miami, who were guarding the communication between the Maumee and Wabash Rivers. Balfour then made his way back to Detroit, which he reached after a march of eleven days.[81]

The British occupation of the Wabash region was completed by the dispatch of Lieutenant Edward Jenkins of the Royal American regiment to Ouiatanon with twenty men and four months' provisions. Like all the commanders of the outposts, Jenkins would be heavily dependent on the cooperation of the local inhabitants, both Indian and French.[82] At nearby Fort Miami, the goodwill of the Miami had already been stretched when Lieutenant Holmes arrived in September 1761 with little ammunition and only four gallons of rum. Holmes had taken refuge in the excuse that the Miami, Kickapoo, and other Wabash nations should have gone to Detroit, where Johnson and Croghan would have given them what they needed. Nevertheless, for the moment relations remained amicable, though the Indians made it clear that with regard to prisoners "they could do nothing" about the matter "as they [the captives] were in the place of others which we had killed." However, "They would do all in their power to persuade their masters to give them up." Their spokesmen also promised to supply the garrison with venison. Two days later, three Miami chiefs even asked Holmes to look after their sick while they were away hunting.[83] It was a reasonable beginning to the new relationship, though in reality the lack of gifts and the bombastic attitude of the British officers could not but give offense. Perhaps the newcomers would ameliorate their language and treat the Wabash peoples in accordance with the spirit of the "middle ground." It was a tall order, given the cultural differences.

3
The Uneasy Peace, 1762–1763

Unresolved Problems

The occupation of the western posts and confirmation of peace with the Great Lakes nations seemingly left Britain secure in its conquests in eastern North America. Johnson was certainly of this opinion, his optimism partly fueled by the belief that his plans for the management of the Indian department were about to be accepted by the ministry in England, whatever Amherst's views. He expected that all trade hereafter would be conducted at the posts under licenses issued by Johnson and supervised by commissaries, interpreters, and smiths. He would also be responsible for the conduct of diplomacy. The one cloud in the sky was the continued involvement of Pennsylvania.[1] Prior to the Detroit conference, the governor of that province, James Hamilton, had held his own meeting at Easton with the Six Nations, eastern Delaware, Nanticoke, and other small local tribes.[2] However, Johnson was confident that he would get sole responsibility to strengthen British imperial control. He never doubted that such arrangements would benefit the Indians.

Meanwhile there was to be no alteration in British policy, despite the obvious discontent of the native peoples and the plea of Tahaiadoris for greater consideration. The British affected to believe disingenuously that they were the injured party following the revelations concerning the Seneca. Accordingly, it was the Indians who had to change regarding gift giving, the adoption of a market economy, the supremacy of English law, the return of prisoners, and the retention of the forts. Acceptance of these was the route to peace and happiness for the native peoples.

The British desire for economy meant that the ending of gift giving remained a priority, as Croghan emphasized to Thomas Hutchins when leaving him in charge at Fort Pitt in October 1761. Hutchins was to break the Indians' habit of visiting the commanding officers, "as they have no business to give him any trouble, and their view is only to get a dram or beg some presents." He was to be equally frugal in feeding them, whether they were "on public business or to trade." Instead, he was to send them away "as soon as their business is done to save [the] expense of provisions."[3] Nevertheless, Amherst was still not satisfied, especially when he received the accounts for Johnson's Detroit conference, which amounted to twice what had been estimated. Since the money had already been spent there was little he could do, but he warned the superintendent that such largesse must not be repeated. "The now tranquil state of the country and the good regulation you have put the trade under" meant that there was "very little reason for bribing the Indians, or buying their good behavior."[4]

However, ending the custom of gift giving still posed difficulties, as Croghan reminded Bouquet. One reason was that the chiefs "seldom or ever hunt which makes it impossible to transact any business with them without making them some presents." This had become accepted practice over a long time: "The British and French colonies, since the first settling of America, have adopted the Indian custom and manners by indulging them in treaties and renewing friendships, making them large presents, which I fear won't be so easy to break them of as the General may imagine." The worse time was the summer, "when the Indians have nothing else to do but travel about .... When they don't go to war they are always visiting their friends, wherever they can get anything or have any expectations."[5]

But even in wartime, the Indians still expected presents for their warriors. This too was a long-standing tradition which had been given fresh impetus by the war with the Cherokee in 1759.[6] However, by the fall of 1761, peace had been made and the British wanted to discourage further sorties because of the disruption caused along the southern backcountry. Consequently, when a party of Six Nations warriors arrived at Fort Pitt in April 1762, their request for powder, lead, vermilion, and "some other trifles" was refused. The warriors immediately protested to Croghan that "it has always been the custom long before this war, by both the British and the French, to give Indian warriors of all nations a little ammunition and necessaries going and coming from war." During the recent conflict, the British had constantly promised the Indians that they would be supplied with everything they "wanted as soon as the French should be drove out of this country." Now it was clear that the British had "spoken with their lips" and "not from their hearts." Croghan surreptitiously gave the war party a little of what they wanted to prevent "such a number" from going "away dissatisfied."[7] He was mindful that the warriors' position in Indian society would otherwise be undermined. Here was yet another example of the British indifference to the traditions of "the middle ground."

The unsatisfactory nature of Amherst's policy led Johnson to write to the Board of Trade in the summer of 1762, observing the dangerous consequences that must follow from a "sudden retrenchment of some yet necessary expenses." Johnson believed that the Indians should be "gradually weaned" from the custom of gift giving: "By a prudent conduct, and due distribution of some little favors to them for a time, we may effect without much trouble ... a quiet possession of our distant posts, and an increase of settlements on the back parts of the country." The British would then "have a well settled frontier, in itself strong enough to repel any sudden attempt from the Indians."[8] After this, there would be no need to buy Indian friendship.

The need for a more sympathetic approach was confirmed by Thomas Hutchins following a tour of the western nations during the spring and summer of 1762. The purpose of his visit was "to examine into the state and behavior of the Indians … and deal with any matters that may be for the good of the service." He was to offer wampum belts but no other presents.[9] The response everywhere was the same. At Michilimackinac, the Ottawa and Ojibwa expressed their dissatisfaction after Hutchins failed to redress their being in want. At La Baye, the Sauk, Fox, and Menominee similarly stressed their poverty, though more discreetly through their interpreter, informing Hutchins privately that they "were a good deal displeased" at not being "given any presents." The importance of presents was more openly stated in early August 1762 when he reached St. Joseph, where the Potawatomi were experiencing widespread sickness which prevented them from hunting. Surely Johnson would send them "some few presents to keep their Women and Children from the Cold," for they could not disguise their surprise that Hutchins had nothing to give them. The sickness may have been typhus.[10] Whatever the cause, the Wabash, Kickapoo, Mascouten, and Piankashaw were equally afflicted when Hutchins addressed them later that month. Their chiefs accepted that death was a matter for the Deity, but continued, "What we think hardest of, is that the British have never so much as given us the least present, or even allowed a smith to be at this post to mend our guns," though other nations had received both. However, they intended to comply with the desire of their British brethren not to resort to the French in the Illinois. Lastly, at Fort Miami, Hutchins heard yet again a story of deprivation and discontent. The Miami were distressed not only by the lack of a smith but also by the need of "presents as their people were mostly sick and could not hunt to support their families."[11]

Hutchins noted in his report to Croghan that he was constantly told how the French, "both in time of Peace and during the late War," had made "these people great presents three or four times a Year, and always allowed them a sufficient quantity of ammunition at the posts." They complained that the English traders currently "were not allowed even to take so much ammunition with them as to enable those Indians to kill game sufficient for the support of their families." Although the officers at the posts were doing their best to alleviate the distress, their efforts were dismissed "as mere trifles," since all the nations were "in great Expectation of having Presents sent them from Sir William Johnson." Not surprisingly, the officers were experiencing "the greatest difficulty" in keeping the Indians "in good humor."[12]

Apart from the lack of presents, Indians everywhere were angered by a ban on the sale of rum which Amherst instituted at the end of 1761. The belief was widespread among the British that the Indians spent a disproportionate amount of their income on alcohol, leaving them unable to feed their families. Balfour had complained about this at Michilimackinac. Campbell at Detroit similarly informed Amherst in November 1761, "The Indians sold all their skins at Niagara for rum and are now in a starving condition for want of ammunition, which I'm afraid may drive them to despair."[13] But many observers believed that a ban on rum might serve a second purpose: that of ending drunkenness among the Indians, which made them dangerous to friend and foe alike. As the trader James Kenny reported from Tuscarawas in August 1761, "The Indians frequently get drunk, pawning their clothes, wampum, and all they have for it." In a recent drunken brawl between two Mohawk, one was killed and the other seriously wounded.[14] Without rum the incident would not have happened, and the need for relief reduced.

Amherst was quickly convinced by these views, agreeing with Johnson at the end of December 1761 that a ban on the sale and distribution of rum would be "the most effectual method of avoiding these expenses at the outposts.... The Indians would then barter their skins for clothing and necessaries that would be of real use to them." He also accepted the argument that it would reduce the number of disorders "for which they never fail to plead as an excuse their being in liquor."[15] The ban accordingly went ahead. But despite this, the scheme was unpopular, even with those Indians who blamed alcohol for their troubles. Walters reported from Niagara in April 1762 that since implementing the ban, "I have had some of their chiefs with me begging that I would allow the traders to sell their people a little rum for their refreshment." Walters had tried to convince them that the ban was for their own good, as they would "live many years longer" and be able "to purchase every necessary of life they wanted for their families."[16] Such arguments had little appeal for a people who faced daily hardship and were afflicted with widespread sickness. In any case, as one chief told the interpreter at Niagara, it "was their liberty" to decide the matter for themselves.[17]

Meanwhile, the Indians everywhere remained convinced that Amherst was withholding ammunition to ensure their destruction. In reality, Amherst had only stopped the military from issuing ammunition, believing that the traders should supply it following the conquest of Canada. Unfortunately he was slow to allow the traders access to the western posts, being concerned that the French might exploit the situation if the Indians were supplied with arms. Not until the end of December 1761 did he decide that there was "nothing to fear" from that quarter. Henceforth, he told Campbell, "The traders will be allowed to carry ammunition, which they will of course barter with the Indians for their skins." He concluded, "If the latter can neither get rum from the traders nor ammunition from the officers at the posts, they will become more industrious and provide for their families by hunting."[18]

Sadly, things were not that simple. Without ammunition, the Indians had few furs to sell and no means of buying what they needed, unless they could get credit from the traders. Like Europe after World War II, the Indians needed help reestablishing themselves. Campbell was one person who thought that assistance was required. He told Bouquet, "I hope the General will change his present way of thinking with regard to Indian affairs," since he believed that a supply of ammunition "would prevent their doing mischief" rather than provide an encouragement.[19] He returned to the subject a few weeks later with Amherst himself: "It will be absolutely necessary for the good of the service to send a large quantity of ammunition early in the spring, as all the posts will be in want against that time. I am certain that nothing can alarm the Indians more than to know that there was any design to keep them scarce of ammunition."[20] But even Campbell admitted the need for some restraint in early 1762 on the news of an alliance between France and Spain. He told Bouquet, "The Indians are a good deal elevated on the news of a Spanish war, and there are daily reports that the French and Spanish will soon retake Quebec.... This goes from one nation to another, and it is impossible to prevent. I assume they only want a good opportunity to fall upon us, had they encouragement from an enemy."[21] In these circumstances, a lack of ammunition was no bad thing.

The continued shortage of ammunition and the ban on rum might have been less provocative had the rest of the trade been more favorable. Unfortunately, complaints continued to be received despite the publication of Johnson's table of prices during the Detroit conference.[22] Few traders paid any heed to it. Nevertheless, the need for a fairer system was recognized even in England, where the earl of Egremont, the secretary of state responsible for the colonies, argued that the natives ought to be treated "upon the same principles of humanity and proper indulgence" as the French Canadians. Egremont commended Amherst's general conduct of affairs. However, it appeared that the Indians were often "alienated from His Majesty's government by the shameful manner in which business is transacted between them and our traders," who used "every low trick and artifice to overreach and cheat those unguarded ignorant people." The French, in contrast, "by a different conduct ...worthy of our imitation, deservedly gain their confidence."[23]

Egremont's letter began a fresh debate on how the trade should be conducted. Gage in Montreal, like Johnson, favored restricting it to the posts so that the traders could be supervised. But he was against any form of monopoly, which the French had mostly operated.[24] This led Johnson to raise the subject in his report to the Board of Trade of August 1762. He affirmed that the only way of achieving an equitable system was by a "free and plentiful trade, subject to proper regulation" by "the department of Indian Affairs."[25] Implicit was the need for more personnel. Meanwhile, the abuses continued. Some Miami came to Fort Pitt in June 1762 complaining about the high prices and the want of ammunition at Fort Miami, where a single shroud cost ten buckskins.[26] The refusal of the merchants to issue credit was another cause of contention. The Indians were keen to accept advances, but slow to settle their debts. The result, as Kenny noted at his store in Fort Pitt, was "dissatisfaction on both sides."[27]

The issue of the forts also continued to poison relations, especially after Amherst's authorization of a new staging post at Sandusky. Amherst did this despite a warning from Johnson that it would antagonize the Great Lakes nations, when their goodwill was already strained, following the revelation of the Seneca War Plan.[28] But equally annoying to Indian sensibilities was their continued ill treatment at the existing posts. The Oneida observed yet again how they were, "for the most frivolous causes, abused, threatened to be fired upon and often run at with bayonets." This was very unbrotherly conduct. The situation was all the more galling since the British no longer had "any occasion for the posts between German Flats and Oswego" now that the French were "entirely conquered."[29]

When these concerns were raised at a conference with the Six Nations in April 1762, Johnson insisted that the Indians' own drunken frolics were the cause of much of the trouble. As for "the posts between the German Flats and Oswego," these "would not have been erected if there had not been occasion for them." The British in any case would not "abandon places of that kind even on a peace, as a wise people should at all times be prepared against the worst which may happen." This was a clear breach of the earlier wartime promises to vacate the forts once the fighting ceased. Johnson tried to justify his stance on the usual grounds that the "posts afford a place of shelter and security to the traders and their goods," at the same time serving "as checks to prevent their defrauding you," while keeping "open the communication into your Countries." The Indians should be grateful for their presence. However, Johnson would ask Amherst to look into legitimate complaints about the soldiers' behavior.[30]

Meanwhile, the problem of the prisoners was still to be resolved, especially with the Ohio peoples. Initially, the western Delaware and Shawnee seemed ready to comply following the Detroit conference. In October 1761, the pro-British Delaware George negotiated the delivery of fourteen captives. Nine days later Tamaqua "the Beaver" arrived at Fort Pitt with eight, promising to bring the rest in the spring, once they had been collected after the hunting season. Two weeks later, the Shawnee delivered a further twenty-two. However, they added that the rest of their captives were already at liberty. Only five of them wanted to return to their relatives.[31]

This was not what the British wanted to hear. They believed that the Indians still had three hundred white persons living with them under duress. Previously, Bouquet had given small presents for the return of captives until Amherst instituted his ban on gift giving.[32] This partly explained why the flow of prisoners at Fort Pitt ceased after May 1762. But there were other reasons too, as mentioned in chapter 1. One was the need to keep some prisoners as an insurance against a British attack. Another was the Indian custom of adoption. When a trader finally found James McCullough's son John, living at Mahoning on the Beaver River, the Delaware insisted on keeping him since the boy had been given in lieu of a dead brother.[33] John in any case did not want to be repatriated, as the Indians constantly asserted about their captives. Hence, when his father finally secured his ransom, John ran back to his Indian family.[34] The situation was compounded by the lack of any mechanism within Indian society for compelling the captives to return. As Croghan had earlier observed, the Indians "have no laws to oblige their people but by persuasion," and that was usually ineffective since "the prisoners by adoption are the property of the families they live with."[35]

If the Delaware were uncooperative, the Shawnee were even more so. This partly reflected their remoteness along the Scioto River and greater proximity to the French on the Mississippi. But it was also a response to Bouquet's ban on trader visits to their villages, which he had instituted as a means of stopping the theft of the army's horses. The Shawnee in retaliation insisted that they would surrender captives only in exchange for goods.[36] To break the deadlock, Governor Hamilton proposed a conference at Lancaster in August 1762. But as the date for the meeting approached, even the Delaware doubted the wisdom of surrendering their captives until the intentions of the British were known. This led Custaloga and Netawatwees, the western Delaware "head king" to return home without attending the conference.[37] In consequence, a mere thirty Delaware set out with Tamaqua from Fort Pitt, bringing just eighteen of the two to three hundred prisoners said to be with them. Not one was with the Shawnee.[38]

Nevertheless, the Lancaster conference began amicably on 12 August 1762, when Governor Hamilton visited Tamaqua in the special encampment which had been constructed for him and his colleagues. The conference proper started on 14 August in the old Lutheran Church, with representatives from the Six Nations, Delaware, Shawnee, Kickapoo, and Miami present. Hamilton first thanked the Indians for the return of the eighteen prisoners, though he expressed surprise that so many were choosing to remain behind when it was universally admitted that the English "live better than the Indians." In any case, the prisoners could not remain with their adopted families. "They were born subjects of our Great King and as such he has a right to demand them."[39] Here was a fundamental clash of values.

Tamaqua replied two days later that the Ottawa, Kickapoo, and Miami had no prisoners. All had left for their old homes. But the Delaware would ensure that the European Americans saw their flesh and blood in due course. Miskapalathy, or Red Hawke, similarly promised that the Shawnee would bring their captives to Pittsburgh. In the meantime the trade should be reopened, as they were very poor. The British had to show some reciprocity if there was to be no compensation for bringing in the captives.[40] The need for this was also stressed by Thomas King on 19 August. He explained yet again the role that captives played in Indian society. The expectation was that they would stay for life. Hence, satisfaction must be made for giving up the prisoners. At the very least, those who wanted to remain with their Indian families should be allowed to do so. King then complained that some of those previously surrendered had been made into servants. This was hardly compatible with the stated aim of returning them to their relatives.[41]

Hamilton replied to King's points on 26 August. He acknowledged the Indian practice of adoption but insisted that the situation was quite different in the case of white prisoners. In British eyes, the Indians had no rights over the captives once hostilities had ended. "As we are of a different color from you, so we have different customs. It is a constant rule with White people that upon making peace … the prisoners on both sides are faithfully delivered up." This he claimed was part of the price for reestablishing "the ancient chain of friendship." Clearly a great many European Americans were still prisoners, particularly among the Seneca, who had received them from the Ohio nations. If that were the case, they must be surrendered. As to compensation, the British never paid a ransom, except for legitimate expenses. Finally, King was mistaken about prisoners being made into servants. They were always dispatched to their homes, though if they had "no relations or place of abode, they were sent …where they can best get employment."[42]

The Lancaster conference was conducted with the usual courtesies. When King declared he was uncertain whether he had included everything in one of his speeches, Hamilton agreed to a recapitulation. King's belts were accordingly laid out in the order that he had spoken, while the minutes taken by the Pennsylvanian recorder, were read aloud and interpreted "paragraph by paragraph." The Indians all agreed that the minutes were an accurate record of what King had said, while King acknowledged that he had said everything he intended.[43] Nevertheless, there was considerable underlying tension. This surfaced when Hamilton suggested establishing a new trade post on the west branch of the Susquehanna River. Kinderunte, a Genesee sachem, angrily asserted that it would lead to the building of a fort and the invasion of the Six Nations' lands. One had only to look at Fort Pitt to see what would happen.[44] Not surprisingly, the Six Nations left the conference "much dissatisfied," as did the Shawnee and Delaware. The anger of Tamaqua and his colleagues was compounded by the theft of their horses.[45]

Despite the obvious affection of the Indians for their captives, the European Americans believed that the Delaware and Shawnee were simply trying to extract better ransom terms.[46] A paper drawn up for Bouquet calculated that 412 prisoners had been voluntarily surrendered at Detroit and Fort Pitt in the previous three years.[47] However, Thomas Penn in London, from hearsay evidence, believed that another four hundred remained, and he could only express surprise that Amherst had not done more to secure their release.[48] Hamilton, accordingly, appointed two commissioners, Colonel James Burd and Josiah Davenport, to expedite the return of the remaining captives. This time, expenses would be paid to those Indians traveling from afar.[49] This prompted Croghan to launch a similar mission in early October 1762 on behalf of Johnson's department, headed by Alexander McKee, one of

Croghan's deputies, whose mother was a Shawnee. McKee's orders were to visit the Shawnee towns, where he was to fix a time for the surrender of the prisoners. He was also to secure the killers of three white men murdered on the Carolina frontier. Finally, he was to advise the Shawnee not to listen to the French in the Illinois, who were endeavoring to incite the western nations against the British. For this reason, he was to "find out what was transacted at a recent conference over the lakes."[50]

In the event McKee secured the release of a few prisoners, but for the most part he was told to wait until the spring since the captives were too dispersed to be collected. The Burd-Davenport mission was similarly unsuccessful. One problem was the widespread sickness in the lower Shawnee towns that Hutchins had noted, which made assembly difficult. But the determination of the Ohio Indians to keep their adopted prisoners was admitted by a relative of Delaware George. He told Croghan that the refusal to supply ammunition to the Indians had confirmed them in their opinion that the English were planning an attack once they had secured their flesh and blood. Otherwise, "The prisoners would have been delivered some time ago."[51] Clearly, the tactic of the Indians was to surrender a few captives intermittently until the British had revealed their intentions. Accordingly, five days later the Shawnee arrived with another three prisoners, pleading their recent sickness as the cause of their delay. They assured Croghan that the rest of their captives would be delivered in the spring at a formal council.[52] The Delaware announced shortly afterwards that they would do the same.[53]

To ensure that they kept their word, McKee set off once more early in 1763 for the lower Shawnee towns. Here he found the Indians seemingly better disposed on the issue of the prisoners. But their mood soon changed when McKee informed them on 26 February 1763 about the cessation of arms between Britain and France and the ceding of Canada. Four chiefs came "to know if the French had given up their country and by what right they could pretend to do it." When McKee tried to placate them by saying that the French had only surrendered land actually occupied by the King of France's subjects, they became even more agitated, and added they "had changed their minds" and would "not be able to carry up the prisoners at this time, but such as were already collected." Accordingly they set off on 10 March with just eight prisoners, two of whom absconded on the first night. The Shawnee made it clear that their main purpose now in going to Fort Pitt was to enquire into the peace, as it was "a matter of very great consequence to them."[54]

Finally, relations between the English-speaking peoples and the Native Americans continued to be bedeviled by the perceived threat to their lands. This was particularly the case on the western borders of Virginia and Pennsylvania where access was greatly facilitated by the wartime construction of the Braddock and Forbes roads from Winchester and Carlisle to Fort Pitt. Bouquet attempted to placate the native peoples by issuing a proclamation in

October 1761 forbidding any further intrusion. He did so believing that settlement was contrary to the 1758 Treaty of Easton, whereby "the country to the west of the Allegheny Mountains is allowed to the Indians for their hunting ground." Anyone breaking the edict was to be tried and punished at Fort Pitt "by the sentence of a court martial."[55] Coincidentally, the Privy Council in England was issuing instructions in this vein to the governors of New Hampshire, New York, Virginia, the two Carolinas, and Georgia, "forbidding them to pass grants of or encourage settlements upon any lands within the said colonies which may interfere with the Indians bordering thereon." Persons who had "inadvertently settled" on lands claimed by the Indians were "to remove themselves" immediately, while anyone purchasing such lands in the future must first submit their application to the Board of Trade.[56]

Unfortunately, removing the white intruders was not as easy as either the ministry in England or Bouquet imagined. Within a few weeks, Bouquet received a sharp protest from Governor Francis Fauquier of Virginia that his proclamation was unlawful. Firstly, it infringed various lawful patents along the Monongahela, Green Briar, and New Rivers which had been issued to the Ohio Company and other proprietors in the early 1750s. Secondly, Bouquet was proposing the use of military tribunals to prosecute offenders. Under English law, only serving soldiers were liable to such procedures. Understandably, the "Gentlemen of Consequence" in Virginia were alarmed. Fauquier could only assume that the proclamation was aimed at vagabonds who had no lawful title to settle.[57]

Bouquet quickly retreated from his initial stance, recognizing the sacrosanct status of property and the right of British subjects to trial by jury. Accordingly, he explained to Fauquier on 8 February 1762 that his edict was indeed aimed at white vagabonds against whom the only realistic method of proceeding was by courts-martial. The edict otherwise would protect those with legitimate titles, though they should inform the commander-in-chief of their claims.[58] The proclamation of Bouquet was thus of limited value, as was the edict of the Privy Council, since both overlooked the granting of previous land titles. Troops were sent from Fort Pitt in February 1762 to burn a squatter settlement on the Monongahela River, following a complaint by the Shawnee, but the effect was minimal since the settlers soon returned.[59] Kenny noted how "it grieves the Indians to see the White People settle on these lands and follow hunting or Planting."[60] Their gloom was increased by the killing of a rat on the Allegheny River. A number of older chiefs remembered the prediction of "their grandfathers on finding a Rat on the Delaware before the white people came." The discovery meant ruin for the native inhabitants.[61] Now the same pattern was seemingly happening again. It was for this reason that the Shawnee advised the British not to send an expedition down the Ohio to occupy the French Illinois posts. In a scarcely coded message, they warned the garrison of the "many foolish and evil persons down this river" waiting to strike them. The British should "sit still" where they were "and cultivate a firm and lasting Friendship with your brethren the Indians."[62]

The inability of the British to respect Indian lands was further demonstrated by the relentless activities of the Susquehanna Company. These had become so intrusive by December 1762 that Tamaqua invited Teedyuscung and his people to resettle on the Allegheny River.[63] The company did momentarily suspend its operations after Thomas King and his colleagues threatened the settlers on their way home from the Lancaster conference in August 1762.[64] But this was only a temporary respite. Soon the New Englanders were back, telling Johnson that their claim was good not only by virtue of their Indian deed but also because Connecticut's charter extended its territory to the South Seas. They had besides invested too much in the scheme and intended to settle one thousand families in the coming year.[65] Then, after several warnings from Amherst, Johnson, and Hamilton, the company agreed in May 1763 to suspend its activities until the matter was considered by the Privy Council.[66] It proved an empty victory for the eastern Delaware. Their settlement at Wyoming had already been burnt, most likely by settlers disgruntled at the delays to the project, and Teedyuscung killed as he lay sleeping in his cabin.[67] The company in any case had no intention of honoring its pledge, for within weeks Teedyuscung's son, Captain Bull, was reporting that the New Englanders had returned and were erecting settlements on the very spot where his father had died.[68]

War Belts

Indian discontent over the lack of gifts, the terms of trade, the return of prisoners, and the invasion of their lands inevitably led to the circulation of further war belts similar to those of Tahaiadoris and Kiashuta. Early in 1762 Gladwin, then commanding at Fort William Augustus, believed he had discovered one such scheme involving the St. Lawrence Indians and the Catholic clergy. According to his information, a large belt had been circulated "inviting all the Indians attached to the French in and about Canada, to assemble at [Fort] Frontenac as soon as the River opens."[69] The belt had originally been left by Charles-Jacques Le Moyne, a French officer, and had been carried "through all the nations between Montreal and Onondaga." The message attached to it, Gladwin stated, was for an attack on "the communication to all our posts."[70] Subsequent investigation by deputy agent Daniel Claus revealed that the belt was one from the Seneca in June 1761, which the St. Lawrence Indians had immediately returned, "knowing the Six Nations to be fond of sending alarming news."[71]

However, there was nothing ephemeral about the belts which Governor of Louisiana Louis Billouart de Kerlérec began circulating in the spring of 1762. Kerlérec had long wanted to strike the British through the agency of France's Indian allies. With Spain about to enter the conflict, the French ministry for once acquiesced in his scheme, ordering the dispatch of a regiment of regulars and a large quantity of supplies. Admittedly Kerlérec's principal objective was an alliance with the Cherokee, Creek, Choctaw, and Alabama nations, since they were best positioned to defend the lower Mississippi Valley, where the bulk of the French population lived. Nevertheless he was also responsible for the Illinois, which the northern nations could more readily protect.

When the reinforcements and supplies reached New Orleans late in April 1762, Kerlérec immediately sent belts with news of their arrival. The messages for the northern nations were carried by one of his officials, Monsieur de Lantagnac. De Lantagnac was to tell the Indians that "Onontio" had not been crushed. Rather, the French king was on his legs again and had sent an army to Louisiana which would soon drive the English out of their country.[72]

De Lantagnac's first destination was Fort Chartres on the Mississippi River, where Captain Neyon de Villiers was commander. He then set off for the Shawnee settlements north of the Ohio River. At their principal town of Chillicothe, de Lantagnac repeated Kerlérec's message, saying that the French king "longed much to see them as his children again." Previously the British "had thrown him on his back, which prevented his visiting his children sooner." But now, with the support of the Spanish, "he was grown young again, and therefore determined with the assistance of his children to fall upon and dispossess the English and what they had taken from him, for which end he had brought a very large sharp hatchet." After this, de Lantagnac continued up the Ohio Valley to the Delaware towns. The Delaware commented that although many considered them mere women, only capable of grinding corn, they would use the "pestle and do as much execution with that as with an axe." Finally, de Lantagnac met the "Chenussio" some distance from their habitations, near the Ohio, to whom he offered the hatchet. This they accepted. However, he did not visit the other Six Nations, knowing they "were not his friends." Before returning home, he charged the Seneca "to make good use of his Ax."[73]

Kerlérec intended the northern Indians to act on their own, since he had only arms and encouragement to give them. The Genesee accordingly approached the Cayuga as the first step in winning over the other Six Nations. But despite their support in 1761, the Cayuga surprisingly refused the ax and "endeavored to persuade the Chenussio" to drop "all thoughts of the kind, as that would break the Covenant Chain."[74] The Seneca nevertheless persevered, knowing that the Shawnee and western Delaware were keen to participate. The plan was for the latter to recruit the Great Lakes Algonquian-speaking peoples, since they had long had ties with them. Consequently, the Seneca returned the belt "to the Delaware with this message that if all the other nations would join, they would not be backward." The Delaware in response forwarded Kerlérec's belt to Detroit, inviting the Great Lakes nations to join the alliance.[75] The result was a conference in the summer of 1762 at the nearby Ottawa village "attended by the chiefs and principal warriors of the Wiandot, Ojibwa, Ottawa and Potawatomie, and some other tribes who live amongst those Indians on Lake Superior, above Michilimackinac and La Baye." Also present were two Frenchmen from Michilimackinac disguised in Indian dress. After the conference was over, deputies were sent to the "Miami, Ouiatanon, Kickapoo, and Piankashaw and other Tribes settled on the Wabash, to let them know the determination of the council."[76]

The outcome was that the Great Lakes nations were not ready to engage in hostilities, despite the promises of French support. As they told the Delaware and Shawnee delegates in reply, "It might be that the English had an intention to make war against the Indians by their keeping ammunition from them and settling so many forts in their country; but for their parts they were determined not to quarrel with the English if they could avoid it." Nevertheless, "They would be on their guard and watch the motions of the English for the future," and desired that the Ohio Indians did the same. The Shawnee and Delaware then held a council on what to do. Half of the warriors were for making war, and the rest for keeping the peace. Finally, lacking sufficient support, they returned Kerlérec's belt to Fort Chartres. However, they too would remain on their guard.[77]

The first indication for the British that something had occurred was at Fort Pitt early in September 1762, when a Mingo warrior told James Kenny that "there had been a French officer and three Shawnee Indians and one Mississippi Indian reconnoitering the Fort and taking a Plan of it." The accompanying Indians had added that "the French would soon come up the River in bateaus" to assist an attack.[78] Then in late September, Croghan learned about the conference near Detroit. However, he was still uncertain about the content except that the discussions were hostile and the French were involved.[79] Firm evidence surfaced only when Alexander McKee visited the Shawnee towns in early November 1762 looking for prisoners. Here some visiting Miami told him what had transpired, handing over a war belt as proof. Although they made no mention of a French officer, they confirmed that there had "been a private council between the Seneca and Delaware" in the spring of 1762, at which they agreed "to strike the English now living in their country.... To get all Nations to join them in this Attempt, they had secretly sent a large Belt with a Bloody Hatchet over the Lakes." They also confirmed that only the Seneca, Shawnee, and Delaware were in favor of war. The Miami had disclosed this information because of their "great regard for the English."[80]

When Croghan questioned the Seneca, Shawnee, and Delaware at Fort Pitt in early December 1762, they acknowledged the existence of the belt, which they claimed had originally been given to the Wabash peoples at Ouiatanon in the spring by the French at the Illinois. However, they asserted that their designs had been entirely defensive, as "they have no intentions to make war with the English." But it was "full time for them to prepare to defend themselves," since the British clearly had a "design to make war on them." Why else would they "stop the sale of powder and lead," refusing "their warriors any to carry on their war against the southern Indians, which was an old custom"?

They believed that the British were restrained from implementing their plan only by the need to recover their remaining prisoners.[81]

The rejection of Kerlérec's belt by the Great Lakes nations did not end the Seneca attempts to effect a pan-Indian alliance, since they soon had a new grievance following the murder of a trader and his servant near the castle of Canadasaga. Johnson, with Amherst's approval, immediately demanded that the two Seneca responsible be handed over to stand trial in a British court.[82] Although the culprits were from the small Delaware village of Kanestio, they were related to a Genesee chief. The demand for their surrender was consequently rejected, though the Seneca recognized the need for a conciliatory gesture. They now suggested settling the matter by some form of compensation. They were supported by the other Six Nations, who argued that "it was better to accommodate matters already bad enough, than to shed further blood thereon." Such a resolution in any case would be in accordance with the traditions of the Covenant Chain. Johnson, however, was adamant when he conferred with the Six Nations on 16 March 1763 at Johnson Hall. The guilty men must be surrendered to prevent similar crimes in the future.[83]

The Seneca responded by dispatching further war belts, using the Delaware and Shawnee once more as their emissaries. According to the Miami, the instigator of this latest initiative was one of the Seneca chiefs "that is always doing mischief," suggesting that either Kiashuta or Tahaiadoris was involved. The belt for the Wabash nations proposed that the Miami at Fort Miami and the Kickapoo and Piankashaw at Fort Ouiatanon "were all to rise and put the English to death all about this place and those at the other places."[84] Simultaneously the Seneca sent another belt to the Detroit nations, urging them to take "the upper Posts on the Lakes," while the Six Nations struck the communication between Niagara and Schenectady. Operations were to "begin at the Time the Corn was planted," after the warriors had returned from the winter hunt. To ensure effective coordination, the Seneca proposed a meeting with their prospective allies at the Wyandot village near Detroit early in the spring of 1763.[85] Fortunately for the British, the Miami once again refused to participate, handing their belt to the commander at Fort Miami.[86]

If any further inducement was needed for the dispatch of these recent belts, it was provided by the news of peace between Britain and France involving the permanent surrender of Canada. As Croghan informed Johnson in the second week of March 1763, the Indians had been "very jealous of our growing power" for some time, "but since I acquainted them of the peace and let them know that all North America was ceded to Great Britain, they seem much more so."[87] Post, on a journey from Cuyahoga, commented similarly that Netawatwees was struck dumb on hearing the terms and refused to believe it until it had been confirmed by "their fathers," the French. When Post suggested that all true friends of the British should be glad, Netawatwees replied "that the English were grown too powerful and seem as if they would be too strong for God himself."[88] For many Indians, war seemed the only option, as a Delaware warrior told one of Gladwin's messengers. Since the British meant "to make them slaves by taking so many posts in their country … they had better attempt something now, to recover their liberty, than wait till we were better established."[89]

But few among the British thought the Indians were serious about war. Croghan believed their talk stemmed from delusions about their previous defeat of Braddock: "Their successes [at] the beginning of this war on our frontiers" were "too recent in their memory to suffer them to consider their present inability to make war with us."[90] Croghan deduced, "From the conversation I have had with numbers of the several nations it is clear to me that something was intended against us" last summer, "but I am of opinion they are not yet united so as to attempt putting it in execution."[91] Bouquet agreed: "Their own interest must convince them of the propriety and necessity of submitting to the measures of the government," especially if accompanied by some timely presents and "a kind treatment."[92] The lack of any perceived threat was of course the view of Amherst himself. The previous year, he had approved Bouquet's proposal to reduce the garrisons at Venango and Presque Isle on the grounds of "there being nothing to fear from the Indians."[93] He saw no reason to reverse that decision now. At most, the Indians might be able to murder a few inhabitants. Certainly Gladwin should be on his guard, but "my own opinion is that they can never hurt us, unless we are weak enough to put ourselves in their power."[94] Unwittingly, his prejudice and contempt had done just that.

Neolin: A Prophet Speaks

The anger among Native American peoples about the newly imposed British order was not just political and economic: it was also religious. A prophet had arisen who was urging the Indians to return to their precontact world in order to be free of white domination. The author of this message was a Delaware religious leader called Neolin.

Little is known about Neolin prior to 1761 except that he was a member of the "loup" or wolf nation, meaning the Delaware. The general consensus is that he was young and lived in the Tuscarawas Valley, since the captive, John McCullough, later recalled that his eldest adopted brother had "gone to Tuscalaways" early in 1761 "to see and hear a prophet that had just made his appearance amongst them."[95] It was a region where the western Delaware had several villages.

At some point toward the end of 1760, Neolin had a vision that took him to heaven. Here the Master of Life explained why the Indian world was in turmoil, the principal reason being the corrupting influence of the white people. On his return, Neolin drew a pictograph on a leather skin to show the Delaware the error of their ways. According to James Kenny, who met several converts at Fort Pitt, Earth was portrayed at the bottom and heaven on top.

The two were originally connected by a single path, "which their forefathers used to ascend to happiness." However, following the arrival of the European Americans, those attempting the ascent now had to make a right turn past numerous barriers, representing "all the sins and vices which the Indians have learned from the white people." Most never got to heaven, for "Hell being fixed not far off, there they are led irrevocably." The only way the Indians could avoid that fate was "to learn to live without any trade or connections with the white people, clothing and supporting themselves [instead] as their fore-fathers did."[96] Then after "two or three good talks" from the Master of Life, war would result and the Delaware be freed, though the precise means were not explained.[97] Neolin's vision was of a heaven with "no white people but all Indians," another reason why "a total separation" was necessary.[98]

According to McCullough, many devotees copied Neolin's pictograph so that they could instruct new converts. Although McCullough "never saw nor heard" the prophet in person, his captivity narrative provides one of the most authentic accounts of Neolin's philosophy. "The first or principal doctrine they taught them was to purify themselves from sin, which they … could do by the use of emetics, and abstinence from carnal knowledge." In addition, they were "to quit the use of fire arms, and to live entirely in the original state that they were in before the white people found out their country." Their devotions extended even to the lighting of fires, since "fire was not pure that was made by steel and flint." Instead, "They should make it by rubbing two sticks together." McCullough knew at least one group who "secluded themselves for the purpose of purifying from sin," though he suspected that they did not abstain from sexual relations, since "several women resorted to their encampment."[99]

Among those pondering the new philosophy was John Doubty, an old Del-aware from New Jersey. He commented to Kenny in August 1762 that "the Indians were a much better people before any white people came amongst them." Then, they prayed day and night to the "Good Spirit above." But once the Europeans "brought rum and supplied the Indians with it, they forgot God and lost their former Devotion."[100] However, since the prophet's arrival they were performing "their new devotions by dancing, singing and sometimes kneeling and praying to a little God who carried the petitions and presents them to the Great Being."[101] These devotions had also been committed to parchment, as Kenny discovered when he met another convert called Simon, who "showed me his Book containing their new religion," which had qualified him to become a minister at Kuskuski on the Beaver River.[102] Few of these ideas were original, being a mixture of Indian and Christian beliefs. How-ever, such ecumenism widened Neolin's appeal at a time when so much in the Indian world was being challenged.[103]

The popularity of Neolin among the Delaware was accordingly undimin-ished when Kenny spoke to another devotee, James Mokesin, in March 1763. Mokesin told the Quaker merchant that the whole Delaware nation had agreed "to follow their new Plan of Religion." "All their Boys," Mokesin explained, "are to be trained to the use of the Bow and Arrow for seven years." During this time, they were "to live entirely on dried meat and a sort of bitter drink made of roots and plants and water." The aim of the potion was "to purge out all that they got of the white peoples' ways and nature." However, after seven years the women and old men could "raise and eat corn," but "everyone was to avoid commerce with the White People," which meant clothing "themselves with skins." Mokesin believed that no neighboring nation had adopted their plan, which was fortunate, since "if any of the others was to drink their bitter water, they would die."[104]

Clearly, the Delaware believed that Neolin's message was for their benefit alone. However, this did not prevent his ideas from spreading among the Algonquian nations of the Great Lakes and Ohio region. By September 1762 it had even affected the Iroquoian Onondaga, who informed Johnson that one of them "lately, in a vision, was told by the Great Spirit above, that when he first made the world, he gave this large island to the Indians for their use," reserving at the same time "the other parts of the world beyond the great waters to the rest of his creation." But "he now saw the white people squabbling, and fighting" for the Indians' lands. This was most displeasing to the Great Spirit, and so contrary to his intentions "when the white people first came, like children," unable to support themselves. Hence, "although their numbers were ever so great," he would "punish them if they did not desist."[105] Johnson, an orthodox Episcopalian, brusquely dismissed such views, failing even to recognize the implied threat. He told the Onondaga, "Your romantic notions, custom of dreaming, and seeing visions, however usual amongst you, cannot but appear in a very ridiculous light to white people."[106]

However, the most politicized version of Neolin's message was that told to the Detroit nations by an Ottawa chief. After outlining "Wolf's" journey to heaven and the need for moral reformation, the speaker turned to the issue of white domination. Before contact with the Europeans, "You had no need of gun or powder, or anything else and nevertheless you caught animals to live upon and to dress yourselves with their skins." Neolin's message from the Master of Life was clear. The Indians had brought their current plight on themselves, for "when I saw that you were given up to evil I led the wild animals to the depths of the forests so that you had to depend upon your brothers to feed and shelter you." Nevertheless, all was not lost, for "you have only to become good again and do what I wish, and I will send back the animals for your food."

Despite Neolin's call for a precontact world, the Ottawa speaker made one concession in this respect: "I do not forbid you to permit among you the children of your Father," meaning the French. "I love them. They know me and pray to me, and I supply their wants and all they give you." The core of the Detroit version of Neolin's message was directed elsewhere, against "those who come to trouble your lands," meaning the British and their European American colonists. "Drive them out, make war upon them. I do not love them at all; they know me not, and are my enemies and the enemies of your brothers." The only solution was to "send them back to the lands which I have created for them and let them stay there."[107]

There was one other difference between Neolin and the Ottawa speaker, whose name was Pontiac. He was a warrior, not a prophet, and he was about to attempt the very thing that Neolin seemingly demanded, the destruction of "those dogs clothed in red."[108]

4

Pontiac Takes the Initiative: Detroit

A Leader Emerges

Very little is known about Pontiac before the siege of Detroit.[1] He was born into a family of chiefs, of mixed parentage, having an Ottawa father from Detroit and Ojibwa mother from Saginaw Bay. This proved of considerable advantage, since the Ojibwa and Ottawa were two of the most powerful nations in the Great Lakes area. He was probably between forty and fifty years of age by 1760, judged on his claim to have fought in the second Fox War. He was almost certainly present at the defeat of Braddock in July 1755, when the Great Lakes nations under Langlade comprised the largest contingent in the French army.[2] Two years later he was noted as being at Fort Duquesne, where he made a speech urging the Indians not to abandon their French allies.[3] This indicates that he was an accomplished speaker as well as an experienced warrior, both essential qualities in an Indian leader. But these visits to Fort Duquesne were important in other respects too, since they brought Pontiac into contact with the Delaware and Shawnee, two fellow Algonquian-speaking nations. It is likely that during these travels he met or at least heard about Neolin, since his path between Fort Duquesne and Detroit could easily have taken him via the Tuscarawas Valley.

Pontiac seemingly made at least one other visit to Fort Duquesne, following its capture by the British. According to Gabriel Le Grand, the local judge, "Before Canada was taken, Pontiac and some chiefs from Detroit, suspecting a complete conquest on the side of the English, had gone down to Fort Pitt and other forts on that communication toward Pennsylvania to enquire what treatment they would have, should the English succeed." The British answered "that all the rivers were to flow with rum; that presents from the great King were to be unlimited, that all sorts of goods were to be in the utmost plenty and so cheap as a blanket for two beavers." This was accompanied by "many other fair promises." Pontiac and his companions accordingly repeated these statements "on their return with much joy, in consequence of which they allowed [Major] Rogers with a handful of men to take possession of the Fort and Colony." However, Le Grand noted that "about a year after, *Pontiac* in particular had been heard to complain and say the English were *Liars*, which opinion then became general." His "chief complaint was the prohibition of rum and that the English took six raccoons for a beaver, when the French never took but four." Other grievances included the lack of "annual Congresses," which were "promised" but never called, in violation of diplomatic protocol.[4] This suggests that Pontiac's change of heart began some time in 1761, possibly during the visit of Tahaiadoris and Kiashuta.

However, Pontiac was seemingly constrained from acting by the lack of support from the other Great Lakes chiefs, as the reply to Kerlérec's war belt in the summer of 1762 indicated. Nevertheless, Pontiac was by no means inactive during this period. According to Menominee tradition, he visited the Milwaukee some time in the fall of 1762 or early spring of 1763 for a grand council, where he introduced the Wisconsin peoples to Neolin's vision of a Native America free of white intrusion, including apparently the French. "It is now in our power to force the whites back to their original settlements." "We must *all join in one common cause*, and sweep the white men from our country." Only then could they be "happy ... having nothing more to do with the hated race." The native peoples had no need of the European peoples, "as we have an abundance of game in our forests—our rivers and lakes teem with all kinds of fish, fowl and wild rice." They could accordingly "live as did our forefathers" and be a happy people once more.[5]

Two factors now altered opinion sufficiently to allow Pontiac to launch an attack early in May 1763. One was the news of peace between Britain and France involving the surrender of their country to their former enemy. There was a widespread belief that the terms which the British were promulgating at Detroit were not credible. As John Rutherford, an early captive, commented shortly, the Canadians "could not bring themselves to believe that *Le Grand Monarch* would ever cede their country to Great Britain and they still flattered themselves that if they could excite the savages to maintain the war against us for a little while, a reinforcement might come to their assistance from France."[6] The native people in any case needed little encouragement to accept these views, following the promises of Kerlérec the previous year. Both groups accordingly concluded that the declaration by the British was a stratagem to conceal the arrival of a French army and fleet at Quebec and New Orleans. Gladwin, now the commander at Detroit, lacking official notification from the French government, was unable to dispel these illusions.[7]

But equally important in explaining Pontiac's actions at this point was the arrival of another war belt, this time from the Delaware, asking for help to revenge "their former loss at Kittanning and for the death of one of their chiefs," meaning Teedyuscung. Initially the council at Detroit resolved to put the belt "under their feet to be considered upon leisure," since Kittanning was not a recent incident.[8] However, the death of Teedyuscung was another matter. A number of Detroit chiefs were already receptive to the idea of war, among them Ninivois, the chief of the Potawatomi; Takay, a sachem of the Wyandot; and Mackatepelecite, who was second only to Pontiac among the Ottawa.

According to Robert Navarre, the local French notary, whose *Journal ou Dictation d'une Conspiration* provides the best account of the first three months of the conflict at Detroit, their support and the news from the Delaware now galvanized Pontiac into calling an emergency council for 27 April 1763 on the Ecorse River, attended by the Detroit Ottawa, Potawatomi, and Wyandot.[9]

At the council, Pontiac went straight to the point. Those gathered "all knew the meaning of the belt" from the Delaware. For his own part "he was determined to help his nephews in procuring revenge, for which purpose he would attack Detroit within three days."[10] However, to win over his audience, Pontiac held up a war belt of his own which he claimed to have received "from his Great Father, the King of France, inviting them to attack the English." He also reminded his listeners of the many insults they had received from Gladwin, especially the lack of gifts.[11] Gladwin, like Amherst, had no comprehension of the importance of gift giving to the Indians. To him their constant importuning was mere begging, leading him on more than one occasion to call them "hogs and dogs," who should get "out of his house."[12]

Before the council ended, Pontiac related the story of Neolin's vision and his journey to see the Master of Life. He also recited what Neolin claimed was a prayer from the Master of Life, similar to the Ten Commandments of the Bible, which the Indians were to remember by heart. Converts were to have only one wife, drink sparingly, avoid conflict among themselves, give rather than sell what the earth provided, and cease making medicine for talking to "evil spirits."[13] But despite an inspirational delivery, Pontiac still lacked unanimous support. The Ottawa were solidly behind him, as were the Potawatomi, whose chief, Ninivois, was under Pontiac's sway. Indeed, both nations "told him that he had only to speak and they were all ready to do what he demanded of them."[14] The Wyandot, however, were split. One faction was headed by Teata, who was a Christian and influenced by Father Pierre Potier, the mission priest. Teata had not been present at the meeting on the Ecorse River and had refused to listen to Pontiac's subsequent messengers. The other faction, led by Takay, supported Pontiac.[15] Pontiac now gave Teata and his group two days to consider their response in the light of his plea for united action.[16]

Pontiac's plan, as he explained on 27 April, was to visit the fort with forty warriors, ostensibly to perform the "peace-pipe dance" before the officers. While this was in progress, other warriors were to inspect the garrison's defenses and the location of the English-speaking traders. Once they had this information, they could then determine their plan of attack. Accordingly at 3.00 p.m. on Sunday, 1 May 1763, Pontiac and his group arrived at the fort. A slight delay occurred before the gates were opened and the dance performed, which was watched by Gladwin and several officers. During this performance the warriors recounted their military exploits, not least that "they had beaten the English at various times and would do so again." Simultaneously ten other warriors wandered around the town, checking its layout and the location of the English merchants and garrison.[17]

This foray persuaded Pontiac to hold another council on 5 May, this time at the Potawatomi village on the west bank below Detroit, to finalize the plans and ensure that he had the full support of his allies. To preserve secrecy, all women were ordered to leave the village and sentinels were placed at the exits and entrances. Pontiac then began a harangue on the need to "exterminate from our lands this nation which only seeks to destroy us." Among the list of British crimes was the high price of trade goods, the absence of credit, and Gladwin's lack of respect for the Indian customs, especially his failure to hold proper condolence ceremonies. Finally Pontiac reminded his listeners that their "Great Father," the king of France, was urging them "to strike." What was there to fear? The British were few in number, while the Indians could expect reinforcements. Pontiac had that day sent war belts appealing for support to the Ojibwa of Saginaw Bay, the Ottawa at Michilimackinac, and the Ojibwa of the Thames River. However, there was no need to wait for these allies to appear. They would be needed later, for he made it clear that he was not just thinking of the capture of Detroit, but of a wider scheme, similar to the Seneca plan of 1761. "When the English are defeated [at Detroit] we shall then see what there is left to do, and we shall stop up the ways hither so that they may never come again upon our lands."[18] It would be a war to benefit all Indians in the region.

Those present on 5 May were finally won over, including Teata's group. The plan was for Pontiac and sixty warriors to ask for a council with Gladwin while another three hundred inspected the merchants' wares and milled about the fort. Weapons with shortened barrels were to be concealed under blankets and brought into the compound by the Ottawa women. At the same time, the Wyandot and the Potawatomi would take up positions outside so that they could intercept anyone attempting to flee or rescue the garrison. The signal for the attack was to be a war cry from Pontiac, which he would give when showing the reverse side of a wampum belt to Gladwin.[19] Critical to the success would be the killing of the officers, for the Indians believed that without them the soldiers would lack discipline and be quickly overpowered.

Unfortunately for Pontiac, his scheme was betrayed. A disaffected Ottawa named Mahiganne came to the fort on the night of Friday, 6 May 1763, and told Gladwin in broken French what was about to happen.[20] Gladwin quickly doubled the sentries and ordered the whole garrison under arms. In addition, loaded cannon were trained on likely gathering places, while the sloop *Michigan* and schooner *Huron* were deployed so that their cannon covered the front and sides of the fort. All this was done with the minimum of fuss so that many French inhabitants did not notice what was happening. However, Pontiac and his entourage were soon aware as they entered the fort that the entire garrison was under arms, with a large detachment on the parade ground with fixed bayonets under Captain Hopkins ready for action. They also noted that all the English merchants' shops were closed.[21]

Pontiac expressed his surprise to Gladwin, both at the warlike preparations and the lack of officers at the council. Gladwin merely replied that he expected some foreign Indians shortly and that he would have to be on his guard. Pontiac responded angrily that Gladwin had been listening to "bad birds" who were trying to stir up trouble with the British. However, he realized that he had been outsmarted. Not wishing to attack the soldiers in combat formation, he and his followers left for their village "seemingly very discontented" about two o'clock in the afternoon.[22]

Gladwin's intention had been to provoke the Indians into starting hostilities in the most disadvantageous manner. Nevertheless, some believed he had taken an unnecessary risk in allowing so many warriors to enter the fort. John Porteous, one of the merchants, commented that Gladwin "despised them so much" that he would allow "as many as pleased to come according to their usual custom," believing that his "preparations made to receive them would sufficiently scare them from their intentions."[23] Gladwin had proved correct in thinking that the Indians would avoid a frontal assault, but wrong that they would abandon their plan, as events quickly revealed.

Pontiac's first task on leaving the fort was to discover who had betrayed his plan. Suspicion soon fell on an Ojibwa woman called Catherine who was living with the Potawatomi. She was dragged before Gladwin, who merely affirmed her innocence. She was then marched back to Pontiac's village and almost beaten to death. More importantly, Pontiac had to reestablish his authority. According to Porteous, many younger warriors criticized him for not giving the signal to attack, arguing that the loss of a dozen warriors would have been a price worth paying. This put Pontiac in a quandary. His original plan to take Detroit by stratagem had clearly been compromised. On the other hand, a frontal attack would be extremely bloody. In the event, he decided to make a further attempt to persuade Gladwin that his only intent was the holding of a peace conference. He promised the warriors that this time the scheme would be successful.[24]

The next day, Sunday, 8 May, the warriors of the three nations played lacrosse at the Ottawa village, a traditional way of preparing for combat. Meanwhile Pontiac, Mackatepelecite, and two other chiefs, together with Pontiac's nephew from Saginaw, came to the fort with a pipe of peace. Here they regaled Gladwin with promises of their good intentions, presenting him with a calumet and a promise to return the following day with all their people to consummate their friendship in the traditional way.[25] However, when Pontiac returned on 9 May with an advance guard of fifty followers, he found the gates closed. Only the chiefs were to be admitted since the young men had "no business being there." Pontiac replied that "they would either all come to council or not at all." If the latter was the case, Johnson's belt of friendship would be thrown away, for no friendship was possible in such circumstances.[26] Gladwin as a goodwill gesture suggested that the Indians might enter thirty or forty at a time, but Pontiac, realizing that his scheme was hopelessly compromised, said defiantly that the British "might stay in our Fort" but the Indians "would keep the country."[27]

The Siege Begins

Unknown to either Pontiac or Gladwin, hostilities had already begun on 6 May 1763 when the St. Claire River Ojibwa had ambushed a small party under Lieutenant Robertson, who were surveying the channel leading to Lake Huron. The Ojibwa there had been alerted early on the morning of 6 May to the impending hostilities by Pontiac's messengers en route to Saginaw Bay and Michilimackinac, who carried "a belt inviting all the nations they met to fall on the English wherever they found them."[28] Robertson's group had left Detroit on 2 May with no inkling of danger until the morning of 6 May, when they were warned by some Canadians that the St. Claire Indians were waiting in ambush further up the river. Robertson discounted the warnings, being anxious to finish his task. The surveying therefore continued. As the current carried them close to a thickly wooded stretch of the river bank, they were lured into a trap by some Indian women offering food. At a given signal the women ran away, allowing the warriors concealed close by to open fire. Robertson and Sir Robert Davers, a young gentleman on a visit to the area, were killed, as were two of the soldiers. Five more were taken prisoner. Among them was the seventeen-year-old John Rutherford, who was working for his father at Detroit. Since he was deemed suitable for adoption, he was invited to eat Robertson's roasted flesh as part of the adoption process.[29] He refused but was still accepted by his new family.

Pontiac now carried out his threat about possessing the country. First he moved his village to Parents Creek across "the river to the side where the Fort was, in order to harass it the better." His plan was to isolate the British and, with the help of the French inhabitants, force them into abandoning their position. A widespread opinion prevailed that the garrison could be frightened out of Detroit. Accordingly, Pontiac divided his forces into two war parties. One went to the rear of the fort, where they scalped a woman and her two sons working on their farm. The second party crossed to Hog Island, where three soldiers were tending some cattle. These too were killed, as were the adult members of the Fisher family, whose three children were taken into captivity.[30] Various groups then commenced firing on the garrison from the safety of nearby barns and houses.

The next day Pontiac's army renewed its fire, paying particular attention to the two vessels, since they protected the flanks of the compound as well as the main entrance on the waterfront.[31] But Pontiac also recognized the importance of psychological tactics. After three hours of firing, he allowed a party of

Wyandot to approach the fort, offering to arrange a peace conference. Soon a number of French inhabitants also suggested a meeting at one of their houses halfway between the fort and Pontiac's encampment. Gladwin was hesitant about sending emissaries on such a dangerous mission. However, Campbell and Lieutenant George McDougall persuaded him to agree, pointing out that the inhabitants were guaranteeing their safety. The proposal would also allow Gladwin more time to search for supplies. An inspection the previous day had revealed sufficient food for just ten days, or three weeks on half rations.[32]

Accordingly Campbell and McDougall set off on the afternoon of 10 May 1763, in the company of several leading inhabitants. Their destination was the house of Antoine Cuillerier, a relative of the last French commander, François Bellestre. Here they found Cuillerier sitting in an armchair, dressed in a lace coat and hat, with the Indians addressing him as though he was the French commander. Cuillerier's exact intentions are not known. He seemingly believed that a French army and fleet were about to appear and that it was his duty to arrange an orderly transfer of authority. He probably intended announcing a ceasefire pending news from the French authorities in the Illinois. Pontiac, however, could not wait that long: his warriors wanted action. Accordingly he brusquely told Campbell and McDougall that if they desired peace, it had to be on the same terms as those given to Bellestre in 1760. The British must surrender their arms and go back across the mountains under escort. Cuillerier feebly suggested that these were actually his terms, which otherwise would have been much harsher.[33] In reality Cuillerier had little control of the situation, for Pontiac now announced that he was detaining Campbell and McDougall, pending a satisfactory outcome to the negotiations. He believed the British commander would do almost anything to secure his two officers. The French inhabitants who had accompanied Campbell and McDougall were accordingly forced to return and report to Gladwin that if these terms were rejected, the fort would be stormed by Pontiac with a thousand warriors. No quarter would be given.[34]

Gladwin responded that he must first hear the views of his two officers. In one respect the suspension of hostilities had proved fortunate, since it had allowed a search of the surrounding buildings, producing a two-month supply for both the garrison and those members of the French community who wished to stay inside.[35] Otherwise the situation was dire. Gladwin had just one hundred soldiers and twenty English merchants, while the schooner and the sloop each had a crew of six or seven. The fortified compound, which was Detroit's sole defense, was a thousand yards in circumference. Its walls consisted of twelve-foot poles, set in the ground with a raised platform inside for the defenders to stand on.[36] There were also three protruding bastions to improve the field of fire. However, such a small garrison meant that Gladwin had no option but to place his men on alternate six-hour shifts, a wearisome prospect.[37]

The next day, 11 May 1763, began quietly as the Indians and their French neighbors debated what to do. The inhabitants wanted to save their lives and property, the Indians to avoid the need for a bloody assault. Eventually it was decided to dispatch another emissary to the fort with revised peace terms. This time the British could sail away in their ships with their firearms, but they were to leave all the merchandise, artillery and an African American lad as a chamber boy for "Marshal Pontiac." Despite these concessions, Gladwin's response was the same as before. He would not negotiate until his two officers returned safely. In the meantime he would defend the fort to the last man.[38] Many French inhabitants believed this was about to happen since Pontiac's forces were visiting all their homes, demanding ammunition, apparently in preparation for a final assault. They accordingly took advantage of the lull to remove their belongings from the fort.[39]

Since Gladwin had refused to accept his revised surrender terms, Pontiac was faced with the necessity for a fresh assault. The Potawatomi and Wyandot therefore placed themselves on one side of the fort and the Ottawa and Ojibwa on the other, both concentrating their fire on the two vessels, since the destruction of these would weaken the British defenses and chances of escape. The Indians also endeavored to use various barns and houses as sniper cover. Some six to seven hundred warriors participated but with little effect, despite several hours of firing. Indeed, they suffered the greater casualties, having three men killed compared to five wounded for the British. The muskets of the Indians, especially those with shortened barrels, were sadly ineffective against the walls of the fort. The firing eventually ceased in the evening, leaving both sides as before.[40]

The threat posed by the Indian snipers and the danger of a sudden assault led Gladwin during the next couple of days to send out parties to burn the nearby barns and houses while the Indians recuperated in their villages. Other detachments sallied forth to cut down fences, orchards, and anything else that gave the Indians cover near the fort. In addition, two cannons were mounted to take advantage of this improved field of fire. After this, Pontiac's forces found it prudent to maintain their distance. The result was a considerable reduction in the intensity of the fighting and in British casualties. Nevertheless, the defenders were dangerously stretched, especially at night when it was difficult to see their enemy. Even without a frontal assault, the fatigue of defending the ramparts for long periods seemed likely to deliver the fort into Pontiac's hands, according to French sympathizers.[41]

Widening Visions

From the start, Pontiac recognized that it was essential to involve as many nations as possible in the war so that they could strike simultaneously in different areas, as envisaged in the plan of 1761. Initially he believed that the news from Detroit would spontaneously ignite the whole region, since war belts to this end had been circulating for some two years. However, his failure to take Detroit by stratagem meant that he now needed more specific assurances of allied support. He accordingly made three new diplomatic initiatives. The first was the dispatch of a scalp and war belt to the Seneca at Kanawagus, a town high up the Allegheny River. Initially, Pontiac had been against "listening to any news from that Quarter," perhaps fearful that the Seneca and their Six Nations confederates would not support his initiative.[42] However, the Iroquois were inordinately sensitive about their position as the foremost league in eastern North America. Any diplomatic snub on Pontiac's part could have cost him dearly. Their participation, in any case, was essential if the English were to be driven back across the mountains. Only the Six Nations were capable of securing the communication from Albany and Oswego, closing one of the principal routes to the Great Lakes.[43]

The same reasoning led Pontiac to dispatch messengers to the Delaware. He had not replied immediately to their call for help, wanting to be reinforced by the northern Ottawa and Ojibwa before going to the aid of the Ohio peoples. The delay in the capture of Detroit now meant that the Delaware and Shawnee would have to attack Fort Pitt on their own. Nevertheless, Pontiac's envoys were to assure the Delaware that while the Ohio peoples "were engaged in that affair ... they the Twightwee [Miami], Ottawa, Huron and others would demolish Detroit and Niagara." Then "they would all join them in a body and march towards Philadelphia."[44] Here was an objective more ambitious than that set by Tahaiadoris and Kiashuta.

Pontiac's third initiative was the dispatch of envoys to appeal for help from the French in the Illinois. This was critical to a restoration of the "middle ground," especially if an experienced officer was sent who could assist with the siege. It would also help reassure the residents of Detroit that they were fighting in a common cause. Accordingly, after several days of deliberation, Pontiac and Cuillerier each dispatched five emissaries to de Villiers at Fort Chartres, requesting assistance and the appointment of an officer to take command at Detroit.[45] There were, however, significant differences in the tone of the French and Indian delegations. Pontiac's message and that of the Ojibwa began with a recital of the lies told by the British and the warnings of the Delaware about the consequences for the Great Lakes nations if they became masters. They also recounted Bellestre's promise that their domination would not last and that the French would return. Accordingly, "we pray our Father at the Illinois to hasten to our succor" and take pity on "these poor children."[46]

The message from the French inhabitants was also supplicatory, but different in intent. It began, "Gentlemen, we are obliged to submit to what the Indians exact from us," affirming that "God alone can prevent our becoming the victims of the English and the Savages." The inhabitants had neither encouraged the Indians to take up the hatchet, nor had the British given them cause to do so. Nevertheless, the situation was dire. Only the French officers in the

Illinois could save them from the dilemma of "two contending parties" who threatened them with "desolation."[47] However, the French delegation included Jacques Godfroy and Mini Chêne, who were intent on a more active part. It is not clear how they reconciled their support for Pontiac with the desire of their colleagues to remain neutral. Most likely, they believed that they were legitimately assisting the restoration of French authority. The rest of the inhabitants were cowards, who were only concerned for their lives and property, not the honor of France. Whatever their reasoning, Godfroy and Chêne readily participated in a mission which they must have known would lead to further hostilities, for Pontiac had instructed his envoys on route to incite the Miami, Kickapoo, Piankashaw, and Wea to capture Forts Miami and Ouiatanon.[48]

Meanwhile the siege still had to be prosecuted. From the beginning Pontiac recognized the need to isolate the fort, especially from assistance coming via the Detroit River. Parties of Potawatomi and Wyandot accordingly patrolled the woods and banks along the river, capturing on 13 May the trader Chapman Abraham and five bateaux containing a large quantity of goods, including seventeen barrels of gunpowder. A considerable amount of rum was also seized, which led to reports of the Indians being drunk.[49] This prompted Gladwin to send the sloop *Michigan* to attack the Wyandot village, but without success when the wind prevented the vessel from reaching its objective. It was subsequently discovered that the reports about drunken Indians were a ruse to lure the sloop into an ambush.[50]

Although Pontiac had been careful not to offend the French inhabitants, it was soon clear that his hoped-for alliance was not forthcoming. Yet their support was crucial to his success, since he needed help in the construction of entrenchments, now that the British had destroyed most of the cover near the fort. The desire of most inhabitants for a bloodless outcome prompted Pontiac to renew his proposal to Gladwin that the garrison should evacuate the fort and sail away in the ships. The British would save their lives, the Indians recover their lands, and the French regain the fort. Pontiac added that if Gladwin refused these terms and was captured, he would be treated as an Indian rather than a European, meaning he would be tortured to death. Pontiac still believed he might frighten the British into leaving Detroit. He certainly did not expect Gladwin's droll reply that he would remain in that case, since his own king would execute him if he abandoned his duty by running away.[51]

If Pontiac thought that his offer to Gladwin and appeal to the French authorities in the Illinois would win over the inhabitants, he was to be disappointed, since most of them still feared that the conflict would lead to their ruin. Indeed, after consultation with their priest, Father Potier, twelve of them arrived on 14 May to ask Pontiac what his intentions were. Pontiac in response tried to quiet their fears by affirming that "he had no other design than to expel the English from the fort and from their lands" in preparation for "the French commander, who as he heard, was about to arrive." But when the delegation suggested that the Indians remain quiet until the French troops appeared, Pontiac refused, arguing that he must have the fort ready for the arrival of "his Father."[52]

For Pontiac, this was a period of frustration and anxiety. The random shots of his warriors were having little effect, few reinforcements had yet arrived in response to his war belts, and there was no word from the more distant theatres of the war along the Ohio Valley and eastern Great Lakes. In addition, Pontiac found that he was short of provisions. Unless more merchant convoys could be seized, the situation could only be remedied by taking supplies from the French, who were already resentful at the requisitioning of their crops to feed the warriors and their families.[53] Moreover, while the British could resupply Detroit with their two armed sailing ships, they would never be starved into surrender. With this in mind, he ordered two hundred warriors in canoes to intercept any bateau traffic entering the river. However, Gladwin now felt sufficiently confident to place the schooner *Huron* near the entrance to Lake Erie to prevent anyone else from being surprised. He calculated that the schooner, with its raised deck, swivel guns, and four-pounder cannon, would be more than a match for the enemy in flimsy birch bark canoes. The master of the schooner was to patrol the entrance until an expected reinforcement under Lieutenant Cuyler arrived from Niagara. Then, after two weeks, he was to sail to Niagara for help.[54]

Meanwhile, Pontiac still had to win over the majority of the French inhabitants. Indeed, on 25 May he received a second delegation of fifteen inhabitants asking him to remember his promise to Bellestre not to harm the French. Pontiac responded by reminding them of his role during the Fox Wars: "I am the same French Pontiac who helped you seventeen years ago. I am French and want to die French." He was not asking them to fight, only to provide provisions and agree "that our women may have permission to raise our corn upon your fields and fallow lands."[55] The Indians had been unable to prepare the ground for their crops because of the hostilities. Pontiac knew what the consequences would be if winter arrived and the fort was still in British hands and no crops planted.

This appeal for help with their agriculture got a better response, since it was not so overtly treasonous, should the British ultimately prevail and seek retribution. Accordingly, offers were made to plough the Indians' fields and plant their corn.[56] Not everything, in any case, was gloomy for it was about this time that Pontiac had news of a double success. After the opening assault on Detroit, Pontiac and Takay had sent envoys to the Wyandot of Sandusky to attack the post established there in 1761. As always the Indians preferred stratagem to a formal assault. Accordingly, on 16 May the local chiefs, who had previously seemed friendly, called on the post's commander, Lieutenant Christopher Pauli. Still blissfully unaware of his danger, Pauli invited four Wyandot and three Ottawa to enter his chamber to smoke a pipe of peace.

After sitting down, he was suddenly seized while the garrison outside were killed, along with a number of merchants. The result was the capture of a large quantity of ammunition and other supplies.[57]

Takay's envoys then returned to Detroit, bringing news that the schooner was anchored near the river entrance with a crew of only six. Such a target was not to be missed, and Pontiac decided on an immediate attack. Unfortunately, he undertook the enterprise on 25 May with only six canoes. These were quickly driven off by the crew using their cannon and swivel guns. Next day nine canoes were sighted, one with Campbell and the interpreter, La Butte, on board.[58] Pontiac calculated that "the presence of this officer would lead the people of the vessel to surrender." Campbell did issue a half-hearted instruction that the vessel should "come on shore." But he then added that "the master knew his orders and advised him to get off from thence as soon as possible." The vessel accordingly set sail for Niagara.[59] Pontiac could only hope that the Seneca were now besieging that post, just as he was doing at Detroit.

However, the attack on the schooner was not entirely wasted since the warriors shortly afterwards discovered that the long-awaited British reinforcement, a company of the Queen's Rangers commanded by Lieutenant Cornelius Cuyler, was bivouacked about twenty-five miles from the entrance to the Detroit River at Point Pelee. This was on the evening of 28 May 1763. Cuyler, like Pauli, was completely unaware of the hostilities, his main concern being to secure his boats. The first intimation of danger was when a soldier, sent to fetch wood with a boy, came running back to say that his companion had been scalped. Soon the Wyandot and Potawatomi appeared, using the woods as cover to get within forty yards of the British position. The Queen's Rangers were a new unit and not well disciplined. When the warriors charged the center of the British line, the whole unit fled for its boats. In the melée sixty were killed or captured, while the other thirty-five, including Cuyler, rowed for their lives back to Niagara, where they arrived on 5 June.[60]

The captives were not so fortunate, being taken to Pontiac's camp. Here they were stripped and made to run the gauntlet. Most were either killed by youngsters practicing their archery skills or made to endure the agony of death by burning, though a few were spared for their skills as craftsmen.[61] Cuyler's men were not the only soldiers to undergo such ordeals, for about the same time Sergeant Shaw and fourteen men of the Royal American regiment were captured near the place where Robertson and Davers had been ambushed. Shaw had set out from Michilimackinac in early May to secure provisions, not knowing about the hostilities around Detroit. This contingent was also brought to Pontiac's camp for similar treatment.[62] Although barbaric from a European viewpoint, such torture allowed captives to demonstrate their courage and prove their worth as warriors.

For Pontiac the situation was now looking brighter, not least because his calls for assistance were finally being answered. On 21 May, Chief Sekahos of the Thames River Ojibwa arrived at Detroit with 120 warriors.[63] Ten days later Wasson, chief of the Ojibwa at Saginaw Bay, appeared with a further two hundred.[64] By early June the besieging forces numbered some 850 warriors, including 250 Ottawa under Pontiac, 150 Potawatomi under Ninivois, 50 Huron under Takay, 250 Ojibwa under Wasson, and 170 Ojibwa under Sekahos. Although each group was led by its own chief, they were "under the authority of Pontiac, their over chief," according to Navarre.[65] These additional forces allowed Pontiac to widen his military effort, which he had always planned to do. Accordingly, the day after Wasson arrived, a council was held in Pontiac's camp at which it was "decided to harass the Fort no longer but to bar the approaches so that no more assistance could reach the English." The fort would then be starved into submission. The change in tactics would in turn release three hundred Ottawa, Ojibwa, Wyandot, and Potawatomi to "prowl round the lake and capture the English they should find there."[66] Since Sandusky had already fallen, the one remaining British fort on Lake Erie was Presque Isle, and it was to this objective that the force set off.

The first part of June also brought news of the capture of Fort Miami by the Miami and Fort Ouiatanon by the Kickapoo and their allies, following the arrival of Pontiac's emissaries. Similar success greeted Ninivois at Fort St. Joseph.[67] Then on 18 June, Kinonchamek, "the son of the Great Chief" of the Ojibwa, arrived, announcing that Michilimackinac had fallen to stratagem during a game of lacrosse.[68] In addition, two canoes of Delaware and Shawnee appeared "to see what was going on," as well as to report their own progress.[69] So far, the Delaware had killed fifteen merchants after receiving Pontiac's belt. However, most of the Ohio warriors were still below Fort Pitt, waiting to ambush the British expedition which was expected down the Ohio.[70]

In the light of these developments, Pontiac called a grand council to discuss the conduct of the war. He was certainly disappointed that Kinonchamek had arrived with only a small delegation of Ottawa and Ojibwa rather than the expected reinforcement. Also disturbing was the decision of the Delaware and Shawnee to go directly to his camp rather than that of Pontiac. Indeed, the new arrivals first held a separate council to which "two or three Frenchmen were called to give information about matters since the beginning of the siege." Particular attention was paid to "all that had been done by Pontiac's orders."[71]

When the grand council started later that day in Pontiac's camp, it proved an acrimonious affair. Kinonchamek told the assembly that he and his companions were not impressed with what they found at Detroit. He accused Pontiac not only of harming the French inhabitants, but also of indiscriminately killing prisoners after they had surrendered. This was in stark contrast, he disingenuously claimed, to the conduct of the Ojibwa, who had studiously protected the survivors by sending them to Montreal. One problem was that Pontiac had not given sufficient attention to the feeding of his people, which accounted for his imposing on the French inhabitants. The "Great Father," whom they were all awaiting, would not be pleased at his conduct.[72] The Shawnee then delivered a similar rebuke on behalf of themselves and the Delaware. They had joined the attack "because the Master of Life" in communication with "one of our brother Delawares [Neolin] told us to do so." But the Great Spirit had expressly "forbade us to attack our brothers, the French." He had similarly given instructions about the proper treatment of prisoners. They would not therefore come to Pontiac's assistance, since his actions were not in accordance with "the wampum belts which we have sent."[73]

These comments were so severe that Pontiac for once said nothing. He was later also criticized by Father Du Jaunay, the Jesuit priest from Michilimackinac, who had accompanied Kinonchamek on his own fact-finding mission. This time, Pontiac replied with more spirit. Du Jaunay "would see soon that he had done a good deed, and his Father would be there again and that he was sure the French and English were fighting at Quebec."[74]

Stalemate, July 1763

Although Kinonchamek departed for Michilimackinac soon afterwards, Pontiac recognized that he must do something to restore his authority. The key to Detroit still seemed to lie with the destruction of the British vessels. He knew that the schooner was likely to return shortly with provisions. Indeed, it had been reported in the vicinity of the Detroit River as early as 21 June. Pontiac now saw an opportunity to recover his lost prestige. In the relatively narrow confines of the river, the schooner would be more vulnerable than on the lake. On 23 June, he ordered a much larger detachment than previously to mount an immediate assault. One group hid on Turkey Island behind a makeshift barricade of tree trunks, while a second detachment waited out of sight in canoes. Unfortunately the schooner kept clear of Turkey Island, leaving it to the warriors in the birch bark canoes to effect a capture. Unknown to Pontiac, the schooner was carrying not only provisions but also the remnants of Cuyler's unit, some fifty men, who deliberately stayed below decks until the moment of the attack. These additional defenders and the ship's cannon proved too formidable for Pontiac's men in their fragile craft. The engagement ended as swiftly as it began, with the loss of fourteen warriors and a similar number of wounded.[75]

Pontiac attempted to make light of his defeat by telling Gladwin that he should surrender immediately before Kinonchamek and his father arrived with eight hundred warriors from Michilimackinac, whom Pontiac would not be able to control.[76] Gladwin answered politely that Campbell and McDougall must first be released. Pontiac replied that he had too high a regard for Campbell and McDougall "to boil them in the same kettle as the rest of the garrison."[77] He still hoped to frighten the British out of Detroit. He was also heartened by the capture of Presque Isle and the return of the task force with several prisoners, including the commander of that post, Lieutenant John

Christie.[78] However, the schooner finally reached the fort on the afternoon of 30 June, bringing Gladwin a small but much needed reinforcement of men, provisions, and ammunition. Two days later, Pontiac suffered another setback when Lieutenant McDougall and three other prisoners escaped while their guards were asleep. The only consolation was that Campbell had declined to join the escapees because of his weight and poor eyesight.[79] He was shortly to pay dearly for his decision not to leave.

Pontiac, meanwhile, still hoped for a more positive response from the French inhabitants. Toward the end of June he began issuing receipts for sequestrated goods, promising repayment once the war was over. These bills were made from the bark of a tree and contained a drawing of the items taken. Pontiac's signature was also engraved in the shape of an otter or racoon.[80] But he did not endear himself by forcing the inhabitants on one occasion to carry him around in a sedan chair.[81] Recognizing the need to win over his neighbors, he addressed them once more on 2 July, hoping that his oratory if not his generalship would secure a favorable response. He first assured the inhabitants that he had started the war as much for their interest as for the Indians'. The Master of Life had made victory certain. The French therefore should do his bidding because Pontiac was fighting on their behalf. At the very least, they should stop informing the British about his movements. Neutrality was not an option. "There is only one way open today; either remain French as we are, or altogether English as they are. If you are French, accept this war belt for yourselves, or your young men, and join us."[82]

Despite Pontiac's implied threats, the principal inhabitants declined this appeal, knowing that they would be committing treason if peace really had been concluded by Britain and France. Navarre pointed out that the inhabitants were still bound by Vaudreuil's surrender terms of September 1760.[83] Zachariah Cicotte then suggested a compromise. He believed "there were above three hundred young men in the settlement, who had neither parents or much property to lose that might and ought to join him." Some were *coureurs de bois*. Eventually, about forty of these men agreed to assist Pontiac.[84] Among them was Antoine Cuillerier's son, Alexis, who was already "carrying messages back and forth from the Indian camp, giving information on the French who assisted the fort."[85] Others openly espousing Pontiac included Pierre Labadie, who put war paint on his two sons and son-in-law before sending them out against the fort.[86]

At this point, there were in effect four groups among the French inhabitants. The first was the relatively small section that supported the British as the lawfully constituted authority. Among them were Navarre, Le Grand, Jacques Baby, and the interpreters La Butte and St. Martin. They were motivated by either their oath of loyalty or a realization that French authority would not be restored and that they must work with the new order. The second, most numerous group was the neutrals who hoped for a restoration of French rule but were fearful of backing the wrong side and being branded as traitors. They kept their heads down, waiting for the storm to pass. The third category comprised those who were prepared to given material help without actually taking up arms. They included Cicotte, Cuillerier, Baptiste Campeau, Jean Chapotin, and the two Meloche brothers, Frank and Baptiste. Finally, there was a group of young Frenchmen who were ready to fight. The leaders of this group were Charles Ducette and Pierre Barthe, to whom Pontiac gave wampum belts as commissions to raise volunteers.[87]

Although Pontiac announced the ending of all forced levies of food, several leading French inhabitants took refuge in the fort following the meeting on 2 July, believing the arrival of a British relief force was more likely than the appearance of a French army and fleet. The refugees were undoubtedly influenced by a letter from Pontiac warning Gladwin that unless he gave up the fort, the inhabitants would be forced to participate in the affair. Pontiac naïvely asked Navarre to write this letter, unaware of the notary's attachment to the British.[88] However, Gladwin made no reply this time. Instead, he ordered Le Grand to summon the inhabitants to the church, where he read the details of the definitive peace between Britain, France, and Spain. A band then played celebratory music for an hour.[89]

The siege nevertheless continued, for on 4 July Gladwin sent Lieutenant Jehu Hay with a detachment to level an entrenchment that Pontiac had started to construct with the assistance of his French volunteers. This led to a skirmish in which Wasson's nephew was shot and scalped.[90] The result was an eruption of bad feeling between Pontiac and his Saginaw allies. Wasson bitterly complained that Pontiac "was very brave in taking a loaf of bread or a beef from a Frenchman who made no resistance, but it was them [the Ojibwa] that had all the men killed and wounded every day and for that reason they would take that from him which he intended to save himself by in the end." This latter point was a reference to Campbell, whom it was believed Pontiac was holding as security for a pardon, should the siege fail.[91] The dishonor to Wasson's nephew had to be revenged. Wasson's men accordingly seized Campbell and took him to a nearby bridge. Here he was stripped, then tied to a stake; his lips were cut off, and arrows shot through his body. Finally his heart was torn out, still beating, so that those eating it would be imparted with the victim's courage.[92] His torso was then dumped in the river.

Perhaps hoping to regain control of the situation, Pontiac called a further council of the chiefs and his principal French supporters. Much time was spent debating whether the reports of a peace were genuine. Rutherford was brought in to translate some correspondence of Campbell in the hope that it might shed light on the question.[93] Among those present were Campeau, the Meloche brothers, Gabriel St. Auban, an interpreter named Louis Denler, Duchette, and Barthe. Not all of them were so wholehearted as before. The events of the preceding day had clearly shocked Denler and Barthe, who admitted to Rutherford that they felt a noose tightening around their necks. Both were considering flight to the Illinois.[94]

Nevertheless, even Barthe thought that the reports of peace were false and that the war should continue. A new plan of action was accordingly agreed on, whereby "the garrison was to be attacked without by the savages and French, and within by the French inhabitants in the fort." Those outside would dig trenches to make the siege more effective. At the same time Barthe, a gunsmith by trade, and Chopoton, another inhabitant with access to the fort, were to assist from inside, where Barthe had a duplicate set of keys to the three main gates.[95] But before Pontiac could put these plans into execution, his own camp was attacked. Angered by the death of Campbell, Gladwin ordered the sloop to exact revenge. Although no one was injured, many dwellings were destroyed, necessitating a second move for the Ottawa. This time Pontiac chose a site six miles away, protected by a swamp, making an attack difficult by either road or river.[96]

These events only reinforced Pontiac's realization that he must destroy the British ships if he was to capture Detroit and assist his Delaware allies in the wider struggle for freedom. He now devised a new scheme for destroying the schooner and sloop by means of fire rafts, perhaps inspired by the French attempt to burn the invading British fleet at Quebec in 1759. To aid construction, Pontiac asked Ducette and Barthe to enlist help from the French inhabitants, though few seemingly participated, except for the two Meloche brothers.[97] Nevertheless the Ottawa and Ojibwa were soon hard at work with saws and axes sequestered from the inhabitants. The first attempt was made on 10 July, when several bateaux were tied together and filled with combustibles. Unfortunately they burnt too quickly and missed their target. A similar attempt two nights later was equally fruitless.[98] Clearly, something heavier was required that would burn longer and not drift from the target. Pontiac accordingly ordered the construction of "a new fire float of dry wood." The work, however, progressed slowly.[99] In the meantime, Gladwin reinforced the sides of several bateaux with oak planking so that their occupants could row more safely and fire more accurately. The bateaux were also equipped at each end with swivel guns and grappling irons to drag the raft clear.[100] On a trial run the armored bateaux lured two canoes into action, resulting in the wounding of several Indians. After some French bystanders explained the purpose of the grappling irons, Pontiac abandoned his scheme for fire rafts.[101] Nevertheless, it was another example of his initiative and resolution to bring the siege to a successful conclusion.

Unfortunately, his determination was not shared by all of his allies. Long sieges were alien to Indian warfare, and the commitment of the Detroit Potawatomi and Wyandot was beginning to wane. Many of the latter were members of Father Potier's mission and were troubled by their exclusion from mass.[102] The Potawatomi in contrast were concerned for one of their chiefs, whom Gladwin had seized in retaliation for the holding of Campbell and McDougall. Both nations were alarmed at the bombardment of Pontiac's camp, since their own villages were beside the river. They were also troubled by the rumors of a definitive peace. The Potawatomi were the first to ask for terms, sending a delegation to the fort on 7 July, with the promise that they would inform their relatives at St. Joseph and the Twightwee at Fort Miami what they were doing. They were followed the next day by Teata and his Wyandot, arguing that they had been forced to take up arms by Pontiac. To both, Gladwin replied that they must first surrender their prisoners to demonstrate their good faith.[103] The Wyandot duly complied on 9 July, when they delivered up seven prisoners, including Lieutenant Christie, the former commander of Presque Isle.[104] Twenty-four hours later, the Potawatomi followed with two soldiers and a couple of traders. However, Gladwin knew they had other prisoners and repeated his demand that there could be no peace until all been given up. The sincerity of the Potawatomi was further compromised by the discovery of an Ottawa spy in their ranks.[105]

To stop these defections, Pontiac visited Teata and the Wyandot in their village across the river, though with little effect. By now, Gladwin was sufficiently confident of his position to open the main waterside gate during the day for the convenience of the inhabitants and garrison.[106] But not everything was bleak for Pontiac and his forces. On 22 July, an Abenaki messenger brought intelligence that a French fleet was on its way to Canada.[107] Two days later several Shawnee and Delaware arrived with the news that Fort Pitt was blockaded and the posts on the communication attacked. To show their commitment, they "gave all the nations" of Detroit "belts of wampum," inviting them to sing "the war song again." It was sufficient for the Wyandot and Potawatomi to rejoin the besiegers.[108] Another reason for optimism was the return of Godfroy and Chêne from the Illinois. They affirmed that de Villiers knew nothing about the signing of a peace, thus supporting the view that Gladwin had been lying all along. Unfortunately, they brought no officer. Nevertheless Pontiac was sufficiently encouraged to deliver an oration, explaining that "the Master of Life had ordered him to make war upon the English," pending the arrival of Onontio in the fall. The chiefs of all the nations, therefore, should join in chanting their war songs. It proved a further example of his leadership skills, for those present all agreed to follow him, even though the siege had lasted almost three months.[109] The restoration of unity was fortunate, for a British reinforcement was about to arrive and test the resolve of Pontiac and his allies in battle.

5
The Spreading Conflagration

Fort Pitt Comes Under Siege

While Pontiac was attempting to bring the siege of Detroit to a successful conclusion, much of eastern North America had joined him in the struggle for freedom. This was no surprise, since Pontiac had launched his attack as part of a wider scheme to expel the British west of the Allegheny Mountains according to the Seneca Plan of 1761. For this reason, he had sent envoys far and wide both before and after the outbreak of hostilities to ensure that all played their part.

Among the first to be contacted at the start of the siege were the western Delaware. This was because Pontiac had initiated military action at their request. A joint delegation from the Detroit peoples was accordingly dispatched toward the Ohio. The first of these envoys reached the village of Tuscarawas on 26 May 1763 with the information that Detroit was besieged, and Sandusky captured, and that it was time to take up arms.[1] However, most of the emissaries went to "a Delaware Town below Tuscarawas a good way," where "a large Body of many different Nations" had assembled. Here, according to some passing Seneca, the "Ottawa Confederacy" delivered "the war hatchet to the Delaware, and desire[d] that they would make use of it against the English, who were taking their country from them." The envoys then pointed out "Fort Pitt and Fort Augusta as the greatest eye sore" to Ohio Indians and "desired they would loose [sic] no time in distressing and attacking" them. Once Detroit was captured, Pontiac and his Great Lakes allies would be able to join the Delaware for a "march towards Philadelphia."[2]

This encouragement from Pontiac was naturally gratifying to the Delaware, since it showed that he did not share the Six Nations' opinion of them as "women." They accordingly thanked the envoys "for looking upon them now as men, and asserted they would show by their actions that they were worthy of the confidence reposed in them." However, effective action required the cooperation of the Shawnee, who were momentarily less keen on military action, despite their anger about the captives. A Wyandot member of the delegation accordingly admonished the Shawnee for not being wholehearted in the cause. If their sachems did not "exert themselves in conjunction with the Delaware," the Ottawa Confederacy would make cuckolds of them by encouraging their warriors to desert to other leaders. Faced with this ultimatum, the Shawnee agreed to participate.[3]

The Delaware did not strike Fort Pitt or its communication immediately. They wanted time to move their settlements to safer refuges down the Ohio River. They also required ammunition and other supplies before commencing an attack. Nevertheless they began preparations at once, for on the next day, 27 May 1763, William Trent, a business associate of Croghan, learned that the Delaware above Fort Pitt had overnight abandoned their cornfields and habitations. Simultaneously other Delaware visited Trent to trade, while urging Croghan's deputy, the half-breed McKee, not to stay in the fort longer than four days.[4] James Kenny, at the Pennsylvania provincial store, reported similarly that Turtle Heart, the brother of Custaloga, and a group of warriors had arrived to exchange their skins for powder and lead. He noted that "they seemed in no bad humor but rather in fear and haste." They too expressed concern for McKee's safety.[5] Finally, McKee himself reported that the Mingo had left their village further up the Allegheny River. Before doing so, they and some Delaware "had sold £300 worth of peltry very hastily with which they bought as much powder and lead as they could get." A subsequent visit to their deserted towns indicated that they had gone down the river, perhaps to join the Shawnee in an ambush of the expedition as it made its way down the Ohio.[6]

Next day, news arrived of the first hostilities. Several farms had been established in the area for the support of Fort Pitt, which made tempting targets for small parties that were unable to attack the fort itself. Accordingly a party of twenty-five Delaware set out on 29 May to attack the plantation of Colonel William Clapham, twenty miles to the southeast on the Youghiogheny River. Clapham was a former Pennsylvania colonel who like many of his contemporaries had turned to western lands to make his fortune. Without warning, the farm was attacked and its occupants killed, with the exception of three workmen who escaped through the woods to Fort Pitt.[7] The killings were allegedly the work of Wolf, a leading western Delaware, and his father Kickyuscung. In an attempt to defuse the situation, Captain Ecuyer sent a message to the Tuscarawas villages, saying that he did not blame the chiefs for the actions of their "foolish young men." They should instead return to their homes until some method could be agreed on for bringing the perpetrators to justice. Above all, the chain of friendship must be preserved.[8] But his appeal had no effect on the warriors, for that same evening two men were scalped at the nearby sawmill. The attackers left a tomahawk in the ground, a traditional way of declaring war.[9]

If any further confirmation of hostilities was necessary, it came with the arrival of Thomas Calhoun and three other merchants from Tuscarawas. Late in the evening of 27 May 1763, Tamaqua, Shingas, and several other western Delaware chiefs had advised Calhoun and his fourteen companions "out of regard" for them to depart immediately. The news was bad, Tamaqua said. At

Detroit, all the British had been killed. A similar massacre had occurred at Sandusky, while Hugh Crawford, the trader, had been captured at the mouth of the Maumee River. In addition, five whites had been killed at the Salt Licks not far from Tuscarawas. Tracks on the road from Sandusky indicated that a party of Ottawa and Ojibwa was coming to attack them. The Delaware did not want to be involved, but were caught between the two contending parties. The traders and their men, therefore, should leave immediately, avoiding Indian paths "as we would not desire to see you killed in our town."[10]

To help the merchants escape, Tamaqua and his colleagues gave them three guides. However, Calhoun and his companions were advised to leave their goods behind and were not permitted to take any arms. The following day, they were ambushed at the confluence of the Beaver and Ohio Rivers. All but four were killed.[11] The ambush appeared to have been staged by Tamaqua to avoid any obvious complicity should the war turn against the Indians. However, the perpetrators were probably a war party from the village of Mahoning. It was this group that had killed the five merchants at the Salt Licks. Indeed, their murderous spree started with the slaying of a trader, Thomas Green, after he had gone to recover a stolen horse. Mahoning and Salt Licks were both on the Beaver River and in the direction of Fort Pitt, whither the war party was probably heading when they discovered Calhoun and his party.[12]

Meanwhile, Captain Ecuyer was endeavoring to put Fort Pitt into a state of defense. His forces consisted of about 230 men, half of them regulars, and the rest male inhabitants organized as a militia. There were also about 150 women and children. Unlike Detroit, Fort Pitt was now a proper European-style stone structure with bastions covering every angle of approach. It also had sixteen cannon. Less imposing was the stockade on the eastern side containing a garden, in which the inhabitants' cattle were lodged. There were also a number of nearby houses grouped in what were called the upper and lower town. These were now destroyed to ensure that the Indians had no cover. However, the garden and stockade were retained, since provisions were likely to be in short supply. Indeed, the situation was potentially worse than at Detroit, since there were no sympathetic French farmers to give surreptitious aid. This meant that Ecuyer would have to conserve his salt provisions until a relief force arrived from the inhabited areas. The settlers were accordingly put on half rations, while the "poorer women and children" had to be satisfied with "a little Indian corn and meat." But to strengthen his position, Ecuyer ordered the garrison of Fort Burd on the Monongahela River to withdraw to Fort Pitt. He also sent warnings to the garrisons at Venango and Le Boeuf, though without success. Each time, his messengers were forced to return.[13]

The intrinsic strength of Fort Pitt meant that Ecuyer had little concern for his own safety. On the other hand, he could not be so confident about the posts on the communication to Carlisle. The position was most critical at Fort Bedford, where Captain Ourry had a corporal and six privates. The town itself had a mere thirty-six men capable of bearing arms, of whom just nineteen had guns but no powder. Concern was not diminished when on 31 May 1763 Wolf's brother arrived "on the pretense of returning a horse," but clearly with the intention of spying.[14] This led the population to take refuge in the fort so that Ourry soon had ninety-three families staying with him, giving him a nominal militia of 155.[15] So far there had been no sign of the enemy, which had allowed them to bring cattle into pens under the walls of the fort.[16] Intelligence from John Hudson, a Cayuga, indicated that Teedyuscung's eastern Delaware were not involved in the hostilities. Rather it was the Miami, Ojibwa, Ottawa, and Sandusky Wyandot who were causing the trouble. The latter included Wolf, who was technically a Wyandot, since his mother was from that nation, among whom family ties were matrilineal.[17]

The main reason for the quiet at Fort Bedford was because the western Delaware had decided to attack Fort Ligonier, which was further beyond the line of settlement. Its isolation therefore made it a tempting target. The commanding officer here was Lieutenant Archibald Blane with a garrison of twenty-five. The first assault began early in the morning of Thursday, 2 June 1763. The Indians, however, only fired from the edge of the woods. The garrison accordingly greeted them with cheers rather than bullets to conserve their ammunition.[18] Like Ecuyer, Blane quickly demolished the nearby buildings to deny the enemy cover. Hence, when the Delaware made another attempt three weeks later, they had no success, despite firing a thousand rounds. They were equally unsuccessful when they attempted to lure a detachment to the woods, where a hundred warriors lay in ambush.[19] Nevertheless, the Delaware were not unduly discouraged, for they let it be known "that all the country was theirs; that they had been cheated out of it, and that they would carry on the war till they had burnt Philadelphia."[20]

The fighting at this point was still relatively scattered because many Delaware and most Shawnee were still below Fort Pitt awaiting the anticipated expedition down the River Ohio. But the Indian offensive was also weakened because the western Delaware were divided about what to do. According to four Shawnee who visited Fort Pitt, the older Delaware chiefs had advised their warriors to reject Pontiac's belt and bloody hatchet. Unfortunately, they had been ignored by the captains and warriors.[21] Nevertheless, Wolf and Kickyuscung had barely a hundred men, which restricted them to firing on small parties cutting hay. Ecuyer, however, was resolved to leave nothing to chance. He had his cannon permanently loaded and a trench dug to protect those working outside the walls. Beaver traps were also set, though without result. The garrison itself was divided into three companies, armed with additional muskets and rifles in case of an emergency. Ecuyer's main fear now was an outbreak of smallpox. To limit its spread, he formed a hospital under the drawbridge, safe from musket fire.[22]

The four Shawnee, who spoke to McKee on 16 June, requested another meeting the following day. This time they reported a much more threatening situation. A general Indian war had broken out, they said. All the "nations had taken up the hatchet" against the British and were intending to attack Fort Pitt, as "Venango and all the other posts that way were already cut off." So many nations had seized the hatchet that the Shawnee themselves "were afraid to refuse" it, a gentle hint to leave.[23] Ecuyer was initially dismissive of the threat to Fort Pitt, but he soon discovered his mistake on 22 June, when the Indians attacked from three sides. The western Delaware and Shawnee had now been reinforced by the Mingo, following the entry of the Seneca into the war. Nevertheless, they ended their assault once Ecuyer ordered his artillery to fire.[24]

As siege warfare was alien to Indian methods, the Delaware and Shawnee decided to try diplomacy once more to gain their objective. Accordingly, around nine o'clock on the morning of 24 June, Turtle Heart addressed McKee near the fort. He began by pointing out that all the strong places linking Pittsburgh and the inhabited areas had been destroyed, and "This is now the only one you have left in our country." He then informed McKee that "six different nations of Indians" were ready to attack. They had only delayed their assault to give the garrison at Fort Pitt time to retreat, which it should do immediately, "as there is every day great numbers of Indians coming here," meaning Pontiac's forces from the Great Lakes. When they arrived, no quarter would be given.[25]

McKee thanked Turtle Heart on Ecuyer's behalf but assured him that Fort Pitt was strong enough to resist "all nations of Indians." He then tried a little exaggeration in return, asserting that three armies were advancing: one of six thousand men to relieve Fort Pitt, another of three thousand men from Canada to strike the Ottawa and Ojibwa "in their own country," and one from Virginia to protect the backcountry with the support of the southern Indians. The Delaware, therefore, should have pity on their women and children. In a second meeting that afternoon, the envoys softened their tone, affirming that they were still friends of the British.[26] Despite this, Trent, now one of the militia officers, presented them with two small blankets and a handkerchief from the smallpox hospital, in the hope that they would "have the desired effect."[27] For the first time in history, germ warfare had been added to the catalogue of human misery.

For the next few days little happened except for the odd skirmish, though the garrison received confirmation from the survivors of Fort Le Boeuf that Venango had been taken and that Detroit was under siege. Shortly afterwards another soldier, Private Gray, arrived with news that Presque Isle too had fallen to a combined force of the Ottawa, Ojibwa, Wyandot, and Seneca, suggesting that Turtle Heart's warnings to McKee about a large Indian army from the Great Lakes were not entirely fanciful.[28] But until the allied Indians arrived, the Delaware could do little, since they still had insufficient warriors to press home their attack.

The failure of the Ohio Indians to make any impression on Fort Pitt now prompted them to reassess their strategy with regard to the frontier settlements. The Shawnee had warned Ecuyer before the outbreak of hostilities that the whites should consider the plight of their women and children if peace broke down.[29] The backcountry was certainly an inviting target, as Captain John Stuart of the 42nd regiment confirmed at the start of July 1763. He told Bouquet that most of the inhabitants in Lancaster County were destitute of arms, ammunition, and provisions, and their spirits were low as they contemplated ruin. In this frame of mind, they were certain to abandon the country on the first attack.[30] This led Governor Hamilton to appeal to the Pennsylvania Assembly for help, though with little hope of success, given the pacific nature of the Quaker majority.[31] Hence he was pleasantly surprised on 6 July 1763 when the assembly agreed to raise seven hundred men for bringing in the harvest. A bill was also to be passed allowing the impressing of carriages "for the King's service."[32]

Sadly for the backcountry inhabitants, the assembly's decision proved too little too late, for by this time attacks on the settlements west of Carlisle had begun in earnest. On 2 July 1763, Ourry reported from Bedford that a party of twenty Indians had fired upon some haymakers on a farm owned by Croghan, killing and scalping three, despite the presence of a guard.[33] A week later, a party of eight Indians carried off a boy from the fort's garden, while two men were scalped near Fort Cumberland on the border with Maryland.[34] Not long afterwards Colonel Thomas Cresap's nearby plantation was attacked, resulting in several deaths.[35] Meanwhile, another war party of twenty western Delaware was devastating the Juniata Valley and adjacent areas. This detachment was led by Shamokin Daniel, a former Moravian convert and an acquaintance of Post. It had initially come from the Ohio "to see if any troops were marching up the roads, but finding none they took to scalping."[36] Their first target on Sunday, 10 July 1763, was the homestead of William White, where they killed all the family except one boy, who managed to escape. Daniel then crossed over to the adjacent Tuscarora Creek, where he similarly surprised and dispatched the family of Robert Campbell. After this the warriors went to Sherman's Creek. Here they split into two groups to increase the attacks. However, they found only abandoned farms. Then, having reunited in the Juniata Valley, they successfully ambushed a party of twelve whites, killing five of them, before outwitting another small group, of whom four were killed. Their final engagement was with a party of militia under Captain Dunning.[37] Despite inferior numbers, Daniel and his men successfully retreated back through the mountains with several horse loads of plunder. However, the raid was not the success they imagined, for some of the warriors unwittingly caught the smallpox virus after scalping their victims in the Juniata Valley, some of whom had recently contracted the disease. Several warriors died in consequence before reaching home.[38]

At least fifty European Americans were killed in these raids. But even more important was their effect on the general population. By the middle of July, fifteen hundred families were estimated to have left Cumberland County alone.[39] The situation was no better in Virginia, where Governor Fauquier reported a scene of devastation from the Potomac to the Carolina border following raids by the Shawnee.[40] For the Indian combatants, these incursions promised a means of recovering their former lands while protecting their present hunting grounds.

At Fort Pitt, meanwhile, the besiegers had decided to try diplomacy once more, lacking sufficient warriors to obtain their objective. They were prompted to do so by the arrival of some Ottawa from Detroit, seemingly sent in response to Pontiac's war council with Kinonchamek. Four of the newcomers approached the fort on 3 July with a "Friendship Belt." The essence of their message was that their chiefs would be arriving the next day for a conference, similar to one at Detroit, where they claimed everything had been amicably settled between Gladwin and the Indians.[41] The proposal was clearly part of an elaborate ruse to take Fort Pitt in the way that Pontiac had wanted to effect at Detroit. In any case, the pretense was discovered the following day when the Ottawa tried to capture two soldiers who had been sent to ferry them across the river.[42]

During the next couple of weeks shots were occasionally exchanged, though matters were sufficiently quiet for some inhabitants to return to their fields. But the lull did not last long, for on 18 July a large body of warriors was seen crossing the Monongahela, most probably the Delaware forces which had attacked Fort Ligonier and the frontier settlements. However, three days later the Shawnee informed McKee that the Ohio Indians were still hopeful of an amicable outcome in view of the news from Detroit, where the Indians had gone home on being promised that their grievances would be redressed.[43] The conference with Ecuyer, accordingly, began near the walls of the fort on 26 July 1763. The Indians were led by Shingas, Tessecumme, Winginum, Grey Eyes, and Turtle Heart for the Delaware, and by Big Wolf and four other chiefs for the Shawnee. Tessecumme, the Delaware speaker, began by asserting that the British were the cause of the trouble: they had repeatedly broken their promises. They had come into the Indians' land with large armies and then built forts, despite the Delaware request not to do so. Now things would be different, for the "Nations over the Lakes," meaning the Ottawa and Ojibwa, intended "in a short time to pass in a very great body" through the Delaware country on their "way to the Forks of Ohio." They would "stop at nothing." Tessecumme pleaded with Ecuyer: "Brother you have heard of their design; if you go quietly home, to your wise men, this is the furthest they will go: if not you will see what will be the consequence." The Ohio allies were giving Ecuyer terms similar to those offered by Pontiac to Gladwin. It was the garrison's last chance to leave alive.[44]

The following day, Ecuyer gave his response. He denied that the British had broken their treaties. The forts were for the protection of the Indians and their trade. As to their lands, the British had taken nothing except what the French possessed. Ecuyer in consequence would never surrender Fort Pitt. He despised the Ottawa and was surprised that the Delaware should ask him to leave, since he was confident of defending Fort Pitt for three years against all the Indians in the world.[45]

After this reply the besiegers returned to a close investment of the fort, aided by the Sandusky Wyandot. Wolf's relatives had been inactive since the fall of Pauli's post, not being required for the siege of Detroit. This meant they could aid the Ohio peoples with whom they had both trade and familial ties.[46] From the early afternoon of 28 July 1763, the Indians fired on the defenders continuously for four days. As Bouquet subsequently learned, the attack was mounted by "the Delaware and part of the Shawnee, Wiandot and Mingo to the number of 400 by their account, but many more as we found out afterwards." The allied nations were sufficiently confident of victory that they brought "their women and children ... to carry away the plunder from the Place, not doubting they would take it."[47] During the night of 30 and 31 July, the besiegers crept up the river bank to target the garrison from close quarters. The latter responded with grenades.[48] Bouquet later commented to Amherst: "The boldness of those savages is hardly credible. They had taken post under the banks of both rivers close [to] the fort, whereby digging holes they kept up an incessant fire, and threw fire arrows. They are good marksmen, and though our people were under cover, they killed one and wounded seven."[49] Among the latter was Ecuyer. The fighting continued till three o'clock on the afternoon of 1 August, when the Indians withdrew.[50]

The next day, Hudson arrived with letters from Ourry. He also brought information about the besiegers, having been detained by them for three days while they read his correspondence. Hudson confirmed that the Indians were divided over what to do, now that a British army was approaching under Henry Bouquet. After Hudson's letters had been translated by a white captive, Tamaqua and his men went home, believing that peace was better than war. However, the Wyandot responded that the Delaware and Shawnee "might do as they pleased," but they would "carry on the war against" the British "while there was a man of them living."[51] Hudson believed that if the Indians attempted to ambush Bouquet on his march, they would do so at either Turtle Creek or Chestnut Ridge. Despite this information, Ecuyer remained confident that Bouquet was in no danger, even if the Wyandot did attack, because the western Delaware had "cut a very poor figure for five days."[52] He was shortly to find his judgment seriously flawed.

Michilimackinac Falls during a Game of Lacrosse

While Fort Pitt was under siege, dramatic events had been happening five hundred miles to the north at Michilimackinac, the most important Great Lakes post after Niagara, Detroit, and Oswego.

The British were not without advice of impending trouble. The previous September, Lieutenant Leslie had been warned about the intentions of some visiting Indians, though they departed after they saw he was on his guard. Certainly the situation was volatile, as Leslie reported to Gladwin soon afterwards. The French inhabitants were spreading stories to discredit the British, while the Indians assumed they could always retire to the Illinois should an attack fail, and both subscribed to the notion that the "country will soon be in the hands of its late masters."[53] Nevertheless these alarms died away during the winter of 1762, though Leslie's successor, Captain George Ethrington, received at least two further warnings, one from Charles Langlade. Ethrington dismissed such information as the "stories of old women," a foolish attitude given Langlade's Indian connections.[54] Alexander Henry was also warned by a friendly Ojibwa family about "evil birds" and advised to leave. Henry ignored them and stayed in his store.[55]

As elsewhere, the reasons for Indian hostility at Michilimackinac were varied. In part it was a matter of tradition since the nations there had long been associated with the French and their policy of the "middle ground." Only the need for European goods had induced them to permit the fort to be reoccupied. But despite promises of better trade prices and quality, the situation had not improved. However, both the Indians and French were consoled by the thought that the British presence would be temporary, since it was inconceivable that Canada would be given up permanently. Then news of the peace arrived.

As noted previously, Pontiac and his allies had dispatched belts to the Michilimackinac area in early May. The journey of 350 miles should not have taken more than eight to ten days. Nevertheless, the nearby Ojibwa claimed they only "received belts of wampum from Pontiac" and the other Detroit chiefs "a few days before the blow" on 2 June 1763.[56] The reason was probably because they, like the other nations in this cooler climate, were still returning from their winter hunt. This was certainly the case with the Ottawa of L'Arbre Croche, twenty miles to the west, the intended recipients of Pontiac's belt. The invitation to attack was accordingly only given to the Ojibwa at the nearby villages of Cheboygan and Michilimackinac. But they may have used their alleged last-minute notification as an excuse for not consulting their Ottawa neighbors so that they could monopolize the spoils of any attack.

Meanwhile, nothing disturbed the thoughts of Ethrington. The plan, as at Detroit, was to take the fort by stratagem, to avoid the necessity for a frontal assault against a fortified place. But rather than asking for a council inside, Menehwehna, "the great chief of the village of Michilimackinac," decided to adopt a more novel approach.[57] The fort, as at Detroit, comprised a compound protected by a wall of stakes set in the ground. On 2 June 1763 Ethrington was informed that the Ojibwa were to play a game of lacrosse against some visiting Sauk near the main gate. About a hundred warriors participated and in due course Ethrington and Leslie came out to watch, knowing nothing of events elsewhere. They also failed to notice that a considerable number of Indian women had passed into the fort carrying blankets under which guns with cut-down barrels and tomahawks were concealed, just as Pontiac had planned at Detroit.[58]

About noon one of the Indians lobbed the ball over the gate of the compound, whereupon most of the warriors ran inside. Others simultaneously seized Ethrington and Leslie, carrying them into the woods. Once inside the fort, the warriors seized their weapons from the women and attacked the garrison, killing fifteen soldiers, including Lieutenant Jamette and a trader named Tracy. The rest of the garrison, some twenty soldiers and a dozen merchants, were then made prisoners, though two of the latter, Henry and Henry Bostwick, hid for a time in the houses of their neighbors before being discovered. No violence was offered to the French.[59]

Fortunately, Langlade was on hand to rescue Ethrington and Leslie from burning at the stake. Like a number of influential Frenchmen, Langlade seems to have accepted the permanency of British rule. Langlade now offered to stand surety for the two men. Langlade's reputation as "the bravest of the brave" and "defender of his country" was too great to ignore. Ethrington and Leslie were accordingly taken back and lodged inside the fort. This maneuver gave Langlade time to send for his Ottawa relatives at L'Arbre Croche.[60] The Ottawa responded immediately, though wounded pride was their main motive for coming to the British rescue. They were angry that the Ojibwa had failed to consult them about the attack. As they later claimed to Gage in Montreal, they had just returned from their winter hunt "when we received the unexpected and disagreeable account of that garrison being treacherously surprised" by the Ojibwa Indians. As compensation, they demanded custody of the surviving prisoners.[61]

This was effected eventually but not without a struggle, for at a joint council the Ojibwa upbraided the Ottawa for not allying with them, since all the other nations had now joined the war. They asserted that Pontiac had taken Detroit, while "the King of France had woke[n], and repossessed himself of Quebec and Montreal." As a result, "The English were meeting destruction, not only at Michilimackinac, but in every other part of the world."[62] Menehwehna also lavished plundered goods on the Ottawa to implicate them in the affair according to Henry, whose journal provides the best account of these events.[63] The pressure to join increased on 6 June, when Henry noted the arrival of another chief, "Le Grand Sable," with a large number of his tribesmen, following the conclusion of their winter hunt.[64] Henry, still inside the fort, misheard a reference to the Grand Saulteur, thought by many to be the supreme chief of all the Ojibwa[65] According to the explorer Jonathan Carver, who met the "Great Chippewa Chief" in 1766, the Grand Saulteur had sworn to "remain the avowed enemy" of the British, since "the territories on which" Fort Michilimackinac was "built belonged to him." By this time, he had "passed the meridian of life," but was still "remarkably tall and well made," and "of so stern an aspect that [even] the most undaunted person" could not but feel "some degree of terror."[66] He certainly conformed to that image now, since he promptly killed seven of the remaining traders to show his support for the capture of the fort, feasting on one victim's corpse to impart courage to his warriors.[67]

Nevertheless, the Ottawa insisted on keeping the remaining prisoners until it was known what had happened at Detroit. To this, the Ojibwa reluctantly agreed. The disapproval of Langlade was undoubtedly one factor in their climb down. Tradition required the victorious war chief to sacrifice his principal captives to ensure the continued support of the spirits. Langlade's intervention on behalf of Ethrington and Leslie had prevented this.[68] Lack of support from other neighboring nations was another reason for caution. The previous year, the Ojibwa had been embroiled in a feud with the Menominee. Then, on 10 June ambassadors arrived from Detroit with the news that the fort had not been captured. Instead, the northern Indians were required to go "to the assistance of Pontiac." The discovery that the grand project to expel the British was incomplete meant that "fear was now the prevailing passion."[69] A joint council accordingly agreed to send a fact-finding mission to Detroit while the warriors retreated to the island of Michilimackinac. The Ojibwa chose Kinonchamek as their envoy, while the Ottawa nominated their priest, Father Du Jaunay. The delegation left that same day and reached Detroit on 18 June. Here, as we have seen, the Ojibwa made various criticisms of Pontiac to justify their refusal to send aid.[70]

Whatever the result of the mission, the Ottawa of L'Arbre Croche were determined to pursue their own diplomatic course. They calculated that if they escorted the remaining soldiers and traders to Montreal, they would be generously rewarded. The British might even reopen the trade by way of the Ottawa River, since this route avoided the area of hostilities.[71] To maximize their bargaining power, the Ottawa had already agreed to Ethrington's suggestion that Lieutenant Gorrell at La Baye be invited to join the party as the only way of saving that isolated garrison. This was on 15 June 1763. Fortunately, the Indians at La Baye were friendly. The last thing the Menominee, Sauk, Fox, and Puan Indians wanted was an interruption to the trade. Accordingly, when Gorrell told them that he needed to go to Michilimackinac to reopen the road, they agreed to protect him on his journey.[72] Even the distant Sioux affirmed that they would not allow the trail to be blocked by their old enemy, the Ojibwa. Gorrell accordingly set off on 21 June, accompanied by ninety warriors, arriving at L'Arbre Croche on 30 June. With the support of his allies, Gorrell was able to ensure that his men retained their arms and did not become prisoners of the Ottawa. Indeed, the La Baye Indians even suggested that Ethrington be installed as the commanding officer of the fort.[73]

This suggestion was quickly rejected by the Ottawa, who insisted on taking the captives to Montreal, though they intended to keep several back to ensure the need for additional talks and presents. As a result, the road to Montreal was not finally declared open until 12 July 1763. On the next day, the principal Ojibwa warriors came to shake hands with Ethrington, suggesting that if Amherst forgave them they would never do the same again. Ethrington replied that the only way they could obtain Amherst's favor was by giving up all the prisoners. Despite this, Henry and two soldiers remained behind when the party finally set off on 18 July 1763, leaving Langlade in nominal command.[74] The war was still far from over, though much depended on what the Grand Saulteur decided to do.

The Capture of St. Joseph, Miami, and Ouiatanon

As already mentioned, one of Pontiac's early decisions in his bid to expel the British west of the Allegheny Mountains was the seizure of Forts St. Joseph, Miami, and Ouiatanon. The first of these guarded the overland route from Detroit to the southern end of Lake Michigan. Pontiac assigned this task to Ninivois, the chief of the Detroit Potawatomi. The plan was for Ninivois to visit his relatives at St. Joseph and incite them to attack. He arrived there on 25 May and promptly asked for a council with the commanding officer, Ensign Francis Schlosser. Schlosser was warned by one of the French inhabitants that the Indians intended no good. But before he could get the garrison under arms, he was overpowered and ten of his men killed, all in the space of a few minutes.[75] Only Schlosser and two soldiers were spared, along with the merchants Richard Winston and Henry Hambach.[76] Ninivois and his men then returned to Detroit, taking Schlosser and the two soldiers with them.[77] All three were exchanged on 15 June for the Potawatomi chief detained by Gladwin at the start of the hostilities.[78]

By the time St. Joseph's had been taken, Forts Miami and Ouiatanon had also been captured as a result of Pontiac's initiative. Both forts were on the route from Lake Erie to the Mississippi, which Pontiac's emissaries were taking in their quest for French help at Fort Chartres. Hence, his envoys carried not only letters for the French commandant but also war belts for the nations along the way. Their first objective was Fort Miami on the Maumee River, where the Miami had their principle village. On their way the envoys met a British trader, John Welsh, whom they seized and plundered.[79] They then went to the Miami village to deliver their news.

The Miami were not entirely pleased at the prospect of attacking Fort Miami. Fifteen years earlier, they had welcomed George Croghan to their village of Pickawillany. However, like the other northern nations, the Miami were dissatisfied at the lack of presents and the price of goods, as Hutchins found during his visit in August 1762. They were in addition suffering from widespread sickness, most likely typhus, which some blamed on the British. Nevertheless, they had cooperated as late as March 1763 in disclosing the Seneca war belt. The possibility of a French army at Montreal or New Orleans may have helped their change of heart. Whatever the cause, the Miami were ready to do for Pontiac what they would not do for the Seneca.

Fort Miami was commanded by Lieutenant Robert Holmes and had a garrison of just twelve men. Holmes was not without warning of what was coming, for a French trader advised him on 23 May 1763 that Detroit was under siege. Holmes immediately ordered the garrison to stay inside and make cartridges in preparation for an assault. However, on the morning of 27 May 1763 "a squaw that lived with Mr. Holmes" came to see him, pleading that one of her relatives was sick and required bleeding. Holmes agreed to help and left the fort. He had not gone more than two hundred yards before he was shot dead. His sergeant rushed out to see what was wrong and was promptly seized himself. The soldiers then closed the gates and prepared to defend the post. At this point, Godfroy and Chêne compelled Welsh to speak to the garrison, promising them their lives if they surrendered. There were just nine soldiers in the fort. Given their isolation and the presence of two hundred enemy warriors, they decided to open the gates.[80] The previous friendship with the Miami may have counted in their favor, as there was no massacre, though all were taken prisoner. Some were sent to Detroit, and the rest dispersed to an unknown fate. Accompanying the prisoners were eighteen warriors, whom the Miami claimed were all they could spare for Pontiac's siege, being still at war with the Cherokee.[81]

With their work completed at Miami, Godfroy, Chêne, and their Indian companions set off for Fort Ouiatanon on the River Wabash. This was commanded by Lieutenant Edward Jenkins with eighteen men. The principal nations in the area were the Algonquian-speaking Kickapoo, Mascouten, Wea, and Piankashaw. On the morning of 1 June, Jenkins was asked to visit one of the Indian villages, unaware of events elsewhere. On arrival, he was immediately bound and placed in a cabin where he discovered some of his soldiers already in custody. His attackers then told him that "Detroit, Miami and all these posts were cut off and that it was a folly to make a resistance." Jenkins should order the remaining soldiers in the fort to surrender. If he refused, they would all suffer death. Jenkins decided that surrender was the better option. Nevertheless, he believed they were about to be killed when two French traders, Alexander Maisonville and Monsieur Lorraine, intervened. They offered the Wabash nations generous quantities of wampum in return for the lives of their prisoners. By now the initial ardor of the attackers had cooled, and they agreed to this suggestion. Indeed they were beginning to regret what had happened, asserting that they had been obliged to act "by the other nations." In consequence, they determined to send Jenkins and his men to the Illinois to be held by the French.[82] For the moment, the area returned to calm. Godfroy, Chêne, and the other envoys continued on their way to Fort Chartres, while the local Indians and French inhabitants awaited the return of Onontio.

The Seneca Join the War: Venango, Le Boeuf, and Presque Isle

While Pontiac's allies were capturing the western British posts, his forces were also enjoying success elsewhere. As already mentioned, the arrival of reinforcements at Detroit had allowed Pontiac to dispatch three hundred warriors toward Presque Isle, which guarded the northern end of the communication between Lake Erie and Fort Pitt. However, unknown to Pontiac, another army was also hastening there. The Seneca had entered the war.

Initially it was uncertain whether the Seneca would participate, even though they had circulated war belts for two years. The rest of the Iroquois Confederacy wanted them to remain neutral, sentiments that they were bound to respect. On the other hand, resentment ran deep over Johnson's demand for the surrender of the Kanestio murderers. Nevertheless the Seneca, including the Genesee, agreed by way of compromise to attend another conference with Johnson starting on 22 May 1763. Their case was presented by Teyawarunte, an Onondaga chief, who pointed out that the English had killed many Indians since their first settlement in America. Despite such provocation, they had "never sought for any revenge or satisfaction (although in our power) after the party offending had condoled the death of the slain agreeable to our custom" by offering compensation. The British should respect the traditions of the Covenant Chain and do the same.[83] Johnson, however, was adamant. Giving compensation for those killed was unacceptable. He could only reaffirm, as he subsequently told Amherst, the "unreasonableness of their custom of not giving up offenders, which was the only means of giving satisfaction."[84]

For the Seneca this was the last straw, not least because Johnson's refusal coincided with the arrival of two war belts, the first from Pontiac calling for war against the redcoats, and the second from the "Indians about Pittsburgh," asking the Seneca to "take up the bloody hatchet." According to Jean de Couagne, the interpreter at Niagara, the Seneca delayed answering the Delaware until their chiefs had returned from the conference with Johnson.[85] But the arrival of Pontiac's belt was a different matter. Here at last was the support which the Seneca had been seeking over the past two years. As Serrehoana, a Genesee chief, subsequently commented, it was this belt which "set some of our people upon mischief."[86]

Before taking action, the Seneca made one last appeal to the other Six Nations. They informed the grand council at Onondaga "that they had given a lease to their warriors and desired they would do the same." Then, "the women of the Seneca spoke with a belt to the women of the other nations desiring they would persuade their men to do the same."[87] In reality the rest of the confederacy, including the Cayuga, wanted the Seneca to desist, at least until another meeting with Johnson at the German Flats to avoid destroying the Covenant Chain. Nevertheless, the response of the "the departing Seneca" was emphatic. The others "might follow their plan of peace," but the Seneca were determined "to follow the resolution they had taken, which was to carry on the war against the English." "Those who acted differently" would surely "repent" their decision.[88] Only the two most easterly Seneca towns of Canadasaga and Canandaigua failed to join the war party.

Since the rest of the Iroquois Confederacy refused to participate, the Seneca had to abandon their original plan of attacking the communication between Oswego and Fort Stanwix, as envisaged by Tahaiadoris and Kiashuta in 1761. Instead, they would assist the Mingo in seizing the forts guarding the road between Lake Erie and Fort Pitt. Their warriors accordingly set off for the Ohio to see if a French army was on its way.[89] It is not known who led them, but on approaching Venango they were almost certainly joined by Kiashuta and the Mingo who lived nearby. Their presence may explain why the assailants were able to enter the fort as friends on 15 June 1763.[90] After massacring the eighteen private soldiers, the assailants forced the commanding officer, Lieutenant Francis Gordon, to write a letter listing their grievances, which were the scarcity of powder, the high price of goods, and the retention of so many military posts. Gordon was then killed, and his letter taken by the Mingo, who "were going down to Fort Pitt in order to do all the mischief they could there … and along the Communication."[91] The hope was that the discovery of Gordon's letter would frighten the garrison into running away.

The main body of the Seneca meanwhile headed north for Fort Le Boeuf, which guarded the top of French Creek and the path to Presque Isle. This post was under the command of Ensign George Price and had a garrison of fifteen men. The first sign of trouble occurred on the morning of 18 June, when five Indians called asking for tobacco and food, which Price gave them. Not long afterwards, another thirty arrived from the direction of Presque Isle, whom Price identified as "Six Nations Indians." The latest arrivals pretended to be on their way to fight the Cherokee and laid down their arms near the fort before asking permission to come inside. By now Price knew of Cuyler's mishap on Lake Erie and suspected their design. He accordingly refused them entrance. The Indians then took up their arms and went to the rear of a storehouse which formed part of the outer compound. Here they removed the foundations so that they could get inside. Next they fired burning arrows at the blockhouse itself, which was constantly set alight. By nightfall, Price recognized that his position was untenable. He accordingly evacuated his garrison via a small window, miraculously without being seen. Since his attackers had come from the direction of Presque Isle, Price headed south for Venango, only to find it a blackened ruin. This left him no option but to continue to Fort Pitt, where he arrived with most of his men on 26 June.[92] Several others, including a woman, straggled in two days later.

The Seneca did not pursue Price, but turned northwards for the more important target of Presque Isle. Here, more by accident than design, they met Pontiac's task force sometime on 19 June.[93] Presque Isle had been rebuilt by Bouquet after its destruction by the French in 1759, and was designed for a larger garrison than was currently there. Its commander was Lieutenant John Christie. His first warning of trouble came on 3 June 1763, when the remnants of Cuyler's rangers appeared during their flight back to Niagara. Cuyler agreed to leave an additional six men to help defend the fort, making a total garrison of twenty-four.[94]

Christie, accordingly, should have been well prepared when the siege began at daybreak on 20 June. Unfortunately, the central blockhouse was situated close to two hillocks which allowed the allied Indians to approach unseen to within forty yards. They immediately started using fire arrows against the fort's wooden defenses and built two log bastions, one on each hill, which allowed them to shoot at the defenders with impunity. They also began digging a passageway to get to the foundations of the blockhouse, indicating that they had learned the lessons of European siege warfare. They next broke into Christie's quarters, which were set on fire, along with the wooden fascines, which were supposed to support a protective entrenchment round the blockhouse. The garrison, meanwhile, were hard-pressed for water. The main well was on the parade ground and under constant fire, while the fort was too far from the lakeside to provide relief. An attempt to dig an emergency well inside the blockhouse itself was to no effect. Not surprisingly, everything was soon burning. Toward midnight on 21 June, a voice in French suggested that further resistance was futile. If they did not surrender, they could expect no quarter.[95]

Christie, desperate to give his men some respite, asked if any of the attackers spoke English. He calculated that talks might give him a chance of reconnoitering the enemy with a view to launching a counterattack. The Indians replied that they had a former prisoner who was now fighting on their side. During further exchanges, the Indians acknowledged that they were the Wyandot from Detroit and had been coerced into the war by the Ottawa. For this reason, they were accompanied by a contingent from that nation. This reply momentarily raised hopes that Christie might be able to exploit these tribal divisions. Hope also briefly flourished when the schooner reappeared, carrying Lieutenant Cuyler and the remnants of his unit back to Detroit. Unfortunately, the water was so shallow that the crew was unable to get within two miles of the shore. In addition, the vessel had only one small rowing boat capable of carrying ten men. This made any attempt at relief perilous, given the Indians' possession of canoes. With the Indians about to tunnel under the blockhouse itself, Christie finally agreed to talks. The terms were that the garrison might either go to Fort Pitt or be ferried out to the vessel. But the garrison had no sooner left the compound than they were seized, bound, and divided among the captors.[96] After this, the two armies separated. Pontiac's task force returned to Detroit with their spoils. The Seneca set off for Irondequoit at the mouth of the Genesee River to intercept British convoys passing along Lake Ontario.[97] As for Christie, he was taken by the Wyandot to their village at Detroit. His ordeal was unexpectedly short, for on 9 July he was handed over with eight of his men as part of the Wyandot diplomatic maneuver to get out of the war.[98]

Christie's military reputation, however, took somewhat longer to recover. Bouquet, as the constructor of Presque Isle, had a vested interest in blaming the destruction of the fort on "the shameful conduct" of an officer who had dishonored his "corps by an infamous capitulation with savages."[99] Six weeks later he was still asking by "what means the Indians" had taken Presque Isle, "that strong post," since reports that the Indians had "undermined it" were "too improbable to deserve credit."[100] Bouquet and his colleagues still failed to appreciate the ability and determination of the native warriors, who had learned new skills from watching European siege warfare at Fort William Henry, Niagara, and Quebec. As a result, Pontiac and his allies now controlled every post west of the Allegheny Mountains except Fort Pitt, Detroit, and Niagara, with its two dependent posts at the foot and top of the falls. At least two hundred soldiers had been killed or captured.[101] By the standards of any previous war, it had been a remarkable achievement. The question was, could Pontiac and his allies sustain their effort, and what would be the British response?

6
The Empire Fights Back

Amherst Plans a Counterattack

While Britain's western empire was collapsing under the relentless assault of Pontiac and his allies, Amherst in New York was quietly considering the outlines of the new peacetime military establishment, which he had just received from the ministry in England. The plan was for an army of twenty battalions or regiments in North America and the Caribbean. A number of units therefore would have to be sent home or disbanded, among the latter being the 80th Light Infantry, 77th Highlanders, and third and fourth battalions of the 60th Royal American regiment.[1]

The new peacetime arrangements were good news for Amherst since they indicated that he too might be returning home. He had been in North America five years and rightly felt his task was completed. Canada had been conquered and added to the British Empire. He did not wish, in any case, to remain in America. He had been previously offered the lucrative governorship of Virginia, but made it a condition of acceptance that his duties could be performed by a deputy. Though he was always polite about America and its people, it is clear that he found the country too "democratic" for his taste. Amherst, like many scions of the gentry, yearned to join the ranks of the nobility and enjoy the deference that went with it, something deficient in colonial America. Only in England could he build an estate and perhaps receive a peerage from a grateful sovereign. There was also the matter of his wife, Jenny, from whom he had been estranged for several years. It was time to return home and enjoy the rewards of his victories.[2]

If these were Amherst's thoughts, they were rudely interrupted on the afternoon of 6 June 1763 by the arrival of two express riders from Bouquet in Philadelphia, forwarding dispatches from Ecuyer at Fort Pitt. The first, dated 29 May 1763, detailed the murder of Colonel Clapham and his family, together with Ecuyer's fear that the expedition down the Ohio would be ambushed.[3] The second, of 30 May, reported the attack on Thomas Calhoun and the alleged destruction of Sandusky and siege of Detroit. In short, Ecuyer commented, "I think the uprising is general."[4]

The news did not disturb Amherst unduly. Despite the allegations about Sandusky and Detroit, he believed the trouble was local to Fort Pitt. The most likely explanation, he told Bouquet, was that it was another of those "rash attempts of that turbulent tribe the Seneca." Nevertheless, Amherst ordered the three light infantry companies of the 17th, 42nd Black Watch, and 77th Highland regiments, totaling close to three hundred men, to assemble on Staten Island under the command of Major Allan Campbell, which Amherst judged to be "more than sufficient to quell any disturbances the whole Indian strength could raise." He acknowledged that the Indians might cut off "defenseless families, or even some of the small posts ... particularly while we ourselves supply them with powder and lead." But "the post of Fort Pitt or any of the others commanded by officers, can certainly never be in danger from such a wretched enemy as the Indians are at this time, if the garrisons do their duty." Amherst was "only sorry, that when such outrages are committed, the guilty should escape," for he was "fully convinced the only true method of treating those savages is to keep them in proper subjection and punish, without exception, the transgressors."[5]

Amherst continued in this opinion for several more days, writing on 11 June to his former mentor, General Sir John Ligonier in England, that the whole affair would probably end with the killing of the Clapham family and a couple of soldiers.[6] He acknowledged the next day to Johnson that "the affair is more general than I had once apprehended," but he still refused to believe that the trouble had spread to the Great Lakes.[7] Nevertheless, as a precaution he ordered two of the light infantry companies to proceed to Philadelphia, where Bouquet was to deploy them as he saw fit. Amherst was vexed at having to do this "when I am in hourly expectation of receiving directions from home for the movement of the several corps" according to the new peacetime establishment.[8] But, he noted in his journal, "I think it necessary to be prepared for the worse that the Indians can do."[9] It was in this spirit that he ordered the remaining light infantry company to Fort Stanwix for service on the lakes if required.

Within a few days Pontiac's forces were demonstrating that they could inflict damage far beyond what Amherst imagined, for on 16 June he learned about the attack on Cuyler's rangers. Clearly he could no longer pretend that the trouble was limited to Fort Pitt, or ignore the possibility that Detroit was indeed under attack. A relief force in consequence would be necessary for that theatre too. This placed Amherst in an awkward dilemma. The army that had conquered North America was no more. Many of the units had gone home to Britain, after serving on expeditions to Martinique and Cuba, and many of those returning to America did so in hospital ships, stricken with disease. Most of the remaining regulars, totaling nine thousand, were either in the St. Lawrence Valley guarding the king's new Canadian subjects or doing similar duties in Florida. Finally, the few provincial troops still in service were due to be released at the end of the month. To raise fresh men would take months, even if the colonial assemblies agreed. The military cupboard was almost bare.[10]

Nevertheless Amherst ordered his aide-de-camp, Captain James Dalyell, to take command of the light infantry company destined for Fort Stanwix, with instructions to gather such other men as he could from the posts on his way to Oswego. On reaching Niagara, he was to "be ready to proceed from thence to Detroit, should there be occasion."[11] To ensure his safe passage, Amherst ordered Captain Joshua Loring, the naval officer, to take command of "thirty seamen" whom Amherst was dispatching "to man the vessels on Lakes Ontario and Erie."[12] Amherst might be contemptuous of the Indians, but he was aware of the importance of naval power. Lastly, he informed the governors of the northern colonies that he would have to detain the remaining provincials until the "occasion" for their services had passed.[13]

Bouquet in Philadelphia, meanwhile, was considering how best to deploy the light infantry. He told Amherst on 16 June, "We are yet too much in the dark to form a plan, but if things are as represented, I propose to march these two companies to Fort Pitt with a convoy of flour, sheep and some powder." He would then "clear the forts of all useless people," before securing the communication and forwarding fresh supplies. To allow him to concentrate his resources, he suggested abandoning Venango and Fort Le Boeuf, though not Presque Isle since it "can conveniently be supplied by the Lake." "To support the other two," in contrast, "is very precarious and would require more men than we can spare without any visible advantage."[14]

Amherst approved the sending of a relief convoy to Fort Pitt, telling Bouquet that he had found him another company of the 42nd Highlanders. Other remnants of that regiment would also be available in due course. Unfortunately the remains of the 77th regiment, amounting to about one hundred men, were "so feeble and weak with West Indian distemper" as to rule them out of the service. However, Amherst was totally against Bouquet's proposed withdrawal from Venango and Le Boeuf: "The abandoning of any posts at a time when the Indians are committing hostilities, must be attended with the worst of consequences," since it "would give the Indians room to imagine themselves more formidable than they really are." He continued, "There is no doubt but it is in the power of the Indians … to cut off some of those small posts before we can send the necessary reinforcements, as the troops at present here are so few and so widely scattered, but an attack on any fenced post, though thinly garrisoned, ought to cost the Indians so dear that they should not make a second attempt of the kind."[15]

Amherst wrote again to Bouquet on 23 June 1763, reminding him of the twin objectives of "keeping entire possession of the country" while "punishing those barbarians who had perfidiously massacred His Majesty's subjects." Hence Bouquet was not to scatter his men along the communication. Instead he was to concentrate his forces at Fort Pitt, sending as many men as possible to Presque Isle to join Dalyell.[16] Bouquet, now at Lancaster, quickly reassured Amherst that he understood his orders perfectly: "The reinforcement you have ordered this way … will fully enable me to crush the little opposition they may dare to offer along the road, and secure that part of the country against all their future attempts." He would then await further orders "to act in conjunction with the rest of your forces to extirpate these vermin from a country they have forfeited, and with it all claim to the rights of humanity."[17]

The shortage of men led Johnson to suggest enlisting the southern Indians.[18] Unsurprisingly, his proposal elicited little enthusiasm from either Amherst or Bouquet. Bouquet commented, "I should be sorry we should ever appear to be under the least obligation to the perfidious Cherokee..... I would rather choose the liberty to kill any savage that may come in our way, than to be perpetually doubtful whether they are friends or foes."[19] Amherst agreed, since he wanted any Indians found in arms to be executed.[20] Accordingly, when Johnson more modestly suggested recruiting the Stockbridge Indians, Amherst reiterated what "a worthless tribe" they had proved during the war with the French. He took a similar view of the seven St. Lawrence mission settlements: "I really cannot say I approve of employing any of the Canadian Indians. All I ask of them is to remain quiet."[21] However, he approved Johnson's idea of calling a conference with the Six Nations at the German Flats. If the latter were not placated, they might join the enemy, thus threatening the communication to Oswego and Detroit. Even Amherst agreed this was a dangerous scenario.[22]

The need for men induced Amherst to approach Governor Hamilton to convene the Pennsylvania Assembly, despite the lateness of the season.[23] Hamilton duly obliged. However, as already noted, the assembly raised only seven hundred men to protect the backcountry during harvest time. This was of little use to Bouquet, who needed troops to guard the communication with Fort Pitt.[24] Similar disappointment was experienced in New York, where Amherst requested three hundred men to protect the road to Oswego. Cadwallader Colden, the lieutenant governor, replied discouragingly that this would mean calling the assembly, which "would have been attended with too many delays to have answered the end proposed."[25] Nor were attempts to find men at a local level more successful. At Albany, Dalyell asked John Van Rensselaer, the largest landlord in the area, whether he could raise men from his tenants. Van Rensselaer replied unpromisingly that he had "little influence with his people." An appeal to the local militia received a similar response.[26] Clearly, if anything was to be achieved in this campaign, the army would have to do it from its own limited resources.

Detroit: The Battle of the Bloody Brook

Despite the lack of numbers, Amherst expected the dispatch of Dalyell and Bouquet to bring a speedy end to the conflict, as he explained in his orders to Gladwin on 2 July 1763. First, Gladwin was to take Dalyell's force under his command together with such men as Bouquet had forwarded to Presque Isle. He was then to act "as you shall judge best for regaining the entire command of the country." He was to pay particular attention to recovering Sandusky, where he was to build a "proper blockhouse" for "sixteen or twenty men, which with an officer, are full sufficient to defend it against any number of Indians, unless the garrison is surprised," a remarkably ill-judged assessment in view of what had just happened. After this, "Our chief attention must be to make ourselves entire masters of the Lakes," for which purpose Amherst had ordered Loring to build two or three additional vessels. Finally, Gladwin was to use every endeavor to punish those "concerned in the present insurrection." "It is my positive order that should Pontiac, who is undoubtedly the ringleader of the mischief," or "any other of the Indians, who it can be proved have been, or are found in arms against us, fall into our power, they are immediately to be put to death." Amherst believed "their extirpation" was "the only security for our future safety," and was fully justified in view of "their late treacherous proceedings." Of course, such "nations as have upon this occasion behaved quietly and peaceably, are to be treated as friends and in the usual manner."[27]

By now, Dalyell was preparing to leave Oswego for Niagara. His journey so far had been uneventful, a testimony to Johnson's success in keeping five of the Six Nations neutral. However, the loss of Presque Isle meant that the military situation in the area had deteriorated since Dalyell received his initial orders. Nevertheless, he decided that the relief of Detroit should remain his first priority. After this, more offensive operations should be possible. He confided to Amherst, "The most effectual means to get free of being shut up by those savages, who invest Detroit, will be to find out their deposits [stores] and the places they have left their wives and children." The former could then be destroyed, and the latter taken captive, after which affairs would wear a very different complexion. He intended making these points to Gladwin.[28]

With no time to lose, Dalyell set off for Niagara. He was about to enter hostile territory, since the latest intelligence indicated that the Seneca had "sent parties to Irondequoit and Sodon ... to way lay any Boats going to and from Niagara." Irondequoit was near the mouth of the Genesee River, the heartland of the Seneca nation. Amherst could only hope that "Captain Dalyell will have proceeded with such precaution as to have been able to defeat any attempts that could be made by those villains."[29] Fortunately, Dalyell's force of 255 men proved too formidable for any ambush and he reached Niagara without incident. Not that he tarried long, for he set off almost immediately without waiting for the schooner to provide an escort, as Major John Wilkins advised. Wilkins was afraid that bad weather might force Dalyell to take shelter on an open beach, exposing him to the perils that Cuyler had experienced.[30] His pleas, however, were to no avail.

Dalyell reached Presque Isle, his first objective, on 15 July 1763, where he found the post, as expected, burnt to the ground. As there was no time to reoccupy it, Dalyell suggested that Wilkins send sixty Canadian "volunteers and artificers" to perform this task.[31] The following day he embarked again, this time for Sandusky, where he arrived on 25 July. The Sandusky Wyandot had been responsible for the massacre of Lieutenant Pauli's garrison and twenty traders. Some punitive action, therefore, seemed in order. Leaving a detachment to guard the boats, Dalyell marched for the Wyandot town, which was some eight miles inland. He arrived to find that its inhabitants had all departed. Unknown to Dalyell, the warriors had gone to join Wolf in the siege of Fort Pitt while the rest of the population took refuge in the woods. Dalyell accordingly destroyed the houses and crops before ordering the troops back to their boats.[32]

After this Dalyell faced the most difficult part of his journey, the navigation of the Detroit River.[33] Pontiac was known to be expecting reinforcements from the "Saulteurs" of Lake Superior and even the Illinois, while the Detroit Wyandot and Potawatomie had once again taken up arms after their abortive peace talks with Gladwin.[34] However, the final approach during the night of 28 July was undertaken in thick fog so that Dalyell was able to pass between the Potawatomi and Wyandot villages on the morning of 29 July 1763 with only a few casualties. For the besieged in Detroit, it was a glorious sight.[35]

Dalyell, perhaps flushed with success, adopted the stance of the arrogant staff officer who had the confidence of the commander-in-chief. He was also well connected, being an officer in the First Foot regiment. However, he was not without experience of fighting in North America, having accompanied Rogers on several ranger missions during the previous war.[36] He now proposed a scheme similar to what he had indicated to Amherst, namely, an attack on Pontiac's camp by means of a night march, all within forty-eight hours of arriving! Gladwin immediately objected. The ground between the fort and Pontiac's encampment had not been adequately explored. In addition, the army would have to march along the river, silhouetted against the water, with houses and woods close by. He also doubted the possibility of surprising Pontiac, knowing that sympathizers would soon give him warning of the British approach. Nevertheless, the more Gladwin prevaricated, the more determined Dalyell became, asserting that the commander "might do as he pleased, but that really he saw no difficulty in the execution and giving them an irrecoverable blow." Gladwin, though of superior rank, was of inferior regiment and social status, and in consequence felt obliged to concede against his better judgment. It was agreed, therefore, that Dalyell would command a force of 250 men and be escorted to the target by Jacques Baby and St. Martin, two Frenchmen of proven loyalty.[37]

The force left in the early hours of 31 July in a column two abreast, protected by armed bateaux from the edge of the river. Accompanying the expedition was Rogers, who had come to Detroit with Dalyell as a volunteer in the Queen's Rangers. After marching for a mile and a half, the men formed into platoons, thirty strong.[38] So far all had been quiet, but as Gladwin predicted, the news of the army's advance had spread quickly. Barthe, the gunsmith, hastened from the fort to Pontiac's camp, calling out, "Go to the woods, go to the woods."[39] Admittedly, some Ojibwa were caught by surprise. According to Rutherford, many of his Saginaw captors only knew of the action when they heard the gunfire and had to run two miles to join the fight.[40] But Pontiac was sufficiently prepared to have fascines ready adjacent to the bridge where Campbell had been executed. A number of entrenchments had also been dug. It was while the army was endeavoring to cross the brook that Pontiac's forces opened fire, wounding Dalyell and killing several men in the first platoon.[41]

Despite this surprise, the troops continued to press forwards but found it difficult to engage in the dark.[42] During a lull in the proceedings Captain Grant, in charge of the rear, was informed that the Indians, numbering three hundred warriors, had been "well apprized of our design" and were planning to cut off the detachment. Shortly afterwards war cries were heard from the woods, making it clear that Pontiac's forces were moving to the rear of Dalyell.[43] At this critical moment Dalyell went to the front for information, which resulted in another hour passing before he gave the order to retreat. The rearguard under Grant now became the army's vanguard. Half a mile down the road, Grant discovered that Pontiac's warriors had occupied some new entrenchments and were firing all along the road. While attempting to deal with this situation Dalyell was killed and his successor, Captain Gray, wounded, leaving Grant in command. The situation was critical, since Rogers reported that the Queen's Rangers were trapped in "a house with the rear of the Troops." Without boats to cover his flank, he would not be able to retreat, "being hard pushed by the enemy from the Enclosures behind him."[44]

Up to this point, the armored bateaux had been ferrying the injured and dead back to Detroit. Now they were able to give Rogers cover with their swivel guns, thus allowing his men to rejoin the main group. At the same time, Grant methodically secured a succession of strong points on the road back to Detroit. His men finally reached the fort in good order as dawn broke. Nevertheless, the escapade had cost eighteen dead and thirty-eight wounded. Most of the casualties were in the 55th regiment as they advanced across the bridge over the "Bloody Brook."[45] Pontiac's losses in contrast were estimated as seven killed and a dozen wounded. Among the bodies left behind was that of Dalyell, who died trying to regroup his forces. The Ojibwa, in recognition of his bravery, ate his heart.[46]

The battle was a notable success for Pontiac. Not only had he protected his encampment from assault, but he had also forced the enemy back with three times as many casualties, despite the British having control of the river. James Sterling, the merchant, had no doubts that the Indians had given the army a "damned drubbing."[47] Only a lack of tactical discipline had prevented Pontiac from destroying the expeditionary force as it retreated. The British in consequence were once more penned up in Detroit, despite their reinforcement. Pontiac was reported as being exultant, calling himself "King from the rising of the Sun to the setting" thereof. He was "well entrenched" and determined to stay in this stronghold "till he has possession of the Fort.[48] The action was a testament to his leadership and the determination of his allies.

In his covering letter to Amherst, Gladwin attempted to make light of the affair. The main reason for the setback, he acknowledged, was that "the enemy are numerous and much braver than could be expected," being "elevated by the destruction of so many posts and the defeat of several parties." But in private, Gladwin laid much of the blame on Dalyell. He subsequently told Gage that the "affair was entirely his own seeking. He requested command of the party and put it on such a footing it was impossible to refuse him."[49] Others agreed. One officer commented that Dalyell had caused the setback because of "his natural obstinacy and a too despicable opinion of the savages." Hopefully, "this unlucky check … will be of service to others, as most of our misfortunes have happened from the contempt we have of our Indian enemies."[50]

Amherst, however, remained unrepentant. He acknowledged that Gladwin might have had cause for objecting to Dalyell's scheme. Nevertheless, he said, "It appears to me to have been a very feasible one and promised success, had not the Indians been apprized of the design." As to the retreat, Dalyell would have done this earlier but for his wounds, which perhaps led him to seek "revenge, by which the King was deprived of a brave officer, and his friends of a very worthy companion."[51] Dalyell's disregard for the safety of his men seems to have escaped Amherst's notice, perhaps because he desired to protect his own reputation from the charge of having made an unsuitable appointment.

As a result the army at Detroit was once more on the defensive, unable even to search for firewood, "as the enemy are masters of the country." Gladwin calculated that six or seven hundred men would be needed to evict Pontiac from his present encampment, protected as it was by a swamp. He could only hope that a considerable body of troops was on its way from Niagara. "Fourteen or fifteen hundred will be sufficient force to chastise the Indians."[52] Any smaller number would not do, since Pontiac was expecting a substantial reinforcement. "In a few days I shall be invested by upwards of a thousand" warriors, Gladwin told Amherst on 11 August 1763, referring to the expected arrival of the Grand Saulteur and St. Joseph Potawatomi. This made a further reinforcement all the more important to prevent the "many other nations entering into this war, who are now only waiting to see what turn affairs take."[53] Even then Gladwin was dubious of a meaningful victory, especially over the seminomadic northern nations. Any campaign against them was likely to result in a pointless chase, leading to nothing more than the burning of a few easily replaced huts. Admittedly the enemy's food supplies around Detroit offered a tempting target, where the Ojibwa and Ottawa "plant abundance of corn," the destruction of which "will distress them more than fire and sword."[54] Beyond this, he was at a loss how the conflict could be ended on terms favorable to the British.

Fort Pitt: The Battle of Bushy Run

While the British were suffering a setback at Detroit, dramatic events were also happening to the south, where Bouquet was attempting to relieve Fort Pitt as the prelude to the occupying of the Ohio Valley.

Bouquet, a Swiss soldier of fortune, had served with various European armies before securing a colonel's commission in the first battalion of the 60th Royal American regiment, which had been formed in 1756 to raise men from the German inhabitants of Pennsylvania.[55] To help recruitment, a special act of Parliament had been passed allowing the appointment of foreign German-speaking officers.[56] Bouquet first saw service in 1757, when his unit was ordered to the assistance of South Carolina and Georgia. The next year, he served with Brigadier John Forbes and later became acting commander for the southern department. By the time of Pontiac's War he was an experienced officer, familiar with combat in both the Old and New World.[57]

Amherst issued his orders to Bouquet on the same day as his instructions to Gladwin. The first task, as Bouquet had suggested, was the escorting of a relief convoy to Fort Pitt, after which the noncombatants there could be sent back home. But, as Amherst had previously indicated, Bouquet was also to forward some men of the 42nd and 77th regiments to Presque Isle to support Gladwin's expected offensive. Bouquet himself was to stay at Fort Pitt to look after the communication "and to be in readiness for going down the [Ohio] river."[58] However, by the time these orders arrived, Bouquet had learned about the loss of Presque Isle, Le Boeuf, and Venango, raising doubts over the advisability of sending men there. He was also becoming concerned about the Indian raiding parties which had started to appear along the frontier. On first arriving at Carlisle, he observed that "a general panic" had seized the country, even though there appeared "to be few savages on the frontiers." The problem was that "every tree is become an Indian to the terrified inhabitants." But now that the Delaware and Shawnee had begun their attacks in earnest, Bouquet suggested that it might be advisable to await assistance from the provinces before advancing on Fort Pitt, which was relatively secure.[59]

Amherst replied on 7 July, assuring him that the loss of Presque Isle would mean no change to his orders, though he admitted that its capture gave "him great concern." As to Bouquet's anxiety for the countryside, Amherst believed the Indians would retire once Bouquet advanced toward their habitations. He should therefore abide by his previous instructions of sending men to Presque Isle, though such force must be adequate "to encounter any body of Indians that can attack them." However, Amherst would write to the commanding officer at Niagara to send troops for the rebuilding of Presque Isle. If any more men arrived from the West Indies, they too would be sent there. Amherst then added philosophically, "In the meantime we must do the best we can with the numbers we have." But in a postscript on the inside of the envelope, he had a novel suggestion to make, prompted perhaps by Ecuyer's report of smallpox among the garrison at Fort Pitt. "Could it not be contrived to send the Small Pox among those disaffected tribes of Indians?" Such action would be fully justified, since "we must, on this occasion, use every stratagem in our power to reduce them."[60]

Bouquet responded cautiously to this unorthodox proposal: "I will try to inoculate [i.e., infect] them with some blankets that may fall in their hands and take care not to get the disease myself." There was the difficulty: such weapons might rebound on the users. However, Bouquet had his own suggestion for dealing with the Indians: "I wish we could make use of the Spanish method to hunt them with English dogs, supported by rangers and some light horse," which he believed would "effectually extirpate or remove that vermin."[61] Amherst replied in a second postscript, reaffirming his earlier suggestion: "You will do well to try to inoculate the Indians by means of blankets, as well as to try every other method, that can serve to extirpate this execrable race." As to Bouquet's own proposal, "I should be very glad your scheme for hunting them down by dogs could take effect, but England is at too great a distance to think of that at present."[62] Both men were seemingly unaware that William Trent had already attempted to spread smallpox by just such means.[63] In reality, germ warfare was as dangerous to the perpetrator as it was to the victim. It was, nevertheless, an indication how far the British and their colonists would go to defeat a foe deemed to be both heathen and uncivilized.[64]

Meanwhile Bouquet was alerting subordinates to his newfound caution, telling Captain Ourry at Fort Bedford, "Prudence requires we should proceed with the greatest circumspection. The body of troops I expect daily is the only present resource in this part of the country, open to all the ravages of that bloody race. Should we meet with a check the consequences are obvious."[65] Four days later he was writing similarly to Governor Hamilton, warning, "Their various successes will have elated the Indians and I am of the same opinion, as you, that there will be some risk in forcing a convoy to Fort Pitt with the troops I have, partly composed of men taken from the hospital." For this reason, could Hamilton obtain some of the Pennsylvania harvest guard to escort the inhabitants to safety from Fort Pitt?[66] Sadly, the answer was the same as before: the Quaker assembly would not countenance such use.[67]

But the full extent of Bouquet's doubts only surfaced in his next letter to Amherst of 13 July 1763: "I do not like to state difficulties so long as I can see how to get clear of them." However, since he was "for the present totally disappointed in the assistance I expected from the province of Pennsylvania … I must represent to you that I think it equally precarious to leave Fort Pitt and its communication too thinly guarded, or to weaken Major Campbell's detachment." There were "considerable magazines at Ligonier, Bedford and

Cumberland, and no dependence to be had on the inhabitants who all desert those posts." In consequence, "Each cannot have less than thirty men." In addition, "The extensive and open works of Fort Pitt require more men than would otherwise be necessary against an enemy who has no chance but by surprise." Bouquet then turned to the proposed advance on Presque Isle: "The distance from Fort Pitt to Presqu'Isle is 142 miles, through a narrow crooked path, difficult creeks, and several long defiles. The Mingo and Delaware who live in that part of the country may consist of four to five hundred men, exclusive of the Shawnee or western Indians who may accidentally be among them." Any body of troops, therefore, would have to be respectable. Another problem was that of getting sufficient carriage along such a difficult route. It would take at least twenty days to get supplies to Fort Pitt, and another ten days to Presque Isle. Finally, the Indian attacks on the frontier were increasing, not diminishing, as Bouquet advanced: "The situation of this country is deplorable and the infatuation of their government ... highly blamable.... They have not paid the least regard to the plan I proposed to them on my arrival here, and will lose this [Cumberland] and York Counties, if the Savages push their attack."[68]

Amherst replied somewhat testily on 16 July, "I never expected impossibilities, nor would I attempt anything that does not promise to succeed: the detachment that goes to Presque Isle ought certainly to be very respectable, and capable of encountering any body of Indians that can be on that route." Otherwise, they should not be sent. At the same time the army must act offensively, and if Bouquet could attack any of the Indian towns en route, so much the better. Much would depend on whether the provincials were willing to help.[69] With this in mind, Amherst had written once more to Hamilton asking him to place the provincials under Bouquet's command. He had entrusted his letter to a senior officer, Colonel James Robertson, to argue the case in Philadelphia that the men raised for the harvest should be redeployed along the communication.[70]

The pleas were to no avail, even though Robertson addressed the leading Quaker assemblyman, Isaac Norris.[71] Bouquet therefore had no option but to continue with what he had, though he told Amherst in his next letter, "I meet everywhere with the same backwardness, even among the most exposed of the inhabitants, which makes every thing move on heavily, and is disgusting to the last degree." Nevertheless, he reached Fort Loudoun on 19 July and Bedford on 25 July, despite the appalling roads. But even as the army advanced, the killings among the inhabited areas continued with three people slain near Shippensburg, thirty miles to the rear. Bouquet also had to contend with desertion, though he hoped that the severe punishment of four absconders would stem the flow. Another problem was that the 77th Highlanders tended to "lose themselves in the woods" and could not "be employed as Flankers." He was attempting as a remedy to hire thirty woodsmen as substitutes. But morale had not been improved by the news that the 77th regiment and the second battalion of the 42nd were to be disbanded in consequence of the new peacetime establishment. Nevertheless, Bouquet told Amherst that "we march on the 28th," adding, "I shall not write to you before we get to Pittsburgh unless something extraordinary should happen on the way."[72]

Four days later Bouquet reached Fort Ligonier, the last post before Fort Pitt. Here he was greeted by a very relieved Lieutenant Blane. Unfortunately for Bouquet, Blane was unable to provide any intelligence about the Indians or the state of Fort Pitt, since all "the expresses sent since the beginning of July" had "been either killed or obliged to return." In this uncertainty and with "all the passes being occupied by the enemy," Bouquet decided to leave the wagons and most of his stores at Ligonier, traveling with just 340 horses loaded with flour.[73]

The army accordingly set off again on 4 August intending to make for Bushy Run, approximately twenty-five miles from Fort Pitt. Here the men and horses would be rested prior to a night march "over Turtle Creek, a very dangerous defile of several miles, commanded by high and craggy hills." Everything went to plan until one o'clock the next day, when, after a seventeen-mile march, the Ohio Indians "suddenly attacked our advanced Guard which was immediately supported by the two light infantry companies of the 42nd regiment who drove the enemy from their ambuscade and pursued them a good way." But despite repeated charges, the Indians constantly "returned to the attack." Even a general charge to secure some high ground achieved little, "for as soon as they [the Indians] were driven from one post, they appeared on another, till by continual reinforcements, they were at last able to surround us, and attacked the convoy left in our rear."[74] The full force of the Mingo, Shawnee, Delaware, and Sandusky Wyandot, some four hundred men, had joined the action under the leadership of Kickyuscung and Wolf, following their withdrawal from Fort Pitt on 1 August. Now they could strike Bouquet in the hilly wooded countryside that had proved Braddock's undoing in 1755.

The movement toward the British rear obliged Bouquet to march back to protect the convoy. "The Action then became general, and though we were attacked on every side, and the savages exerted themselves with uncommon resolution, they were constantly repulsed with loss." Nevertheless, in a letter to Amherst that night, Bouquet ended with an ominous warning: "Whatever our Fate may be, I thought it necessary to give your Excellency this early information, that you may at all events, take such measures as you will think proper with the Provinces for their own safety, and the effectual relief of Fort Pitt." In the event "of another engagement, I fear insurmountable difficulties in protecting and transporting our provisions; being already so much weakened by the losses of this day in men and horses, besides the additional necessity of carrying the wounded, whose situation is truly deplorable." Sixty were already dead or wounded, and many of the latter were in excruciating pain, made worse by the lack of water.[75]

As night fell Bouquet formed a circular camp on some high ground, with flour bags stacked to protect the wounded. Early next morning, the Ohio Indians resumed their attack. Kickyuscung and Wolf knew that if Bouquet was prevented from relieving Fort Pitt, the fortress must fall or be evacuated. Winning the battle had become crucial to the outcome of the war. The Indians began with their usual war cries to scare the British into running away. After this, Wolf and Kickyuscung pressed forward on every side, though always giving way when the troops attacked in formation before resuming their ambuscade. Another problem was that the troops were fatigued from the previous day's action. They were also distressed by the lack of water. The convoy was increasingly under threat, having lost many horses, while the terrified drivers hid in the bushes. Another defeat like that of Braddock threatened. Kickyuscung in particular reminded the troops of their likely fate as he shouted to them from behind the trees.[76]

It was at this point that Bouquet resorted to stratagem. The problem had been his inability to draw the Indians into the open so that the regulars could deliver a telling blow at close quarters. Bouquet now ordered the most advanced units to withdraw toward the center of the camp, while two light infantry companies marched round the rear of the army, concealed by trees and high ground, to strike the Indians on their right flank. The sight of the troops in the center apparently withdrawing finally induced the allied Indians to charge what they thought was an enemy in flight. As they rushed in, the British suddenly turned and fired a volley at close range before attacking with fixed bayonets. The sudden change in the British tactics proved too much for the warriors, who now had to retreat past the light infantry, exposing them to a deadly flanking fire. Within minutes, the battle had ended and Bouquet was able to advance to Bushy Run, where the men and horses finally got water. Even so it was not quite the end of the affair, for as Bouquet noted in his report to Amherst, "We had hardly fixed our camp when they fired upon us again." However, another charge by the light infantry brought the action to a close. But in grudging respect for the Indians, Bouquet noted that "our brave men disdained so much as to touch the dead body of a vanquished enemy so that scarce a scalp was taken, except by the rangers and packhorse drivers."[77]

The action had been a desperately close affair. Had Bouquet's stratagem not worked, he would almost certainly have had to abandon the convoy and wounded to escape back to Fort Ligonier. Fort Pitt would then have been in the greatest danger. The Indian leaders, Wolf and Kickyuscung, had shown great tactical skill, while their warriors fought with courage and determination. Kickyuscung paid for it with his life.[78] The British estimated the Indian losses as about the same as their own, though the Delaware chief Killbuck subsequently claimed that they had not had above 110 men engaged, of whom just 5 were killed. However, he was almost certainly talking about Delaware casualties, not those of the whole Indian army.[79]

Bouquet spent a couple of days reorganizing his force before setting off for Fort Pitt. Some war whoops were heard in the distance, but no further attempt was made to prevent him from reaching Fort Pitt on 10 August 1763. By now, most of the Delaware and their allies were in retreat down the Ohio toward Tuscarawas. But despite the Indian failure to stop the redcoats, the battle was still a Pyrrhic victory for the British, since Bouquet was unable to fulfill Amherst's objective of sending men to Presque Isle or down the Ohio. He noted: "After the heavy loss we have sustained, the troops we have left will barely be sufficient for the service of this department and the escorts of Provisions." The most that Bouquet could do was to dispatch four hundred men to take the civilians down to Bedford before returning with the remainder of the convoy. The blame for this disappointing outcome lay with the provincials: "Had the provinces assisted us, this would have been the favorable moment to have crushed the Barbarians, a service we cannot effect with our forces alone."[80] In reality, the setback was due to the stubborn resistance of the Native Americans.

Bouquet repeated these points to Hamilton, though he put more gloss on his achievement, claiming a "complete victory in which the most warlike of the savage tribes have lost their boasted claim of being invincible in the woods." Hence, if the provinces had supported him, "this lucky blow" would have allowed the British "to drive the Indians over the lakes or compel them to sue for peace." The danger was that "if we give them time to recover of their panic, we may have the whole to do over again." The lesson was clear: "The only method of protecting our settlements is by carrying the war into the enemy's country." But to do that, Bouquet needed additional troops.[81] The war for the Ohio was still in the balance.

7
Amherst Tries Again

The Tribulations of Command

Although Amherst believed that Dalyell and Bouquet would be successful, he recognized that they might need reinforcement if the enemy were to be completely defeated. The problem was where to find additional men, since provincial help was unlikely so late in the season. The arrival of six transports from the West Indies on 29 July with twelve hundred men, hence, was good news, even though 20 percent were sick.[1] Amherst in consequence was able to order four companies of the 80th Light Infantry to Niagara from Montreal, along with the 46th regiment under Lt. Colonel Browning.[2] Amherst had also recruited a small "alert corps" from some former ranger companies, under Captain Valentine Gardiner, comprising 120 men. These too were ordered to Niagara, making a total reinforcement of over six hundred men.[3]

Although the dispatch of Browning and Gardiner gave Amherst an opportunity to reassess the conduct of the war, he did not do so. He told Gardiner that the Seneca and "all the other nations of Indians on the Lakes [that] have committed hostilities, must be deemed our enemies, and used as such." This did not mean treating them "as a generous enemy, but as the vilest race of beings that ever infested the earth and whose riddance from it must be esteemed a meritorious act for the good of mankind." "You will therefore take no prisoners, but put to death all that fall into your hands of the nations who have so unjustly and cruelly committed depredations." As an incentive, Amherst was offering "a reward of one hundred pounds to the man who shall kill Pontiac, the chief of the Ottawa, a cowardly villain, but who was the first instigator of the mischiefs that have been committed." A similar reward was to be paid for slaying the killer of Captain Campbell, who had gone to see the Indians "at their desire as a friend, and on promises of his being sent back safe."[4]

With the dispatch of these reinforcements, Amherst felt additionally confident about the situation. The Indians must surely now be reduced to the utmost misery and "lasting impression of our just wrath."[5] The first indication that all was not well was the arrival on 23 August of Bouquet's letter of 5 August, implying that his mission might fail. Though Bouquet reached Fort Pitt, his subsequent correspondence made it clear that he would be unable to take further offensive action. "So many men are fallen sick, that the number

115

fit for duty in the 42nd and 77th is reduced to 245." This made it impossible to send a detachment to Presque Isle "agreeable to your Excellency's Orders."[6] In any case, Bouquet had another reason for being cautious. Daniel, one of the Indian messengers, reported that although the Delaware were "much dejected by their recent defeat," they had been reinvigorated by the return of a hundred Shawnee warriors from Detroit, "where they had spirited up" Pontiac's forces "to continue the war." As a result, "The Delaware were preparing to join the Shawnee" for another offensive. Hence, Bouquet believed he could not act offensively unless suitably reinforced.[7]

Amherst in consequence wrote to Gladwin on 28 August that he might have to send men to Presque Isle himself to secure the communication with Fort Pitt.[8] Although Amherst claimed that Bouquet's letters gave him "the highest satisfaction," he was clearly disappointed at the outcome of the battle at Bushy Run.[9] With no further regulars available, Amherst would have to find other sources of manpower if an offensive was to be launched down the Ohio. He accordingly wrote to Governor Fauquier of Virginia, suggesting that the colony use its forces against the Shawnee towns along the Scioto River. The province had recently raised two volunteer battalions under Colonel Stephens and Colonel Lewis to defend the frontier. Could these not be used for such an objective?[10] Amherst also wrote to Stephens directly. The time for such a blow was favorable and would add "greatly to the security of the frontiers for the future" as well as "reflect the highest honor on the Dominion of Virginia."[11]

But even as Amherst was writing these thoughts, Fauquier was affirming that the laws of Virginia did not allow its forces to proceed "one foot out of the colony." If Amherst wanted these men, it must be "by act of the assembly."[12] But summoning an assembly so late in the season was not practical. Amherst therefore had no alternative but to make one last plea to Bouquet to attack the Delaware and Shawnee. If Bouquet was unable to forward the 42nd and 77th regiments to Presque Isle, he should at least employ them offensively down the river. "Although the getting up [of] the convoy of provisions was very essential for subsisting the troops, yet were we to make that the only point of view, the punishment of the savages can never take place."[13] Bouquet, however, was unmoved. A second Indian messenger, Andrew, had confirmed that the Delaware, Shawnee, and Mingo were regrouping along the Muskingum and Scioto Rivers for an attack on the communication to Fort Pitt.[14] Amherst's hopes for an advance down the River Ohio were not advisable.

Although he was disappointed at the lack of momentum on the Ohio, Amherst still had high expectations of Dalyell. As he told Fauquier on 29 August 1763, he was "in hourly expectation of hearing" from Detroit, and "I flatter myself that the Accounts, when they do come, will be as favorable as I could wish."[15] Nothing, of course, could be further from the truth, as Amherst learned four days later when he heard that Dalyell had been killed and his men forced back to Detroit. There was little Amherst could immediately do, since he had already dispatched his last reserves with Browning and Gardiner. Nevertheless, he was convinced that the forces going to Niagara might still enable Gladwin to strike a decisive blow against Pontiac before the winter. As a further consolation, he increased the bounty on Pontiac's head to £200.[16]

With these thoughts in mind, Amherst ordered Wilkins at Niagara to take command of the forces now gathering there. Wilkins's first task was to reestablish Presque Isle to secure the communication between Niagara and Fort Pitt. Indeed, Amherst was surprised that Wilkins had not already done this, since the risk in rebuilding the post appeared minimal. Dalyell had not seen a single Indian on his journey down Lake Erie, indicating that the enemy was either at Detroit or below Fort Pitt. The abandonment of Sandusky was seemingly further proof of this.[17] This obsession with the posts reveals a serious lack of judgment on Amherst's part, for unknown to him, Pontiac had already sent a new force to reoccupy Presque Isle.[18] Soon the British commander was to receive another even nastier surprise.

Niagara: The Battle of the Devil's Hole

One area that had been relatively free of trouble was Niagara. Three men had been scalped on the road to Lake Erie in the early days of the conflict, and two sailors later killed when they went fishing up the Buffalo River,[19] but otherwise there had been nothing more than the occasional sighting of small reconnaissance parties. The lack of activity at Niagara was surprising, since it was relatively close to the Genesee settlements. In addition, the twenty-mile communication between Lake Ontario and Lake Erie made it vulnerable to attack.[20] The first part of the journey was by boat along the Niagara River. But a mile from the falls, everything had to be unloaded for the nine-mile journey to the top of the escarpment and point of reloading. Originally there had been only a steep path, but in 1751 Daniel Joncaire had widened it to allow the passage of horses and carts. A mile beyond the falls was Joncaire's former trading house of Little Niagara, now called Fort Schlosser.[21] However, Fort Schlosser was judged too close to the rapids for the schooner and sloop to operate. The wagon trains in consequence had to transfer their goods onto bateaux for the last leg of the journey to the mouth of Lake Erie, where another temporary landing place had been established, later called Fort Erie.

At the start of the second week of August, the garrison nominally had 346 men. However, sixty had been sent as part of Dalyell's force to reinforce Detroit. Of the rest, 36 were at the lower landing, 85 above the falls, and 120 in the main fort itself.[22] This latter was a relatively compact structure, in contrast to Detroit, and like Fort Pitt was constructed of stone according to the best principles of European warfare.[23] Nevertheless, this was a small number for such extensive responsibilities. Particularly vulnerable were the wagon trains taking supplies from the lower landing place to Fort Schlosser, an eighteen-mile round trip. Wilkins could only express his relief at the end of August that the oxen at the portage had so far "miraculously escaped."[24]

But although the Niagara portage remained unscathed, the calm was about to end, for early in September news arrived that the *Michigan* sloop had gone aground at Catfish Creek, a few miles away on the southern shore of Lake Erie. The boat had been carrying Lieutenant John Montresor with a detachment of the 17th regiment. Its loss threatened the supply line to Detroit and with it Amherst's ability to wrest the initiative from Pontiac.[25] The situation was dangerous since Pontiac had a new force of 150 Ottawa and Ojibwa at Presque Isle, following the arrival of the Grand Saulteur in early August. Pontiac's men had been there since 18 August, partly to recover some swivel guns for use in the siege, but also to ambush any "troops which might be sent to the relief of Detroit." A party of fifteen warriors was also scouring the other side of the lake for possible targets.[26] Catfish Creek was a mere seventy miles from Presque Isle and within easy reach of the Genesee settlements. The danger of discovery and attack was obvious.

Montresor alerted Wilkins to his predicament while he set about salvaging what he could from the wreck. He also took the precaution of simultaneously constructing a breastwork for the protection of his men.[27] Wilkins quickly dispatched a company of the Royal American regiment to assist. Their arrival on 2 September 1763 proved opportune, for at 8.00 a.m. the following morning, Montresor and his men were attacked by two large bodies of Indians, one from each flank. The firing continued until 10 a.m., when the defenders made a counterattack, supported by the sloop's swivel guns.[28] The British losses were three men; the Indian casualties were unknown. The Mohawk messenger Daniel identified the attackers as Seneca. However, he only spoke at a distance with one detachment.[29] Montresor later concluded that the Wyandot, Ojibwa, and Potawatomi had all participated in the attack, confirming that Pontiac's task force had been involved.[30]

This action was the first by the Seneca since the capture of Presque Isle. The reasons for their subsequent inactivity are not known. It may have been the result of diplomatic pressure from the other Six Nations, following their conference with Johnson at the German Flats in mid-July when he had demanded a return to the Covenant Chain.[31] Early in September, the confederacy requested another meeting with Johnson in an attempt to resolve the differences between the British and the Seneca. Unfortunately, this conference proved even more acrimonious than previous ones. The Six Nations began brusquely by demanding an account of Dalyell's defeat, despite Johnson's protest that this was an unusual way of proceeding before the main business. The various chiefs then asserted that only two Genesee towns were involved in the hostilities and that their anger might yet be abated. The confederacy had accordingly sent emissaries to talk with them and expected a reply shortly. In the meantime, they reminded Johnson of the reasons why the Seneca had gone to war: the presence of the posts, the scarcity of ammunition, the dearness of goods, and the need for a plentiful trade.[32] Johnson, however, was not in a conciliatory mood. Despite the recent British setbacks, he warned the delegates that Amherst was determined to punish the Seneca. In the meantime, all trade remained suspended.[33] It may have been this unsympathetic reaction that prompted the Seneca into a resumption of military action, just as it had incited them at the end of May when Johnson refused to compromise over the surrender of the Kanestio murderers.

However, the Seneca had another reason for acting at this point, being widely criticized by their allies for their failure to attack Niagara according to the plan of 1761. As Major Thomas Moncrieffe subsequently informed Amherst from Niagara, "The Upper Nations are much incensed at the Five Nations for doing nothing on this Carrying Place, as they were led by them into the war."[34] Early in September, rumors began to circulate that the western nations were coming to do the task themselves. Andrew, the messenger, was told in a chance encounter with some of his Wyandot relatives that "800 western Indians in eighty canoes" were heading "towards Niagara to take post at the Carrying Place to cut off all communication with Detroit." Part of this force included "the Ottawa and Chippewa, who were at Presqu'Isle" and "not yet come back."[35] The Seneca were about to be sidelined in their own backyard.

Meanwhile, Wilkins was more confident of his situation. The sloop had been partially salvaged, and some eight hundred barrels of provision saved. Wilkins was also buoyed by the arrival of Amherst's reinforcements. Most important was the appearance of the four companies of the 80th regiment from Fort Augusta, totaling 374 men. An advance company of Browning's 46th regiment had also arrived, with the remaining 270 men close behind.[36] The opportunity for the Seneca to strike a telling blow had seemingly passed.

Browning arrived on Tuesday, 13 September 1763.[37] On the next day, the convoys made their way as usual between Fort Schlosser and the lower landing place, where two platoons of light infantry were now stationed. About ten o'clock, a civilian sutler, Mr. Stedman, arrived with the news that a convoy, escorted by a sergeant and twenty-four men, had been ambushed. Stedman himself had only escaped by being on horseback.[38] The two lieutenants in charge of the light infantry, Fraser and Campbell, assumed that the attackers were a raiding party, not realizing that the incident had been staged to provoke just such a response. They accordingly marched to the rescue along Joncaire's road as it wound its way up the cliffs, flanked on the left by thick woods. It was a perfect place for an ambush since the troops had little cover on the path and no obvious retreat down a two-hundred-foot precipice. According to subsequent Indian intelligence, the warriors were drawn from all the Seneca castles except Canadasaga and Canandaigua. Some 350 warriors took part, led by Oghnawaisse, Korihonti, Tagadareghsera, Adungat, Oguaghwaunda, Ouaqudecka, and Kayenquerego.[39]

The ambush itself occurred at a point called the Devil's Hole, where the cliff's face had become fractured, resulting in a deep hollow. The officers as always were the first target. Strung out in a thin line, the soldiers were quickly forced back, whereupon "the Indians filed off to the right and made a wing so as to cut them off from the fort." The troops, exposed to "the heavy fire by the Indians in the woods," attempted to take cover by scrambling down the cliff face. Many fell to their death or got caught in the branches of trees, where they were scalped while struggling to free themselves. In a few minutes, the affair was over. Seventy men were dead and another ten captured, including two officers. A number did get to the river below but were then swept away by the current and drowned. Only a handful got back to the lower landing. When added to the convoy's casualties, the British had lost over one hundred men. The Seneca, in contrast, had just one man wounded.[40]

When news of the first attack reached Niagara, Wilkins hastened to the lower landing with part of the 60th regiment to reinforce Fraser and Campbell. Here he found several dirty, disheveled, and wounded individuals, two or three of whom had been scalped and were about to die. The survivors told him that the attacking force comprised between four and five hundred warriors. Wilkins accordingly set off toward the field of battle, beating a drum to alert any soldiers still hiding in the woods. But after a short advance, he decided to await reinforcements before going to the scene of the fighting, which was still three miles away. The next day he set out once more. On the road itself, he found the bodies of Lieutenant Campbell and sixteen men, all stripped and scalped. The bodies of another thirty-two were discovered thrown over the precipice. Most of the oxen and wagons of the convoy had suffered a similar fate. Among the dead were presumed to be Lieutenant Rosco of the artillery, and Captain Johnson and Lieutenant Dayton of the New York provincials. However, the bodies were so badly disfigured that it was impossible to identify either Rosco or Dayton. After burying the corpses, Wilkins proceeded to Fort Schlosser, where he found two more survivors.[41] Of the Seneca, there was no sign.

The Seneca had returned home, as was customary after a battle. Here they could celebrate their victory, especially the ritual distribution of captives for adoption or torture. Some oxen were also brought back, the first seen in the Genesee Valley. According to one survivor, a sergeant in Gardiner's corps, at least four light infantry were among the captives and two officers, presumably Rosco and Dayton, both of whom were put to death.[42] The young Mary Jamison, who had been adopted seven years earlier, asked if she could see the warriors feasting and "frolicking" with the two prisoners, on whom "they proposed to glut their revenge." Her fictive mother refused, fearing it would alienate her from the nation. She advised Mary, "With war we have nothing to do: our husbands and brothers are proud to defend us ... let our warriors alone perform on their victims their customs of war." As Mary was subsequently told, the prisoners were first tortured and then "executed by having their heads cut off, their bodies cut in pieces," before being "burnt to ashes."[43]

Amherst himself learned of the affair on 30 September. Publicly he affected to believe that it made little difference to his plans, since Wilkins still had sufficient troops to advance on Detroit. Nevertheless, he acknowledged privately in his diary that the news from Niagara was "very disagreeable ... an unfortunate affair" which rendered "the supply of Detroit very difficult."[44] Clearly, the sloop would have to be rebuilt to ensure that Detroit ran "no risk of want during the winter," for this was necessarily now "the grand point."[45] The punishment of the Seneca, therefore, would have to wait, though Browning should deploy some men against the Genesee castles "to show the Indians the distinction we make between Friends and Foe."[46] Certainly some kind of action was required to restore the reputation of the British, as the Mohawk informed Johnson. Otherwise, the Six Nations "would be obliged to abandon the English," resulting in the severance of communications between Albany and Oswego. As it was, the Seneca and Delaware were planning a sortie via Cherry Valley, after assembling their forces high up the Susquehanna River. The Mohawk were mystified why Amherst had been so slow to take effective action. His constant dispatch of such a "small number of troops" had merely made them "an easy prey for the enemy Indians." What was required was a large reinforcement.[47]

Johnson was rightly alarmed by this intelligence, for another of his informants reported that "the Chenussio were waiting at home for the arrival of more of our troops, for whose coming they kept a good look out." Their plan was to "be ready to attack them whenever they attempted going over the Carrying Place." The other Seneca castles that had participated in the Devil's Hole episode were similarly prepared "on hearing of more Troops coming that way."[48] The determination of the Seneca to prosecute the war was further confirmed by some recently released traders. Their plan was to attack the Carrying Place in 1764 in cooperation with the Delaware and Shawnee, while the Great Lakes nations took Detroit. The remaining Six Nations would then be compelled to support the allied Indians. The belief was universal that arms and ammunition would be available from the Illinois French.[49] Clearly, the grand plan of 1761 was still very much alive.

Nevertheless, Amherst remained oblivious to these dangers, dismissing the traders' reports as "too well formed for the Indians to execute."[50] This was despite all the evidence that the Indians were capable of fighting coherently. Even at this late stage he was still obsessed with reestablishing Presque Isle as part of his scheme for decisive action at Detroit, though he was beginning to doubt the practicality of the latter.[51] As he admitted to Gladwin on 6 October, "the lateness of the season" might "prevent such offensive operations as I could have wished to have been pursued." Nevertheless, he was hopeful that "the Troops under you and that will soon join you, with the supplies that we are forwarding, are sufficient proofs that everything has been done, that could be done to reinforce you." For once, Amherst seemed to recognize that he himself might be accused of not doing enough to help.[52] This was certainly Gladwin's own opinion. He told Johnson, "I am brought into a scrape and left in it; things are expected of me that can't be performed." He was only sorry he had not "quitted the service seven years ago, and that someone else commanded here."[53]

Meanwhile, Wilkins continued his efforts to reinforce Gladwin, though hopes of an early departure proved misplaced. As Wilkins's major of brigade, Thomas Moncrieffe, confessed to Johnson, the various setbacks had "greatly retarded the necessary supplies being sent to Detroit." The "want of sufficient carriages" following the battle at the Devil's Hole meant that "we are obliged to transport the provisions every day on men's shoulders." Consequently, "the reinforcement" that Amherst "thought was long ago with Gladwin, is still here."[54] Another problem was that the Seneca continued to watch Wilkins's camp. Fifty warriors attacked a cattle guard at Little Niagara early in October, killing eleven of the sixteen oxen, further slowing the forwarding of supplies.[55]

Wilkins finally embarked for Detroit on October 20 with 650 men. As the expedition set off, its rearguard was fired upon by a large group of Indians. As a result two bateaux were swept downstream to Fort Schlosser with the loss of fifteen dead and wounded, including an officer. The attack confirmed Johnson's intelligence that the Seneca would continue to attack British forces in transit for Detroit.[56] Gardiner's company immediately gave pursuit but ran into hostile fire, having three men killed and another eight wounded, including Gardiner himself. This compelled Wilkins to land with a further two companies, only to find "the enemy posted in a thick cover on the other side of an impassable swamp." Wilkins had little option but to reembark, whereupon "many savages appeared on the shore when we were about two miles off."[57] It was not an auspicious start to the reassertion of British authority on the lakes.

Unfortunately for Wilkins, his troubles were by no means over, for on the evening of 7 November the flotilla was caught in a storm near the western end of Lake Erie and had to land in a high swell, during which eighteen bateaux were destroyed and sixty men drowned. Most of the provisions and ammunition were also lost. A hastily convened council of war agreed unanimously to return to Niagara, since to proceed would merely increase the number of mouths at Detroit, where provisions were known to be short.[58] The council also recognized that it was too late to do anything effective. The expedition finally reached Niagara on 25 November 1763. During its absence the Seneca had surrounded a wood-cutting party near the lower landing and scalped nine men, putting the communication once more at risk.[59] One soldier was executed, and his head severed in sight of the post.[60] It was symbolic of Amherst's ignominious failure to reestablish British authority in the area.

Detroit: The Siege Suspended

Ironically, had Wilkins reached Detroit, he would have found that the siege had been lifted and a truce agreed to while the Indians went hunting. However, until the middle of October the garrison had remained confined to the fort, leaving the countryside to Pontiac. His position had been strengthened in early August by the arrival of two hundred Ojibwa from Lake Superior led by the Grand Saulteur.[61] Although the Michilimackinac Ojibwa had opted for peace after the capture of that fort, the "Saulteurs" had not seen action and were still keen to fight, encouraged perhaps by the rumors of impending French help. The hope of further spoils was almost certainly another factor. They had also not received the pardon which they had demanded from Amherst when bidding Ethrington goodbye. [62]

The arrival of the northern Ojibwa, however, did not end the stalemate at Detroit. Pontiac still feared a frontal assault, while Gladwin was too weak to counterattack. It was partly to break this deadlock that Pontiac had sent his task force back to Presque Isle to recover two swivel guns previously buried there.[63] In the meantime Pontiac continued the blockade, positioning his army to repel further sorties by the British. In this he was highly successful, for as Gladwin confessed to Amherst in his next report, Pontiac had divided his forces after the battle of the Bloody Brook into "three distinct bodies." They were "so situated that I did not think it prudent to attempt anything against them for fear of a second defeat." The best Gladwin could do was to establish a post four hundred yards from the fort to protect the houses of some loyal Frenchmen, which the besiegers were threatening to burn. This led to the only fighting in August when Pontiac's army attacked for three successive days, suffering several casualties in the process. The British had six men wounded.[64]

Nevertheless Gladwin's position was not entirely secure, since he remained short of provisions, underlining once more the importance of the schooner and sloop. Pontiac was equally aware of Gladwin's predicament and determined to attack, now that he had over a thousand warriors in support. Early in September, the schooner was seen approaching the Detroit River. On board, coincidentally, were five Mohawk on a diplomatic mission to detach the Wyandot from their alliance with Pontiac.[65] On the evening of 3 September, the Mohawk went ashore, leaving the eleven crew to wait for daylight before proceeding up the river. It was at this moment that Pontiac launched his attack with 350 warriors. In the gloom, his men were able to get alongside the vessel so that they were shielded from the cannon and even the swivel guns. Several clambered onto the bowsprit, while others climbed through the windows of the master's cabin. The crew, unable to reload their muskets fast enough, used spears to repel the boarders. In the melée the master and another member of the crew were killed, and four others wounded. The vessel was on the point of being captured when an overzealous warrior cut the anchor cable. The vessel spun round from the force of the current, scattering the canoes while simultaneously exposing them to the fire of the cannon.[66] The fighting had lasted one hour, and as James Sterling readily acknowledged, "The attack was the bravest ever known to be made by Indians." Nevertheless, Pontiac's losses were eighteen dead and twenty wounded.[67]

On hearing of the attack, Gladwin sent four armored bateaux to the ship's assistance, in case the Indians renewed their attempt the next day.[68] Not surprisingly, they declined to do so. Nevertheless, the outcome had been a lucky escape for the British. Had Pontiac's attack succeeded, the garrison at Detroit would have been in jeopardy, given the loss of the sloop at Catfish Creek. It was partly for this reason that Gladwin gave the crew £100 in reward. The action otherwise changed little. As Gladwin again reminded Amherst, "The enemy are still masters of the country, and are likely to be so, if your Excellency does not send a body of men to disperse them." Indian confidence was increased by the apparent lack of British forces on the way. "The crew report and the enemy clearly believe that there are few troops at Niagara," Gladwin reported, though he found this hard to believe.[69]

But the situation facing Pontiac was also full of predicament. The attack on the schooner had been costly, the hunting season was approaching, and Detroit remained in British hands. Siege operations were not part of the Indian military tradition, and desertions were beginning to occur. On 18 September 1763, Lieutenant Jehu Hay recorded that the "Ottawa, Potawatomie and Wiandot were to go off" the next day. Surprisingly among those preparing to join the exodus was Pontiac himself. Most likely he saw the withdrawal as a temporary necessity during the hunting season. But not everyone accepted such reasoning, for Hay also learned that many Ottawa were angry with Pontiac "for proposing to go." They had in consequence chosen "Manitoo [Manitou, an Ottawa sachem] for their chief in his Place."[70] As Monsieur La Ville, one of the French inhabitants, subsequently reported, "The Indians began to tire and Pontiac would actually have gone off, but he had been spirited up again and made to stay by the Grand Saulteur."[71]

Unfortunately for the allied Indians, their forces suffered a further setback on 2 October 1763 when Gladwin sent the armored bateaux to look for firewood. After traveling four miles upstream, they were fired on from the shore and then attacked by two hundred warriors in twenty-five canoes. The Grand Saulteur and his northern Ojibwa mistakenly believed the bateaux would be easy prey. They soon learned their error when they received several charges of grapeshot from thirty yards. The British lost just one man killed and two badly injured.[72] The Indian casualties were estimated to be twelve dead and at least as many wounded.[73]

Despite this setback, Pontiac still had 180 warriors on the southern side of Detroit near the Rouge River, keeping watch to prevent the inhabitants from sending provisions to the fort. Three hundred Potawatomi, Ojibwa, and

Wyandot led by the Grand Saulteur were similarly posted on the northern approaches, making nearly five hundred warriors in all.[74] The possibility of starving the British out of Detroit had not been forgotten, nor had the idea of offensive action, for Rogers reported on 7 October that the Indians knew about Wilkins's force and were "determined to attack them at Point a Plee," where Cuyler had previously been ambushed.[75] The allies were also boosted by the arrival on 8 October of sixty Miami, indicating that the wider Indian community was still supporting the Native American cause.[76] Lastly, Pontiac had not given up hope of French assistance, for it was at this time that he persuaded the Shawnee chief, Charlot Kaské, to carry another message to the French at Fort Chartres asking for help.[77]

Nevertheless, the alliance was in a fragile state. Most of the Detroit Wyandot had long been lukewarm to the cause, and only threats of punishment kept them from deserting.[78] Their morale was further undermined by "an epidemical disorder," most likely typhus, which led to "shivering, then a fever attended with blotches," followed by death forty-eight hours later.[79] Furthermore, the armored bateaux were hurting the settlements along the river, the hunting season had started, and the combatants urgently needed food. On the evening of 8 October 1763, Montresor noticed much agitation among the Indians as they crossed and recrossed the river for a council. Three days later Wabbicommicot from Mississauga appeared outside the fort, offering to act as a mediator, being one of the few Ojibwa leaders who had not participated in the hostilities.[80]

Gladwin had no authority to negotiate since Amherst's instructions were that the Indians should first be "chastised." It was for this reason that Wilkins had been dispatched, though Gladwin had no idea how he would feed the newcomers, given his lack of supplies. Indeed, he had concluded in a letter to Amherst on 7 October that it was too late to undertake further operations: "The enemy are master of the country, the season is far advanced, not a stick of firewood in the garrison, and but little provisions owing to the loss of the sloop."[81] The offer of Wabbicommicot, accordingly, was not rebuffed. Indeed, it gave Gladwin an opportunity to secure wheat and other provisions from the surrounding countryside. But as a gesture of goodwill, he ordered the armored bateaux to remain at the fort while the discussions took place.[82]

The Ojibwa from the Thames River were the first to arrive for talks on 14 October. Next day it was the turn of the Detroit Potawatomi, followed by the Ottawa of Manitou and the Saginaw Ojibwa on 17 October. Montresor, who took the minutes at these negotiations, noted that Wasson, the killer of Captain Campbell, was among those present on 17 October. Nevertheless no attempt was made to detain him, even though Amherst had also placed a price on his head. The next day the Detroit Potawatomi informed Gladwin that their "whole tribe proposed breaking up their camp" for the winter hunt. Gladwin responded approvingly, though he warned that any Indians remaining in the settlement would be treated as enemies. Two days later, "the greatest part of the Potawatomi" were reported to have "dispersed."[83]

Attention now turned to Pontiac's forces on the Rouge River, where sixty canoes arrived on 20 October for a council. On the next day, groups of Indians were seen paddling away or filing off through the woods with their horses and goods. The question was, were they going to hunt or were they regrouping to fight? The latter remained a possibility, for Navarre reported on 25 October that Pontiac's men were still "skulking about the edge of the woods and about the fort" for scalps, hoping "to break the treaty the other nations are making."[84] The conundrum was not resolved until 30 October 1763, when it was revealed that Monsieur Dequindre, a cadet in the French army, had arrived from the Illinois with letters from de Villiers. These informed the Indians and inhabitants that the war between the European nations was over and that the two monarchs had "ordered all their chiefs and warriors to lay down their arms." The Indians in consequence should also "bury the hatchet," since the blessings of peace would far outweigh the uncertainties of war. De Villiers's letter assured them that the French king had only surrendered those lands "which he had amongst you." His great aim now was to avoid another war. For this reason, he had allowed the English and French east of the Mississippi to become one people. Hence, if the Indians attacked the British, they could expect no supplies from the French. However, if they made peace they could always visit their "Father" on the other side of the Mississippi, where their wants would be supplied.[85] Dequindre then confirmed that he had delivered similar messages to the Piankashaw, Wea, Mascouten, Kickapoo, and other nations allied with the French.[86]

Dequindre's message left Pontiac with little option but to talk. Nevertheless he was not about to make an abject surrender, as he made clear in a letter to Gladwin dated 30 October 1763. First he acknowledged that his "Father," the French king, had urged him to make peace, which advice he accepted. Accordingly, "All my young men have buried their hatchets." He hoped in consequence that both sides could forget "all the evil things which have occurred for some time past." Pontiac, the Saulteurs, and Takay's Wyandot were ready to visit Gladwin to discuss these matters. He finished his letter with a polite "I wish you good day."[87]

Gladwin replied to Pontiac as he had to the other chiefs. Final peace lay in the hands of Amherst. "If you conduct yourselves well in the future, as soon as the General is convinced of this, I have no doubt that everything will be well." He finished similarly with a polite "I wish you good evening."[88] But he refused Pontiac admission to the fort. The Ottawa chief still had a £200 price on his head, and Gladwin was under orders to execute him summarily, even though he had overlooked Wasson's offense.[89]

In his account to Amherst, Gladwin commented that he had agreed to talks, being "so circumstanced for want of flour that I must either abandon my post or hear them." He calculated that keeping "possession of the country" was better than refusing to see them. Nevertheless, Gladwin had made the Indians no promises. "I told them the affair of peace lay wholly in your breast; but I did not doubt, when you was [sic] thoroughly convinced of their sincerity, everything would be well again." The spring would be the best time for completing the negotiations, when the Indians had used up their reserves of powder for hunting. "I don't imagine there will be any danger of their breaking out again." One reason was that the Detroit Indians had lost between "eighty and ninety of their best warriors." However, if Amherst wanted to punish them further, he could do so. But, as Gladwin tried to explain, "No advantages can be gained by prosecuting the war, owing to the difficulty of catching" the Indians. Moreover, "the expense of such a war" must lead to "the entire ruin of our peltry trade ... and the loss of a prodigious consumption of our merchandises." Another consideration was that "it will be the means of their retiring" across the Mississippi, where they would prejudice all the nations "against us, and make them our enemy for ever." This in turn "will render it extremely difficult (if not impossible) for us to possess that country, as the French have promised to supply them with everything they want."[90]

The appearance of Dequindre and the peace talks with Gladwin resulted in the depopulation of the three Indian villages around Detroit. Pontiac himself retreated to the Maumee River, a favorite Ottawa hunting ground, with three hundred followers. Not long afterwards, Manitou and his group followed him, camping a little further down the river.[91] Gladwin's refusal to negotiate with Pontiac meant that he was free to continue the struggle, as were most of the chiefs who looked on their talks with Gladwin as a truce to see how the British behaved. Johnson understood this when he commented to Colden in New York, "Their offers of a peace arise principally from an expectation that they will for the future obtain their desired ends, which they could not get by any other means than by having recourse to arms."[92] The British accordingly must mend their ways if they hoped to enjoy peaceful relations with the Indians in the future. That had been the message of Tahaiadoris in July 1761. It remained so now.

The departure of the Detroit Indians meant that Gladwin could punish those French inhabitants guilty of abetting them in their war. He had identified thirteen such men, though most had fled to the Illinois.[93] But two of the most prominent were still at large in the settlement. Accordingly, on 3 November a detachment of thirty men set out to arrest Jacques Godfroy and Mine Chêne. As Montresor noted in his journal, the two were "notorious for their disaffection." Neither man resisted, nor was there any opposition from the other inhabitants. By early afternoon, both were lodged in the fort's prison.[94]

Gladwin need not have worried about negotiating a truce with Pontiac and the other chiefs, for unknown to him, Amherst was about to return to England. The king had finally granted him permission to retire, providing he did not leave before "the danger is passed."[95] Amherst ignored this stricture, though he admitted to Egremont that he "would have liked to report an end to the Indian ravages."[96] But that would mean another year in America, which he was not prepared to accept. Accordingly he informed Gage that he was to succeed him as commander-in-chief, though he made a point of outlining his thoughts about the next campaign before departing.[97] He then issued a proclamation thanking the regulars for their service over the years. It had been an honor to command them.[98] On the afternoon of 17 November 1763, he boarded his ship, the *Weasel*, in New York for the voyage home. His passage was relatively smooth, allowing him to disembark at Plymouth on 24 December 1763.[99] There were no crowds. Amherst was yesterday's man, though he told one confidant, "The gracious reception the King was pleased to honor me with made me very happy."[100] It was one of the few occasions when Amherst gave expression to his personal feelings.

Otherwise, Amherst's reception in England was generally hostile. Captain Thomas Bassett, who had carried some dispatches for Amherst without the customary reward, gleefully reported that "a violent clamor is already begun against him," both "among the civil as the military part of the world."[101] Croghan, who was also in London after resigning from the Indian department, confirmed this, commenting that Lord Halifax, the secretary of state, "found great fault" with Amherst. He "has been pelted away in the papers, [and] the army curse him in public," as did "the merchants." "In short he is nobody here, nor has he been asked a question with respect to the affairs of America since he came over which a gentleman might not ask his footman."[102] Opinion was equally unflattering among many of his former colleagues in America. Loring, the naval commander, asserted that Amherst's campaign had revealed the folly of thinking "that the chastisement of these nations" would be easy. It seemed that "nothing will convince some people of their mistakes but a hearty drubbing."[103] Colonel William Eyre was similarly critical. Amherst's "attempt to maintain posts without the consent of the Indians or without having them by their own desire" was both "vain and delusive."[104] It was for this reason that Croghan had quit the service in September 1763. When Amherst assured him that he would soon be needed, Croghan replied that he believed he might get to Britain and back twice before Amherst could chastise the Indians and establish a durable peace.[105]

These were harsh criticisms, but not entirely unmerited. Amherst was mainly responsible for Pontiac's War, due to his unsympathetic policies after the fall of Canada. In addition, he consistently underestimated the martial abilities of the native peoples after the campaign began. Throughout, Amherst lacked a sense of what was possible. In consequence, he expected miracles from subordinates like Gladwin and Bouquet.[106] It had not been a distinguished performance.

Winter Operations

Gage Takes Command

Thomas Gage, the new commander-in-chief, was different from Amherst in several respects. He was a scion of the Irish nobility rather than the English gentry. His family had also been devoutly Catholic before converting to Anglicanism to protect its estates, which may account for his greater open-mindedness. Another difference was that he had been in America longer than Amherst and had put down roots by marrying into one of New York's elite families, making him more sympathetic to his surroundings.[1] His military career was also different from that of Amherst. He had arrived in 1755 as a lieutenant colonel, commanding the advance guard of Braddock's army when it was attacked after crossing the Monongahela River. The events that day had been a sobering experience which led Gage to realize the need for different tactics in the wilderness conditions of North America. Accordingly he ordered his regiment, the 44th infantry, to practice marksmanship and wood fighting, commenting that "if we intend to beat them, we must fight them in their own way."[2] But he also recognized that more specialist troops were required for reconnaissance, raids, and flanking parties. When Rogers's rangers failed to acquire the necessary discipline, Gage proposed a regiment of regulars instead, appropriately equipped for wilderness warfare. The result was the 80th Light Infantry.[3]

Finally, Gage was readier than Amherst to acknowledge that the Indians were not just mindless savages. He recognized that they had attacked the British "through motives of Policy, which would have engaged more enlightened nations to take measures ... of the same nature." The key to avoiding future conflict was to prevent "purchases of lands from the Indians, by private people," since it would "prevent the evil practices" which had all too often prevailed.[4] There were, however, limits to Gage's empathy. The Indians were still savages who would "cut our throats whenever we are so unfortunate as to disagree with anyone of them."[5] It paid to be on one's guard.

Gage's moderation reflected changing attitudes in London. Since the spring of 1763, the ministry had been debating how to administer the newly acquired American territories. Apart from establishing new colonies in Canada and Florida, the ministry recognized the need to address the future relationship with the Indians with respect to trade and the protection of their hunting grounds.[6] The result was the Proclamation of 7 October 1763. In future a boundary line was to be established along the watershed of the Allegheny Mountains to protect the Indians' hunting rights. No colony hereafter was to claim territory beyond that line or allow the purchase of lands by private individuals. At the same time, those settled beyond the mountains were to remove themselves to the inhabited parts. The Proclamation then turned to the vexed question of commerce. In the interests of "a free and open trade," all those engaging therein first had to take out a license from a governor or commander-in-chief, giving "security to observe such regulations" as had been promulgated. The trade itself was to be supervised by "commissaries," as Johnson had long advocated. Although the Proclamation did not fully address the issue of law and order, other than the arrest of white fugitives, it seemingly promised a new era for relations between the British and Indian peoples.[7]

News of the Proclamation reached Gage on 30 November 1763. He immediately sent a copy to Johnson so that he could inform those nations still friendly to the British of what was intended.[8] It was for the same reason that he approved Gladwin's negotiations with the Detroit nations.[9] But although Gage was less prejudiced, this did not mean he was abandoning the idea of force. He told Halifax that there was no alternative "but the carrying on [of] an active and vigorous war against the savages, till their distress shall oblige them to sue for peace." Only then could the British expect to obtain "a proper satisfaction for the injuries we have received by their treacherous and bloody massacres."[10] Clearly the shadow of Amherst had not been entirely removed.

The Frontier: The Paxton Boys

It has already been noted that while the regular army was advancing westward, a vicious parallel war was being waged along the frontiers of Pennsylvania and Virginia between the white inhabitants and the Delaware and Shawnee. However, until September 1763 the attacks were relatively low-key, since the warriors concentrated on the forts and the advance by Bouquet. In addition, the eastern Delaware had yet to become involved. Hence, the death toll among the Pennsylvanian frontier settlements in the first three months numbered perhaps fifty persons.[11]

However, after Bouquet's successful relief of Fort Pitt, the frontier became a more tempting target. Many Delaware saw the raids as an alternative way of recovering their homeland while simultaneously avenging the deaths of their people. The Shawnee were similarly motivated regarding the protection of their hunting lands south of Fort Pitt, threatened as they were by intruders from Virginia. Accordingly in the second week of September the raids resumed, though initially on a small scale. In Berks County in eastern Pennsylvania, a Delaware war party of eight attacked the homestead of the Quaker John Finder, killing four of his family, after being invited into the house to have breakfast. They then went to the house of Nicolas Miller, where four children were slain. The local militia successfully overtook the Indians and rescued two of the captives. However, the warriors escaped without loss.[12] This allowed them to strike the homestead of Franz Hubler in the Bern Township, carrying off Hubler's wife and three of his children while scalping three others, two of whom died.[13]

To deal with this renewed threat, the Pennsylvanians decided to retain the seven hundred men raised to protect the harvest. Unfortunately, they were insufficient to cover the whole frontier and many communities had to make their own arrangements. Great Cove in Cumberland County was one such settlement, hiring "thirty men, accustomed to hunting, inured to hardship and well acquainted with the country." Their commander, James Smith, was a former captive and thus familiar with Indian warfare. He organized long-range scouting parties so that the inhabitants had early notice of impending danger. The people of Great Cove had been forced to employ Smith because "the soldiers voted by the assembly were not acquainted with the country or the Indian manner of fighting." But Great Cove was a poor community and needed help.[14] Nevertheless, their petition to the provincial assembly was denied.[15]

Governor Hamilton was similarly rebuffed when he sought assistance for Northampton County, after several raids in mid-October. He told the assembly that there was urgent need for "effectual aid so that the inhabitants can be induced to stand their ground," otherwise Philadelphia would be at risk.[16] Ironically this was what Pontiac had promised his Delaware allies at the start of the war. But Hamilton's appeal was to no avail. The assembly believed it had done as much as possible. It was fatuous to suppose that they could provide for the defense of a three-hundred-mile frontier without help from New Jersey and Maryland.[17] In reality, the assembly was motivated by the Quaker dislike of violence and their desire to thwart the proprietary government. The general indifference of the coastal areas outside New England for the plight of the frontier people was another factor.*

In this situation, the backcountry inhabitants of Pennsylvania had to follow the example of Great Cove and do what they could to help themselves. Some bolder spirits had already taken the initiative at the end of August 1763, when Captain William Patterson organized an expedition of one hundred men from Cumberland County to attack the eastern Delaware at Great Island on the west branch of the Susquehanna River. He and his companions believed that the Indians there had been responsible for the earlier raids by Shamokin

---

* The divisions between the frontier and the coastal regions continued after the American Revolution in the guise of the piedmont versus the tidewater. New England was the exception because it was more homogeneous, having received little external emigration since the end of the seventeenth century. Most frontier families consequently had eastern relatives concerned for their welfare.

Daniel, despite advice from the garrison at Fort Augusta that the eastern Delaware at Great Island were friendly.[18] After losing several men in a firefight, Patterson withdrew, only to be pursued during the night by his would-be victims. Nevertheless, his detachment managed to escape. But before reaching Fort Augusta, they met three Wyalusing Nanticoke Indians who had been trading at Bethlehem. The desire for revenge and the opportunity for plunder overcame any feelings of humanity. The three Nanticoke were brutally shot in the back.[19] Two months later Colonel John Armstrong led a second force from Cumberland County of 250 volunteers and succeeded this time in destroying the settlement at Great Island. However, the Delaware had all fled, as was the case at the next settlement of Myonaghquea. Armstrong returned at the end of October 1763 with a meager £70 in plunder.[20] Indeed, he and Patterson had achieved little other than alienating the eastern Delaware, who until this time had been trying to abstain from the conflict. During the same period, over fifty people were killed in neighboring Northampton County.[21]

While Pennsylvania was attempting to defend itself from the Delaware, the Virginia backcountry was also coming under assault from the Shawnee. This second phase of the frontier war began with a success on 12 September 1763, when Captain William Ingles with thirty men routed a group of twenty-three warriors, killing several of them and putting the rest to flight.[22] However, on 30 September a detachment of sixty men under Captain Moffatt and Captain Philips was attacked on Jackson's River in Augusta County by a superior force and compelled to leave behind twelve dead.[23] In response, Colonel Lewis with 150 volunteers surprised the attackers at the forks of the Potomac River on 3 October, killing six of them and wounding another fifteen, as their tracks indicated. However, the war party still managed to escape through a laurel thicket.[24]

It subsequently transpired that the group ambushed by Ingles was a genuine Cayuga war party going to attack the Cherokee. Fortunately for the English colonists, the Cayuga subsequently announced that they would not seek revenge.[25] Nevertheless, this inability to distinguish friend from foe was a major weakness in the British and colonial attempts to establish a genuine relationship with the Native American peoples. Johnson was especially indignant when the New York papers claimed that a detachment under Captain Westbrook had been defeated on the borders of Pennsylvania by some Mohawk, who had been identified by their caps and style of hair. As Johnson angrily told Gage, the fidelity of the Mohawk over a period of one hundred years deserved better recognition. The Mohawks in any case "do not wear caps nor any nation of the Confederacy except the Seneca and some Cayuga."[26]

Among those involved in the attacks on the Pennsylvania backcountry was Captain Bull, Teedyuscung's son. A desire to avenge his father was undoubtedly one factor, though Bull had not gone to war on the burning of Wyoming. He had been a member of the Moravian Church and still hoped that the

Pennsylvania authorities would do him justice. For a moment it seemed that his hopes were to be fulfilled, when in early June 1763 Governor Hamilton issued a proclamation and sent two justices to evict the Connecticut squatters from Wyoming.[27] Unfortunately, it was too little too late, now that the frontier was ablaze. Then Bull suffered a further blow when his cousin Zacharias, another Moravian convert, was murdered along with his wife and child by the Northampton County militia, after stopping at a tavern for refreshment.[28] This time, Bull did not expect or seek justice from the white man.

Instead, he set about planning his revenge with a war party of twenty eastern Delaware. He had already, like most combatants, moved his family to safety on the west branch of the Susquehanna River, following the destruction of Wyoming.[29] On 8 October 1763, he struck the murderers of his cousin at a tavern owned by John Stenton between Bethlehem and Fort Allen, where the militia had gathered. After killing several inmates and burning the building, Bull proceeded to the Wyoming Valley.[30] Here he killed nine Connecticut homesteaders, one of them a woman, who was roasted over a fire, perhaps in retaliation for the death of his cousin's wife. When a rescue party under Captain Clayton arrived a few days later, they found a grisly scene. Two metal hinges had been driven into the woman's hands, while several of the men had spikes in their eyes, as well as spears, arrows, and pitchforks sticking in their bodies.[31] This led the Reverend John Elder, the minister at Paxton, to comment that "till that branch [of the Susquehanna River] is clear of the enemy, the frontier settlements will be in no safety."[32]

Bull's party meanwhile had proceeded up the east branch of the Susquehanna toward Wyalusing before crossing over toward the Jersey frontier, where they struck Westbrook and his detachment.[33] Wyalusing itself was occupied by some Christian Delaware and small groups from other neighboring nations. The threat to their safety from both Indian and white combatants was obvious. A conference was accordingly held in Philadelphia in early December 1763, attended by Hamilton and the Quaker leaders in the assembly and council. John Curtis, a Nanticoke from Wyalusing, began by asserting that his people had accepted all the governor's peace belts, even though three of their people had been murdered by Patterson and his men. The Delaware Wyalusing had attempted to stop the attacks but had been threatened with death for taking the white man's part. The enemy Indians asserted that since the fall of Montreal, the British had "killed more people than during the war." The warriors, therefore, "were not to be stopped," especially "after the killing of the four Indians at Fort Allen," a reference to another incident in Northampton County.[34]

Every raid, of course, created the desire for fresh retaliation. In the event, the anger of the white population was to be directed elsewhere. For the past seventy years a community of Indians had been resident at the town of Conestoga, near Lancaster, where they had taken refuge from the Iroquois during the seventeenth-century Beaver Wars. Suspicion was rife among neighboring whites that the Conestoga were acting as messengers and spies for the alleged war parties from Wyalusing.[35] As the killings continued, the anger of the inhabitants at Paxton boiled over. Since Wyalusing was too distant, the Paxton "boys" chose the settlement of Conestoga to vent their anger. Any moral doubts about such action were easily reconciled by the call of the biblical prophet Joshua to destroy the heathen. The Reverend Elder subsequently claimed that he had attempted to prevent the affair but to no effect.[36] Eighty armed men descended on Conestoga on the morning of 13 December, killing six Indian inhabitants. The rest of the community, fourteen in number, including several women and children, took refuge in Lancaster, where the authorities placed them in the local workhouse for safety.[37]

Governor John Penn, on hearing of the outrage, issued a proclamation for the arrest of the perpetrators. He also announced that friendly Indians like the Wyalusing were to be moved to Philadelphia for safety. No one was to molest them en route.[38] Several groups had already accepted the offer of sanctuary, including 140 Moravian Indians from the mission at Shamokin. They were wise to have done so, since the governor's proclamation had no effect on the backcountry inhabitants. On 27 December 1763, a second party set off from Paxton for Lancaster to complete their work of butchery. As Edward Shippen, one of the local justices, recorded, "Between 2–3 pm upwards of 100 armed men rode very fast into town, turned their horses into Mr Slough's, the Innkeepers yard, and proceeded with the greatest precipitation to the workhouse, where they stove open the door and killed all the Indians." They "then took to their horses before I could get half way to the work house." However, the sheriff, coroner, and several others "got down as soon as the rioters, but could not prevail with them to stop their hands." Some of the mob declared that they would proceed to Philadelphia, where the remaining Indians were lodged, and destroy them too.[39] Poignantly, the Lancaster victims were found holding copies of their various treaties with the governments of Maryland and Pennsylvania.[40]

The attack was widely condemned among the elite. Even Armstrong found it prudent to assert that no one in Cumberland County was involved: "I should be very sorry that ever the people of this county should attempt avenging their injuries on the heads of a few inoffensive superannuated savages, whom nature had already devoted to the dust."[41] But he was clearly divorced from the sentiments of his neighbors, for the threat to march on Philadelphia was no idle one, nor was it confined to the Paxton Township. The discontent in the backcountry was so widespread that Governor Penn requested Gage for assistance from the army.[42]

The killings threatened to have other consequences too. Pontiac and his allies had justified their war because the British and their European American colonists were aiming to destroy the native peoples. Here was graphic evidence of that intent. Johnson was especially concerned that the Six Nations might construe the incident as an attack on their territory and dependents. At a hastily arranged meeting at Johnson Hall, he explained "in the most favorable manner, of the murder of the Conestoga Indians by some rash indiscreet people." He also informed the Iroquois that £600 was being offered "for apprehending the ringleaders" and bringing them "to condign punishment," to prevent "any thing of that kind being attempted for the future."[43] In reality, the Conestoga were friendless even among the wider native community because of their long acculturation among the whites. The Six Nations readily accepted Johnson's condolences, though they could not help observing that he "had often upbraided them for not keeping their people in order." Now it seemed that the British were just as bad.[44]

Meanwhile, the frontier raids continued, as each atrocity justified further retaliation. Several communities in Northampton County had formed volunteer companies to protect themselves. Nevertheless, early in January 1764 twelve people in Whitehall, six in Heidelberg, and four in Lynn became "unhappy victims to the merciless savages." Numerous houses, barns, and other possessions were burnt at the same time.[45] Great Cove was among those to suffer. Without assembly help, David Scott, its leading inhabitant, had been obliged to discontinue the scouting parties. Nine days later a Delaware war party attacked the residents, butchered several of them, and carried a number into captivity. "The rest were compelled to abandon their habitations," Scott said in a petition to the Council, leaving them "in great distress and poverty."[46]

It was this sense of neglect which finally led the backcountry settlers to march on Philadelphia. As Richard Peters, the former provincial secretary, commented, "The government, in failing to do its duty," had broken "the compact between the people and the government." In this situation "the laws of nature obliged" the inhabitants "to preserve themselves." "The most effectual way of doing this" was "to kill these barbarians wherever they meet them."[47] Some 1,500 Westerners set off for Philadelphia to do just that.

The news of their marching caused consternation in Philadelphia, where the normally pacific Quakers rushed to support the militia. Governor Penn attempted to prevent further confrontation by sending the Wyalusing and Shamokin refugees to join Johnson and the Six Nations.[48] Unfortunately, the New York council refused them entry, asserting that they were "the most obnoxious to the people" of their province.[49] The bedraggled group accordingly retraced its steps through New Jersey to Philadelphia. Here the refugees were lodged in the local barracks, protected by a company of the 60th regiment under Captain John Schlosser. Simultaneously the assembly passed a riot act, giving the soldiers immunity from prosecution if they killed anyone while performing their duties.[50] The council also announced that 150 armed gentlemen were offering their support to Schlosser.[51]

In the event, a violent confrontation was avoided. At Germantown, six miles from Philadelphia, the frontiersmen were met by Benjamin Franklin and a delegation from the assembly. Killing the Indians in the barracks was only a subsidiary aim of the marchers and their leaders, Mathew Smith and James Gibson. What the backcountry inhabitants wanted were political changes which would protect them in the future. Accordingly, their first demand was for greater representation in the assembly to counter the dominance of the Quakers. This would then give the previously underrepresented western counties more influence over Indian policy, especially the practice of allowing the natives to reside in the province "in time of war." In addition, they wanted a bounty for Indian scalps and help in retrieving their captive relatives. Finally, they objected to the Quakers giving presents to the Indians in such dangerous times.[52]

The result was a political revolution in Pennsylvania, with the Quakers finally losing power in the provincial assembly. The native peoples in consequence lost their principal advocates in this important province. Pennsylvania was no longer a showcase for the ideals of the "middle ground" where Native and European Americans could live in harmony. Instead, it was to be the killing fields, for as Franklin commented, "The spirit of killing all Indians, Friends and Foes, spreads amazingly through the whole country." The action of the Paxton boys "was almost universally approved by the common people."[53] In consequence, Penn commented that "it now seems more than ever necessary that all the Indians should be removed out of the province, in order to put a stop to the present disturbances and murmurs of the people."[54] It was a sad end to the ideals of the Quaker colony and a grim indication of the fate awaiting its remaining native inhabitants. Pontiac and his allies had been more than justified in striking how and when they did.

Johnson's Winter Offensive

Although winter had brought an end to major operations, this did not preclude smaller raids, especially by the British and their colonists. Winter was a propitious time for such operations, since the native combatants were preoccupied with hunting. Amherst had suggested striking the Genesee before his departure for England, though his proposal had elicited little support.[55] Browning at Niagara thought the weather was too variable and insufficient snow shoes were available.[56] Johnson, on the other hand, believed an attack on the Seneca would forfeit the goodwill of the other five members of the Iroquois Confederacy and put the communication between Oswego and Albany at risk. He asserted that if the support of the confederacy was retained, it "will effectually secure our troops from surprises, obtain proper intelligence, and enable them to pursue their destination with small hazard." Many of these "friendly tribes" were keen to act and had been "greatly disgusted" at Amherst's refusal to accept their services. Most were ready to engage the Delaware and Shawnee, "our most inveterate enemies." Johnson also believed some Canadians should be recruited since it would help break the bond between them and their former allies. This measure too had been vetoed by Amherst. But if Gage was determined to strike the Seneca, it should be done by two forces advancing "from Irondequoit and Niagara." Such a pincer movement would "disconcert and divide the enemy," though hardly surprise them.[57]

A month later, Johnson reiterated the need to avoid alienating the other Five Nations by attacking the Seneca. The advantages of treating them lightly meant that the whole confederacy "would readily join against their perfidious dependents, the Shawnee and Delaware, as well as any others who have acted as principals in the war."[58] The British would then have significant Indian support for the first time in the conflict. Herein, Johnson believed, lay the answer to many of the problems which had previously bedeviled the British military effort. It was for these reasons that he had started negotiations once more with the Six Nations, including representatives from the Seneca.[59]

Unlike Amherst, Gage acknowledged that "friendly" Indians might have some military usefulness, especially against their own kind since "they know the woods, dwellings, and hunting grounds of every nation."[60] He was similarly flexible about the use of the Canadians.[61] Accordingly, at the start of 1764 Johnson began formulating a plan to attack the town of Kanestio with volunteers from the Six Nations. Kanestio lay near the source of the east branch of the Susquehanna River and was the place, Johnson believed, where many of the attacks on the Pennsylvania frontier had been launched. Technically it was a Delaware settlement, but it had become home to "renegades of profligate fellows from several nations," including the Seneca who had murdered the two traders in November 1762. Hence the inhabitants were "very proper objects of our resentment," having "been principals in carrying on hostilities."[62] Gage agreed, telling Johnson on 23 January 1764, "I very much approve of your sending the Indians on immediate service."[63]

On 9 February Johnson accordingly gave orders to Captain Andrew Montour to attack Kanestio with a party of two hundred Indians and thirty woodsmen.[64] Montour was of mixed French and Oneida blood, a classic example of the diverse cultures found on the frontier. He was, however, no newcomer to the British cause, having cultivated the patronage of Croghan, Johnson, and Conrad Weiser, the interpreter, for the past twenty years.[65] Montour's presence accounted for the large number of Oneida on the expedition as well as a number of Tuscarora, Onondaga, and Mohawk.[66] Great care was to be taken to distinguish friend from foe, though to animate the men, Johnson proposed a reward of £50 for the heads of the eastern Delaware chiefs, Squash Cutter and Long Coat. He told Montour that Gage had "great expectations" about the operation.[67]

On this occasion Johnson did not have to wait long, for a week later he learned that an eastern Delaware encampment near the main branch of the Susquehanna had been surprised. Twenty-nine captives had been taken, including Bull.[68] With such a haul, Montour decided to return to Johnson Hall. Here the captured warriors could be interrogated, while the women and children were divided among the victors for adoption "agreeable to the Indian custom."[69] Johnson's interrogation revealed that all the prisoners were from Kanestio and were principally eastern Delaware. Bull himself admitted to twenty-six killings. However, he refused to explain why he had struck his former friends, merely saying that "he was advised to it and his party followed his example."[70] This raised erroneous suspicions of Quaker involvement and led to further questioning in New York City, where the warriors, fifteen in number, were lodged for security. Bull acknowledged to Witham Marsh, the provincial agent, that he had received encouragement from the Genesee, as had the other Delaware. But when "asked whether any white men of Pennsylvania … had desired them to strike," he said "he did not understand the question." Even so, Marsh was convinced that "some quaking devils" were behind Bull's activities.[71]

Montour's raid was simultaneously supported by a smaller group led by Thomas King. He too succeeded in intercepting nine Delaware on their way to the settlements, "singing their war song against the English." One Delaware was scalped, and three others taken prisoner. Johnson commented that this was "the first blood drawn by our Indians, which will prove of great consequence." He believed that the two expeditions had caused a "general Panic" among the enemy Indians, who had not expected the British to employ "their own sort against them," given Amherst's previous refusal. The enemy in consequence had had to retreat to protect their families, thus easing the task of the regular troops.[72] Johnson was so enthusiastic about his operations that he even invited the Stockbridge Indians, Amherst's old bugbear, to take part in future raids.[73]

He was accordingly delighted when Montour suggested that Kanestio and the other Delaware settlements along the Tioga River should be the next target, since the destruction of these would bring peace to the frontier communities, as Elder had argued.[74] Toward the end of March 1764, Montour set out once more with 140 Indians and some 60 rangers, to attack the remaining villages of the eastern Delaware. He was accompanied by Johnson's son, Guy.[75] The first settlement to be struck was Kankaghto, which they found abandoned. This contained thirty-six log cabins with stone chimneys, all of which they burned. They similarly attacked another town of thirty houses on Cayuga Creek, north of Tioga. This too had been abandoned and was quickly destroyed. Finally, the war party marched to Kanestio, the largest of the eastern Delaware towns, consisting of sixty well-built houses, which were also torched. Great quantities of corn and numerous horses, hogs, and cattle were simultaneously destroyed. Among the dwellings were many items, such as saddles, apparently taken from the English-speaking inhabitants. As to the recent occupants, there was no sign, though it was assumed that they had retreated toward the Ohio River. The Six Nations were consequently preparing "to go in pursuit of them" and their Shawnee and Delaware allies on the Scioto

Plains and Muskingum River. Johnson speculated that if the Iroquois carried out their plan, both the eastern and western Delaware would have to flee to the Miami and the Shawnee seek refuge among the Cherokee, with whom they had once been connected.[76]

The success of these raids led Johnson to suggest their use during the main 1764 campaign, though he believed they should operate as a separate unit, accompanied only by a few white officers and rangers. This would enable them to distress the enemy far more effectively than if they were tied to the regulars, since they would "be able to go to places where our troops cannot follow." Only fellow Indians could drive the enemy "from their retreats, destroy many of them, and reduce the rest to a state of despondency."[77] The honor of such an outcome would naturally fall to Johnson, consolidating his position as the indispensable intermediary with the Six Nations. Perhaps he might even be appointed commander.

Rapprochement with the Seneca

While Johnson was pursuing his winter offensive, he was as mentioned conducting peace talks with the Seneca. Publicly Johnson argued that this was necessary to protect the communication between Albany, Oswego, and Niagara as well as ensuring Six Nations support for the 1764 campaign. But Johnson also knew that by securing peace for the Seneca, he would be sustaining his own power and influence among the Iroquois, which had been the key to his career for more than twenty-five years.

Johnson was not the only self-interested party. The Seneca, too, had an agenda to serve. By entering peace talks now, they hoped to lay the blame for the war on the Delaware, Shawnee, and Detroit nations, a deception in which their Six Nations allies were more than ready to assist. Accordingly, at the start of December 1763 the confederacy announced their intention of visiting Johnson to discuss the state of the Covenant Chain. Initially only representatives from the Seneca towns of Canadasaga and Canandaigua were present at Johnson Hall.[78] However, further delegations arrived until all nine Seneca castles were represented, including the Genesee. The main conference began on 15 December when the Genesee chief, Serrehoana, acknowledged the receipt of several peace messages from Johnson. Most important had been one carried by Silver Heels which had led them "to drop further hostilities and lay hold of the chain of friendship with the rest of the Confederacy." Serrehoana then asserted that the Delaware were principally to blame for what had happened. They had approached the Detroit nations, who in turn had contacted the Genesee. This had drawn some of the Seneca to do mischief. Fortunately, the other members of the confederacy had refused to become involved.[79]

Johnson said little in reply other than that the arguments of the Seneca would have to be related to Gage.[80] His aim now was to persuade the other five members of the confederacy to participate in the forthcoming offensive.

However, when the conference resumed on 17 December, Teyawarunte, the Onondaga speaker, begged Johnson not to "push or move the Five Nations to carry on the war against the Shawnee and Delaware" before settling "this affair of the Chenussio." Johnson answered churlishly that he would explain the Seneca position to Gage but "did not think the General would overlook their vile behavior."[81] The conference then adjourned while Johnson wrote to Gage and the Six Nations consulted among themselves in their grand council chamber at Onondaga..

In his report to Gage, Johnson emphasized that the Genesee request for peace had been earnestly supported by all those attending the conference. If the issue could be settled, the rest of the Six Nations "would cheerfully join the operations against the Shawnee and Delaware," who they claimed were "the principal authors of the late troubles."[82] But Gage was not convinced by these arguments. Writing to Johnson on 12 January 1764, he commented that the culpability of the Genesee Indians for entering the war "seems very plain, however they may endeavor to excuse it." Indeed, their conduct was no different from that of the other combatants, who had all "acted upon the same principles." The Seneca were especially culpable since it was "their inveteracy and hatred" that had "animated those nations" in the first place. So far they had escaped physical damage and were suing for peace solely because the French had failed to send help. Hence, at the very minimum they must surrender either the devisors of the war or the two Kanestio murderers. They must also cede ownership of the Niagara portage.[83]

Despite the strength of these arguments, Johnson continued to argue for an accommodation with the Seneca. He told Gage on 27 January 1764 that the Genesee had only been drawn into the war as auxiliaries of the French, the Delaware, and the western Indians. "The defection of the Chenussio" was understandable, given their loss of the carrying trade at Niagara, "where they used to earn a good deal by transporting the traders and western Indian goods." The same was true of "the peremptory (but reasonable) demand" for the surrender of the two Kanestio murderers.[84] This partiality for the Six Nations did not go unnoticed and led Colden, who had written a history of the Iroquois, to question Johnson's judgment in the matter. He told the earl of Halifax, "The Indian nations are a mob directed by popular leaders who are governed by their passions and love of war and revenge."[85] Nevertheless, Johnson determined to persist in his plan. Early in March, he learned that the Five Nations were ready to resume talks and would be accompanied by three hundred Seneca. Johnson blanched at the cost of such a gathering and directed that only the chiefs and principal warriors should appear. So many negotiators in time of war was unprecedented. Two hundred then turned back, but over a hundred continued as the representatives of their nine castles.[86]

The conference opened on 24 March 1764. However, the first few days were spent conciliating the Cayuga for the killing of their warriors by Captain

Ingles and his Virginians.[87] As a result, Johnson was unable to broach the issue of peace terms for the Seneca until 30 March 1764, when he indicated uncompromisingly that they would have to make "proper satisfaction ... such as the General desires." This seemingly contradicted the need for leniency to win over the rest of the confederacy. Nevertheless, Johnson still invited the assembled Mohawk, Oneida, Onondaga, Cayuga, and Tuscarora to accept the "English axe" and make war on the king's enemies "in conjunction with the troops." By way of encouragement, he presented them with a belt six feet long, portraying "two men and an Axe." He also performed a war dance with accompanying song.[88]

The next day a Seneca warrior responded by taking the ceremonial axe in his hand, declaring "war against the Shawnee, Delaware and others his Majesty's enemies." He was followed by the rest of the confederacy, together with the Caghnawaga from Canada. This was a personal triumph since Johnson had yet to state the terms of peace for the Seneca, which he only did on 1 April 1764. First, they must surrender the two murderers who had fled to Kanestio. Next, they must deliver up all prisoners, including deserters and Frenchmen. Third, they must cede the land along the Niagara Carrying Place, allowing the British unimpeded passage between the lakes. In addition, they must cease all dealings with the Shawnee and eastern and western Delaware, adhere to the Covenant Chain against the king's enemies, and leave hostages for the fulfillment of the terms.[89]

The Seneca replied the next day, accepting the terms, except those concerning the Kanestio murderers and the surrender of their remaining prisoners.[90] But after Johnson had reiterated that they must agree to every article, the Seneca reluctantly agreed, adding the qualification "if found" in the case of the Kanestio duo.[91] This provoked a further confrontation in Johnson's study, where he affirmed that Gage would not be happy with such vagueness. The Seneca replied that the two men belonged to one of their chiefs and that "they could do nothing more than press him to deliver them up, which they expected would be complied with."[92] There for the moment the matter rested until the terms were ratified at a conference which Johnson was planning at Niagara as a prelude to the 1764 campaign. In the meantime, the Seneca were to hand over their prisoners. The Six Nations' envoys finally left Johnson Hall on 14 April, "well satisfied," according to Johnson, "and determined to join the army when called."[93]

Unfortunately for Johnson, his satisfaction quickly evaporated with the news from Montour that the eastern Delaware refugees had sought protection with the Seneca, not their relatives down the Ohio, as previously assumed. This was a flagrant breach of article 6 of the treaty just negotiated. Among the refugees was the chief Squash Cutter![94] Confirmation of this extraordinary development came on 30 April 1764, when three Seneca envoys visited Johnson to explain their conduct. "Our nephews the Delaware have begged forgiveness for what they have done and are willing and desirous to put themselves under our protection." The eastern Delaware had agreed to return to their former dependent status as "women." Therefore, "We beg brother you will regard their submission and repentance and forgive them, as you have our nation." Johnson in reply could only express his astonishment at this outcome, reaffirming vehemently that the Seneca must fulfill all their obligations, including their promise to kill and capture as many Delaware as possible. The envoys then promised to deliver his message to their nation.[95] Nevertheless, Johnson's hopes of uniting the Six Nations under his direction in the forthcoming campaign were clearly compromised. The eventual outcome was far from certain.

9

The Campaign for the Great Lakes, 1764

Indian Defense Plans

Although Johnson had successfully detached the Seneca from the enemy coalition and humbled the eastern Delaware, Indian opposition had by no means collapsed. One reason was that most combatants had entered the war as the allies of Pontiac, not the Seneca. Even those who had sought peace at Detroit were prepared to resume hostilities, if the British failed to offer satisfactory terms. Another factor was their ability to fight. As Gage told Halifax, "It is thought they will either break this truce or conclude a peace," depending on "the condition they shall find themselves in the spring." Their reception by the French would be critical.[1]

Among the nations determined to continue the struggle in 1764 was the western Delaware. As early as November 1763 Louis Chevalier, a French merchant, reported from St. Joseph that four Delaware had arrived from the Ohio with six belts "to renew their true alliance" and ensure "one heart" among the combatants. The Potawatomi in consequence had sung their war song, as had the Miami, despite Chevalier's advice that the recent news from Fort Chartres meant there would be no French help. The plan was to resume hostilities in the spring.[2]

A similar refusal to accept a British presence was evident along the Mississippi. As de Villiers reported to Governor Jean D'Abbadie, Kerlérec's successor at New Orleans, the nations around Fort Chartres, principally the Illinois, were delighted that he was still there. They constantly urged him to "take courage" and "not abandon your children. The English will never come here as long as there shall be a red man." De Villiers speculated that he might have to evacuate Fort Chartres completely as "the only means of making them stop their enterprise," for he knew it was essential "to avoid all reproach from the English government" following the conclusion of peace.[3]

One reason for the continued opposition to the British was the influence of Neolin and his ideas. When the officers at Fort Chartres urged reconciliation, the warriors responded that "it was the Master of Life who was exciting them to war." De Villiers explained, "A prophetic spirit has been introduced among the Abnaki," meaning the Algonquian peoples. "A man of that nation" has convinced "all his own people and in turn all red men that God had appeared

143

to him." The message was simple. The "Master of Life" alone could protect the native peoples. "If you suffer the English among you, you are dead men. Sickness, smallpox, and their poison will destroy you entirely." But moral reformation was also required. According to de Villiers, the Potawatomi were particularly affected. They had "thrown away their altar mats and manitous [meaning false spirits], live no longer with more than one wife, offer up prayers evening and morning and wish to be baptized." However, "all the nations of the Lakes" were influenced by the new creed, which remained a mixture of Christianity and traditional Indian beliefs.[4]

Among the latter were the Wyandot of Sandusky. Their God also called on them to make war and peace for seven years, during which time the British would be defeated by a mixture of force and stratagem. Consequently when Teata, the moderate sachem from the Detroit, brought a peace message from Johnson, they laughed behind his back, calling him a fool for believing such promises. The reality was that the Wyandot could never be friendly with the British while they occupied Detroit. Only their traders were welcome. Moreover, the white people might be as numerous as leaves on a tree, but one Indian was "better than a thousand English." Consequently, they had agreed with the Shawnee that they would "try to take Fort Pitt by treachery" in 1764. "If they failed there," they would then "go to the Frontiers."[5] The one problem for the allied nations was a lack of ammunition, though the Sandusky Wyandot themselves still had a supply following the capture of that fort in 1763, which Gladwin believed was the reason why they had "been reinforced" by so "many villains from all the nations concerned in the war."[6] The shortage of ammunition elsewhere was confirmed by a fifteen-year-old captive, who had spent the winter of 1763 at Captina Creek with the Shawnee. He noted that they had been compelled latterly to hunt with their bows and arrows. Nevertheless, they too intended to plant their corn early and lay in provision for their families, after which they would advance on Fort Pitt to burn it. Living among them were several other captives, two of whom had adopted the Shawnee way of life.[7]

Among these acculturated whites was Gershom Hicks, who had twice been a prisoner of the western Delaware. He was sufficiently dedicated to the Indian cause to visit Fort Pitt in April 1764 to "find out what Provisions, Ammunition and troops were in this Fort." Hicks initially pretended that he had escaped from his captors. But after three days of questioning, his true purpose was exposed and he was forced to confess, under the threat of death, what the Ohio Indians intended. He told his interrogators that the Delaware currently had several small parties from the Salt Licks, Hochhockin, Wacatomica, and Scioto searching for targets on the frontier. The eventual plan was for the Delaware, Shawnee, Sandusky Wyandot, Miami, and Ottawa to gather their forces at the start of May, amounting to eight hundred men, for an attempt on Fort Pitt. If that scheme failed, they would attack Ligonier and

Bedford, which were less well fortified.[8] Hicks also confirmed what his British interrogators suspected: that the Indians were seeking help from the French. One of the Delaware chiefs, White Eyes, had visited Fort Chartres, though he had been told to leave by the French commandant. However, he had managed to purchase nine horse loads of goods from French traders with promises of more. Payment had been made in furs and skins. White Eyes in addition had approached the nations along the Mississippi, requesting them to stop the British from coming up the river, which they had readily agreed to do. Finally the Delaware had sent messages to the Six Nations, inviting them to join the alliance.[9] Tamaqua had even visited the Genesee to plead their cause. Despite this the Seneca had refused the invitation because of their continuing negotiations with Johnson and had counseled patience instead, much to the dismay of the envoys.[10] Hicks confirmed that "the Delaware were not pleased with this answer, having already owned themselves to be women to them," meaning acknowledgment of Iroquois suzerainty. In consequence, they would now fight them too.[11]

The resolution of the Ohio Indians to continue the struggle was confirmed by some Onondaga warriors, whom Johnson had ostensibly recruited for a raid against the Shawnee.[12] The Onondaga reported that the Ohio nations were gathering at Scioto in company with the Miami. However, their plans were different from those stated by Hicks, since they intended "to fight in the woods" where the cannon of the British "would be useless." Morale was high and they were "constantly dancing their war dances," in anticipation of victory over both the British and the Six Nations.[13] Their confidence was confirmed by two Mohawk who witnessed the arrival of Johnson's Onondaga [Six Nations] war party. On being asked by the Shawnee what they came for, the warriors replied jocularly, "We are come to scalp you." At this point Kiashuta said, "Here take these, giving them two old scalps that he had newly painted. Go home and tell Sir William you have scalped some Shawnee," which they did.[14] However, the Ohio allies still lacked powder. It was for this reason that the Shawnee had sent a further delegation of sixty warriors to Fort Chartres pleading for French help.[15] A lack of powder may also have been the reason why the Shawnee and Mingo sent peace messages to Fort Pitt via one of their captives, Major Thomas Smallman, a former provincial officer and cousin of Croghan. All the differences, they asserted, could be resolved, if only the British were honest and admitted they were "entirely to blame."[16]

As winter gave way to spring, it became apparent that the Great Lakes nations too had by no means given up the idea of hostilities. According to one report, the Ottawa along the Grand River were planning to attempt a repeat of Pontiac's stratagem in 1763. Their chief, Manitowby, would visit Detroit for a council with Gladwin "under the pretence of trading with the merchants." His real design, however, was to "massacre the colonel and the other officers in Council," which they proposed to do with fifty warriors. Manitowby believed, like many of his colleagues, that the rest of the garrison would offer little resistance once the officers were killed. The Saginaw Ojibwa were assembling in support of the scheme.[17] Indeed they had sent a party to recruit the Ojibwa at Michilimackinac, as Alexander Henry witnessed. Matchekewis, one of the Michilimackinac warrior chiefs, similarly visited Sault Ste. Marie "to raise a party of warriors" for the Detroit venture.[18] A considerable army was in prospect.

Pontiac, meanwhile, had spent the winter of 1763 with his followers on the Maumee River. His main encampment, two leagues above the rapids, contained twenty-two cabins, each accommodating six to eight warriors. Another six cabins were occupied by some Ojibwa.[19] A second Ottawa band under Mackatepelecite was fifteen miles further up the Maumee River, occupying a further six cabins, suggesting that Pontiac could call on two hundred men.[20] News of the warlike intentions of the Delaware, Shawnee, Great Lakes, and Illinois nations naturally reinforced his belief that war was the only way of obtaining justice from the British. Like the Shawnee, he was hoping for French support, following the dispatch of Kaské the previous September. In reality, Kaské had been refused assistance at Fort Chartres and had departed for New Orleans instead.[21] Consequently, when Pontiac had still heard nothing by March 1764, he set off for the Illinois himself. The campaigning season was approaching and it was time to make preparations. Before leaving, he instructed his men to prepare cornfields so that their families did not suffer in the ensuing campaign, as in 1763.[22] Pontiac, like any sensible commander, was always ready to learn from previous mistakes.

Pontiac arrived at Fort Chartres on 15 April 1764 and immediately went to see de Villiers. First, he referred to the "Master of Life" who had guided him to Fort Chartres. Then he boasted disingenuously, "I have left my army at Detroit who continue there the war against the English." They would do so "until there are no more red men," since "they would rather die with the tomahawk in their hands than die in slavery." At recent meetings, the British had gloated how they no longer needed the natives, calling them "hogs," who like lumps of clay would be blown away with the wind. This was the reason he had ignored the French call for peace last October. However, he hoped that de Villiers would not be angry at his disobedience, but carry the "words of all the red men" to the French king, for nothing would please them more than to see Bellestre return to Detroit. Last summer Pontiac and his warriors had "cleared the road" to Fort Chartres, despite the efforts of the British to stop him. Surely, when the French monarch knew of their devotion, "he will take pity on us," for Pontiac was not talking solely for himself. "The Abenaki, the Iroquois, the Shawnee and the Saulteurs, in short all the nations of the continent hold this discourse."[23]

De Villiers replied that King Louis XV's words were mandatory for every Frenchman. De Villiers had been ordered to make peace with the British and that is what he had done. However, he reminded Pontiac that he could still visit his "father" on the other side of the Mississippi, providing he ended hostilities with the British. When Pontiac interjected angrily that he could not accept what his "father" was saying, de Villiers repeated that the king had ordered his subjects to live as brothers with the British. He then tried to reassure Pontiac that Louis XV had not ceded any Indian land. He had only given up what the French occupied. Therefore, he again appealed to Pontiac to bury the war hatchet: "Return to your village, be quiet, love and remember the Frenchmen." Above all, "Make peace with the English." The appeal proved in vain, though Pontiac promised to continue his friendship with the French. No blood would be spilt on lands occupied by them, showing that he understood de Villiers's predicament.[24]

De Villiers's official account suggests that decorum was maintained throughout the meeting. But according to some Potawatomi envoys from St. Joseph, when Pontiac persisted in offering his war belt, de Villiers "grew angry and kicked it away from him, asking him if he had not heard what he had said to him." The French commander then turned to the Illinois, telling them that they would shortly see the British in the fort and that they should "live in amity with them." After this rebuff, Pontiac asked for some rum, which he took to a nearby Illinois village. Here he invited the inhabitants to sing their war song, which they did, though many regretted doing so afterwards.[25] Nevertheless, de Villiers ruefully acknowledged to D'Abbadie that Pontiac had "succeeded in destroying in an hour in the hearts of our domesticated [Illinois] Indians what I believed I had inculcated in eight months."[26]

Given such support, Pontiac decided to stay in the Illinois to await the expected British invasion. Perhaps the French would change their mind. At La Baye, it was said that the heir to the French throne had arrived with a fleet at Quebec and would soon be master of all Canada.[27] Alternatively, the Spanish might assist. All that was needed was a letter from one of these kings. The power of written documents was something with which Pontiac had become familiar. According to D'Abbadie, he kept two secretaries: one to write his letters, the other to read those sent to him "so as to keep each of them ignorant of what is transacted by the other." Even Gage acknowledged that this indicated "a person of extraordinary abilities."[28]

One of those secretaries was Baptiste Campeau, who had fled Detroit following the collapse of the siege. Pontiac now employed him to write to his warriors on the Maumee River, telling them they must be patient. The British were sending five hundred troops to the Illinois via the Mississippi River. Pontiac in consequence had decided "not to return till he had defeated the English; that then he would come with an army from the Illinois to take Detroit."[29] This was no idle boast. He already had the support of the Illinois. Soon he received promises of help from the Miami, Kickapoo, Mascouten, Wea, and Piankashaw, who arrived at Fort Chartres toward the end of June 1764. Their mission, like that of Pontiac and Kaské, was to convince the new commandant, Captain Louis St. Ange, of their determination to continue the struggle.

But first they must have supplies. When St. Ange reminded them that their poverty was a result of the war, they replied unanimously that "they all preferred dying to making peace with the English."[30] The St. Joseph Potawatomi gave the same response when they visited Fort Chartres once more the following month.[31] As a result Pontiac was able to leave the Illinois on 1 July 1764 confident that the Wabash nations, like those of the Illinois, were solidly in support.[32] Even if French officialdom refused to help, the merchants were more than willing to supply him and his allies with what they needed.

Pontiac returned to the Maumee River because there was no sign of the British advancing up the Mississippi River. However, reports suggested that a British army was about to appear at Niagara. Pontiac's forces comprised two hundred Ottawa and Ojibwa, and four hundred Wabash warriors, making an army of some six hundred men. The falls of the Maumee River were a good location for his army, since it allowed him to challenge any British advance toward the Illinois from Lake Erie. At the same time he would be within striking distance of Detroit, should Manitowby's plans take effect.[33] He might even be able to strike the British rear, should they ascend the Sandusky River to attack the Delaware and Shawnee. Once again he was showing that strategic and tactical ability that Gladwin had noticed during the siege of Detroit. With the Mingo, Wyandot, Delaware, and Shawnee preparing to attack Fort Pitt, there was still much to play for from the native perspective.

British Preparations: The Niagara Conference

Since Pontiac and his allies remained defiant, Gage had no alternative but to prepare a new campaign. The belief was widespread, in any case, that a durable peace was only possible after the British had appeared with "such forces as must convince them of our ability to chastise them if they break it."[34] Before departing, Amherst had proposed the deployment of two armies: one under Colonel John Bradstreet to deal with the Great Lakes nations, and the other under Bouquet to attack the western Delaware and Shawnee settlements along the Muskingum and Scioto Rivers.[35] Letters requesting support from the provincial authorities had accordingly been sent late in the fall of 1763.

Despite this, the raising of men and supplies only progressed slowly. As Gage informed Halifax in early March 1764, Massachusetts had refused to supply troops unless war was formally "renewed," though the real reason for its prevarication was that its own borders were not affected. New York, which was "more exposed to the incursions of the enemy," had offered only five hundred men with another three hundred for the protection of the frontier; while New Jersey had so far voted just four companies of sixty men each, half of what he had asked for.[36] The one positive note was Governor James Murray's promise in Quebec to raise two companies of Canadian volunteers.[37] Gage was pleased about this since they would help "convince the Savages of the folly of looking to the French for assistance."[38] Nevertheless, the provincial total was far below what Gage had expected.

The parsimony of New York was surprising since it had the most to gain from a successful campaign, opening as it would a route to the west. But if the northern governments were remiss, the situation was even worse in the southern department, where nothing had been determined, despite Amherst's previous requests. By the end of February Gage was telling the governors of Pennsylvania, Maryland, and Virginia that unless their provinces voted a substantial number of men, he would be reduced to fighting a defensive war.[39] Most critical was the situation in Pennsylvania, where the assembly voted to raise a thousand men but insisted on taxing the Proprietary estates for their support. When Governor John Penn vetoed this, the assembly adjourned for six weeks.[40] The best that could be apparently expected for the war on the Ohio would be the raising of a corps of rangers from Maryland and Virginia.[41]

The fate of the campaign therefore rested seemingly on the progress of the northern army under John Bradstreet. Bradstreet was one of the few regular officers to have been born in the colonies. His father had served in the 40th foot regiment in Nova Scotia and Newfoundland, where he secured his son's first commission. Bradstreet rose slowly to the rank of captain, restrained by his birth and lack of money. Then in 1755, the outbreak of war gave him an opportunity to show his organizational skills. Soon he had become the army's indispensable logistics expert, serving as deputy quartermaster to both Abercromby and Amherst with the rank of lieutenant colonel. But such work, though essential, was hardly glamorous, since field command was what every officer dreamt about. Only once did Bradstreet escape the tedium of the supply services when he organized a successful raid on Fort Frontenac in the summer of 1758. During this brief interlude, he showed considerable skill with a force consisting largely of provincials. His one setback was the refusal of the Six Nations to accompany him. It was perhaps an omen of things to come.[42]

Gage issued his formal orders to Bradstreet on 2 April 1764. His force would comprise 500 New Yorkers, 250 men from Connecticut, 240 from New Jersey, plus 300 Canadians. In addition he would have 314 regulars of the 17th foot regiment and four companies of the 80th Light Infantry, plus ten pieces of field artillery, the whole amounting to 2,000 men. Bradstreet's first objective, after securing Niagara, was to complete the destruction of the Wyandot village at Sandusky, where it was believed large stocks of corn and ammunition were being held "with which they supply the other nations." Then he was to attack the Delaware and Shawnee on the Muskingum and Scioto Rivers, the first by way of Cuyahoga Creek and the second via the Sandusky River. After this, Bradstreet was to journey to Detroit to ensure that the nations there were ready to conclude a formal peace. If they refused, he was "to extirpate them by every means" possible. Then, after improving the defenses of Detroit, he was to find a channel through Lake St. Claire so that he could proceed to

Michilimackinac, where the French inhabitants were reported to be out of control. If true, he was to seize the offenders, confiscate their goods, and help the British merchants recover their property. As to the Indians, he was not there "to caress or flatter them." On the contrary, his mission was "to chastise such nations who shall continue in arms against us." At the same time, he was to offer "peace and protection to those" who "choose to conclude a lasting peace."[43] It was not clear whether this included Pontiac.

These were ambitious orders, especially the requirement to advance by separate routes against the Delaware and Shawnee. Another weakness, as Bouquet observed, was the difficulty Bradstreet would face getting to the Scioto without horses to carry his provisions, for the rivers in that region were unlikely to allow much water carriage.[44] However, one consolation was that Bradstreet would have considerable latitude during the campaign, for as Gage informed Halifax, the expedition would "be at too great a distance to receive any orders" from headquarters. Hence, "It is left with him in such circumstances to determine thereon according to his best judgment."[45]

Despite this concession, Bradstreet was not happy with his command. The reduced provincial levies meant that he would have barely half the three thousand originally indicated by Amherst. The quality of the provincial troops was also a cause for apprehension. He asked Gage, "What service may one expect from fourteen hundred men, one half of them new raised levies and the half of the other but lately subjects of the French King, operating in the heart of the savages' country?"[46] A third concern was the dependability of his Six Nations allies who were expected to contribute five hundred warriors. Rumors had circulated that the Genesee were planning an attack on Niagara, supported by the Sandusky Wyandot and Delaware.[47] Now, following Johnson's negotiations, he was being told to confide in these same warriors.[48] To Bradstreet, this was tantamount to telling potential enemies his plans! He could only hope that the rest of the Iroquois were not coming "to watch our motions, according to custom, instead of doing real service."[49] Finally, Bradstreet had expected to take the field early to surprise the enemy before they returned from their winter hunt. The subsequent delays had prevented this, making it likely that many more Indians would resume hostilities. In that case, he told a correspondent in England, "I shall have the sad mortification of acting mostly on the defensive."[50]

One development to cheer him was the implementing of a scheme for hauling boats and provisions over the cliffs near the Niagara Falls by ropes and pulleys. The advantage was that it would limit the need to use Joncaire's road, thus reducing the danger of another ambush.[51] The hauling gear itself was to be located in a small gully, protected by redoubts at the top and bottom of the cliff.[52] By 30 April 1764, Browning reported that the system was beginning to operate. The Carrying Place itself was now "free from any appearance of an enemy," though the peace talks with the Seneca had produced this rather than the new lifting mechanism.[53]

By the end of May, Bradstreet was ready to leave Schenectady. But first he asked Johnson for some hints on the management of the Indians.[54] Johnson readily obliged, drawing up a list of points for consideration. Bradstreet should address the Indians affably while reminding them of their promises to the British. He should also remember the Indian custom of holding councils. The French had always done this, pretending artfully to follow the Indians' advice, thus ensuring their wholehearted support. Johnson then speculated on various ways in which the Indians might be deployed with the light infantry.[55] In his enthusiasm for military detail, he neglected to clarify their respective roles in the making of peace. It was an omission he would regret.

Bradstreet's arrival at Oswego meant that the Great Lakes nations now had to decide whether to turn their ceasefire with Gladwin into a permanent peace. They had much to consider: their losses during the siege of Detroit, the disruption to their economy, and the need for European goods. On the other hand, they had not been defeated, and the French and Spanish might yet come to their aid. Most importantly British intentions remained uncertain, despite calls from Johnson for a renewal of friendship. Nevertheless, the Detroit Wyandot at least had few doubts about the advisability of peace. Accordingly, after a Mohawk had delivered Johnson's message, their speaker acknowledged that his nation had been foolish to take part in the war, having acted contrary to the will of "the Great Spirit." Now their women prayed continually for peace.[56] Gladwin told Gage that he was inclined to pardon the Detroit Wyandot as they "were led into the war" and had "done little mischief." In contrast the other nations had not contacted him since the previous October, preferring to send "deputies to the Illinois." Clearly "their submission in some measure depends on the supplies and encouragement they meet with there, for at present they have not the means either to annoy us or support their families."[57]

Though it was increasingly clear by early June that French help was unlikely, the Ottawa continued to threaten the Wyandot for submitting to the British terms, which led Gladwin to demand the "extirpation" of "that bloody enterprising treacherous villain Pontiac and his crew."[58] Indeed, Gladwin noted that "some bands of Chippewa," meaning Wasson and Matchekewis, still seemed "determined to hold out, being in expectation of an army from the Illinois, so blind are these people to their own interest."[59] Nevertheless, the trend toward an accommodation continued, the next supplicants being the Wyandot of Sandusky, who were on Bradstreet's line of march. Like others, they claimed that "what they had done was in consequence of the messages and lies" sent them by the Ottawa. They now surrendered five prisoners as a token of their sincerity. Gladwin advised them to complete their contrition by visiting Johnson at Niagara.[60] However, he told Bradstreet that he might still attack the Sandusky Wyandot, if he thought it appropriate. Peace in the area was not assured, despite the negotiations, for Pontiac and his Ottawa were still "sending belts and messages everywhere" from their camp on the Maumee River.[61]

In the event, Bradstreet's approach proved a stronger inducement for the remaining Great Lakes nations than the diminishing hope of French assistance. However, in the case of the northern Ojibwa, an important role was also played by the French Canadian trader, Jean Cadotte. Cadotte had married an Ojibwa and enjoyed a status at Sault Ste. Marie similar to that of Langlade at Michilimackinac. It was Cadotte who had successfully restrained the Sault Ste. Marie Ojibwa from accompanying the Saginaw Indians in the spring of 1764 for an attack on Detroit which Wasson was planning. Even more importantly, according to Henry, it was Cadotte who prevented "the Chippeways of Lake Superior … from joining Pontiac."[62] This refusal to take up arms was undoubtedly a severe blow for Wasson and his colleagues. Accordingly on 21 July 1764, he and his followers arrived at Detroit with a prisoner, "asking pardon in a most submissive manner."[63] Their capitulation was followed a few days later by that of the Ottawa under Manitou, who was equally apologetic. He pleaded that he did not know the reason for the conflict, only that Pontiac who had "set them on … was no more heard" by the Ottawa. As to the future, Manitou promised that he and his people "would reside in Sandusky until given liberty to settle in their ancient village." Gladwin replied by noting that this was Manitou's first request for peace since October, indicating that he had only appeared after despairing of help from the Illinois. He should therefore demonstrate his sincerity by surrendering those who had "set you on," meaning Pontiac. Gage would then be more inclined to forgive him and his people.[64]

In reality the British attitude to Pontiac was changing, for in early July 1764 Gage wrote to Johnson suggesting that Pontiac should either "be gained" to the British interest or "knocked in the head." The Ottawa leader had "great abilities." The one obstacle to an accommodation was "his savage cruelty" which "destroys the regard we should otherwise have for him." Nevertheless, Gage still hoped that Johnson would "see him at Niagara."[65] This was in contrast to his sentiments earlier, when he had talked about putting "the whole to the sword."[66] One reason for his change of attitude was the realization that Pontiac might be useful in helping the British gain possession of the Illinois.

At Niagara, meanwhile, Bradstreet found himself surrounded by a thousand Indians with more arriving each day. Apart from the cost of provisioning them, there was the security of Fort Niagara to consider. The Seneca were clearly hostile, while the rest of the Six Nations appeared untrustworthy. His concern was shared by Johnson, who suggested that it would be imprudent "for the troops to leave" until "it was known what part the Genesee Indians would act." Bradstreet was understandably frustrated by this suggestion. He was already two months behind his original schedule. Now the campaign was being stopped because the Indians had to be given the pretended "liberty of coming in and out of the fort at pleasure."[67] The chance of a decisive outcome had all but disappeared.

Johnson finally reached Niagara on 7 July but did not start the main negotiations until 12 July, when he met a mixed assembly of Mississauga Ojibwa, Detroit Wyandot, Michilimackinac Ottawa, and La Baye Menominee. First he explained why the king was sending an army into their country. This was to make them recognize the folly of starting an unjust war. Nevertheless, Johnson was authorized to pardon those who were sincere in their desire for peace. But first, he expected them to "declare who were the promoters of the war and the causes they assign for so high a breach of their agreement." Then they should volunteer to join the king's forces for which they would be well rewarded, as this, more than anything, would facilitate a reopening of the trade.[68] But despite this forceful speech, none of those present confessed any knowledge about who had started the war. A speaker from Sault Ste. Marie admitted that they had received three war belts, but claimed to have disregarded them. The Mississauga Ojibwa from Toronto replied similarly. They were strangers to the conflict, being lovers of peace, and were now in great poverty as a result. However, Wabbicommicot, their chief, announced the next day that eighteen of his warriors would join the army. He at least understood the link between cooperation and the reopening of the trade.[69]

Johnson waited until 17 July before answering his audience. He first emphasized that the nations around Michilimackinac must allow the fort there to be reoccupied if they wanted a resumption of trade. He then pointed out the differences between the British and French systems of commerce. The Indians may have been rewarded for their services in wartime, but the French always exacted a high price. The British, in contrast, had few demands to make other than the possession of some trading posts. In future the Great Lakes nations should ignore rumors spread by "bad birds"; look to the British for justice; protect the soldiers and traders at Michilimackinac; and make restitution for the property stolen the previous year, including slaves and prisoners.[70]

Later that afternoon Johnson met the Detroit Wyandot to complete the negotiations begun by Gladwin. In addition to the return of prisoners and help for the British, the Wyandot now had to acknowledge the king's right to a strip of land on each side of the Detroit River to secure the navigation between Lake Erie and Lake Huron. The British in return would end hostilities; forgive past offences; respect the Indians' "original rights and privileges;" and ensure a properly regulated free, fair, and open trade. Johnson did not explain what the Wyandot's "original rights and privileges" were: it was not his intention or interest to do so. Nevertheless the Wyandot accepted his terms.[71] Two days later the nations around Michilimackinac similarly agreed to Johnson's conditions.[72]

However, the most important item on Johnson's agenda was the conclusion of peace with the Seneca. So far there had been no sign of that nation.

Not until the morning of 23 July 1764 did a messenger report that the Genesee were on their way.[73] Formal proceedings finally began the next day when Johnson berated the Seneca for giving shelter to the Susquehanna Delaware. He also noted that they had only four prisoners with them. However, the British would still grant peace if they fulfilled the prescribed terms. The most important condition was the surrender of the eastern Delaware ringleaders, or at least their dispatch to Johnson "to make a proper submission and satisfaction." Another requirement was that they nominate some of their "best men" to witness the survey of the land ceded by them along the Niagara River. In addition, they were to give six chiefs as hostages. Providing they agreed to these terms, Johnson would abate the article requiring them to surrender the Kanestio murderers.[74]

Johnson was aware of the need for Bradstreet's army to begin its operations. Consequently, he demanded a categorical answer the next day whether the Seneca would accept these terms. The chiefs replied that some envoys were still collecting the prisoners while others had been delayed because of "evil reports" about the British.[75] In reality the Genesee were being duplicitous, as Bradstreet subsequently learned. Shortly after setting out for Niagara, their principal chief heard that four western Delaware and Shawnee envoys had arrived with proposals for continuing the war. The chief immediately returned home to hear their message, giving the envoys "fifteen belts and five strings" of wampum for "the upper nations" as encouragement to continue hostilities.[76]

Perhaps suspecting chicanery, Johnson told the Six Nations that unless the Genesee complied with the terms, the army would march against them.[77] Next day, the Seneca indicated they would accept Johnson's proposals and also take up the hatchet in the British cause. They added that one of the Kanestio murderers had fled while the other had died, and hoped this would not be considered "a breach of our covenants." As to the prisoners, they were all on the road to Niagara. For the moment Johnson said little other than that he would address the Seneca once the prisoners had arrived.[78] Nevertheless an agreement seemed sufficiently close by 29 July 1764 for Bradstreet to ask the assembled Six Nations and Canadian Caghnawaga if they were ready to accompany him on the campaign. They unanimously said they would. Undoubtedly, the prospect of scarce supplies was a strong incentive.[79]

Two days later the Great Lakes Indians set off for home, having declined to enlist with the army. Before leaving, Johnson gave them a large belt commemorating the Covenant Chain which was to be kept at Michilimackinac. Johnson then returned to his talks with the Seneca, giving them another "severe reprimand for their past behavior."[80] The Seneca in response affirmed on 3 August that they would fulfill every article. As to the Susquehanna eastern Delaware, they would submit to whatever terms Johnson proposed, since they were determined to behave well for the future. If not, they could easily be punished by their hosts. The Seneca therefore requested Johnson to cease his resentment. Finally, they reminded Johnson that they had been the first to pick up the war hatchet at Johnson Hall and could offer twenty-three young warriors for the army. The rest would follow as soon as they were sober.[81]

Johnson reiterated once more that the eastern Delaware must surrender Long Coat and Squash Cutter, both of whom were "to be disposed of as the General shall think proper." All white prisoners were to be delivered and hostages left until the Delaware complied with their obligations. However, he thought it inadvisable for the Seneca to join the army in view of their recent hostility.[82] Next day Serrehoana accepted these conditions on behalf of the Genesee. The articles of peace were finally signed on 6 August 1764.[83]

In his account to Gage, Johnson claimed the conference as a great success. The Genesee had made all the concessions desired of them, including the building of a new fort at the entrance to Lake Erie for the convenience of the vessels. They had also surrendered thirteen prisoners, including a deserter, leaving just four to be delivered when their health permitted. In addition the eastern Delaware had made an abject submission, and treaties had been concluded with nearly all the western Indians. Equally importantly, some five hundred warriors were to accompany Bradstreet. This support was already affecting the balance of power, since Pontiac was apparently ready to make peace, "finding himself deserted by so many of his people." Only apprehension about his treatment had prevented him from appearing at Niagara.[84]

Gage was disappointed to hear that Pontiac had been absent, though pleased about his pacific intentions. Otherwise he was not overly impressed with Johnson's achievement. The Seneca had yet to implement all their obligations, while "none of the deputies at the Congress from the Western Nations belonged to any of the tribes who took up arms, except the Huron [Wyandot] and perhaps some of the Chippewa." Admittedly, the Wyandot of Sandusky and Detroit Ottawa had delivered some prisoners to Gladwin, but another campaign was clearly necessary against the western Delaware and Shawnee, for "unless that is done the overtures made by others and the bringing in of a few prisoners are only to amuse us whilst the storm threatens them."[85] Johnson testily responded that all the warring nations had been present, except for Pontiac's Ottawa and the Potawatomi. But he admitted that he had not been able to identify everyone at Niagara, though many had "undoubtedly" been in arms the previous year. As to their sincerity Johnson had no doubt, providing the British showed some reciprocity.[86]

The Search for a Negotiated Peace: The Mission of Captain Morris

The signing of the treaty with the Seneca meant that Bradstreet could finally set out to deal with those nations still in arms. The delay at Niagara had paradoxically seen an improvement in the military situation, since the Pennsylvania Assembly had now made provision for a thousand men without requiring a tax on the Proprietary estates, thus allowing Bouquet to act offensively down the Ohio Valley. But any cooperation between the two armies would not be possible before October, when Bouquet expected to leave Fort Pitt.[87]

By this time Bradstreet had discovered what Bouquet had been predicting about the impossibility of attacking the Shawnee via the Sandusky River. The only route by water to the Scioto Plains would be by Presque Isle and Fort Pitt, and that would take too long.[88] Another problem for Bradstreet was his lack of clear objectives, if the attack on the Delaware and Shawnee was abandoned. The Wyandot at Sandusky were now begging for peace as were most of the Detroit nations. The one exception was Pontiac and his forces on the Maumee River, to which Bradstreet's orders made no reference. His only other objectives were a visit to Detroit and the garrisoning of Michilimackinac. But whatever he did, Bradstreet felt constrained by distrust of his Indian allies. As he told a correspondent in England, "There are few who think the savages will kill savages on our account."[89]

Bradstreet was right to be doubtful, since the Six Nations were not fighting for the benefit of the British. Naturally they wanted to derive the maximum political advantage from being Britain's principal Indian allies. On the other hand, they had no wish to drive the western nations across the Mississippi into the French orbit. Ideally they wanted to restore their authority over all the Delaware and Shawnee while still ostensibly acting as the allies of Britain.[90] If they could achieve this, the result might be the creation of a new Iroquoian sphere of influence, similar in some respects to what they had enjoyed in the seventeenth century.

The flotilla that departed on 6 August consisted of some sixty bateaux and a similar number of canoes. Three days out near Presque Isle, the armada was met by ten chiefs claiming to represent the Sandusky Wyandot, western Delaware, Shawnee, and other nations inhabiting the "Scioto Plains, the Banks of the Ohio, Presque Isle," and elsewhere. Among their number was Kiashuta. Initially they demanded to know where Bradstreet was going and what his "intentions" were. However, they quickly changed their tone when they saw the size of his armada. Instead, they assured him that they had recalled their warriors from the frontier and had come to Lake Erie to beg "for mercy and peace."[91]

At this critical point Bradstreet failed to establish the envoys' credentials, since they had few wampum belts or other symbols of authority. In his anxiety to get an agreement, he naïvely accepted the assurances of the chiefs that they had full power to "to conclude and sign a peace." The delegation in reality was a ploy to spy on Bradstreet's forces and waste time, for each passing day reduced his ability to strike a decisive blow. Hence, to the surprise of many, Bradstreet promptly offered terms without even consulting the Six Nations. He may have decided that negotiations were preferable to a battle with his motley army. He may also have been influenced by the dispatch of Thomas Smallman to Fort Pitt with peace overtures from the Shawnee and Mingo, despite their "impertinent" language blaming the British for what had happened.[92]

His proposals were as follows. All prisoners were to be freed, the British were to be allowed forts wherever they wished with a strip of land as wide as a cannon shot, British traders were to be unmolested, Indians committing offences against whites were to be tried before a joint jury, hostages were to be given for the fulfillment of the terms, and the signatories were to assist the British in any war against their enemies. Ratification was to be in twenty-five days' time at Sandusky to allow time for the collection of the captives.[93]

The envoys quickly agreed to what had been demanded, after which the Six Nations took them by the hand, saying that "they were glad to see they were come to their senses and hoped they would continue so," otherwise they would have to make war on them.[94] So far the Six Nations strategy for orchestrating a peaceful outcome was working, for article 7 of the new treaty required Bradstreet to write to the commander of the army marching by way of the Ohio to prevent his proceeding.[95] Ironically the Six Nations and Ohio peoples were now working toward a common goal, the stalling of the British offensive, albeit with a different outcome regarding their own relationship.

While awaiting ratification of the agreement, Bradstreet decided to proceed to Detroit, which Gage had decreed his next objective after dealing with the Delaware and Shawnee. There he could complete terms of peace with the nations that had not attended the Niagara conference. The armada accordingly set off down Lake Erie, stopping briefly to remind the Sandusky Wyandot of the need to have their prisoners ready by the middle of September.[96] Another call was made at the mouth of the Maumee River for a meeting with the Miami, along with the Ottawa and Ojibwa of Manitou and Wasson.[97] Some chiefs did appear, but in too few a number to determine anything. It was accordingly agreed to leave confirmation of the peace with those nations until the arrival of their chiefs at Detroit.[98]

It was at this point that Bradstreet decided to send a diplomatic mission to the Illinois via the Maumee and Wabash Rivers, which Gage had recently suggested as a means of winning over the peoples there. It was tacit recognition that the army had no chance of occupying the Illinois without the concurrence of its nations. At the very least, the dispatch of emissaries might counter Pontiac's influence.[99] In any case Bradstreet had developed a taste for diplomacy, following his negotiations at Presque Isle. A new initiative might win over the Wabash peoples, thus opening the road to the Illinois. The same process might be repeated along the Mississippi, until a comprehensive peace had been established everywhere.[100] Such proceedings would be a safer way of executing his orders than forcing his way across the continent.

Bradstreet decided to entrust this daunting task to Captain Thomas Morris of the 17th regiment. The mission was perilous, given that the Wabash nations had recently declared to St. Ange their undying opposition to the British.[101] Nevertheless, the Ottawa and Ojibwa near the mouth of the Maumee agreed that he could pass through their settlements, offering hostages for his safe return. Morris also received belts from the Six Nations and the St. Lawrence Caghnawaga requiring his safe passage, which Thomas King would interpret for him.[102] In addition, Morris was to be accompanied by two French Canadians, one of them Jacques Godfroy, who was awaiting execution for treason at Detroit. Godfroy was conversant in several Indian languages and Bradstreet now offered him a pardon if he helped Morris reach the Illinois. Godfroy readily agreed.[103] Finally, Bradstreet gave Morris a letter for St. Ange at Fort Chartres, requesting his protection and assistance in stamping out the "false reports" about imminent French help which had caused so much turmoil among both the inhabitants and Indians.[104]

After this the army set off for Detroit, where it arrived on 27 August 1764. Bradstreet first inspected the fort's defenses and ordered a number of improvements. Preparations were also made for the dispatch of a detachment under Captain Howard to Michilimackinac.[105] Then, four days after reaching Detroit, a belt unexpectedly arrived from Pontiac implying a desire for peace following a meeting with Morris.[106]

Initially Morris had received a hostile reception when he reached the Ottawa village of Rochedebout on 27 August 1764, being "surrounded by the most formidable body of savages I have yet seen collected together." Unwittingly he had stumbled on Pontiac's main army of six hundred Ottawa, Ojibwa, Miami, Kickapoo, and Mascouten warriors, who had been "summoned ... to make war" in the light of Bradstreet's advance.[107] Pontiac lost no time in telling Morris "that the English were liars, [and] that his father (the French King) was not crushed." Indeed, he had a letter from that monarch as proof, though Morris doubted its authenticity, since it was "full of the most improbable falsehoods" about the dispatch of a French fleet and army.[108] Fortunately, Pontiac appeared "quite tractable" and his power "absolute."[109] It was therefore agreed to hold a "grand council" the following day.

At the council on 28 August, Morris explained his mission.[110] However, according to Thomas King, Pontiac spent most of his time addressing the Iroquois, saying that he was very pleased to see the "chiefs from the Six Nations as he understood that they were the occasion of the war." Indeed they were seemingly still its strongest proponents, since he had recently "received Belts from the Seneca for carrying on the war," which they had sent "during the Congress held at Niagara." But since this was apparently not the case, he would "take care for the future how he should be deceived." Nevertheless, when King confirmed the nature of the mission, Pontiac was immediately conciliatory, offering to send "a very large belt to 210 Castles to make the Road clear, that nothing should molest" Morris and his delegation. The belt was to be taken ahead of Morris by St. Vincent, a half-breed trader and onetime drummer in the French army.[111] It was seemingly at this point that Pontiac sent his belt to Bradstreet, proposing talks. Nevertheless, he was not making an abject surrender. War was still an option if the British did not reciprocate appropriately, since he was confident that the French would come up the Mississippi with "sixty sail of vessels."[112]

Morris had good reason to believe that his mission would be successful, even though he had nearly been killed in several drunken frolics following the council.[113] In a letter to Thomas Mante, one of Bradstreet's aides, Morris urged a generous treatment of the enemy. The Indians were "by no means afraid of" the British, though the Miami and others were sending observers to Detroit to hear what Bradstreet had to say. Hence, "a general pardon would remove all prejudices" and make the British "masters of the Illinois and the rest of the country ceded to His Majesty." Pontiac might then be made "a faithful subject of the King of England and become of infinite service." Morris concluded, "This sensible savage wants only to be convinced that no French army is arrived in Louisiana ... to enter into an alliance with us." This report of impending French help was simply being "spread to prevent his seeking our Friendship."[114]

Unfortunately for the cause of peace, Pontiac's belt was delivered to the Six Nations at Detroit, who promptly cut it into pieces and threw it in the river. They were similarly cavalier with his "speech that was to accompany" the belt, which they "entirely rejected."[115] The reasons for their hostility are not clear, though jealousy is the most likely answer. The British were now treating Pontiac as an agent for peace. This was a role which the Six Nations wanted to monopolize. But the incident may also have reflected a belief that Pontiac's influence was in decline. On 2 September fifty of his Ottawa arrived at Detroit to make peace, with the information that the Ojibwa and Potawatomie would follow the next day.[116] In reality the new arrivals had come as part of Pontiac's peace initiative, though Pontiac himself declined to appear "till his pardon should be granted." On hearing this Bradstreet quickly convened a council on 5 September, where he pardoned the Ottawa leader in the presence of the Ottawa, Ojibwa, and Miami Indians. News of this was then dispatched to Rochedebout, where Pontiac was stationed with sixty of his remaining warriors.[117]

After this Bradstreet turned to completing peace with the nations that had been absent from the Niagara conference, notably the Saginaw Ojibwa of Wasson and the Potawatomi of Ninivois. The first to speak on 7 September was Wasson, who addressed the assembly on behalf of the young warriors of both the Ojibwa and Ottawa. He said they were glad to be so well received. Everything "bad" last year "was done by the old warriors without cause." The young warriors had now taken over and were determined to settle everything regarding the future peace and friendship. Wasson also spoke on behalf of two Miami chiefs, saying that they were overjoyed at the prospect of peace and trusted that the army would cast aside all resentment. Finally, Shamindawa, an Ottawa chief, related how Pontiac had spoken to Morris at Rochedebout, holding a belt of wampum while affirming that "he was heartily ashamed of what had happened." "If he could be forgiven, he would be very thankful and do all the service in his power to the English."[118]

Bradstreet acknowledged the apparent sincerity of the Indians and pronounced peace on the now familiar terms. The nations must acknowledge that they were the "subjects and children of His Majesty George III" and that he had "sovereignty over all and every part of this Country." Secondly, if any nation violated the peace, the others must agree to help punish the transgressors. Thirdly, all future offenders against the British were to be surrendered "agreeable to the laws and customs of this colony." Fourthly, all captives had to be given up. In return, their lands would be protected and the trade reopened. The granting of a pardon to Pontiac was then confirmed, providing he came to Sandusky with the Ohio nations. During the proceedings, the Indians repeatedly used the word "brother" instead of "Children of the King of England." When Bradstreet reprimanded them for this, Wabbicommicot agreed that the term "children" should be the new form of address.[119] It was indicative of a change in their relationship with the British. "Brother" implied an equality of status, and "children" one of dependency. The metaphor, of course, had been accepted by the Great Lakes nations in their dealings with Onontio. Consequently, a general peace still seemed possible.

Suddenly news arrived that eight hundred warriors had assembled at Sandusky to fight Bradstreet rather than make peace.[120] Some misadventure had seemingly befallen Morris, as was confirmed a few days later when the bedraggled members of his party arrived after escaping through the woods. Since writing to Bradstreet on 31 August 1764, Morris had continued his mission, encouraged by Pontiac's reception and the decision of the Kickapoo, Mascouten, Miami, and Ojibwa to return home, now that peace was in the offing.[121] On 2 September 1764 Morris had set off for Fort Miami, where the Miami had their main settlement.[122] Here the reception on 7 September was instantly hostile. Morris was confined to the fort and several times in peril of his life, being at one point tied naked to a stake in preparation for burning. Only prompt action by Pontiac's nephew saved him. Simultaneously, King and his Six Nations colleagues were summoned to a council with the Miami to explain themselves.[123]

The situation had deteriorated for two reasons. Firstly, Morris's mission coincided with the arrival of the western Delaware and Shawnee envoys, carrying the fifteen war belts from the Genesee and the message that "they would perish to a man before they would make peace with the English." Although Pontiac had seemingly ignored the envoys at Rochedebout, they had subsequently gone to the Miami and St. Joseph Potawatomi to rally support.[124] Their message to the Miami was that they "must kill the English on their arrival," while the Seneca barred "the road till such time as they could put a better instrument into their hands." King tried to defuse the situation by explaining that "he was sent by Colonel Bradstreet and the chiefs of the Six Nations in order to make peace with them" and ensure that "the Road should be open from the Illinois to the Onondaga." His pleas were to no avail. As the

Miami chief explained, these fifteen belts had "come from the Seneca in the name of the Six Nations" and could not be ignored. Admittedly, the second belt from the Seneca supported King's assertion that the other five nations of the Iroquois Confederacy were not supportive. Nevertheless, the Miami chief "was convinced of the Honesty and Sincerity of the Seneca." It was plain that the British were "the authors" of the hostilities, by "wanting to encroach on our Lands." Indians everywhere ought to "support one another." King and his colleagues, therefore, should return to Detroit; otherwise, they would be killed.[125] No second warning was needed. Morris and his party fled that night, only to lose their way in the forests and nearly die of starvation before reaching Detroit.[126]

However, a second reason for the change of attitude to Morris's mission was undoubtedly the reception of Pontiac's belt at Detroit. As Johnson subsequently learned, Pontiac was "greatly incensed against Colonel Bradstreet for cutting his belt of wampum to pieces with an axe, which he Pontiac looked upon as a threat or challenge, though he meant well by sending it."[127] Bradstreet, of course, was not guilty of the charge. Nevertheless the damage had been done, as St. Ange reported from Fort Chartres. The reception of Pontiac's belt at Detroit demonstrated that the British were "the cruelest of enemies," who had no respect for any agreements they made. Pontiac's immediate response in consequence was to deny having ever thought of peace. As proof, he sent a large war belt urging "all red men to help him."[128] The Miami were the first to hear of this.

The Thwarting of John Bradstreet

The dismal end to the Morris mission left Bradstreet in a quandary as he embarked for Sandusky, uncertain if he was going to ratify the peace treaty of 12 August 1764 or do battle with the eight hundred warriors that were reported to have gathered there. His first stop at the mouth of the Maumee River found Manitou and his Ottawa waiting patiently, all expressing a desire for peace. But reports were simultaneously received that four hundred Delaware, five hundred Shawnee, and two hundred Wyandot were preparing to attack the British when they landed at Sandusky.[129] The army accordingly set off the next day for that destination, only to be told that the warriors were assembling for peace, not war, in accordance with the agreement of 12 August.[130]

These conflicting signals induced Bradstreet for once to confer with his Indian allies. The consensus was that the western Delaware were still distributing war belts and were not to be trusted.[131] The decision was accordingly taken the next day, 20 September 1764, to advance thirty miles up the Sandusky River toward the Wyandot town, where the Delaware and Shawnee were thought to have gathered. If they still refused to ratify the treaty, the army would then be in a position to attack their villages toward the Ohio.[132] The latter seemed the more likely outcome, given the experience of Morris.

Ominously the army had only twenty days' provision left.[133] Even its safety was in question, since the route back to Lake Erie required a march down a narrow twelve-mile defile. Bradstreet accordingly ordered a return to Lake Sandusky. Here he encamped on the site of a former French post. However, eighty allied Indians were left upstream "under the pretence of waiting for the arrival of the enemy Chiefs."[134]

But any hopes of a diplomatic settlement took a further knock on 25 September 1764 when two Ottawa chiefs reported that the Miami, Kickapoo, Mascouten, and St. Joseph Potawatomie had performed the war dance as requested by the Delaware and Shawnee envoys.[135] The final blow occurred later that day with the arrival of a letter from Gage disowning the 12 August 1764 treaty. Gage had learned the details from Bouquet, who was both astonished and angry at the terms granted by Bradstreet. There was not the slightest atonement for "the massacres of our officers and garrisons, and of our traders and inhabitants, in time of profound peace." The terms were especially reprehensible concerning the Delaware and Shawnee, who had continued to kill and take prisoners as late as 22 August 1764. Equally incredible was that Bradstreet had done this "at a time when two armies after long struggles" were about "to penetrate into the heart of the enemy's country." Finally Bradstreet, as a junior colonel, had abused his position in sending Bouquet orders not to proceed against the enemy. Bouquet would therefore continue his operations until he heard from Gage.[136]

Gage was quick to support Bouquet, telling Bradstreet that he had exceeded his authority on 12 August 1764. Treaty making was a matter for Johnson. Bradstreet's orders were to attack the Shawnee and Delaware, unless they gave up the promoters of the war and sent deputies to Johnson. He was in consequence to continue the campaign in cooperation with Bouquet.[137] Bradstreet did not take this criticism lightly. He told Gage that article 8 of his instructions empowered him to make peace with the Delaware, Shawnee, and Sandusky Wyandot. In addition, there was nothing about referring everything to Johnson other than to keep him informed. Moreover, the terms granted at Presque Isle were much more advantageous than those concluded by Johnson "fifteen days earlier with those masters of butchery and treachery, the Seneca," who were circulating fresh war belts even while signing peace terms at Niagara, as Morris had recently discovered. Nevertheless, Bradstreet would remain at Sandusky to support Bouquet, though the weather would be increasingly inclement as winter approached. Certainly an advance to the Muskingum and Scioto Rivers via Cuyahoga Creek or the Sandusky River would not be possible, since both had insufficient water to support such an operation.[138]

This did not mean that Bradstreet intended to be completely inactive. He accordingly asked the Six Nations "to join a small party of our troops and some Ottawa now present to immediately proceed and attack some of the enemy settlements on the Ohio." But to Bradstreet's surprise, the Six Nations refused, arguing that they had been "sent out to make peace."[139] Bradstreet immediately convened a court to enquire "what orders Sir William Johnson had given the chiefs of the Five Nations with regard to Peace or War." They answered once more that their instructions were to make peace with all those nations ready to comply with Bradstreet's terms. Only if these were rejected would they carry on the war.[140] Any hope that the Six Nations might change their mind were further dashed on 5 October when they found a new excuse for inaction, claiming that the Shawnee were relatives of the Onondaga.[141] When Bradstreet protested that the Six Nations had only been asked to strike the Delaware, King merely reaffirmed that the mission of the Six Nations was the making of peace. In any case they intended to await the report of a scouting party, which Bradstreet had dispatched earlier that day before commencing hostilities.[142] Bradstreet in exasperation commented to Gage, "It is clear that the Five nations do not intend attacking the Shawnee and Delaware, and their conduct throughout has convinced me that they never did."[143]

The scouting party returned a few days later, reporting that it had found one abandoned Delaware settlement. Seemingly the inhabitants had run off after receiving "advices from the Six Nations encamped now with us of our design."[144] Here was clear proof that Johnson's allies were playing a double game to thwart the expedition. Indeed, at the next conference on 12 October 1764, they brazenly advocated that the army should immediately return home as the season was too advanced for further action.[145] Unsurprisingly, the camp was awash with rumor and suspicion. Montresor noted in his journal a report that the enemy Indians were planning to attack Bradstreet's camp at Sandusky, while the Seneca were similarly determined to strike the British "when and where we least expect it." Even the "faithful" King was suspect, having been found to possess a French flag which he had acquired from the Miami on his recent mission with Morris. The flag, it was rumored, would be hoisted to signify the arrival of French troops. More reliably, Alexander Maisonville, a loyal French trader from the Illinois, reported that the Wabash nations had assembled twelve hundred warriors at the rapids on the Maumee River near Rochedebout, where Pontiac resided. Their plan was simple. If the army advanced, they would first attack the rearguard protecting the expedition's boats, after which the main body could be destroyed. They would then advance on Detroit.[146]

In reality the army had no purpose now, except to keep an eye on Pontiac, whose forces were likely to disband shortly for their winter hunt. The weather was deteriorating and sickness was widespread. Relations between the provincials and regulars were also deteriorating over the old issue of "rank and seniority."[147] The following day, Bradstreet recognized the inevitable and ordered a return to Niagara.[148] In an explanatory letter to Bouquet, Bradstreet wrote that he had ascended the Sandusky River as far as it was navigable for canoes, but had found it impossible "to put General Gage's orders into execution." Still, he took consolation that his "long stay" had prevented the Wabash and other nations from giving the Shawnee and Delaware any assistance. In any case, Colonel John Campbell would send parties recruited from the Detroit nations against the Shawnee and Delaware. In addition he had dispatched emissaries to all the Indian nations, informing them of General Gage's intentions concerning the peace.[149] This was a reference to Bradstreet's dispatch of Godfroy and Maisonville with a letter for St. Ange asking him to take action against those traders, notably St. Vincent, who continued to propagate lies about the possibility of French assistance.[150] En route, the two men were to "use their best endeavors to persuade all the savage nations" from the Maumee to the Mississippi "that it is the fault of the Shawnee and Delaware that war continues against them." If they wanted a resumption of trade, they must help end these hostilities and send their chiefs for a conference the following June at Detroit.[151]

The next day, 18 October 1764, Bradstreet's whole army, comprising some 1,400 men plus 150 Indians, embarked for Niagara in fifty-nine boats. After rowing all day, the army went ashore near the Rocky River. Soon a swell developed, producing a violent surf which destroyed twenty-five boats before they could be hauled up the beach. Most of the provisions and much of the equipment were also lost. According to Bradstreet the losses were due to the incompetence of the provincials, who neglected to haul their boats to safety on first landing.[152] Part of the army in consequence had to march along the shore in company with the Indians, resulting in further recriminations. Some of the soldiers nearly died of starvation, while others deserted to escape their difficulties. The flotilla finally reached Fort Erie on 3 November 1764.[153]

Inevitably, there were recriminations about this wretched outcome. Bradstreet affirmed to Gage that he had done everything possible in accordance with his orders and believed that the Delaware and Shawnee would have made peace but for the march of Bouquet, which led them to renew their hostilities on the frontier. Privately he blamed Gage's strange and contradictory orders, believing "the public service suffers much for want of Sir Jeffery Amherst in America."[154] He was supported in his views by Mante in his subsequent *History of the Late War*. Mante argued that Bouquet's refusal to recognize the August peace terms had destroyed Bradstreet's chance of concluding hostilities with the Delaware and Shawnee.[155] However, support for Bradstreet was small compared to the criticism. Gage asserted that Bradstreet had been naïve to deal with envoys who had only a few strings of wampum for their diplomatic credentials.[156] Johnson was equally dismissive. Bradstreet's use of the terms "sovereignty" and "subjects" at Detroit could only alarm the Indians when they discovered their true meaning.[157] This reinforced the point that he should have concentrated on fighting the Delaware and Shawnee and left the treaty making to others. Not surprisingly, the Six Nations had become disgusted at his inaction. Consequently, Bradstreet's conduct toward the Six Nations had been unfair and his insinuations about their intentions unfounded.[158]

Bradstreet's erstwhile native allies were inevitably no more complimentary. The St. Lawrence Indians told Johnson that they had never returned naked and starving while serving with the French. It had been a humiliating homecoming.[159] But most damaging was the testimony of Thomas King. He castigated Bradstreet for failing to heed Indian advice about the envoys at Presque Isle. The Canadian and Six Nations thereafter let Bradstreet do as he pleased, though they were disgusted at his precipitate retreat down the Sandusky River when no danger threatened. Another complaint was that he discussed everything in French and left them uninformed as to what had been decided. Finally, he compelled them to return home on foot through dense woods without food. The expedition had been a shambles.[160]

Among the accusations and counterclaims, there was much special pleading. Johnson wanted to protect the reputation of the Six Nations from the charge of being unreliable allies. The Six Nations had to conceal their political and diplomatic agenda, which was very different from what Johnson asserted. Gage in turn wanted to shield himself from the charge that his instructions were inoperable. Finally, Bradstreet had to explain his failure to achieve anything against the Delaware and Shawnee. But for Pontiac and his allies, the campaign had been a notable achievement. Admittedly, the Detroit nations had quit the coalition, though many were ready to fight again if the opportunity or necessity arose. Pontiac himself still commanded widespread respect, while the Wabash and Illinois nations remained in arms. Most notably the Delaware, Shawnee, and Mingo had survived unscathed from Bradstreet's army. The question was whether they could thwart the intentions of a second force under Bouquet now advancing toward the Ohio Valley.

10
Peace Comes to the Ohio Valley

Bouquet Prepares for Battle

Amherst and Gage had been wise to plan a second army on the Ohio in the light of Bradstreet's debacle. However, the preparations for this force had been much delayed by the tardiness of the provincial assemblies. Gage and Bouquet had first discussed the dispatch of an army down the Ohio at the end of January 1764, but little had been settled concerning men and supplies when Bouquet received his orders on 4 April 1764, two days after Bradstreet's.[1]

In the absence of provincial help, Bouquet's command was to comprise eight under-strength companies of the 42nd Royal Highland or Black Watch regiment, and six similarly reduced companies of the first battalion of the Royal American regiment, totaling perhaps seven hundred men. Gage still hoped to get some volunteers from Virginia and Maryland for escort duty. He also thought that Pennsylvania would ultimately make a contribution and that Johnson would provide him with two hundred Six Nations warriors. Nevertheless, Bouquet's objectives for the moment would have to be defensive, his "first consideration" being "the preserving [of] Fort Pitt and the posts of communication." But it was important not to lose sight of the wider picture. As Gage observed, "A defensive war with savages is always greatly disadvantageous." Accordingly, "I would have you, when every place is secured from danger ... to carry on the war offensively." Bouquet's principal targets were to be the Shawnee and Delaware settlements on the Scioto and Muskingum Rivers. Naturally, it would be beneficial if he could coordinate his operations with Bradstreet so that the Indians were caught between the two. However, Bouquet would have to decide such things himself, given the distance between the two.[2]

By mid-May it was clear that no help was forthcoming from either Virginia or Maryland, so offensive operations would have to be postponed while the regulars protected Fort Pitt and the line of communication. Fortunately, there was better news from Pennsylvania. Toward the end of May, the assembly voted to raise one thousand men, organized in two battalions, this time under Bouquet's command. But manpower was still short, given the widespread desertion from the Royal American regiment. The reasons for this were not hard to find. The terms of service for most of its men had long since expired.

This, when "added to seven years of a most disagreeable service in the woods have occasioned this unprecedented desertion." The problem was exacerbated by the readiness of the population to harbor the absconders. This led Bouquet to remind Gage that he too had leave due and request that "when the service will admit," he would be "relieved from this command, as I begin to feel my strength unequal to the burthen and fatigues of it."[3]

From the start, Bouquet was not optimistic about cooperating with Bradstreet as Gage wanted. However, if the Detroit Indians honored their request for peace, Bradstreet ought to be able to send some men to Bouquet's assistance. This would then facilitate an attack on the Muskingum and Scioto settlements while Bradstreet simultaneously dealt with the Sandusky Wyandot. All the towns between the Ohio and Great Lakes could then be destroyed, and the whole country cleared of its native inhabitants. However, if the Delaware and Shawnee asked for mercy, he suggested the following eight conditions be imposed: that they deliver up for execution the murderers of Colonel Clapham and the Beaver Creek traders; that they surrender every white prisoner without exception; that they disavow alliances with other Indians (excepting only the Six Nations); that they renounce all claims to lands east of the Ohio River; that they must never cross the Ohio without permission; that they trade only at places designated by the British; that they compensate the colonial traders for their recent losses; and, finally, that they give hostages for the fulfillment of their agreements.[4] Gage replied that these terms were very proper, though the final details would have to be settled by Johnson. However, he doubted that Bradstreet would have any spare men. On the other hand, Johnson was promising him a large body of Indians.[5]

Despite this news Bouquet began thinking about the conduct of his campaign after he had secured the posts. The main problem was how to transport the army once it left Fort Pitt, whether by land or water transport. There were several objections to the latter. One was a lack of sufficient bateaux. Another was the navigability of the Ohio and its tributaries in late summer. Furthermore the danger of an ambush was a real possibility, as had been demonstrated recently by some Mississippi Indians, who had prevented a force under Major Arthur Loftus from ascending that river to the Illinois.[6] Accordingly Bouquet decided to abandon water transport as a means of getting to the Muskingum and Scioto Rivers, which led him to conclude, "As we are now circumstanced, it seems evident that the only certain way we have left is to go altogether by land, carrying flour upon horses and driving cattle."[7]

As to strategy, Bouquet believed there were two ways of striking the Indians. The first was "to march with the whole force to the lower Shawnee town, and in case of success there, take in on our return all the smaller towns of the Shawnee, Delaware and Mingo." The second option was "to encamp the troops near Fort Pitt and from thence send parties into the enemy's country to harass and distress them, burn their villages and destroy their corn." The first method Bouquet believed would be the most effectual, but at the same time "exposes the success of the expedition to one single chance." It would also be expensive hiring so many packhorses. Moreover, the enemy might still retire beyond the Wabash and Mississippi Rivers. The second method, on the other hand, would be slower. Perhaps a combination of the two might be the answer, especially if Bradstreet was encamped at Sandusky. Terms might then be offered similar to those of the Seneca, giving them "peace and security for their lands" in exchange for immediate compliance regarding prisoners and the perpetrators of the war. If they still refused, the two armies might then attack simultaneously.[8]

Gage replied, advocating Bouquet's middle option. The army should advance in one body but not go so far as to encircle the enemy, which would put the expedition at too great a risk of being cut off. He now accepted that cooperation with Bradstreet would be restricted over such distances and differing states of readiness. The best that Bouquet might do would be to warn Bradstreet when he was ready to leave Fort Pitt. The same flexibility would be required in his conduct of the peace negotiations, since Johnson would be at too great a distance to be consulted on every detail.[9] This was ironic in view of Gage's subsequent denial that he had given such powers to Bradstreet following his offer of peace terms at Presque Isle on 12 August 1764.

Bouquet now started organizing the supply of his army of approximately two thousand men, which comprised six hundred regulars, a thousand provincials, and some four hundred wagon drivers and cattle drovers. To feed such an army, Bouquet would need sixteen hundred cattle and three thousand pack horses. Appropriate contracts were accordingly placed with local merchants.[10] At the same time Bouquet issued orders on the training of the Pennsylvania recruits, which Colonel John Reid, his second in command, was to carry out at Carlisle. The best men were to be selected as rangers or light infantry and organized in companies of fifty. Another fifty were "to be employed as Light horse men," recruited from people "used to riding." The rest of the provincial infantry was to practice three basic exercises: running, marching, and wheeling in "open files." This would allow them to form "a line of march two deep," as well as a battle formation. Finally strict attention was to be given to the making of encampments, which were to be rectangular in shape, similar to the one he had devised at Bushy Run.[11]

Despite his seeming optimism, Bouquet was by no means enamored of the task before him, as he confided to a friend in England. Many of the best officers had gone home "tired of this disgusting work of Indian fighting." The province of Pennsylvania, meanwhile, had recruited "all the vagrants and vagabonds in the street to go immediately upon service without having time to give them any shape." Most of his precious regulars, "the brave men of last year," were guarding Fort Pitt, "so that I must venture myself with this strange mob, who cannot be ready before the end of July." Nevertheless, he added, "I am still confident that we shall do well and once more rout the villains who scalp as fast as ever."[12] This latter was a reference to the outbreak of fighting on the frontier, following the decision of the western Delaware and Shawnee to resume their raiding parties.

The need to train the provincial forces made Bouquet realize that he would not be able to begin his campaign until the fall. This did not worry him unduly: indeed, it might even be an advantage. Campaigning in October would be easier when the leaves had fallen and the undergrowth decayed. The woods would be more open, and he would still have nearly two months in the milder climate of the Ohio Valley. This would be time enough to reach the lower Shawnee towns. If Bradstreet made a diversion from Sandusky at the beginning of October it would be helpful, as would the recruitment of some Indians by Johnson, but Bouquet was prepared to deal with the situation from his own resources.[13] He admitted to Gage that the lack of native support was a heavy blow, "especially for an expedition by land where Indians would have been most useful." However, he was attempting to recruit some Virginian woodsmen as substitutes. Though unpaid, they would receive provisions and ammunition.[14] He was similarly hopeful of a further response from Pennsylvania, following the decision of the provincial council to pay a bounty on Indian scalps.[15] Earlier, Bouquet had again suggested the use of dogs to counter the ability of the Indians to outrun soldiers and seemingly strike the settlements at will. "A few instances of Indians seized and worried by dogs, would I presume deter them more effectually from a war with us, than all the troops we could raise." Unfortunately, no one had thought of asking for such hounds from Britain.[16]

Despite the bounty on scalps, Bouquet's appeal for volunteers in Pennsylvania met with a poor response. This included the inhabitants of Paxton. Bouquet expected their young men would serve enthusiastically without pay given their previous grievances. Instead, they preferred to enlist "as packhorse drivers," employment "for which a coward is as fit as a brave men." He commented to one of the magistrates, "Will not people say that they have found it easier to kill Indians in a jail than to fight them fairly in the woods?" Bouquet believed the backwoodsmen were shortsighted in not serving, even if unpaid, since they were unlikely to get another chance of pacifying the frontier with the support of the army. Next time, they would have to fend for themselves. He personally was so "disgusted at the backwardness of the frontier people" that "I hope this will be the last time I shall venture my reputation and life for their sake."[17]

A similar request to the Virginians for volunteers also appeared fruitless. Here, too, the major stumbling block was Bouquet's inability to pay the men. He had written to Colonel Adam Stephen early in July, asking him to encourage some "good woodsmen" from the Hampshire and Frederick County militias.[18] It proved to no avail, though Stephen's refusal to cooperate was the result of a grudge against Bouquet for his refusal to accept some overdue supplies the previous year.[19] There was similar disappointment with the Augusta County militia, when Colonel Andrew Lewis reported that the assembly would not allow his men to serve outside the province. However, he believed many would volunteer for service on the southeast side of the Ohio River, since that area was adjacent to their own settlements.[20] The problem was that Bouquet's current route largely benefited Pennsylvania. This had caused controversy during the previous war when Washington and his colleagues badgered Forbes to take an alternative route from Virginia.[21]

Meanwhile, the first parties of the Delaware and Shawnee had been sighted near Fort Pitt and the neighboring frontiers.[22] This confirmed a report by two Mohawks that "thirty small parties" had left the Delaware villages to strike "the inhabitants of the frontiers."[23] Several groups infested the communication, sniping at small detachments, hoping to spread sufficient fear and confusion so that the army was diverted from marching against their settlements down the Ohio. Others invaded Virginia's Hampshire County in the region of Patterson Creek, inflicting a "great deal of mischief." At the end of May, one of the larger raiding parties even attacked workers outside Fort Dinwiddie, near the junction of the Monongahela and Cheat Rivers, killing fifteen and capturing a further sixteen before firing on the fort for several hours.[24] A week later, Colonel Armstrong reported that thirteen people had been killed and several houses destroyed four miles south of Fort Loudon. As Armstrong commented to Governor Penn, it "seems that the Indians now intend to concentrate on the frontier and by burning houses, lay as much of the country waste as possible."[25] Shortly afterwards, Armstrong caught up with some raiders and killed five. But the fighting was always sporadic as the raiding parties changed objectives to foil pursuit. Hence, while Lewis was warding off attacks in Augusta County, Major James Livingston at Fort Cumberland in neighboring Maryland was reporting that "we are very quiet on this side."[26]

He spoke too soon. About this time some three hundred Delaware, Shawnee, and Mingo gathered at the forks of the Muskingum River. As the adopted John McCullough noted, "Their intention was to come to the settlements and make a general massacre of the whole people without any regard to age or sex." Total war seemed the only option. In the event, most warriors returned after ten days, "having concluded that it was not safe for them to leave their towns destitute of defense. However several small parties went on to the different settlements."[27] The result was one of the most notorious incidents in the war on 26 July 1764, when a Delaware raiding party stormed Enoch Brown's school in the Conococheague Creek at the southern edge of Cumberland County in Pennsylvania. The master and nine pupils were killed, and another four taken prisoner.[28] Although the war party was only carrying out a previously agreed policy, McCullough noted that "some of the old Indians were very much displeased" with the warriors "for killing so many children." Native peoples did not kill young people indiscriminately. One chief even called the attack an act of "cowardice."[29]

Unfortunately for the attackers, none of this deflected Bouquet from his objective, since he believed this time that the closer he got to the Indians' own habitations, the sooner they would desist from their attacks against the white settlements.[30] By the middle of August, Bouquet had reached Fort Loudon. His main task now was to organize the forwarding of supplies to Fort Pitt in preparation for an advance on 1 October. Because of his experience at Bushy Run, Bouquet gave meticulous orders for the first convoy, which Reid was to escort with 450 men. He was to start early each morning so that he reached the next encampment by one o'clock in the afternoon. This would give the animals time to graze before nightfall. In addition, the drivers of the wagons were to have scythes for cutting grass so that they could be tethered in the camp at night. At each encampment the horses were to be unloaded and seventy flour kegs arranged to form a small redoubt sufficient to protect a guard of eighteen men. A total of eight such redoubts were to be built, one at each corner with an additional one in between. The rest of the kegs were to be stacked two high along the center of the square to form a convenient line for reloading.[31]

Bouquet further refined these tactics when he set out himself for Fort Pitt. Four light horsemen were to proceed in a single file, always keeping sight of the army, with two more on each flank and ten in the rear. Half of the regulars were to follow the light horse marching two deep, ready to form the front of the square. The first battalion of the provincials would march on the right of the road in single file, and the second battalion on the left ready to form the sides of the square. The rest of the regulars would then follow to form the rear, with a company of light infantry to protect them in turn. In case of attack, the troops were to halt immediately and take their allotted positions with each man at least one yard from the next, kneeling on one foot while resting arms. However, they were not to fire until ordered. The cattle and horse would then move into the center.[32] The only uncertainty to Bouquet's scheme was how efficient the two inexperienced provincial battalions would prove in advancing outwards from the road to form their part of the line.

As the various convoys and detachments arrived safely at Fort Pitt, Reid reported on 17 September 1764 that a group of Delaware had intimated a desire for peace and were collecting their prisoners for delivery to Bradstreet at Sandusky. They also wanted to talk to Bouquet. Reid was naturally suspicious that they were attempting to play one army off against the other.[33] Only the previous day news had been received that a messenger had been killed on the road to Sandusky and his head stuck on a pole, signifying death to all intruders.[34] Reid had retaliated by detaining two of the Delaware envoys, one a brother of Hicks, Captain Jonny, and the other the war chief, Captain Pipe.[35]

Twenty-four hours later, Bouquet arrived to join the talks himself. Among the Delaware delegation was Captain Jacob, one of their leading warriors.

However, Bouquet ignored the usual rituals and started his address. First he upbraided the Delaware for playing fast and loose with Bradstreet, pretending that they had recalled all their warriors when they patently had not. Despite this, Bouquet was prepared to give them one more chance "to prevent your total destruction … by giving us satisfaction for the hostilities committed against us." One preliminary requirement was that they give his messengers safe passage to deliver letters to Bradstreet and back. Should the messengers fail to return within twenty days, he would put Captain Pipe and his companion to death. Bouquet was making these proposals to show the Indians that "you have yet a door open to mercy." They should accordingly go directly to their towns and "acquaint your chiefs of what I say." The chiefs should then immediately return to Bouquet with "all their prisoners, if they have not already delivered them to Colonel Bradstreet." They would also be required to give "such other satisfaction for the murders committed by your nations as I shall require."[36]

After this Bouquet put the finishing touches to his expedition. On 22 September he arranged a shooting competition for the Pennsylvanian battalions, offering a reward of £3 to the best shot and £2 to the runner-up.[37] Most heartening was the arrival of a hundred Virginian volunteers under Major Field, with news that another 250 woodsmen were on their way under Lewis's deputy, Lieutenant Colonel John McNeill. These men would be invaluable for the execution of Bouquet's new method of marching. The army was now sufficiently equipped for Bouquet to be confident of handling any situation "without Colonel Bradstreet's assistance." He therefore proposed to march to the Delaware towns, even if they sued for peace, "to convince them that we can penetrate through those woods which they imagine would always screen them."[38]

A Meeting at Muskingum

Just as the army was preparing to cross the Ohio River, two envoys arrived from the Six Nations. They claimed to have been sent by Johnson to resolve the misunderstandings between the British and the Ohio nations, and were sorry to see that Bouquet was still determined on hostilities. He should negotiate instead like Bradstreet. The Ohio peoples were about to surrender all their prisoners at Sandusky, after which they would come and make peace with Bouquet. Alternatively Bouquet could join Bradstreet at Sandusky where everything could be settled.[39]

Bouquet replied that the Six Nations were being duped by the Delaware and Shawnee. Why did the Ohio chiefs not come themselves to speak to Bouquet? Instead they had carried out attacks of every kind, breaking all their promises. Accordingly Bouquet would set off on the road to Sandusky but only as far as the Tuscarawas settlements, where he expected to find that the Delaware were truly inclined to peace. If they still proved obdurate, he would attack their towns. But until he arrived there he would not commit any hostilities, unless attacked.[40] The chance of a negotiated end to the conflict on the Ohio had been considerably increased.

On 2 October, Bouquet issued his orders to the army. Paramount was the need to conserve provisions, otherwise the expedition would fail in "a wilderness that will afford them no relief." For this reason, anyone caught stealing from the stores would be summarily hanged.[41] The army then began to advance with the Virginian volunteers in the front followed by three teams of woodsmen with axes. Their task was to make three parallel paths so that the army could effectively march in a square formation, allowing it to protect its supply train. In an emergency the center column comprising the regulars would form the front and rear of the army while reinforcing the flanks if necessary.[42] This was an improvement on his plan of advance to Fort Pitt, though it was made possible by the less mountainous, more open wooded terrain.

For the next twelve days the army marched through the hilly countryside, constructing bridges and encampments as it proceeded. The troops were constantly watched by Indian scouts, but both sides observed the informal truce as suggested by Bouquet. For the Indians this was largely a matter of necessity, since Bouquet's dispositions prevented the kind of attack that had led to Braddock's defeat. The army accordingly reached the Tuscarawas River on 13 October "unmolested," close to the Delaware settlements.[43]

The situation of the Delaware was now critical. One option was to evacuate the Tuscarawas Valley by canoe. The plan, however, was born of desperation, given that their families would have to leave their crops and possessions just as winter was approaching. But before taking this step, the Ohio nations held another council to consider their situation. According to McCullough, they all acknowledged that "they were scarce of ammunition, and were not able to fight him [Bouquet], that they were then destitute of clothing, and that upon the whole it was best to come on terms of peace with the white people." Least enthusiastic for this course were the Shawnee. Nevertheless, "as the Delaware had left hostages with the commander of the army, the Shawnee acquiesced to come on terms of peace, jointly with the other tribes."[44] A message was accordingly sent to Bouquet intimating a desire to talk. It was signed by several prominent leaders, notably Captain Jacobs, Wingenum, Sunfish, Captain Will, Killbuck, and "Neolan." Their only precondition was an assurance that Captain Pipe and Captain Johnny were alive and well.[45] Bouquet in response assured them that the hostages were safe and suggested a meeting for 16 October 1764.[46] He then had an arbor constructed near the perimeter of his camp where the participants could talk under shelter. He also ordered the army to construct a protective stockade while the negotiations took place.[47]

The first delegation to arrive comprised just four Mingo and two Delaware, but no Shawnee. Also absent were the principal chiefs. Bouquet was understandably irritated. The envoys explained that the delay was because the chiefs had been invited to visit Bradstreet. They added reassuringly, "When you hear our chiefs you will then be convinced that our delay was not through any bad design towards you." Bouquet replied tersely that he was glad to hear this, "as Peace is much better than War." However, he could not wait for the Shawnee. Each nation must answer for itself. He would start with the Delaware the next day.[48]

This had an immediate effect, for twenty-four hours later all three delegations arrived, including a number of principal chiefs, namely, Kiashuta for the Mingo; Custaloga, Tamaqua, and Turtle Heart for the Delaware; and Keissinauch for the Shawnee. Kiashuta spoke first, using the face-saving formula that the Detroit nations and their own "foolish young men" were responsible for the outbreak of hostilities. In consequence, the war was "neither your fault nor ours." Now they had banished every evil thought from their minds and had taken hold of the chain of friendship "which the chiefs of the Delaware, Shawnee and we, who are related to the Six Nations, desire you will likewise do." Moreover, as promised to Bradstreet, they were collecting their prisoners for delivery to either Fort Pitt or Sandusky. Custaloga and Tamaqua then concurred with these sentiments. The exchange ended with Kiashuta producing a copy of the peace granted them by Bradstreet.[49]

Bad weather meant that Bouquet was unable to reply for two days, so that it was not until 20 October that the talks resumed. He first made it clear that he had no time for their excuses about starting the war. The British would have protected them from the designs of the western nations. As to their young men, it was their duty to keep them in order. He was also not convinced about their reason for not appearing sooner, since they had had plenty of time to meet Bradstreet before receiving Bouquet's summons. It was clear they did not intend to deliver up their prisoners. In addition, they had continued their depredations on the frontier long after they had promised Bradstreet that they would cease. However, the British were "a merciful and generous people, averse to the shedding of blood, even of their most cruel enemies." Hence, if the Indians could convince the British of their sincerity, they would be spared. However, the army would not leave until the Delaware and their allies had complied with every condition. They should do so promptly since the Great Lakes nations had made peace while the Six Nations were fighting for the British. The Ohio peoples consequently were surrounded and faced utter destruction. They had twelve days to collect all their prisoners and bring them to Wakatomica, a Shawnee town forty miles away on the Muskingum River, near its junction with the Tuscarawas River.[50]

In a letter to Gage, Bouquet commented on the difficulties of making peace with the Ohio nations. Their representatives had several times been on the point of running away and there was a "total want of government among them" which "renders the execution of my orders very intricate." The danger was that "if they abandon their towns and retire to the mountains, we shall miss our object, which is a safe and honorable Peace." The refugees would in addition "prejudice all the Indians unacquainted with us." A number of recently released prisoners "say that all the chiefs and most considerable warriors of the Delaware have constantly been against the war, and have taken no share in it," while "most of the traders were killed by the Wyandot, Ottawa, and other western Indians who compelled these nations here to join with them." It was difficult to know what or whom to believe and how to proceed, since there was much special pleading and denial of blame.[51] It was for this reason that Bouquet shortly afterwards declared that all the prisoners must be surrendered before peace terms could be discussed.[52]

Coincidentally, that same day Gage was writing his thoughts to Bouquet. He suggested that if the Shawnee and Delaware were sincere in their desire for peace and had recalled their war parties from the frontiers, "you will in that case relax your demands upon them for satisfaction, and get as good terms as you can, keeping up the authority you have always done, which is proper upon such occasions with the Indians." But the ringleaders must still go to Johnson for ratification of the terms.[53]

On 22 October the army set out once more, this time for the mouth of the Muskingum River, where it had been agreed that the Delaware, Shawnee, and Mingo would meet Bouquet with their prisoners. The army advanced in the same methodical manner as before, ready for action while protecting the packhorses and cattle. The troops arrived on 25 October and immediately formed another entrenched camp.[54] The deadline for the arrival of the Indian delegates and their prisoners was 1 November 1764. As the date approached, the Shawnee expressed concern that the British had not shaken hands with them. Bouquet replied that they would only do so once a final peace was concluded, since the British only "took their friends by the hands." Hence, they should send in their prisoners without delay.[55] Four days later Big Wolf, one of the Shawnee chiefs, brought in eight prisoners, for which Bouquet commended him.[56] The following day it was the turn of Custaloga's Delaware, who handed over thirty-two prisoners, while Kiashuta surrendered three on behalf of the Mingo.[57]

It was during these preliminaries that Bouquet received information of Bradstreet's retreat to Niagara. The news caused him little concern, though he was pleased that it was brought by twenty Canadian Caghnawaga under their chief, Peter. These were the only warriors to offer their services, for as Bradstreet confirmed, "Not a man of the Five Nations will act."[58]

Despite this promising start, the deadline for the delivery of the remaining prisoners soon passed. The Delaware and Mingo had given up most of their captives, but the Shawnee had still to make a significant delivery. Accordingly, when the Indians indicated on 4 November 1764 that they were ready to resume talks, Bouquet replied that "he would not admit them to speak until they had delivered the remainder of the prisoners."[59] This produced on the next day eight more captives from Tamaqua and three from Custaloga.[60] A sufficient number had now been surrendered for Bouquet to send them under escort to Fort Pitt. Great care was to be taken to prevent any from escaping back to their adopted families. William Smith, who shortly wrote an account of the expedition, noted the mixed reaction of the prisoners when reunited with their relatives, many of whom had enlisted in the army in the hopes of such a reunion. Some adults were pleased to be returning to white society. But others were distressed, especially the younger ones who had lived with the natives for much of their lives, like John McCullough. Many of these tried to escape, some successfully. Smith could only assume that their conduct was the result of their being "persons ... of the lowest rank." But he was touched by the obvious distress of their Indian foster parents and siblings, who brought corn to their loved ones and even followed them to Fort Pitt in support.[61]

Meanwhile, the negotiations had faltered with the discovery of a dead soldier in the woods. Bouquet immediately sent Kiashuta a message saying that he would hold the Delaware responsible since the killing had taken place on their territory.[62] Even at this stage, Bouquet had become impressed with Kiashuta's apparent business-like approach to the negotiations. But the key to the success of the talks seemed to lie with the Shawnee, who had yet to bring in their prisoners. Fortunately, on 8 November a message arrived from Red Hawk, their principal warrior, explaining that they would have appeared sooner, had they not heard "evil reports that you had some bad designs against us."[63] Suspicion was still rife among the Indians, and with good reason in view of the atrocities perpetrated by the Paxton boys.

Since the Delaware and Mingo had surrendered most of their captives, Bouquet now agreed to discuss terms. The first meeting on 9 November 1764 was with Custaloga, representing the Delaware Wolf phratry, and Kiashuta for the Mingo. Kiashuta began the proceedings by apologizing for the murder of the British soldier, which he hoped would not hinder the friendship already begun. He then handed over three prisoners, the last held by either the Mingo or Custaloga. He ended his oration by expressing the hope that the path between their peoples was once more open.[64] Bouquet replied initially by demanding the surrender of the soldier's murderers, but moved quickly to express support for Kiashuta's hopes that the bones of the fallen should be covered, indicating his desire to end hostilities. Bouquet then spelt out his conditions for a peace. First, hostages had to be given for the fulfillment of the terms, two from the Mingo and two from Custaloga. Deputies must also be sent to Johnson with full powers to make peace. But this would only be granted if all violence had ceased against the king's subjects. At that meeting, Johnson would settle everything regarding trade and anything else necessary to restore normal relations. Finally, Bouquet announced that Captain Pipe and Captain Johnny would be released. He then shook hands with the chiefs "which occasioned much joy."[65]

On 10 November 1764, the other two Delaware phratries made their submissions. Present was Tamaqua on behalf of the Turkey phratry, while the Turtle phratry were represented by the brother of Netawatwees. Also in attendance were Custaloga and Kiashuta. Tamaqua began by surrendering another thirteen prisoners. Next he gave thanks for the return of peace, promising that "our young men shall now think of nothing but hunting, to exchange their skins and furs with their brethren for clothing." He also agreed to return any prisoners who escaped to their Indian families. Bouquet replied with the same speech which he had given to Kiashuta and Custaloga the previous day, adding as a conciliatory gesture his belief that a Pennsylvania soldier who had previously scalped some Indians should be handed over for justice.[66]

The Turtle and Turkey phratries needed little time for deliberation. Within twenty-four hours, they had named their six hostages and five deputies to visit Johnson, the latter led by Killbuck, one of their younger chiefs. Bouquet pronounced himself satisfied with both sets of men. But he announced that he was deposing Netawatwees as chief of the Turtle phratry because of his absence from the conference.[67] In reality it was an empty gesture, since Bouquet could not ensure compliance once he left Muskingum. Indeed, Netawatwees met Croghan at Fort Pitt in May 1765 as though nothing had happened.[68]

Finally, it was the turn of the Shawnee to make their peace. This took place on 12 November. Red Hawk acted as their principal speaker, seemingly having more authority as a warrior chief than Keissinauch. He appealed to Bouquet to set aside all bad thoughts, as the Shawnee were doing on their side. As proof of their sincerity, he now delivered thirty-six captives, promising that the remainder would be given up in the spring. He then adopted Kiashuta's argument that the Ottawa were the cause of the war and that they should take the blame. Lastly, he produced a number of letters and treaties that had been made between the Shawnee and English from 1701 to 1742 to support his claim that they had always abided by their promises.[69]

Bouquet delayed his reply until 14 November 1764 to allow inspection of the documents. However, at a private meeting he roundly condemned the Shawnee for not living up to the preliminary terms agreed by Keissinauch. There could be no peace until all the prisoners were surrendered, hostages given, and hostilities ended.[70] He repeated his tirade the following morning when he included a new condition: all French inhabitants living with the Shawnee must also be given up.[71]

Bouquet was right to be suspicious, for even at this stage some Shawnee were hoping for aid from Onontio. That August they had sent another delegation to Fort Chartres, though their reception on 17 August 1764 had been no more welcoming than that given earlier to Pontiac. St. Ange told his visitors that he could not assist them "in view of the circumstances and their disposition to continue the war."[72] But while St. Ange held firmly to official French policy, the case was far otherwise with the local merchants, who were anxious to trade. In consequence, "The French [inhabitants] had treated" the Shawnee "with the utmost civility, gave them large presents and sent several traders after them to their nation for supplying their wants."[73] A military response to Bouquet might yet be possible.

Fortunately for the cause of peace, the Shawnee delegation, on reaching the Wabash River, heard about the treaty being negotiated at Muskingum. A council was quickly called, where it was unanimously agreed to accept what was being negotiated with the British. This was despite word from the Detroit Ottawa and Potawatomi that their peace with the British "was from their lips, not their hearts, and that they would not stand by it."[74] The Shawnee militants may have been discouraged by the widespread outbreak of smallpox. According to a subsequent report, their nation had lost almost 150 men and a similar number of women and children.[75] The French traders were accordingly sent back.

Bouquet's tirade on 13 November also seemingly had a beneficial effect, though the negotiations were helped in part by the emergence of a new spokesman, Benevissica. He immediately indicated full compliance with the conditions and proceeded to name six chiefs as hostages, among them Red Hawk. He also agreed to gather together all the remaining captives, though he refused to be responsible for the French inhabitants since they were not of his nation. This pacified Bouquet sufficiently to reinstate the Shawnee in the peace process. However, to ensure compliance he announced that Benevissica would be accompanied to the Shawnee towns by some of the prisoners' relatives. Bouquet finished his address by asking the Shawnee to name their deputies to go to Sir William Johnson. After this Peter, the chief of the Canadian Caghnawaga, Tamaqua, and Kiashuta made speeches urging the Shawnee to comply.[76]

In his report to Gage, Bouquet acknowledged that he had been compelled to cede some ground, notably on securing the authors of the war. However, to have attempted to seize the ringleaders would merely have scattered the Ohio Indians and led to a continuation of the frontier conflict. This could be in no one's interest. But there was still much to be done if the peace was to hold. Firstly, the Mingo ought to be repatriated to their Six Nations homeland, being "the most corrupted of all the Indians." Secondly, the traders should be barred from the Indian towns to prevent the kind of cheating which had caused such anger. In addition, Fort Massiac and Fort Chartres must be occupied if the French were to be prevented from causing trouble.[77]

Before leaving the Muskingum River on 18 November 1764, Bouquet gave instructions regarding the Indian hostages. They were to be well fed and given a dram of liquor each morning. Half were to be allowed to hunt, while the other half remained in confinement. However, the officers were not to become "too familiar with them as they are apt to become troublesome and insolent."[78] Bouquet with the main part of the army then set off for Fort Pitt, which they reached on 28 November 1764. Here orders were issued for a suspension of hostilities. However, trade with the Ohio nations remained prohibited until a definitive peace had been made with Johnson.[79] Meanwhile, the majority of the troops prepared to depart for Carlisle and the inhabited areas. The Royal American regiment was the first to march, followed shortly afterwards by the two Pennsylvania battalions, leaving the 42nd regiment to garrison Fort Pitt and the posts on the communication.[80] Most inhabitants by this time had returned to their farms and habitations, in anticipation of a durable peace.[81]

As Bouquet had predicted, problems remained, not least with the hostages. Two of the Shawnee detainees fell sick and had to be sent home, while another was required for a peace mission to the Wabash nations. The remaining three, including Red Hawk, then took flight, "believing the English had bad intentions towards them."[82] The reason subsequently proved to be a scalping by some Maryland volunteers who were hoping to claim the Pennsylvania bounty in gross violation of the recent treaty.[83] As a result, Bouquet had no Shawnee hostages left at Pittsburgh, though Benevissica asserted that he and his colleagues would fulfill their engagements.[84] The Mingo also gave cause for concern since their four hostages promptly absconded with eight of the army's best horses. Bouquet could only hope that their conduct would improve when Kiashuta returned from Sandusky, where he had gone to recover some prisoners. Finally, as Bouquet commented to Gage, there was the continuing problem of how to secure the Illinois country. "The dignity of the nation" was at stake if its possession was deferred any longer.[85]

William Smith, in his account of the campaign, was highly complimentary of Bouquet's generalship. Only one man had been killed at Tuscarawas. The expedition had also been well provisioned, no mean feat in the wilderness.[86] Gage was similarly pleased. "The peace you have made does great honor to yourself and must give the greatest satisfaction to the King. Nothing but the steps you have taken of marching into their country and prescribing your own terms with that firmness and resolution ... would ever have brought those savages to a serious peace. You have by an admirable conduct reduced and humbled them as they deserved, and thereby made a peace upon a solid foundation." Of course, the nations of the Wabash and Illinois peoples still had to be brought to terms, as had Pontiac. But Gage was hopeful that the peace lately made by Bouquet and the dispatch of further belts and messages might bring the remaining enemy into terms.[87] Certainly, he had no hesitation in telling the secretary of state "that the country is restored to its former tranquility." Only the possession of the Illinois remained to be accomplished.[88]

It had been an impressive demonstration of military power, the result of careful planning, which owed much to Bouquet's experience of campaigning in the region. He demonstrated the ability of a regular army to penetrate the woods and stay there without giving its Indian inhabitants an opportunity to surprise him. Moreover, he had demonstrated to the Indians the vulnerability of their habitations and families. Many like Johnson, Croghan, and Gladwin believed that such an advance was impossible, arguing that the Indians would always flee into the interior. Bouquet had proved this was not necessarily the case, though he acknowledged in a subsequent paper that the army must pay more attention to Indian methods of warfare if it was to be effective in North America.[89] But he never forgot that war was only a way of implementing policy. Hence, early in the campaign he kept in mind the possibility of a negotiated peace, recognizing that the British army could never gain control of so extensive a country without an accommodation with its inhabitants. By avoiding a draconian peace, he had done much to prepare the way for a restoration of the "middle ground," if such was to be.

The Ohio peoples, too, had reason to feel a sense of achievement. They had not been defeated in the field, and although families had been broken up by the return of the captives, no blood had been shed and no execution of the "ringleaders" had taken place, as the British had originally demanded. The amnesty even covered the eastern Delaware leaders, Squash Cutter and Long Coat, when they accompanied Killbuck in early May 1765 to ratify the undertakings made at Niagara. Once the articles had been finalized, Johnson took both men "by the hand," signifying that they, like the western Delaware, had been pardoned and readmitted to the "Covenant Chain of Friendship."[90] Most remarkable was the release of Captain Bull after the remaining prisoners had been collected.[91]

Inevitably some concessions had had to be made. The western Delaware had to allow the king's troops passage through their territories, disputes involving whites were to be settled in British courts, while compensation in the form of land was to be paid to those traders who had been robbed during the conflict. In addition, the Delaware were required to accept any future boundary line between the Six Nations and the Crown, leaving them vulnerable to the territorial whims of the former.[92] Indicative of this was the Six Nations' invitation to the western Delaware to return to their habitations at Kittanning, clearly a way of controlling them.[93] For all their bravery, the Delaware had yet to break free of domination by the Six Nations.

The signing of a final peace with the Shawnee and Mingo took somewhat longer to complete, following the flight of Red Hawk. Their envoys only assembled at Johnson Hall in mid-July 1765. The Shawnee were represented by Benevissica, and the Mingo by Kiashuta. In attendance were envoys from the eastern and western Delaware led by Turtle Heart. The Delaware were present because Croghan had told them in a meeting at Fort Pitt that their previous delegation to Johnson Hall had been inadequate.[94] First, Johnson explained the terms of the treaty he had settled with Killbuck. Turtle Heart then confirmed the Delaware acceptance of that agreement and their readiness to pay "due submission and subjection," though only so far as it was "consistent with the Indians' native rights." Next, the Shawnee agreed to an almost identical treaty as that of Delaware. They also accepted the term "children of the Great

King" rather than "brethren of the English." However, like the Delaware, they added the caveat "so far as the same" was "consistent with their native rights." Finally, the Mingo accepted a similar agreement, adding that they would withdraw "from their present places of residence and return to the respective nations to which they belong."[95] Clearly the Delaware, Shawnee, and Mingo had made no abject capitulation, for as children they expected to be protected by their father. Johnson said nothing.

Although peace had been established on the Ohio and Great Lakes, the Wabash nations remained in arms, as did Pontiac and the Illinois peoples. Even nominal British authority over these territories still had to be established. The question was, how could this be done?

11

Pontiac and the Struggle for the Illinois

The Mississippi: Invasion Route or Pathway to Peace?

Despite the treaties with the Delaware, Shawnee, and Mingo, much remained to be done if peace really was to be established between the British and native peoples of eastern North America. Three regional groups still opposed British control of lands supposedly surrendered by France in the Treaty of Paris. The first were the peoples of the Illinois, notably the Peoria, Kaskaskia, and Cahokia. The second were the Wabash Miami, Kickapoo, Mascouten, Wea, and Piankashaw. The third were a mixed group, comprising the St. Joseph Potawatomi, Pontiac's Ottawa, and the Ojibwa of the Grand Saulteur. All three groups believed that France might yet come to their aid and that a successful defense of their lands was possible, thereby ensuring the continuation of the "middle ground."

The British, of course, refused any such outcome that did not recognize their sovereignty. They believed that the failure to occupy territories nominally ceded by the French would be seen as a cause of national failure. Furthermore, the possession of these territories would give the British greater access to the fur trade with distant nations like the Sioux. Finally, possession would make it easier to prevent the French from inciting the Indians, as many believed had been the case.

Amherst had originally planned to occupy the Illinois with four hundred regulars from Fort Pitt in the summer of 1763. The outbreak of war along the Ohio made this impractical. Nevertheless, the need for action prompted Gage early in 1764 to order the commanding officer at Mobile, Major Robert Farmar, to send troops to the Illinois via the Mississippi. An expedition under Major Arthur Loftus accordingly set out on 27 February 1764, comprising 320 soldiers. The first part of the journey was without incident. However, about two hundred miles from New Orleans, Loftus was attacked by a party of Tunica and Choctaw Indians, who killed six of his men and wounded another seven, forcing him to return to New Orleans.[1] The Tunica justified the attack to their French allies by asserting that the British always brought smallpox with them. Once allowed "to settle on the river they would build forts." After this, they would kill the French and poison the Indians.[2]

Loftus initially blamed the French for his setback but was told firmly by D'Abbadie that his preparations had been inadequate. Loftus should have negotiated his way up the river, in which task the French would have gladly assisted.[3] Gage wisely acknowledged the need to follow "the French method of paying tribute to the tribes," since Loftus did not have sufficient troops "to force his passage."[4] A watershed had been reached in the British conduct of the war. Force was being laid aside in favor of the spoken word.

Farmar accordingly ordered one of his junior officers, Lieutenant Philip Pitman, to try diplomacy prior to another attempt at dispatching troops.[5] D'Abbadie agreed to help, assuring Farmar that he would "spare no means to assist this officer to ascend the Illinois in the most prompt and safe manner possible."[6] With this in mind, he invited Pitman to a conference in New Orleans with the Choctaw and Tunica at which the latter agreed to let the British pass, provided they received some presents.[7] Unfortunately, Pitman divulged the information that Louisiana would soon become a Spanish province.[8] This not only angered D'Abbadie, who was fearful of prematurely upsetting the Indians, but also alienated the boatmen who refused to give him a passage. Although D'Abbadie assured Gage that the French were doing all they could to facilitate British possession of the Illinois, the Pitman mission for the moment was doomed.[9]

D'Abbadie was sincere in not wanting to offend the British, since he was responsible for implementing the Treaty of Paris on behalf of the French Crown. For this reason he warned his officers to be careful when dispensing ammunition to the Indians. He had already commended de Villiers for telling Pontiac about "the impossibility of furnishing him with supplies."[10] But as D'Abbadie told the French minister of marine in September 1764, "It is not possible for us to do away entirely with powder and ball as gifts to the savages." The reason was that the Indians "no longer make their living except by hunting with the gun and contribute by that means to our own subsistence and to the commerce of the colony."[11] He had therefore allowed the merchants to send their convoys as usual up the Mississippi, but had repeated his ban on the sale of ammunition by the traders. Unfortunately the French merchants ignored such directives, as did the British, which Gage subsequently acknowledged to be the case.[12]

In the meantime Indian hostility to the British in the Illinois remained as strong as ever, as St. Ange (now in command) confirmed in October 1764: "All the Lake and most distant nations have sent to tell me the same thing," which was that they wanted "to see their Father back ... and to be assured that the English will never come here."[13] Nor had the situation improved the following month, when St. Ange reported that fifty Indians were present every day who "I must nourish since they know no other post where they have a Father from whom they believe they should draw all their necessities." He concluded, "If the English do not take possession of this country in a short time, I shall be overpowered this spring by all the partisans of Pontiac whose number is increasing every day."[14]

The situation of the French officials was certainly invidious. St. Ange had barely forty men at Fort Chartres for policing a territory of several hundred square miles. He was also constrained by the knowledge that the province would soon be handed over to the Spanish.[15] At the same time the influence of Pontiac seemed almost universal. He told the senior military officer, Charles Aubry, "All the savages who ordinarily draw their assistance from here and from the neighboring posts have accepted the invitations which have been made them by Pontiac and his people" to join the war, following the debacle with Captain Morris. Their appeal for support included "all the most distant nations," in which endeavor "I feel that they will succeed very perfectly."[16] Those who refused were threatened with Pontiac's "hatred and that of all his people."[17]

Pontiac's diplomacy was especially effective along the Mississippi, where the Arkansas Indians "searched all the French convoys for Englishmen," putting "to death a deserter of the 22nd Regiment who they discovered amongst them."[18] Nor did the situation improve at the start of 1765. Aubry, now acting governor on the death of D'Abbadie, reported that the Quapaw, a tribe midway between the Illinois and New Orleans, had "received belts from Pontiac to strike the English when they ascend the river." Aubry had immediately dispatched an officer with presents to win them over but was not optimistic about winning the nations to the north, who were "too distant to have any influence over them."[19] His only hope was that the arrival of the Spanish would "cause a revolution favorable to the English." The Indians knew full well the cruelty of the Spanish, especially their methods of conversion, with a sword in one hand and crucifix in the other.[20] But until that happened, the situation was likely to remain tense, since all the northern nations "were extremely incensed with the English." Reports indicated that "fifteen hundred men of the different tribes" were going to assemble at Fort Chartres "in the early springtime," under Pontiac's command, to prevent the British from taking "possession of that post." If that happened, Pontiac would be "celebrated for ever in the annals of North America."[21]

Nevertheless, Gage had little option but to persevere with his new diplomatic approach, since another campaign would not be possible without provincial support, and that was unlikely following the imposition of the Sugar Act by Parliament. The colonies believed they were already making a sufficient contribution to the Imperial treasury without having to pay any further tax. Farmar accordingly ordered Lieutenant John Ross of the 34th regiment, in company with the trader Crawford, to proceed up the Mississippi, where he was "to assemble the different tribes of Indians with proper instructions to gain them over by every possible art and invention."[22] The two men left Mobile on 2 December 1764, accompanied by Lieutenant Charles Stuart, the southern superintendent's nephew. Their appearance in New Orleans coincided with the arrival of some Choctaw chiefs, the most populous nation on the lower eastern Mississippi. D'Abbadie, to show support, invited the British officers to hear his address to the Choctaw in which he stressed "the desirability of peace and union between the Red man and White man."[23] D'Abbadie also offered Ross and Crawford an interpreter to negotiate their way up the Mississippi.[24] The party, however, were delayed for want of money.[25] Ross in consequence returned to Mobile to try a different route to the Illinois, traveling by canoe along the Choctaw, Chickasaw, and Cherokee Rivers.[26] This proved more successful, and he and Crawford reached Fort Chartres on 18 February 1765 without mishap. However, several chiefs immediately went to St. Ange and declared that the British must leave. One Ojibwa chief insolently handed Ross the pipe of peace before snatching it back.[27]

Nevertheless, Ross determined to continue his mission, despite reports that Pontiac would be arriving in a few weeks' time with three thousand men to oppose the British on the Mississippi. Ross was comforted by the thought that since Pontiac was the "great instigator of the savage nations," the rest "might otherwise be easily brought to terms." Consequently, if Ross could appease Pontiac, an agreement might be possible.[28] But St. Ange was not optimistic. He told D'Abbadie, "All the Indians seem resolved on clinging to their resolutions," and none more so than the Illinois, following Pontiac's interference the previous April, when he and "Minawouanon" had destroyed "all that we could do with the Illinois."[29] Nevertheless, St. Ange agreed to invite the various nations to a conference with Ross.

Since the Indians were still on their winter hunt, it was not until the beginning of April that St. Ange assembled the Illinois, Osage, and Missouri peoples at Fort Chartres.[30] First he reminded his audience that their "father," the king of France, wanted them to lay down their arms and receive the British. He then appealed to his audience to think of their wives and children. All to no avail. Tamaroa, the chief of the Kaskaskia Illinois, repeated what he had earlier told D'Abbadie. His nation would "not have the English upon their land." Although the Illinois remained "attached to the French," they could not obey St. Ange on this occasion, since they "must continue the war along with their other brethren." Ross should therefore depart and tell his people to stay in their own country. The Osage and Missouri then expressed similar sentiments: the French were their only fathers, and everyone should remain on their own lands.[31] What made the situation especially threatening was that St. Ange had received information that Minawouanon was on his way down the Illinois River with four hundred warriors to join Pontiac.[32] Among their number were some Potawatomi who intended to seize Ross in retaliation for the detention of two of their men at Detroit. Clearly St. Ange would no longer be able to protect the British officer on their arrival and pleaded with him to leave.[33] Ross finally accepted the wisdom of this advice, having already been threatened by several warriors with tomahawks. He and Crawford accordingly set out for New Orleans, their mission a failure.[34]

Pontiac himself had spent the winter of 1764, as in 1763, on the Maumee River.[35] However, when it became clear that the British were once more trying to ascend the Mississippi, he set off again to aid the Illinois peoples in their struggle for freedom. He was still hopeful of French help. The previous fall St. Ange had sent him a suit of clothes, a hat, and some vermilion, "desiring him to remain quiet till ordered to do otherwise." Now he was determined to visit the French commander "to know if he should make war or peace, which determination the Miami [Twightwee] waited for."[36] However, it was not just the Miami who wanted directions. Pontiac had also circulated war belts to the St. Joseph Potawatomi, Mascouten, Kickapoo, Illinois, and Winnebago from La Baye. His plan in 1765, after repulsing the British on the Mississippi, was to assemble these nations in June for an attack on Detroit, where they were to be "joined by several nations from the northward," meaning the Ojibwa of the Grand Saulteur. The scheme was to be undertaken "entirely by the Indians without the least assistance from the French."[37] Pontiac had learned his lesson about relying on the French inhabitants. The Indians would have to fight their own battles, though they still needed French supplies.

The determination of the northern Ojibwa to continue fighting was confirmed by Marsac, a Canadian interpreter, who asserted that the "great chief of the Chippewa intended to strike somewhere as soon as the Strawberries are ripe." He believed that "all the Indians along the Mississippi, Wabash and Maumee were assembled this spring" and determined "to divide into two parties, one to go to Pittsburgh and the other against Detroit."[38] However, the target for the Grand Saulteur and his Ojibwa, as Croghan subsequently learned, was Michilimackinac rather than Detroit. The St. Joseph Potawatomi and "a chief of the Chippewa from Michilimackinac, called the Grand Sota," were to attack Howard's garrison, once they had finished their business with Pontiac in the Illinois.[39]

Meanwhile, Pontiac's forces on the Maumee River remained ready to repel any British advance from Lake Erie, as a detachment from Detroit discovered. Its leader, Jadot, had gone to arrest some French renegades who were suspected of supplying the Wabash Indians with ammunition.[40] Half a mile from the Miami village, Jadot was ambushed, disarmed, and taken to Fort Miami, just like Morris the year before. Here he was questioned by three Ottawa chiefs and then by the Miami. In the course of his interrogation, he was told that the British had given up Montreal to the French and retreated to Quebec, where they were under siege. Elsewhere the Dutch and Spanish had declared war, compelling the British to surrender their lands east of the Mississippi. As to the recently concluded treaties with Johnson at Niagara, the shaking of hands was a ruse to obtain rum, since the issue of war and peace was a matter for the French king. If their father sent a message to open the road, they would do it: equally, if he ordered them to close it, they would do that too. Finally they told Jadot that de Villiers had been recalled in disgrace for negotiating with the British. His Cross of St. Louis had been taken from him, and he had been hanged. Jadot should take note.[41]

Diplomatic Endeavors: The Fraser and Sinnott Missions

Although the Mississippi seemingly remained the best avenue to the Illinois, peace with the Delaware and Shawnee meant that the British could now approach via the Ohio River. Johnson was one person of this opinion. He argued that the easiest way of making peace with Pontiac and the Miami would be by enlisting the help of the Delaware and Shawnee. The latter had links with the remaining combatants and were obligated by their recent peace agreement to help the British. An appropriate garrison might then follow from Fort Pitt. The best man to carry out this mission, Johnson believed, would be George Croghan.[42]

Gage quickly accepted this proposal. The dispatch of envoys via the Ohio might allow contact with those nations that had hitherto been inaccessible to the offers of peace. This would then permit the British "to enter into alliance with them and ask their consent to take possession of their country." The British failure to do this in 1764 explained why the Indians were now showing "so much umbrage." Nevertheless, this was an extraordinary statement by Gage. The principal representative of the British Empire in North America was pleading with the native inhabitants for permission to occupy their country! It was not how imperial nations supposedly acted. However, it seemed the only way, since force was not an option. As Gage commented to Bouquet, "You have seen what the provinces will do, or rather what they will not do, when the enemy is at their doors. What can be expected of them, do you think, to carry on such operations at such a distance?" The only hope realistically was the use of diplomacy. "From the accounts we have hitherto had from the Illinois, it seems that Pontiac with the Shawnee and Delaware, could put us in possession of that country, whenever they pleased."[43] They were the key. Diplomacy, not force, was more essential than ever to the achieving of British policy.

With this in mind Gage ordered Bouquet to select a suitable officer to accompany Croghan, both for his protection and to check his extravagance. The appointee was to be intelligent and speak good French. Rank was not important: indeed, the nominee might be a volunteer.[44] In the event, Lieutenant Alexander Fraser of the 78th Highland regiment volunteered for the service. Gage immediately accepted, believing "no one so well qualified."[45] The mission of Fraser and Croghan had three parts. The first was to carry dispatches to St. Ange, informing him of the mission and requesting his assistance in securing the Illinois. The second was to deliver a manifesto to the French inhabitants promising protection for their Catholic faith, freedom to emigrate with their possessions, and the rights and privileges of the king's existing subjects if they remained.[46] The third was to tell the Indians about the recent peace agreements and their acceptance as a precondition for a reopening of the trade. The envoys were also to emphasize that no retribution would be sought for acts committed during the war. All would be forgiven.[47]

To ensure the success of the mission, Croghan was to send peace belts informing the remaining combatants of the recent agreements with the Shawnee and Delaware. However, to ensure that the benign intentions of the British were known, an additional belt was to be sent to Pontiac with a message from Gage inviting him to Detroit. The British had made peace with every other Indian nation and would have "none our enemy." But the belt was also to show Pontiac that his good treatment of Morris had been recognized and that "all that is past shall be forgot." In return it was hoped that he would demonstrate "the sincerity of his friendship by some singular marks of service."[48] In other words, would he assist the British in the occupation of the Illinois?

Croghan and Fraser departed from Philadelphia in mid-February 1765, after purchasing a large stock of Indian presents.[49] They arrived at Fort Pitt on 28 February 1765.[50] Here Croghan invited the Delaware and Shawnee to nominate their accompanying envoys, dispatching at the same time a belt to Pontiac on the Maumee River.[51] The invitations necessarily required time to execute. But the mission was also delayed by an attack on the convoy carrying the presents at Sidling Hill, between Bedford and Fort Ligonier. The backcountry inhabitants of Pennsylvania were incensed that the murderers and abductors of their families were receiving gifts while they had to fend for themselves.[52] But as the days passed, the suspicion grew that Croghan was dallying at Fort Pitt to facilitate his trading interests, though he vehemently denied this. The success of his mission depended on his being accompanied by some Delaware and Shawnee envoys.[53]

Fraser, meanwhile, was anxious to begin his task. After two weeks and no sign of either the Indian envoys or presents, he requested permission to set off alone, since his instructions required him to be in the Illinois by early April.[54] Croghan reluctantly agreed, since he believed that the Delaware and Shawnee envoys would be at Fort Pitt before the end of March. To facilitate Fraser's passage, Croghan gave him some wampum and other necessaries. He also engaged Maisonville as an interpreter, in company with several Seneca, Wyandot, and Shawnee, all in a bateau manned by nine soldiers.[55]

The journey down the Ohio, starting on 22 March, was uneventful. Fraser and his colleagues met several small parties of Indians, to whom he explained his mission and gave some tobacco as a gesture of goodwill. However, on reaching the first French settlement on the Mississippi, Fraser was informed about Ross's recent departure and his narrow escape from being burnt at the stake by Pontiac. Fraser affected to think these stories were designed to detain him while they stirred up the Indians. He accordingly hired a small horse-drawn cart and set off on 17 April for Fort Chartres with just one guide. He successfully navigated Kaskaskia without being spoken to until three Indians caught up with him, demanding to know who he was. Fraser told them about the peace with the Ohio Indians and his wish to address their chiefs at Fort Chartres. He was then allowed to continue unimpeded. However, two of his men were detained by the Illinois while going back to Kaskaskia for his papers.[56]

On arrival at Fort Chartres, Fraser delivered Gage's letter to St. Ange explaining the purpose of his mission. St. Ange immediately confirmed what the inhabitants had told him concerning the danger he was in. The two men then had a frank exchange about the activities of the French traders. Despite this, St. Ange invited Fraser to dinner, in company with the local padre. While eating Pontiac burst in with eight of his men, dragging Fraser from the room. St. Ange eventually managed to calm the fracas, though only after telling Pontiac that he would have to kill him first. Eventually a compromise was reached: Fraser could address the Illinois Indians before being handed over to Pontiac. St. Ange's intention was that this would give Fraser time to escape, but the British officer refused to abandon his mission.[57]

Accordingly the next day, 18 April 1765, Fraser informed the Illinois of the peace between the British, Ohio, Six Nations, and Great Lakes peoples. He stressed that the British had never done the Illinois any harm and expressed surprise that they should have seized two of his men. Fraser then met a somewhat calmer Pontiac, assuring him that "the English now looked on him as their brother," which would be confirmed shortly by Croghan, whom he had previously met. Fraser reiterated that the Delaware and Shawnee had made peace. In reply Pontiac asserted that he knew nothing of this, since some recent Shawnee visitors had not spoken about the matter. However, he would hear what Fraser had to say at a council of all the nations then present at Fort Chartres.[58] One problem for Pontiac was that he might have difficulty convincing his allies of the desirability of peace, especially the northern Ojibwa when they arrived. Nevertheless he himself was seemingly more favorable to the idea, given the attitude of St. Ange, for without French support the Indians would have no access to arms and ammunition.

Five hundred Indians consequently gathered that afternoon, comprising the Illinois, Missouri, Pontiac's Ottawa, and some neighboring nations. First St. Ange spoke on a large belt, assuring his audience that peace had been settled between the warring European powers and that he was authorized to speak by the king of France. The Indians accordingly should lay down their weapons and live like brothers with the British, who had sent Fraser "to speak to you about it." If they did not listen, their wives and children would suffer, for peace was the only thing that could rescue them from their current wretchedness, which was caused by the want of trade. He then rebuked the Illinois for detaining Fraser's men in breach of their promise to remain calm after Ross's departure.[59]

The Illinois replied that the two soldiers were safe. They had only seized them on the orders of their elder brothers, the Ottawa. The Ottawa were the people who had made war on the British, and they must decide the issue of war or peace. The Illinois were clearly anxious to exculpate themselves from any blame concerning the soldiers.[60]

The mention of responsibility for the war prompted Pontiac to speak. He accepted St. Ange's peace belt, since "his father" advised him to do so. He also accepted Fraser's assurances that the Delaware, Shawnee, and Iroquois had made peace. But though he had been a principal in the war, he had not begun it. On the contrary he had received the war belt from those nations whom Fraser now said were at peace, meaning the Seneca, Delaware, and Shawnee. In future, the British should be more sincere. But he welcomed the impending visit by Croghan, "as he could not think he would be imprudent enough to come to tell them lies now, as they had detected him before in so many." It was accordingly agreed that the various chiefs should meet Croghan at Ouiatanon, being "the most central place" in the region. Here a formal peace could be settled. The conference ended with Fraser treating the assembly to 130 pots of brandy and a bullock.[61]

Four days later the chiefs set off with Maisonville for Ouiatanon, leaving St. Ange hopeful that he had finally ensured his primary aim, the safety of the French inhabitants. He told Fraser that most inhabitants were not *coureurs de bois* like St. Vincent and Joncaire, who had lived for years with the Indians as "true Republicans," beyond the rule of the law. Certainly these men had never been authorized to act for the French king and should be punished, though the British would have to do this, since St. Joseph, Miami, and Ouiatanon lay within the jurisdiction of Canada. But the rest of the inhabitants were blameless of stirring up the Indians. They were simple farmers whose only wish was to grow their crops and live in tranquility.[62]

Unfortunately, for St. Ange much remained to be resolved. Pontiac had not accompanied Maisonville to Ouiatanon, since he was still expecting an answer to a letter which he had sent to the king of France, "desiring to know" for certainty "whether he had made peace with the English." He had entrusted his letter with de Villiers on the latter's departure for New Orleans. Clearly Pontiac had yet to make a final determination about war and peace. One reason was a recent report that some Shawnee envoys had disappeared en route to Fort Pitt, raising fears that they had been taken prisoner or killed. Could Pontiac trust the British in view of all that had happened previously? In the meantime, waiting for clarification was naturally frustrating. Fraser noted in his account to Gage that "Pontiac and his ruffians are most always drunk. He himself is too sensible to abuse me but his followers who are a set of idle abandoned rascals, strike me and threaten at times to scalp me or burn me." They did this thinking that they had the approval of the French. They also taunted Fraser with the information that the "chiefs of the Sautou [Saulteur] nation with a great many of their warriors" were coming to Fort Chartres and were "determined to prosecute the war against the English."[63]

Next day, 28 April 1765, the threat turned into reality with the arrival of several hundred Saulteurs, Potawatomie, Kickapoo, and Mascouten. They had come in response to Pontiac's war belts the previous fall following the abortive mission of Captain Morris. As the Grand Saulteur subsequently explained to Croghan, he had favored peace in the fall of 1764 "but was then sent for to the Illinois" to help keep "the English out of possession of that country." The new arrivals first called on St. Ange to exchange greetings. This gave him and Pontiac an opportunity of informing them of the new situation and the reason for Fraser's presence. The chiefs responded that the British officers treated them like animals rather than as men. Nevertheless, they promised to follow the advice of Pontiac and their "elder brothers." They would accordingly return the following day for further talks. Unfortunately, the warriors did not agree with their chiefs or Pontiac's arguments in favor of peace. Two hours later they appeared at Fort Chartres demanding brandy. St. Ange quickly closed the gates, having a garrison of just thirty-eight men. However next morning the warriors surged forward when the gates were opened for the inhabitants. St. Ange had taken the precaution of hiding Fraser and the soldiers in various parts of the fort. Even so, they were eventually discovered and carried off to the Indian encampment. Their incarceration was mercifully short, for the next day the chiefs brought them back, reaffirming their intention of following Pontiac's advice.[64] Clearly, Pontiac's standing as a pan-Indian leader remained important, for without his influence the chiefs would probably have been swept into further hostilities.

Nevertheless, the arrival of so many angry warriors placed Pontiac in a difficult situation. He accordingly decided to go himself in search of Croghan rather than wait at Fort Chartres, inviting Fraser to accompany him. St. Ange immediately urged the other chiefs to join the two men in this mission. Shortly afterwards, the whole party set off for Ouiatanon.[65]

However, they got no further than Kaskaskia when news was received that fourteen Illinois Indians had been killed by some British and Cherokee, while waiting to ambush a French convoy. Fortunately Pontiac and his warriors were on hand to protect Fraser and his men until the report proved false, when "everything then was on the best footing once again." But a few days later Kaské arrived with a war belt from New Orleans, saying that Aubry had instructed him to kill the British. Kaské had gone to the French capital with his wife, following St. Ange's rebuff in August 1764. Now he asserted that not only would the French merchants supply the Indians with ammunition but also the king of France would declare war on their enemy within a month.[66] In reality Kaské's treatment at New Orleans had been no different from his reception from St. Ange. The British and French had ended their differences, and the Shawnee should make peace.[67] Fraser visited Kaské in an attempt to soften his hostility and found him far from the stereotypical bloodthirsty savage. "He told me his father was German and that since his infancy he had taught him to hate the English." Despite this, he was married to an Englishwoman who had been adopted when a child. Unusually for Indians he only drank water, and was "much respected amongst all the nations for his sense." He told Fraser that he was sorry that the Shawnee had given up their prisoners to Bouquet, as it was his intention "to meet Croghan and send him and his presents back." But they would not harm Fraser and his men, for he never treated any messenger ill.[68]

Three days later, the plans of Pontiac and Fraser had another setback when Maisonville returned after failing to find Croghan. Most of the chiefs responded that they could "wait no longer, [as] they must go to their villages to plant their corn." The peace that St. Ange, Fraser, and Pontiac had constructed with so much difficulty was seemingly about to be lost by default. Nevertheless, Fraser prevailed on Pontiac to remain at Kaskaskia for another ten days in the hope that Croghan would appear. Fraser now looked on Pontiac in a very positive light, noting that "he is the person who seems most inclined to peace of any among them and it must be hoped he can be prevailed on to do this since it will be much the stronger for his support." He then complimented Pontiac for his wider qualities: "He is in a manner adored by all the nations hereabouts and he is more remarkable for his integrity and humanity than either Frenchman or Indian in the colony. He has always been as careful of the lives of my men as well as my own as if he had been our father." The self-opinionated British officer was softening in his views of the native world.[69]

Nevertheless, the arrival of Kaské had seemingly thrown the issue of war or peace into turmoil again, for as Fraser noted, the Shawnee chief got more credit each passing day. Fraser was especially upset that St. Ange made no attempt to contradict Kaské's claim about having the support of Aubry. Fraser was increasingly afraid that he and the soldiers were about to be taken hostage, pending the outcome of negotiations with Croghan. He accordingly sent all his men away, remaining himself with just one servant.[70] Fortunately Pontiac agreed with this decision, though some of his followers called him a coward and British stooge for not putting the soldiers to death. Fraser yet again narrowly avoided being killed. Indeed, his only lifeline was the readiness of Pontiac to believe that the British were sincere in their desire for peace with him and his allies.[71]

Given this volatile situation Pontiac decided to resume his search for Croghan, with the help of three of Fraser's horses to carry his baggage. He invited Fraser to accompany him, but the British officer determined to retire to safety down the Mississippi. Nevertheless, Pontiac affirmed that he would make peace with Croghan, once he was convinced that both the British and the Six Nations had buried the hatchet. He had told "the Iroquois, when they had made him take it up" in 1763, "that he would not bury it till they did." Now "he wanted only to be as good as his word." In the meantime, "He had forbid all the nations to kill the English," while the situation with the Six Nations was clarified. As to terms of peace, Pontiac was still against allowing troops into the Illinois. Only traders would be welcome. However, Fraser believed he would be more accommodating when he learned about the agreements with the Delaware and Shawnee and recognized the need for garrisons to protect the trade.[72] Fraser finally left Kaskaskia on 29 May. By 17 June, he was in New Orleans.[73] Although he and St. Ange had persuaded Pontiac about the benefits of peace, no firm understanding had been reached.

Remarkably, this was not the end to the British diplomatic offensive prior to the appearance of Croghan. Fraser had no sooner left than a new mission appeared under Pierce Sinnott, acting on behalf of John Stuart, the southern superintendent, who was seeking to add the Illinois to his departmental responsibilities. Sinnott was accompanied by Lieutenant Gauterais, whom D'Abbadie had originally offered to Ross as an interpreter. Sinnott's orders were to do everything possible to "ingratiate himself with the French and Indian inhabitants ... by assuring them of protection in their persons and estates, and of the same religious and civil freedoms and privileges" as enjoyed by the inhabitants of Canada.[74] The new mission managed to ascend the Mississippi. Nevertheless, it too was a failure. Sinnott and Gauterais reached Fort Chartres in early June, just after Pontiac had departed for Ouiatanon. Without his calming presence, the Indians at Fort Chartres were mindful of their earlier threats against Ross and Fraser.[75] Despite this, Sinnott and Gauterais distributed presents valued at 150,000 French livres while the Illinois Indians debated their proposals.[76] Five days later, they received "a flat denial." The Illinois "would not suffer the English to take possession of their country." Their reasons were simple: "The French King had no right to cede it to the King of Great Britain, as he had never purchased it of them."[77] What triggered this overt hostility was the news that Croghan had been captured and three Shawnee chiefs killed. A new outbreak of hostilities could be expected. Sinnott and Gauterais fled that night.[78] Peace in the Illinois was seemingly as far away as ever.

Croghan and Pontiac Unlock the Impasse

By the early summer of 1765, peace in the Illinois seemingly hung like a thread on the appearance of Croghan. This was expecting a lot from one individual. However, unlike Ross, Fraser, and Sinnott, Croghan was known to the native peoples, having been a trader in the region in the early 1750s. His robust Irish character undoubtedly put him at ease with his Indian acquaintances. So did his legendary generosity.

Croghan, as already noted, had stayed behind at Fort Pitt to await the Delaware and Shawnee envoys. Unfortunately, both nations were slow to appear. The western Delaware only arrived at the end of April, having been delayed because one of them had "been called up to Heaven by the Great Spirit of Life" and advised that his nation should consult the Quakers before making peace.[79] To substantiate their case, the Delaware brought Neolin to see Croghan. However, the meeting was not a success since the prophet merely repeated what he had previously said while Croghan was adamant that the Quakers could not negotiate a peace for them. Only Johnson could effect that.[80] But the Shawnee were even slower to assemble at Fort Pitt, because they were still collecting their prisoners. As a result the envoys to accompany Croghan were not ready until 15 May, seven weeks after Fraser's departure.[81]

Initially Croghan made good progress. By 23 May 1765 he had reached the Scioto where the Shawnee surrendered a number of French traders, as Bouquet had demanded, to show their commitment to the peace. However, at the mouth of the Wabash River, a breastwork was found with tracks indicating an ambush.[82] This duly occurred on 8 June when the mission was attacked by the Kickapoo and Mascouten, who robbed Croghan of all his possessions and killed three Shawnee chiefs. Croghan himself was tomahawked but saved, as he later explained, by his "thick skull."[83] The assailants subsequently claimed that they thought Croghan was leading a party of southern Indians on a raid, having heard nothing from Pontiac or St. Ange about the ending of hostilities. They were accordingly dumfounded when they discovered that Croghan's escort consisted of Delaware, Shawnee, and Mingo, and that these nations had all made peace with the British. Elation quickly turned to fear as the assailants contemplated the likelihood of reprisals by the Shawnee and the Six Nations. The other Wabash nations quickly disassociated themselves from the action. At Vincennes the Piankashaw condemned the Kickapoo, advising them to take good care of Croghan. The Wea at Ouiatanon were even friendlier to the captives. Many remembered Croghan from his earlier visits and insisted on tending his wounds. The Kickapoo and Mascouten, in response, tamely asserted that they could not release Croghan until they had heard from "their father" at Fort Chartres since he had given them the hatchet to strike such foes.[84]

Nevertheless, by early July even the Kickapoo and Mascouten were "reconciled to the English taking possession of this country." They were confirmed in their decision by the arrival on 11 July of Maisonville with the news that St. Ange wanted the Indians to escort Croghan to Fort Chartres. Maisonville also brought a message from Pontiac saying that "he would be glad to see" the British envoy too and that if he liked what Croghan had to say, "he would do everything in his power to reconcile all nations to the English." This was critical, for as Croghan correctly commented to Johnson, "Pontiac has great sway amongst those nations" in the area. Now this influential chief was on his way to meet him. Croghan suddenly oozed confidence in the success of his mission, not least because Pontiac was "an old acquaintance of mine. I hope I shall be able to settle matters with him on a good footing."[85] His optimism was boosted further by the demeanor of the Kickapoo and their allies, who were now begging Croghan to reconcile matters with the Shawnee and the Six Nations.[86] As Croghan commented to Johnson, the killing of the three chiefs had helped break the confederation of eighteen nations, which the French had been three years in the making.[87]

On 18 July, Croghan and his entourage set off for Fort Chartres, as requested by St. Ange, accompanied by the chiefs of the Wabash peoples. Not many miles "by the way we met with Pontiac together with the deputies of the Six Nations, Delaware and Shawnee, which accompanied Mr. Fraser." Also in the party were "deputies with speeches" from the Illinois nations. Since Ouiatanon was nearby, it was agreed to go there rather than Fort Chartres, a sign perhaps of waning French influence. There, in Croghan's words, "I settled all matters with the Illinois Indians" and with Pontiac, "they agreeing to every thing the other nations had done, all which they confirmed by Pipes and Belts." Pontiac told Croghan that he had continued the war because the French told him that the British intended to settle the Cherokee on their country, after first enslaving them. Now they were better informed. However, they "desired that their father the King of England might not look upon his taking possession" of the French forts as "a title for his subjects to possess their country, as they never sold any part of it to the French."[88]

After this the whole group set off for Detroit to hold the conference which Bradstreet had originally proposed in September 1764. On the way Croghan collected a few captives from the Miami. He also noted nine or ten French families nearby, "a runaway colony from Detroit during the late Indian war." The guilt of these people was palpably obvious, for since coming "to this post … they have spirited up the Indians against the English" in order to prolong their own freedom.[89] Now they would very likely receive a pardon in the new spirit of mutual forgiveness.

Croghan finally reached Detroit on 17 August. During the next two weeks, he and Campbell renewed the agreements with the various nations there. First, they met the Wabash peoples who acknowledged that they were now the "children of the King of Great Britain." According to Croghan, they also reaffirmed having "given up the sovereignty of their country" to him as the king's representative, though this was certainly an exaggeration of what they had said at Ouiatanon. Finally, they promised to support the transference of the posts previously held by "their former Fathers," the French, "to the English now their present Fathers."[90]

Three days later Croghan met Pontiac and the Detroit nations, including those settled at Sandusky and along the Maumee River. Croghan began by observing that a good straight road had been created between the British and their Indian "children." It was accordingly time for the Potawatomi and Ottawa to abandon their settlements on the Maumee River and return to Detroit.[91] Pontiac answered the next day on behalf of the Detroit nations, emphasizing his ascendancy once more over Manitou and Wasson. He began by addressing Croghan as "Father." He asserted that "the Great Spirit and giver of Light" had brought them together "for our mutual good and to promote the good work of peace." Accordingly, "I declare to all nations that I have settled my peace with you before I came here and now deliver my pipe to be sent to Sir William Johnson that he may know that I have made peace and taken the King of England for my father." His people appreciated the invitation to return to their old settlements but preferred to remain where they were along the Maumee River, removed from the soldiers and the insidious effects of liquor. He then made a plea that the trade be resumed as under the French, who allowed "your children credit for a little powder and lead, as the support of our families depend upon it." He completed his oration by requesting the opening of a barrel of rum, "that your children may drink and be merry."[92]

With the hunting season approaching, the Wabash nations set off for home. Before leaving they requested a visit from the traders before the winter; otherwise, they would be obliged to go to the French in the Illinois. They reaffirmed their consent to the British possession of the posts in their country. But, perhaps sensing that Croghan was misinterpreting what they had said previously, they added, "You tell us that when you conquered the French they gave you this country." To avoid any misunderstanding, "We tell you the French never conquered us neither did they purchase a foot of our country nor have they a right to give it to you." Consequently, "If you expect to keep these posts we will expect to have proper returns from you."[93] Two days later Pontiac expressed similar views on behalf of the Detroit nations. The French had settled part of their country, but the Indians had never sold it to them. They acknowledged that "their country was very large and they were willing to give up any part of it that was necessary for their Fathers, the English, to carry on trade." However, this was "provided they were paid for it, and a sufficient part of the country left for them to hunt on."[94] To make his point about Indian sovereignty, he then deeded several small tracts to the white inhabitants.[95]

Other groups also arrived at Detroit to complete their peace with the British. Perhaps the most important was on 12 September, when Croghan met the Grand Saulteur and the remaining northern Ojibwa, who had returned home via Chicago following Pontiac's decision to negotiate with Croghan. Most of the Lake Superior Ojibwa had already made a formal peace with Howard at Michilimackinac at the end of June, when Cadotte, the French trader, brought in a convoy of eighty canoes.[96] The Grand Saulteur now did the same, acknowledging that he and his people had "been fools" to "have listened to the evil reports and the whistling of bad birds." But the British too had bad people who told lies and had equally "been the occasion of what has past."[97] In a second private conference, the Grand Saulteur admitted his part in encouraging hostilities in the Illinois. He and Pontiac had been urged by their French fathers to keep the British out of the Illinois for one more summer, pending help from France and Spain. He had also been told, like Pontiac, that the

British were planning to bring the southern nations to settle their country. He had consequently behaved badly to the British officers at Fort Chartres that spring, meaning Fraser and Sinnott. Now he was better informed about the British and was convinced that the French merely "told them lies for the love of their beaver."[98] It was a notable admission from a leader who had been one of the most resolute opponents of the British. Croghan and Campbell quickly announced that the Ojibwa chief and his people were forgiven. As a token of British friendship, they gave him some presents, with which he "departed very well satisfied."[99]

Finally on 25 September the St. Joseph Potawatomi presented themselves. Like many others, they blamed the Detroit nations and their "foolish young warriors" for their involvement in the war. The problem had been one of leadership: now they saw what they needed to do. They finished by observing that the French had "always sent us home joyful" and hoped that the British would not let them go back "ashamed" to their kinfolk with nothing to show for their efforts. Campbell and Croghan understood this, though they stressed that in future the Potawatomi would be rewarded according to their behavior. The best way of conducting themselves was to stop listening to evil rumors, attend to their hunting, support their families, and enjoy the blessings of peace.[100]

Campbell reported to Gage that the conference had produced a general peace "with all the nations of Indians to the westward" of Detroit. Most importantly, Pontiac had promised to do all that he could for the new understanding. This was crucial, since he still had "great influence over the Indians," an assessment with which Croghan agreed.[101] "Pontiac is a shrewd sensible Indian, of few words, and commands more respect among the nations than any Indian I ever see do amongst his own tribe."[102] Here was testimony to his decisive contribution at a time when the western nations might have plunged into a new war and substantiates the extent of his pan-Indian influence.

With such support, the new peace seemed likely to hold. Even so Croghan acknowledged that the Indians still preferred the French. The two races had "been bred up together like children in that country and the French have always adopted the Indian customs and manners and treated them civilly and supplied their necessaries generously." In consequence, "They gained the hearts of the Indians and commanded their services and enjoyed the benefits of a very advantageous trade." At the same time, they taught the Indians "to hate the English." Hence, the removal of their "misapprehensions" would be a thing of time. Nevertheless Croghan believed that a significant start had been made at Ouiatanon and Detroit.[103]

With the new agreements in place, the British could finally occupy Fort Chartres. This task was given to Captain Thomas Stirling with a hundred men from Fort Pitt. On his way down the Ohio, he ran into some French traders. With them was Kaské, on his way home from Fort Chartres. Kaské wanted the French Creoles to fire on the British. Only the superior numbers of Stirling prevented them from doing so. As it was, Kaské did "his best to dissuade the few Indians with Stirling from continuing." Faced by such hostility, Stirling entered Fort Chartres quietly to avoid giving offense.[104] The fort itself was handed over on 10 October 1765. After the ceremony, St. Ange crossed the Mississippi to build a new post to protect the infant settlements of St. Louis and Genevieve. Most of the inhabitants followed him.[105] Nevertheless, for the moment happier times appeared to be in store for the French, English, and Illinois peoples.

The attempt of the British to take control of the Illinois had been a remarkable episode. The Peace of Paris in 1763 had seemingly inaugurated a glorious era for the British Empire comparable to that of ancient Rome. Yet within two years its leaders had to plead with the Indians for consent to occupy the French forts. Fortunately for the British, Pontiac was able to win over the Illinois nations and most of the remaining combatants. It was a remarkable demonstration of his influence and leadership. The episode also reveals the limited nature of power on the periphery of empire. As Gage and his colleagues had discovered, their ability to control events beyond the Allegheny Mountains was governed by the need to work with the native peoples. Diplomacy and compromise, not force, were the more effective weapons. Paradoxically, the British were about to receive a similar lesson from their colonists on the other side of those mountains.

Conclusions

Pontiac's War was a remarkable episode in the history of eastern North America. In the first few weeks of the conflict, Pontiac and his allies captured nine forts, killed nearly three hundred British troops, slaughtered or captured several hundred settlers, displaced many thousands more, pushed the frontiers back fifty miles in many places, and seized £100,000 worth of merchandise.[1] In contrast, Amherst's attempts to reverse these setbacks signally failed. Bouquet came close to defeat relieving Fort Pitt, Dalyell lost his life trying to end the siege of Detroit, the Niagara garrison suffered a grievous loss at Devil's Hole, while Wilkins's much delayed expedition ended in fiasco. If the Six Nations had shown greater commitment, Niagara and Oswego might have been taken and the Allegheny Mountains made into a more formidable barrier against white aggression.

Although the Indian military effort ceased for the winter of 1763, this did not end their bid for freedom. Pontiac and his allies successfully assembled a new coalition in 1764 drawn from the Ohio, Wabash, Illinois, and western Great Lakes peoples. Admittedly, the Detroit nations were constrained by a lack of supplies to make peace with the British, as did the Mingo, Delaware, and Shawnee when confronted by the armed might of Bouquet. But Pontiac remained unsubdued and so did the Wabash and Illinois peoples, while the French merchants in Louisiana continued to supply them with ammunition. As late as July 1765, Pontiac still had a substantial coalition ready to defend the cause of Native American freedom.

During this time the Indian combatants were often closer to success than they realized, for the British were never in a strong position. The regular army was a fraction of what it had been on the conquest of Canada and no reinforcements were available, since the British taxpayer was tired of funding military adventures in such faraway places.[2] Nor would the colonial inhabitants fill the void. Outside New England, the coastal population was generally indifferent about defending the frontier, believing that the backcountry inhabitants should look after themselves.[3] But colonial reluctance to help was all the greater after 1763 because of the growing political difficulties between Britain and America. It was for this reason that Gage warned Bradstreet in May 1764 that it would be "as well if our Indian broils are finished this year since we will get no more help from the provinces for another campaign."[4]

Although the resources were eventually found for Bradstreet and Bouquet, the challenges facing the British were still formidable. Croghan had warned at the start of 1764 about the futility of continuing Amherst's methods of warfare. What purpose, he asked, could be served by "driving a parcel of wretches before us, who we know won't give us a meeting, but where they have the advantage of either beating us or running away"? The best that could be expected from such operations was the burning of a few bark huts and cornfields. Furthermore, this could only be done at great expense and with dubious benefit, for as soon as the troops appeared small parties of warriors would descend on "our defenseless frontiers ... while the remainder of them are retiring over some mountains, Lakes or Rivers with their Women and Children to a place of safety, where we can't pursue them." Croghan concluded caustically, this cannot be called conquering Indian Nations."[5]

In the event, Bouquet proved that a regular army could penetrate deep into the interior and that the Indians were vulnerable to such attack because of their women, children, and old people. As the Delaware well knew, their ability to flee was additionally limited by the need to respect their neighbors' hunting grounds. Nevertheless, Bouquet recognized the validity of much of what Croghan was arguing. "Peace is much better than war," he told the Delaware at Muskingum, knowing that his army could not stay indefinitely in the wilderness. He accordingly settled for the release of the prisoners and a notional submission on other issues. He was wise to do so, for, as Gage had predicted, further operations proved impossible. During 1765, the British had to rely on diplomacy to achieve their objectives. The result was a compromise peace to end a conflict that neither side could win on their own terms.

This outcome owed much to the leadership of Pontiac, a fact which has often been ignored by historians. Admittedly he was not a military leader in a European sense, and historians have been right to emphasize that he only exercised direct control over the Detroit Ottawa. Nevertheless, it was Pontiac who lit the torch and sustained the coalition for three difficult campaigns during which he showed both tactical and strategic ability. Moreover it was his decision to make peace that brought the hostilities to an end, thus strengthening his credentials as a pan-Indian leader.[6] This is not to claim that he was the only important Indian figure. Tahaiadoris and Kiashuta provided him with a strategic plan. Neolin gave him an ideological justification. Other key figures included the warriors Manitou, Wasson, the Grand Saulteur, Kaské, and the Delaware chiefs Tamaqua, Custaloga, and Netawatwees. Indeed the latter three, with their Shawnee allies, were almost as important as Pontiac in sustaining the cause of Indian freedom during the first eighteen months of the conflict.

The war, of course, was not without cost to the native peoples. The fighting in 1763 claimed the lives of at least two hundred warriors. There was also widespread disruption to Indian society and economy. The repatriation of several hundred captives by the Delaware and Shawnee was especially grievous, since it accelerated the decline in their population. The Seneca and Detroit peoples were also hurt by the ceding of lands along the Detroit and Niagara Rivers, which facilitated a route to the heart of their territories. Finally, the Indians now had to call the British their "fathers" rather than "brothers," acknowledging their status as children of the British rather than the French king.

Nevertheless, the efforts of Pontiac and his allies meant that there was no punitive peace of the kind that usually followed such wars. Instead, leaders like Pontiac and Kiashuta were greeted as friends and allies, while the British seemingly promised a new era of cooperation regarding Indian hunting rights, trade, and gift giving, similar to the French "middle ground." This was demonstrated at Oswego in July 1766, when the Six Nations and Great Lakes peoples met Johnson for a conference. Johnson symbolically lighted "Pontiac's pipe," before explaining his plans to regulate the trade through commissaries and other officials in accordance with the Proclamation of 1763. The Indians in future only had to attend to their hunting and trading to bring the greatest happiness to their families. At the same time, the "King's Great men" would punish the "lawless banditti" who invaded their lands.[7] Johnson then distributed a large quantity of presents. Superficially, there seemed much to be optimistic about as the chiefs made their way home. A new era of understanding and respect was in prospect, symbolized by a final handshake between Pontiac and Johnson. A restoration of the middle ground had seemingly been effected.

In reality the situation was far from what the courtesies at Oswego suggested, since the conflict had done nothing to change the racial prejudices of the white peoples. Although the British military now gave the Indians grudging respect, the European American population still looked upon them as savages who were an obstacle to progress, meaning westward expansion. The use of the terms "children" and "father" in this context was pejorative. The Indians were not children in the familial sense: rather, they were inferiors to be kept in permanent subordination. The Indians consequently remained in a legal vacuum, being neither true dependents (for whom someone was responsible), nor foreign nationals (with their own government to protect them), nor British subjects (with substantive rights). This anomalous status continued long after the American Revolution, when the United States followed a similar repressive policy of denying them citizenship.

These attitudes made a mockery of the middle ground, since it could only function through mutual respect. As a result, all the problems previously experienced during Amherst's new order quickly resurfaced. The lack of European American respect for the Indians was symbolized by the brutal murder in January 1768 of ten Delaware by a German settler, Frederick Stump. Stump was eventually arrested but rescued by a mob before he could be put on trial.[8] Even if he had been brought before a court, no backwoods jury would have convicted him.

The same disregard was also true regarding Indian land rights. In New York, the courts continued to uphold patents, no matter how fraudulent; while in Pennsylvania and Virginia, backcountry squatters and speculators invaded the Delaware and Shawnee hunting grounds, disturbing the game and destroying their way of life. Here the brutal savagery of the recent frontier war had not dampened the thirst of whites for land or their readiness to cross the mountains to get it. Unfortunately for the Native American peoples, their ability to resist these depredations had been weakened rather than strengthened by the war, because of their losses in manpower and the continued prevalence of disease. However, the westward movement of the white population was an epochal force which neither the British nor later federal governments could control. Hence, the feeble attempts of the British to enforce the Proclamation of 1763 merely alienated the backcountry settlements, preparing them for war and revolution, as David Dixon has demonstrated.[9]

Another indication that the middle ground was meaningless was the failure of the British to ensure an equitable trade. In reality, Johnson had exaggerated his authority at Oswego when promising the implementation of a well-regulated commerce. Gage allowed the appointment of some commissaries, interpreters, and smiths, but it proved only a temporary measure.[10] Within eighteen months the ministry in London had decided that the burgeoning expense of the empire was too high, whatever the promises implicit in the Proclamation of 1763. The decision was accordingly taken to reduce the number of western forts to Niagara, Fort Pitt, Detroit, Michilimackinac, and Fort Chartres.[11] The abandonment of the smaller posts should have been welcomed by the Indians, being one of their original war aims. But without a network of posts, there could be no system of regulation as envisaged by Johnson. The Board of Trade in any case believed that the colonies had learned their lesson regarding the treatment of the Indians and that the management of the trade could safely be returned to their care.[12] This rosy view was entirely illusory, even in Pennsylvania where the Quakers, who did empathize with their Indian neighbors, were politically in decline following the march of the Paxton boys. The result was widespread Indian dissatisfaction.[13]

A further blow to the hopes of restoring the middle ground was the refusal of the British to resume gift giving. This was shortsighted because the peace treaties gave them an opportunity of developing better relations with the Indians, especially their leaders. Although Johnson and Croghan did hold occasional conferences, they did not make them a regular forum for renewing the Covenant Chain, as the Indians expected. The reason, of course, was the continued obsession of the British government with economy. Leaders like Pontiac were neglected, though the British were sensible not to make too much of him, since Indian society never accommodated easily to a supreme leader, especially in peacetime. Before the Oswego conference, Johnson was informed that "the Indians are very jealous of Pontiac and want to choose another chief....They think we make too much of him."[14] Admittedly, Pontiac did not help his own cause. To some extent, his talents were not suited to peacetime pursuits. He became embroiled in the murder of one of the Fisher children captured at Detroit, which damaged his credibility with the British. As a result he increasingly became an itinerant hunter, eking out subsistence with a few companions.[15] His past violent behavior finally caught up with him in May 1769, when he was stabbed near Cahokia by a Peoria warrior seeking revenge for the wounding of a chief three years earlier.[16] The Grand Saulteur ironically met a similar death the following year near Michilimackinac at the hands of an aggrieved trader.[17] As to the other leaders prominent during Pontiac's War, Tamaqua became a Moravian convert for the last few years of his life, while Neolin, Custaloga and Netawatwees faded into obscurity. Only Kiashuta remained prominent as an intermediary and diplomat. Otherwise a new generation of chiefs had to guide the native peoples through the difficult challenges posed by the War of American Independence.

One final expedient remained whereby the lives and properties of Native Americans might have been protected and a semblance of the middle ground retained. This was the drawing of a boundary along the watershed of the Allegheny Mountains in accordance with the Proclamation of 1763. Most Indian leaders welcomed the idea as a means whereby the two races could at least live in peace. Unfortunately, the northern boundary was left to Johnson to determine, which he did to suit his political and financial interests, when the line was finally drawn at the Treaty of Fort Stanwix in October 1768. He argued that the boundary could be effective only if it provided for the future needs of white Americans, and that necessarily meant a new land cession.[18] Johnson was abetted in his scheme by the Six Nations, who saw the drawing of the boundary as a way of protecting their lands along the Mohawk Valley. By ceding territory elsewhere, they hoped to save their ancestral territories west of Schenectady. They accordingly surrendered the hunting grounds of the Delaware and Shawnee south of the Ohio River, arguing that these lands were theirs to sell by right of conquest. The result was a massive breach in the natural barrier of the Allegheny Mountains, leading to the rapid settlement of eastern Kentucky.[19] All the efforts of the Ohio peoples to defend their lands and way of life in the period 1755–1765 had been for nothing.

Not surprisingly, the Ohio peoples did not take kindly to these developments, though they should not have been surprised at their betrayal by the Six Nations. Many Delaware, however, had joined the Moravians in the intervening years in an attempt to acculturate to the white man's ways.[20] For these converts, force was not an answer. The Shawnee, however, had no intention of being so meekly dispossessed. During 1770 they sought to form a new pan-Indian alliance with the Wabash, Illinois, and Great Lakes nations.[21] Unfortunately for the Shawnee, these tribes were not immediately threatened by the Treaty of Fort Stanwix, and though dissatisfied with many aspects of the British relationship, they doubted the efficacy of another war.[22] The Shawnee also lacked a leader of Pontiac's stature, while Neolin's influence had declined since the negotiations with Bouquet and no comparable prophet had taken his place. The result was the isolation and speedy defeat in 1774 of the Shawnee and the loss of their hunting lands on the southern bank of the Ohio.[23]

Hence, within ten years of Pontiac's bid to defend the rights of the native inhabitants of eastern North America, the position of its peoples was worse than ever. Unfortunately for the Indians, this reflected a fundamental vulnerability in their political, social, and economic structures. The reality was that they had no chance *ultimately* of prevailing against the European Americans, whatever their short-term tactical successes or strategic insight. They may have been more adept at frontier warfare, but by the second half of the eighteenth century they had neither the numbers nor technology to succeed in the long term. The relentless advance of white settlement meant the progressive destruction of their habitat, thus eliminating any advantages they previously enjoyed fighting in such terrain. Only the intervention of some outside force could have halted this process.

Suddenly this seemed a possibility, with the outbreak of the War for American Independence. The British, like the French previously, needed allies to match the more numerous Americans. A new version of the "middle ground" seemed possible, one that offered the native inhabitants the protection of their lands and way of life under the aegis of their British father.

Unfortunately for the native peoples, most of them were once again on the losing side. After seven years of conflict, the United States proved the more enduring power. The British in consequence surrendered most of the Great Lakes and all the territory south and east of the Mississippi. The Six Nations in particular paid a high price for their choice of ally. Most had to make new settlements in Canada. Those who remained were condemned to reservation status. Nor was the fate of the Ohio and Wabash peoples much better. Though they retained the northern bank of the Ohio, it was not long before white settlement was encroaching there also. Pressure also began to be exerted on the Great Lakes peoples, especially of Lake Ontario and Erie. The course of European American aggrandizement had been set for the next one hundred years. Only after the native peoples had little to surrender did they receive citizenship. Even then, justice remained an elusive entity.

Notes

Introduction

1. J. Clarence Webster, ed., *The Journal of Jeffery Amherst, recording the Military Career of General Amherst in America from 1758 to 1763* (Toronto, 1931), 246.
2. Articles of Capitulation for the Surrender of Canada, 8 September 1760, *NYCD*/10:1107–20.
3. Louise Phelps Kellogg, *The French Regime in Wisconsin and the North West* (Madison, Wisc., 1925), 291–96.
4. Ibid.
5. Michael A. McConnell, "Charles-Michel Mouet de Langlade: Warrior, Soldier, and Intercultural 'Window' on the Sixty Years War for the Great Lakes," in *The Sixty Years War for the Great Lakes, 1754–1814,* eds. David Curtis Skaggs and Larry L. Nelson (East Lansing, Mich., 2001).
6. Frank H. Severance, "The Story of Joncaire: His Life and Times on the Niagara," *Buffalo Historical Society Publications* 9 (Buffalo, N.Y., 1906). For Daniel Joncaire and his son Tahaiadoris, see the first section of chapter 2.
7. See Frank H. Severance, *An Old Frontier of France: The Niagara Region and Adjacent Lakes under French Control,* 2 vols. (New York, 1917), 1:268–69.
8. Louis Kerlérec to Minister of Marine, M. de Machault, 12 December 1754, printed in *Illinois on the Eve of the Seven Years' War, 1747–1755,* vol. 3 of Collections of the Illinois State Historical Library, ed. Theodore Calvin Pease, XXIX, French Series (Springfield, 1940), 923–24. See also Kellogg, *French Regime,* 268–69, 364–66.
9. Brett Rushforth, "Slavery, the Fox Wars, and the Limits of Alliance," WMQ 63:53–80; and Kellogg, *French Regime,* 314–40.
10. Richard White, *The Middle Ground: Indians, Empires, and Republics in the Great Lakes Region, 1650–1815* (Cambridge, 1991), 215–32.
11. Ibid.
12. Ibid., 198–209.
13. Even here, not all the occupants were converts to the white man's religion.
14. Quoted in Stephen F. Auth, *The Ten Years War: Indian-White Relations in Pennsylvania, 1755–1765* (New York, 1989), 19.
15. See Timothy J. Shannon, *Indians and Colonists at the Crossroads: The Albany Congress of 1754* (Ithaca, N.Y., 2000).
16. Fred Anderson, *Crucible of War: The Seven Years' War and the Fate of Empire in British North America, 1754–1766* (New York, 2000), 67–71.
17. Kellogg, *French Regime,* 425–26.
18. Stephen to Sir John Hunter, 18 July 1755, *Newcastle Papers, BL*/Add Mss 32,857, fols. 215–18.

19. Francis Jennings, *The Ambiguous Iroquois Empire: The Covenant Chain Con-federation of Indian Tribes with English Colonies from Its Beginnings to the Lan-caster Treaty of 1744* (New York, 1984), 325–46.
20. Eric Hinderaker, *Elusive Empires: Constructing Colonialism in the Ohio Valley, 1673–1800* (Cambridge, 1997), 126–28.
21. Ibid., 140. The Quaker trader James Kenny was later told that no Delaware and only three Shawnee were present at Braddock's defeat; "Journal of James Kenny, 1761–1763," *PMHB* 27:183.
22. Thomas Pownall to Johnson, 21 December 1755, *JP*/13, 76–77. The Delaware sub-sequently handed back their "skirts" to the Seneca after launching a war against the white frontier settlements; information from Alexander McCluer, 6 March 1757, *JP*/2, 681–82.
23. Hinderaker, *Elusive Empires*, 27–29; and Bruce Trigger, ed., *The North East*, vol. 15 of *The Handbook of North American Indians* (Washington, D.C., 1978), 622–35.
24. Captain Thomas Butler to Johnson, 7 April 1757, *JP*/2, 704–6.
25. Ian K. Steele, *Betrayals: Fort William Henry and the "Massacre"* (Oxford, 1990), 79–108. Steele points out that the number killed was half that asserted by the British, the discrepancy being explained by a similar number of men being made prisoner; ibid., 109–83.
26. Quoted in D. Peter MacLeod, *The Canadian Iroquois and the Seven Years' War* (Toronto, 1996), xv.
27. Speeches of the [Canadian] Iroquois, Nipissing, Algonquian, Abenaki, and Mis-sissauga to Governor Vaudreuil, 30 July 1758, *NYCD*/10:805–6.
28. Pennsylvania Council Minutes, 21 July–7 August 1757, *PCR*/VII, 649–714; and Jennings, *Empire of Fortune*, 347–48.
29. Conference in the State House, Philadelphia, 11–12 July 1758, PA, First Series 1, ed. Samuel Hazard (Philadelphia, 1852–1854), 3:461–69.
30. Reuben Gold Thwaites, ed., *Early Western Journals, 1748–1765* (1904; reprint, Lewisburg, PA, 1998), 198–99.
31. Archibald Loudon, ed., *A Selection of the Some of the Most Interesting Narra-tives of Outrages Committed by the Indians in Their Wars with the White Peo-ple,* 2 vols. (Carlisle, PA, 1808, reprint, Lewisburg, PA, 2001), 1:202–3; and Ian McCulloch and Timothy Todish, eds., *Through So Many Dangers: The Memoirs and Adventures of Robert Kirk, Late of the Royal Highland Regiment* (Limerick, Ireland, 1775; reprint, New York, 2004), 38–40.
32. Conference at Easton, 8–26 October 1758, *PCR* 8:175–223.
33. "Life and Travels of Colonel James Smith," printed in Loudon, *Indian Narra-tives*, 1:202–3. Smith was an adoptee of the Ohio Indians at this time.
34. C. Hale Sipe, *Fort Ligonier and Its Times* (Harrisburg, PA, 1932; reprint, Ligo-nier, PA, 1976), 67–74.
35. Reuben G. Thwaites, ed., *Early Western Travels, 1748–1846*, vol. 1 (New York, 1966), 252–80.
36. Indian Conference Minutes, 26 February 1759, *PCR* 8:306–7; and Mercer to Bouquet, 1 March 1759, *BP*/3, 164–65.
37. "George Croghan's Journal," ed. Nicholas B Wainwright, *PMHB* 71:318–25.
38. Johnson to Amherst, 21 April 1759, *NA/WO*/34/39 fol. 84; and Johnson to Board of Trade, 17 May 1759, *NYCD*/7:76.

39. Pierre Pouchot, *Memoirs on the Late War in North America between France and England,* ed. Brian Leigh Dunnigan, trans. Michael Cardy (Youngstown, N.Y., 1994), 202–8.
40. Ibid., 215–16.
41. Johnson to Amherst, 25 July 1759, *NA/WO/34/39* fols. 39–40. Johnson makes no comment about the dubious role of the Six Nations. Another account of the battle can be found in Captain De Lancey to Governor James De Lancey, 25 July 1759, *NYCD/7*:402–3.
42. Mohawk Intelligence, 20 December 1759, *NA/WO/34/46,* fol. 66; "Croghan Journal," 22 May 1760, *PMHB* 71:370–71; and Vaudreuil to Berryer, 24 June 1760, *NYCD/10*:1092–3.
43. Journal of the Niagara Campaign, 27 July 59, *JP/13,* 115.
44. "Croghan Journal," 26 January 1760, *PMHB* 71:365–66.
45. "Croghan Journal," 7–9 August 1759, *PMHB* 71:336–41; ibid., 3–4 September 1759, *PMHB* 71:347–51; ibid., 16–17 October 1759, *PMHB* 71:356–58; and list of Indian nations at Fort Pitt, 5 November 1759, *BP/4,* 84.
46. "Croghan Journal," 3 September 1759, *PMHB* 71:348, 350.
47. Ibid., 17 October 1759, *PMHB* 71:356–57.
48. "Croghan Journal," 23 August 1759, *PMHB* 71:344–45.
49. Post to Peters, 11 March 1760, *NA/WO/34/33,* fol. 47.
50. Amherst to Hamilton, 30 March 1760, *JP/3,* 204–5.
51. Declaration to the Ohio Indian Nations, 27 April 1760, *NA/WO/34/38,* fols. 101–2.
52. Post to Amherst, 30 October 1760, *NA/WO/34/83* fol. 158.
53. Gertrude Selwyn Kemble, ed., *Correspondence of William Pitt When Secretary of State with Colonial Governors and Military and Naval Commissioners in America,* 2 vols. (London, 1906), 1:237–42.
54. Amherst to Johnson, 23 February 1760, *NA/WO/34/38* fol. 97.
55. Proceedings with the Deputies, 13–14 February 1760, *JP/3,* 188–92; and Pouchot, *Memoirs,* 287–88. The readiness of the Iroquois to support their St Lawrence relatives was a long standing practice, see Jon Parmenter, "After the Mourning Wars: The Iroquois as Allies in Colonial North American Campaigns, 1676–1760," WMQ, LXIV (2007), 39–82.
56. Amherst to De Lancey, 3 August 1760, *NA/WO/34/30* fol. 120.
57. Conference with the deputies of the Twightwee, Potawatomi and Kickapoo, 2–12 August 1760, PA, first series, 3:744–52.
58. Journal of Jelles Fonda, 13 August 1760, *JP/13,* 169.
59. "Croghan Journal," 30 July 1760, *PMHB* 71:379–80.
60. Conference with the Western Nations, Fort Pitt, 12–17 August 1760, PA, first series, 8:744–52.
61. Webster, *Journal of Jeffery Amherst,* 239.
62. List of Indians on the Campaign, 13 September 1760, *JP/10,* 180–85.
63. MacLeod, *Canadian Iroquois,* 171–72.
64. Indian Conference, 16 September 1760, *JP/13,* 163–66.
65. Amherst to Rogers, 12 September 1760, *BP/5,* 33–35.
66. *Journal of Major Robert Rogers, containing An Account of the Several Excursions He Made under the Generals Who Commanded upon the Continent of North America, during the Late War* (London, 1765), 214–15.

67. "Croghan Journal," 5 November 1760, *PMHB* 71:387–88.
68. Ibid, 388–89. One of these younger men may have been Pontiac, since Rogers claimed subsequently to have met him at this time; Robert Rogers, *A Concise Account of North America* (London, 1765; reprint, Ann Arbor, Mich., 1966), 239-43.
69. "Croghan Journal," 22 November 1760, *PMHB* 71:392–93.
70. William Renwick Riddell, "Last Indian Council of the French at Detroit," Transactions of the Royal Society of Canada 25 (1931): 165–68.
71. Croghan Journal, 3 December 1760, *PMHB* 71:394–95.
72. *Proceedings of an Indian Conference*, Detroit, 3 December 1760, *JP*/10, 198–201.
73. Ibid., 202–4.

Chapter 1

1. Amherst to Gage, 26 February 1759 *NA/WO/34/46A* fol. 144.
2. Memoir on Canada, by Monsieur Bourlamaque (circa 1760), *NYCD*/10:1139–55.
3. Amherst to Colonel William Farquar, 11 September 1759, *NA/WO/34/23* fol. 11.
4. Croghan to Johnson, 22 December 1759, *JP*/10, 131–32.
5. Claus to Johnson, 27 October 1760, *JP*/10, 189–91.
6. Kenny Journal, 4 February 1762, *PMHB* 37:40.
7. Ibid.; and Kenny Journal, 17 February 1763, *PMHB* 37:187.
8. For Johnson's ambitions to own a European-style estate, see James Thomas Flexner, *Lord of the Mohawks: A Biography of Sir William Johnson* (Boston, 1959); and Milton W. Hamilton, *Sir William Johnson, Colonial American, 1715–1763* (Port Washington, 1976). For Croghan, see Nicholas B. Wainwright, George Croghan, *Wilderness Diplomat* (Chapel Hill, N.C., 1959).
9. Johnson to Goldsbrow Banyar, 5 June 1761, *JP*/3, 400.
10. For Johnson's associations with the Brant family, see Isobel Thompson Kelsey, *Joseph Brant, 1743–1807: Man of Two Worlds* (Syracuse, N.Y., 1984). For Johnson's suggestion to provide alcohol "to let them shorten their days," see Johnson to Gage, 11 May 1764, *JP*/11, 190.
11. Thomas Pownall to Johnson, 16 August 1755, *JP*/1, 835–36.
12. Amherst to Johnson, 8 November 1760, *JP*/3, 277–78.
13. Commission of Sir William Johnson, 11 March 1761, *NYCD*/7:458–59.
14. Amherst to Johnson, 22 February 1761, *JP*/3, 345.
15. Amherst to Monckton, 2 August 1760, *NA/WO/34/43* fol. 145.
16. Monckton to Bouquet, 26 October 1760, *BP*/5, 86–87.
17. Amherst to Johnson, 22 February 1761, *JP*/3, 343–47.
18. Amherst to Johnson, 1 February 1761, *NA/WO/34/38*, fols. 131–32.
19. Bouquet to Monckton, 15 September 1760, *BP*/5, 38–39.
20. Gage to Amherst, 2 December 1760, *NA/WO/34/5*, fol. 10.
21. Amherst to Gage, 27 May 1761, *NA/WO/34/7* fol. 34
22. Speech of Delaware George, 26 May 1761, *BP*/5, 509–10.
23. Campbell to Amherst, 14 February 1761, *NA/WO/34/49* fol. 19.
24. Johnson to Amherst, 21 March 1761, *JP*/10, 243–47.
25. Campbell to Monckton, 22 May 1761, Aspinwall Papers, Massachusetts Historical Society Collections, Fourth Series, vol. 9, 414–15.
26. Johnson to Amherst, 15 November 1760, *JP*/10, 197.

27. Amherst to Johnson, 19 November 1760, *JP*/10, 198–99.
28. Amherst to Johnson, 1 February 1761, *NA/WO*/34/38 fol. 131.
29. Johnson to Amherst, 12 February 1761, *NA/WO*/34/39 fol. 169.
30. Journal of Indian Affairs, 8 March 1761, *JP*/10, 237–38.
31. Richard White, *The Middle Ground: Indians, Empires, and Republics in the Great Lakes Region, 1650–1815* (Cambridge, 1991), 264–65.
32. Journal of Indian Affairs, 8 March 1761, *JP*/10, 238–39.
33. Campbell to Bouquet, 8 June 1761, *BP*/5, 533.
34. Speech Delivered by the White Mingo, 6 June 1761, *BP*/5, 532–33.
35. Walters to Amherst, 29 June 1761, *NA/WO*/34/21 fols. 172–73.
36. Amherst to Walters. 2 November 1760, *NA/WO*/34/23 fol. 45.
37. Journal of Indian Affairs, 23 February 1761, *JP*/10, 221–23.
38. Johnson to Amherst, 12 June 1761, *NA/WO*/34/39 fol. 186.
39. Johnson to Amherst, 21 June 1761, *NA/WO*/34/39 fol. 190.
40. Journal of Frederick Post, printed in Reuben Gold Thwaites, ed., *Early Western Journals 1748–1765* (Lewisburg, PA, 1904; reprint, 1998), 278–79.
41. Conference Held by Colonel Bouquet with the Delaware Chiefs, 4 December 1758, *BL*/Add Mss 21655 fols. 19–20. Ibid, *BP*/2, 621-24.
42. Reuben G. Thwaites, ed., *Early Western Travels, 1748–1846*, vol. 1 (New York, 1966), 284–85. Croghan was seemingly responsible for this piece of deception, which Post wanted to reveal to Bouquet.
43. Declaration to the Ohio Indians, 27 April 1760, *NA/WO*/34/38 fols. 102–3.
44. Amherst to Monckton, 29 April 1760, *NA/WO*/34/43 fols. 136–37.
45. Gregory Evans Dowd, *War under Heaven: Pontiac, the Indian Nations and the British Empire* (Baltimore, 2002), 44.
46. Brigadier Stanwix to Amherst, 17 September 1759, *NA/WO*/34/45 fol. 100; and Dowd, *War under Heaven*, 52–53.
47. Croghan to Johnson, 22 December 1759, *JP*/10, 131–32.
48. Johnson to Gage, 17 March 1760, *JP*/3, 200–1.
49. List of Houses and Inhabitants at Fort Pitt, 12 April 1761, *BP*/5, 407–11; and Eric Hinderaker, *Elusive Empires: Constructing Colonialism in the Ohio Valley, 1673–1800* (Cambridge, 1997), 149–50.
50. Meeting with Oneida and Tuscarora Chiefs, 7 July 1761, *JP*/3, 432–33.
51. Meeting at Oswego with the Sachems and Warriors of Onondaga, 21 July 1761, *JP*/3, 443–44.
52. Ibid, 446–47.
53. Kenny Journal, 6 July 1761, *PMHB* 37:10.
54. Speech to the Indians, 29 June 1761, *BP*/5, 590–92.
55. Kenny Journal, 3 August 1761, *PMHB* 37:16.
56. Johnson Detroit Journal, 25 July 1761, *JP*/3, 453. In reality, only one "young Seneca" was killed; ibid., 12 September 1761, *JP*/3, 494.
57. Amherst to Johnson, 24 June 1761, *JP*/10, 297.
58. Hutchins to Bouquet, 22 December 1760, *BP*/5, 193–94; and John Blair to Bouquet, 5 February 1761, *BP*/5, 279.
59. Indian Conference at Fort Pitt, 1 March 1761, *BP*/5, 324–25.
60. Bouquet to Campbell, 30 June 1761, *BP*/5, 596–97.
61. Bouquet to Monckton, 10 July 1761, *BP*/5, 626–27.

62. Declaration to the Ohio Indians, 27 April 1760, *NA/WO/34/38* fols. 102–3.

63. Bouquet to Thomas Cresap, 12 September 1760, *BP/5*, 32–33.

64. Bouquet to Monckton, 20 March 1761, *BP/5*. 354–55.

65. Colden to Johnson, 18 January 1761, *JP/3*, 306–7.

66. For a history of the patent, see Johnson to the Lords of Trade, 30 October 1764, *NYCD/7*:670–75.

67. Meeting with the Lower Mohawk, 20 March 1760, *NYCD/7*:435–36.

68. Johnson to Goldsbrow Banyar, 10 February 1761, *JP/3*, 326–29.

69. Journal of Indian Affairs, 18 February 1761, *JP/10*, 220; and Johnson to Cadwallader Colden, 20 February 1761, *JP/3*, 338–39.

70. Johnson to Colden, 18 June 1761, *JP/3*, 410.

71. Colden to Johnson, 7 March 1761, *JP/10*, 233–34.

72. Petition to the Council, 27 March 1761, *JP/10*, 248–50. For a discussion of Johnson's conflict of interests, see Flexner, *Lord of the Mohawks*; and Hamilton, *Sir William Johnson*.

73. James Hamilton to Amherst, 10 May 1761, *PCR* 8:622–25; and declaration of Thomas King, 18 February 1762, *CAN/C/1222*.

74. Conference with Teedyuscung, 18 September 1760, in 1756–1767, vol. 2 of *The Susquehanna Company Papers*, ed. Julian P. Boyd (Ithaca, N.Y., 1962), 24–25; and Hamilton to Johnson, 12 May 1761, *JP/3*, 390–92.

75. Hamilton to Fitch, 10 February 1761, *Susquehanna Company Papers*, 2:54–57. Fitch replied that as the venture was a private one and lay in a separate jurisdiction, there was nothing that he could do as governor of Connecticut; Fitch to Hamilton, 7 May 1761, *Susquehanna Company Papers*, 2:84–85.

76. Pennsylvania Council Meeting, 3 April 1760, *PCR* 8:467–72.

77. John Demos, *The Unredeemed Captive: A Family Story from Early America* (New York, 1994).

78. Banyar Goldsbrow to Johnson, 24 September 1755, *JP/2*, 80.

79. Stephen Williams to Amherst, 16 October 1759, *NA/WO/34/78* fol. 87.

80. Post to Amherst, 30 October 1760, *NA/WO/34/83* fol. 158.

81. Stanwix to Amherst, 26 January 1760, *NA/WO/34/45* fol. 125.

82. Petition of James McCullough, 3 June 1761, *BP/5*, 525–26.

83. Bouquet to Monckton, 24 July 1761, *BP/5*, 654.

84. Croghan: Indian Conference at Fort Pitt, 1 March 1761, *BP/5*, 324–26.

Chapter 2

1. Johnson to Colonel John Vaughan, 18 April 1765, *JP/11*, 700–1.

2. Frank H. Severance, *An Old Frontier of France: The Niagara Region and Adjacent Lakes under French Control*, 2 vols. (New York, 1917), 1:144–329.

3. Colonel William Eyre to Amherst, 18 May 1760, *NA/WO/34/20*, fol. 41.

4. Croghan: Uneasiness of the Iroquois, 27 July 1761, *BP/5*, 664.

5. Ibid., 317.

6. Amherst to Rutherford, 10 April 1761, *NA/WO/34/88* fol. 158; and Amherst to Pitt, 4 May 1761, *NA/CO/5/61*.

7. Rutherford to Amherst, 28 April 1761, *NA/CO/5/61*.

8. Amherst to Loring, 4 May 1761, *NA/WO/34/65* fol. 180; and Amherst to Gladwin, 22 June 1761, *WO/34/53* fols. 61–62. The French previously had vessels on Lake Ontario, but never on Lake Erie.

9. Croghan to Johnson, personal, 25 July 1761, *JP*/10, 317.

10. Johnson Journal, 24 July 1761, *JP*/13, 227.

11. Croghan to Johnson, personal, 13 January 1761, *JP*/3, 303.

12. Vaudreuil to Langlade, 3 September 1760, in *Report and Collections of the State Historical Society of Wisconsin for 1877–1879* (Madison, 1879), 8:215–16; and William Renwick Riddell, "Last Indian Council of the French at Detroit," *Transactions of the Royal Society of Canada* 25 (1931): 165–68.

13. Johnson Journal, 4 August 1761, *JP*/13, 233; and Severance, *Old Frontier of France,* 1:308.

14. Johnson Detroit Journal, 28 July 1761, *JP*/3, 456.

15. Croghan Journal, 27 July 1761, *PMHB* 71:410–11.

16. Croghan: Indian Intelligence, 10 December 1760, *JP*/3, 336–37; and Carl A. Brasseaux and Michael J. Le Blanc, "Franco Indian Diplomacy in the Mississippi Valley, 1754–1763: Prelude to Pontiac's Uprising?" *Journal de la Société des Américanistes* 68 (1982): 61.

17. Conference with the Northern Indians, 23 August 1762, *PCR* 8:753.

18. Croghan Journal, 27 July 1761, *PMHB* 71:410–11.

19. Uneasiness of the Iroquois, 27 July 1761, *BP*/5, 664–65.

20. Croghan Journal, 27 July 1761, *PMHB* 71:410–11. Campbell at Detroit got a similar version from the Wyandot interpreter, St. Martin, which he related to Amherst, 17 June 1761, *NA/WO/34/49* fols. 38–39.

21. Campbell to Amherst, 17 June 1761, *NA/WO/34/49* fols. 38–40.

22. Johnson Official Detroit Journal, 17 July 1761, *JP*/3, 440–41.

23. Indian Conference, 22 April 1762, *JP*/3, 695–96.

24. Report of an Indian Council, 18 June 1761, *BP*/5, 563–64. The exact date of the conference is uncertain. Campbell, the commanding officer at Detroit, sent his first warning in a letter to Bouquet, 16 June 1761, *BP*/5, 555–56.

25. Report of an Indian Council, 18 June 1761, *BP*/5, 561–65.

26. Campbell to Amherst, 8 July 1761, *JP*/3, 448–50.

27. Kenny Journal, 1 October 1761, *PMHB* 37:23–24.

28. Conference held at the Wyandot town near Fort Detroit, 3 July 1761, *JP*/3, 450–51.

29. Information from an Onondaga Indian, 28 July 1761, *JP*/3, 456. See also Johnson to Claus, 9 August 1761, *JP*/10, 324. The Genesee later admitted to Johnson that Tahaiadoris's belt "had formerly been left by Joncaire when he had his last Interview with our Nation," Indian Conference, 22 April 1762, *JP*/3, 696.

30. Conference held at the Wyandot town, 3 July 1761, *JP*/3, 450–51.

31. Campbell to Amherst, 17 June 1761, *NA/WO/34/49*, fols. 38–39.

32. Campbell to Bouquet, 7 July 1761, *BP*/5, 619.

33. Ibid.

34. Ibid., 619–20.

35. Croghan Journal, 27 July 1761, *PMHB* 71:410–11; and Croghan to Monckton, 27 July 1761, Cadwalader Collection, series IV, box 5, *PHS*.

36. Bouquet to Monckton, 27 July 1761, *BP*/5, 659–60.

37. Kenny Journal, 1–4 July 1761, *PMHB* 37:8.

38. Amherst to Walters, 8 July 1761, *NA/WO/34/23* fol. 70.

39. Amherst to Johnson, 9 August 1761, *NA/WO/34/38* fol. 161.

40. See in particular, William R. Nester, *"Haughty Conquerors": Amherst and the Great Indian Uprising of 1763* (Westport, Conn., 2000).

41. Amherst to Johnson, 30 May 1761, *JP*/10, 274–75.

42. Amherst to Johnson, 11 June 1761, *CAN*, C/1221.

43. Johnson Detroit Journal, 1 July 1761, *JP*/3, 428–29. There are two versions of Johnson's trip to Detroit. The formal version, which Johnson sent to the Board of Trade, is published in volume 3 of the Johnson Papers, 428–503, and is referred to here as the Johnson Detroit Journal. The more private draft version can be found in *JP*/13, 215–74, and is listed here as the Johnson Personal Journal. The two versions differ in places but generally complement rather than contradict each other.

44. Johnson Detroit Journal, 13 July 1761, *JP*/3, 439–40.

45. Amherst to Johnson, 8 July 1761, Northcliffe Collection, 37, Canadian National Archives.

46. Johnson Detroit Journal, 21 July 1761, *JP*/3, 442–48.

47. Ibid., 28, 30 July 1761, *JP*/3, 454–58.

48. Ibid., 1 August 1761, *JP*/3, 458–59.

49. Ibid., 4 August 1761, *JP*/3, 459–63.

50. Ibid., 9 August 1761, *JP*/3, 463–64.

51. Ibid., 9 August 1761, *JP*/3, 465–66.

52. Ibid., 4 September 1761, *JP*/3, 468–69.

53. Ibid., 470–71; and Croghan Journal, 21 August 1761, *PMHB* 71:413–14.

54. Johnson Detroit Journal, 5–6 September 1761, *JP*/3, 471–72.

55. Johnson Personal Journal, 6 September 1761, *JP*/13, 251.

56. Johnson Detroit Journal, 9 September 1761, *JP*/3, 474–80.

57. Ibid., 10 September 1761, *JP*/3, 483–87.

58. Ibid., 487–88.

59. Ibid., 491.

60. Johnson Personal Journal, 10 September, 1761, *JP*/13, 254.

61. Johnson Detroit Journal, 12 September 1761, *JP*/3, 493.

62. Conference with the Six Nations, 22 April 1762, *JP*/3, 695–96. The Genesee also claimed that "one half" of Joncaire's belt "represented war and the other half peace," and that it was the latter "which the deputies [Tahaiadoris and Kiashuta] were charged earnestly to recommend."

63. Johnson Detroit Journal, 17 September 1761, *JP*/3, 495–98.

64. Ibid., 498.

65. Johnson to Amherst, 5 November 1761, *JP*/3, 559–60.

66. Gage to Halifax, 7 January 1764; and Clarence E. Carter, ed., *The Correspondence of General Thomas Gage with the Secretaries of State, 1763–1775,* 2 vols. (New Haven, Conn., 1931–1933), 1:10–11.

67. Kenny Journal, 1 October 1761, *PMHB* 37:23–24; and Croghan to Monckton, 3 October 1761, Cadwalader Collection, series IV, box 5, *PHS*.

68. Amherst to Johnson, 1 February 1761, *NA/WO/34/38* fols. 131–32; and Robert Rogers, *Journals of Major Robert Rogers, containing an Account of the Several Excursions He Made under the Generals Who Commanded upon the Continent of North America during the Late War* (London, 1765), 230–31.

69. Campbell to Amherst, 14 February 1761, *NA/WO/34/49* fol. 19; and Father Du Jaunay to Father St. Pé, 24 June 1761, *JP*/3, 412–17.

70. Father Du Jaunay to Father St. Pé, 24 June 1761, *JP*/3, 412–17.
71. Alexander Henry, *Travels and Adventures in Canada and the Indian Territories between the Years 1760 and 1776* (New York, 1809; reprint, Ann Arbor, Mich., 1966), 43–44.
72. Henry, *Travels and Adventures,* 49–51.
73. Instructions for the Officers, 8 September 1761, *JP*/3, 473–74.
74. Henry Balfour's Conference, 29 September 1761, *JP*/3, 537.
75. Ibid., 540–41.
76. Ibid., 30 September 1761, 541–44.
77. Ibid., 30 September 1761, 544–45.
78. Balfour to Amherst, 29 December 1761, *NA/WO/34/40* fol. 131.
79. Journal of James Gorrell, 23 May 1762, *JP*/10, 700–2.
80. Ibid., 702–4.
81. Balfour to Amherst, 29 December 1761, *NA/WO/34/40* fol. 131.
82. Campbell to Bouquet, 8 November 1761, *BP*/6, 26.
83. Lieutenant Holmes: Indian Conference, 25 September 1761, *JP*/10, 325–27; and ibid., 27 September 1761, 327.

Chapter 3

1. Johnson to Amherst, 27 June 1761, *JP*/10, 300–2.
2. Minutes of Indian Conferences, 3–12 August 1761, *PCR* 8:721–72. The Pennsylvania authorities claimed that the Indians came of their own accord, not by invitation.
3. Croghan to Hutchins, 25 October 1761, *BP*/5, 841–42.
4. Amherst to Johnson, 26 December 1761, *NA/WO/34/38* fol. 171.
5. Croghan to Bouquet, 27 March 1762, *BP*/6, 68–70.
6. Croghan to Monckton, 19 March 1761, Cadwalader Collection, series IV, box 5, *PHS*.
7. Croghan Journal, 23 April 1762, *PMHB* 71:423.
8. Johnson to Board of Trade, 20 August 1762, *JP*/3, 865–69.
9. Croghan to Hutchins, 3 April 1762, *BL/Add Mss* 21655 fol. 179.
10. Mathew C. Ward, "The Microbes of War: The British Army and Epidemic Disease among the Ohio Indians, 1758–1765," in *The Sixty Years War for the Great Lakes, 1754–1814,* ed. David Curtis Skaggs and Larry L. Nelson (East Lansing, Mich., 2001), 65.
11. Journal and Report of Thomas Hutchins, 4 April–13 September 1762, *JP*/10, 521–28.
12. Hutchins to Croghan, 24 September 1762, *JP*/10, 528–29.
13. Campbell to Amherst, 8 November 1761, *BP*/6, 28–29.
14. Kenny Journal, 3 August 1761, *PMHB* 37:16.
15. Amherst to Johnson, 30 December 1761, *NA/WO/34/38* fol. 172.
16. Walters to Amherst, 27 April 1762, *NA/WO/34/22* fol. 19.
17. De Couagne to Johnson, 26 May 1763, *JP*/10, 684.
18. Amherst to Campbell, 31 December 1761, *NA/WO/34/49* fol. 290.
19. Campbell to Bouquet, 28 November 1761, *BP*/6, 32.
20. Campbell to Amherst, 10 January 1762, *NA/WO/34/49* fol. 68.
21. Campbell to Bouquet, 3 July 1762, *BL/Add Mss* 21648, fols. 243–44.
22. Johnson to Bouquet, 18 September 1761, *BP*/5, 761–62.

23. Egremont to Amherst, 12 December 1761, *WCL/AP/5*.

24. Gage to Amherst, 20 March 1762, *NA/CO/5/62* fols. 85–89.

25. Johnson to the Board of Trade, 20 August 1762, *JP/3*, 865–67.

26. Edward Ward to Bouquet, 15 June 1762, *BP/6*, 95–97.

27. Kenny Journal, 20 July 1762, *PMHB* 37:163; and see Richard White, *The Middle Ground: Indians, Empires, and Republics in the Great Lakes Region, 1650–1815* (Cambridge, 1991), 480.

28. Johnson to Amherst, 29 July 1761, *JP/10*, 322.

29. Conference with Six Nations, 25 April 1762, *JP/3*, 707.

30. Ibid., 26 April 1762, 710–11.

31. Croghan Journal, 18 October 1761, *PMHB* 71:416; ibid., 27 October 1761; and ibid., 8 November 1761, 417.

32. Bouquet to Amherst, 30 March 1762, *WO/34/40* fol. 147.

33. Edward St. Leger to Bouquet, 22 June 1762, *BP/6*, 98.

34. James McCullough, "Narrative of Captivity," in *A Selection of Some of the Most Interesting Narratives of Outrages Committed by the Indians in Their Wars with the White People*, ed. Archibald Loudon, 2 vols. (Carlisle, PA, 1808, reprint, Lewisburg, PA, 2001), 1:276–77.

35. Croghan to Johnson, 25 July 1761, *JP/10*, 317.

36. Kenny Journal, 21 May 1762, *PMHB* 37:156–57; and Baird to Bouquet, 8 June 1762, *BP/6*, 89–90.

37. Kenny Journal, 8 July 1762, *PMHB* 37:161.

38. Bouquet to Amherst, 11 July 1762, *BP/6*, 99–100.

39. Conference with the Indians, 14 August 1762, *PCR* 8:729–33.

40. Ibid., 16 August 1762, 735–36.

41. Ibid., 19 August 1762, 741–44.

42. Indian Conference, 26 August 1762, *PCR* 8:759–61.

43. Ibid., 24 August 1762, 757. The written record could be the occasion of controversy at such meetings. For a discussion of the subject, see James H. Merrell, *Into the American Woods: Negotiators on the Pennsylvania Frontier* (New York, 1999), 254; and James H. Merrell, "'I desire all that I have said…may be taken down aright': Revisiting Teedyuscung's 1756 Treaty Council Speeches," *WMQ* 53 (2006): 777-826.

44. Ibid., 27 August 1762, 766–67.

45. "Croghan Journal," 14 September 1762, *PMHB* 71:426; and Thomas McKee to Johnson, 1 November 1762, *JP/3*, 921–22.

46. Kenny Journal, 8 September 1762, *PMHB* 37:168.

47. Return of Prisoners, 9 October 1762, *BP/6*, 121.

48. Penn to Hamilton, 10 December 1762, in 1756–1767, vol. 2 of *The Susquehanna Company Papers*, ed. Julian P. Boyd (Ithaca, N.Y., 1962), 2:187–89. As mentioned in chapter 1, apart from deserters, Amherst showed little interest in the repatriation of the captives.

49. Hamilton to Burd, 25 September 1762, *PCR* 8:776–77.

50. Croghan to McKee, 5 October 1762, *NA/WO/34/39* fol. 301. See the second section of this chapter.

51. Croghan Journal, 22 January 1763, *PMHB* 71:435.

52. Ibid., 27 January 1763, 436.

53. Ibid., 5 February 1763.

54. McKee to Croghan, 12 April 1763, *BP*/6, 180–82.

55. Proclamation, 31 October 1761, *BP*/5, 844–45.

56. Board of Trade to George III, 2 December 1761, *NYCD*/7, 477–79. The western boundary of Pennsylvania was already limited by charter to 80.5 degrees longitude; similarly, Maryland to 79.5 degrees.

57. Francis Fauquier to Bouquet, 17 January 1762, *BP*/6, 39–40.

58. Bouquet to Fauquier, 8 February 1762, *BP*/6, 44–45.

59. Croghan Journal, 5–7 February 1762, *PMHB* 71:420–21.

60. Kenny Journal, 12 April 1762, *PMHB* 37:152.

61. Kenny Journal, 19 March 1762, *PMHB* 37:45.

62. McKee: Indian Conference Minutes, 16 April 1763, *BP*/6, 183–84.

63. Conference with Teedyuscung, 19 November 1762, *PCR* 9:6–9. However, Tamaqua and his colleagues had earlier failed to support Teedyuscung's claim to some land along the Delaware River which he asserted had been taken fraudulently from his people by the Penn Proprietors, Conference with the Indians, Lancaster, 18 August 1762, *PCR* 8: 739-40.

64. Daniel Broadhead to Governor Hamilton, 27 September 1762, *JP*/10, 530–33.

65. Johnson to Amherst, 30 March 1763, *JP*/4, 70–72.

66. Fitch to Johnson, 30 May 1763, *JP*/4, 130.

67. For a discussion of those responsible, see Anthony F. C. Wallace, *King of the Delawares: Teedyuscung, 1700–1763* (Syracuse, N.Y., 1990), 258–61.

68. Hamilton to Johnson, 18 May 1763, *JP*/10, 671–72.

69. Gladwin to Amherst, 24 February 1762, *JP*/10, 384–85.

70. Gladwin to Amherst, 25 February 1762, *JP*/10, 386.

71. Conference with the Canadasaga Indians, 15 March 1762, *JP*/10, 398–99. Another similar belt was left by the Canadian officer Louis-Luc La Corne with the Mississauga Ojibwa, which also circulated in the years following the French defeat; Testimony of John Seger, 12 October 1763, in Charles Moore, "The Gladwin Manuscripts," *Michigan Pioneer and Historical Society* 27:652–53.

72. Carl A. Brasseaux and Michael J. Leblanc, "Franco-Indian Diplomacy in the Mississippi Valley, 1754–1763: Prelude to Pontiac's Uprising?" *Journal de la Société des Américanistes* 68 (1982): 62–63.

73. Indian Intelligence, 7 July 1763, *JP*/10, 767–68. Although Johnson received this information from a Mohawk sachem in July 1763, it is clear from the reference to a French officer and prospect of Spanish help that the chief was talking about events in 1762, not 1763. Also, the movements of the "French Officer" are consistent with Lantagnac's orders from Kerlérec; see *French Archives, Archives des Colonies,* 13a, vol. 43 (Ottawa: Correspondence Générale, various years).

74. Indian Intelligence, 7 July 1763, *JP*/10, 768.

75. Shawnee Intelligence, 30 January 1763, *BP*/6, 155–56.

76. Intelligence from Croghan, 28 September 1762, *JP*/10, 534. Croghan got this intelligence from "[a]n Indian of good character amongst all the Western Nations who lived near Detroit." The two Frenchmen have not been identified.

77. Shawnee Intelligence, 30 January 1763, *BP*/6, 155–56.

78. Kenny Journal, 4 September 1762, *PMHB* 37:167. Bouquet accepted that the information was correct but believed the season was too late for the French to attempt anything.

79. Intelligence from Croghan, 28 September 1762, *JP*/10, 534–35.

80. Journal of Alexander McKee, 1 November 1762, *JP*/10, 578–79.
81. Croghan to Johnson, 10 December 1762, *JP*/3, 964–66.
82. Johnson to Amherst, 12 November 1762, *JP*/10, 568–69; and Amherst to Johnson, 26 December 1762, *NA*/*WO*/34/38, fol. 214.
83. Indian Council, 16 March 1763, *JP*/10, 629–30; and Johnson to Amherst, 18 March 1763, *JP*/10, 623–25.
84. Speech of the Chiefs of the Miami [Twightwee], 30 March 1763, *BP*/6, 171.
85. Robert Rogers to Johnson, 7 October 1763, *JP*/10, 871–72. Rogers obtained this information from Aaron, a Mohawk messenger, who attended a council near Detroit on 6 October 1763 when "all the nations" asserted that the war in May 1763 had begun at the desire of the "Five Nations" (i.e., the Six Nations excluding the Tuscarora). Aaron repeated this account to Johnson, stating that the Ottawa, Delaware, and Shawnee all named the Seneca as the instigators of the conflict; 1 December 1763, *JP*/10, 939.
86. Speech of the Chiefs of the Miami, 30 March 1763, *BP*/6, 171.
87. Croghan to Johnson, 12 March 1763, *JP*/4, 62–63.
88. Kenny Journal, 21 February 1763, *PMHB* 37:187.
89. Gladwin to Amherst, 20 April 1763, *NA*/*WO*/34/49 fol. 176.
90. Croghan to Bouquet, 10 December 1762, *JP*/3, 964–66.
91. Croghan to Bouquet, 8 January 1763, *BP*/6, 139–40.
92. Bouquet to Amherst, 19 May 1763, *BP*/6, 190–91.
93. Amherst to Bouquet, 2 March 1762, *BP*/6, 50–51.
94. Amherst to Gladwin, 29 May 1763, *NA*/*WO*/34/49 fol. 325.
95. "A Narrative of the Captivity of John McCullough," in Loudon, *Selection of Some of the Most Interesting Narratives,* 1:272.
96. Kenny Journal, 15 October 1762, *PMHB* 37:171–72. Kenny's account of Neolin's road map is corroborated by John McCullough, except that the latter's version shows the earth divided into four squares, representing the different degrees of virtue and wickedness. McCullough's map also has two roads, one in the center taking the virtuous to heaven, and the other on the left taking the "abandonly wicked" to hell. However, the latter were given three chances of escaping their fate by submitting themselves to an ordeal by fire to purge themselves of their wrongdoing; Loudon, *Selection of Some of the Most Interesting Narratives,* 1:272–76.
97. Kenny Journal, 15 October 1762, *PMHB* 37:171.
98. Ibid., 12 December 1762, 175.
99. Loudon, *Selection of Some of the Most Interesting Narratives,* 1:272–75.
100. Kenny Journal, 20 August 1762, *PMHB* 37:165–86.
101. Ibid., 18 October 1762, 172.
102. Ibid., 4 November 1762, 173; and Loudon, *Selection of Some of the Most Interesting Narratives,* 1:272–73.
103. For a further discussion of the links between Christianity and Neolin, see Gregory Evans Dowd, *War under Heaven: Pontiac, the Indian Nations, and the British Empire* (Baltimore, 2002), 99–100.
104. Kenny Journal, 1 March 1763, *PMHB* 37:188.
105. Indian Conference, 10 September 1762, *JP*/10, 505–6.
106. Ibid., 13 September 1762, 511.

107. Milo Milton Quaife, ed., *The Siege of Detroit in 1763: The Journal of Pontiac's Conspiracy and John Rutherford's Narrative of a Captivity* (Chicago, 1961), 14–15.
108. Ibid., 16.

Chapter 4

1. For an overview of Pontiac's background and leadership qualities, see Richard Middleton, "Pontiac: Local Warrior or Pan Indian Leader?" Michigan Historical Review 32 (2006): 1–32.
2. Louise Phelps Kellogg, *The French Regime in Wisconsin and the North West* (Madison, Wisc., 1935), 425. Kellogg based her statement about Pontiac's presence at the battle on an assertion by a grandson of Charles Langlade, who had led the Great Lakes Indians against Braddock.
3. "Speech of Pontaigue, Ottawa Chief, Fort Duquesne" (undated but placed among Johnson's papers for 1757), in Richard E. Day, *Calendar of the Sir William Johnson Manuscripts* in the New York State Library (Albany, N.Y., 1909), 92. The original was unfortunately destroyed by fire in 1911, together with many other Johnson papers at the New York State Archives.
4. Declaration of Monsieur Jadeau, 5 April 1764, *JP*/13, 320.
5. Louis B. Porlier, "The Capture of Mackinaw, 1763: A Menomonee Tradition," in *Report and Collections of the State Historical Society of Wisconsin*, vol. 8 (Madison, 1876), 227–29.
6. Milo Milton Quaife, ed., *The Siege of Detroit in 1763: The Journal of Pontiac's Conspiracy and John Rutherford's Narrative of a Captivity* (Chicago, 1961), 250.
7. The Peace Preliminaries were announced in Philadelphia on 26 January 1763, *PCR*, IX, 13–15. Amherst received the definitive articles, which contained few changes, on 4 May 1763; Amherst to Governor Fauquier, 4 May 1763, *NA/CO/5/63*, fols. 53–54.
8. Conference with Six Nations, Speech of Serrehoana, Speaker for the Genesee, 15 December 1763, *JP*/10, 965–66. Kittanning had been destroyed in 1756 by a Pennsylvania force under Colonel John Armstrong; see Mathew C. Ward, *Breaking the Backcountry: The Seven Years' War in Virginia and Pennsylvania, 1754-1765* (Pittsburgh, PA, 2003), 106–7. It is not certain that the chief referred to here was Teedyuscung, nor that the information of his death on 20 April 1763 could have reached Detroit at such short notice. However, Indian messengers traveling by horseback, foot, and canoe could cover incredible distances.
9. Quaife, Siege of Detroit in 1763, 5–7, 20–21. Navarre's authorship of the first item in this publication, cited hereafter as "Navarre Journal," is not absolutely certain. However, it was clearly written by someone who had not only access to the British in the fort but also close contact with the Indians and French inhabitants. Navarre fits both profiles, since he lived outside the fort during the siege but had ready access to it as the local notary. Moreover, being the local notary meant that he was sufficiently literate to compose such a document, a scarce talent in a frontier community like Detroit. His freedom to come and go was demonstrated by his presence at a meeting of the French inhabitants on 2 July, when Pontiac appealed for help; Declaration of Mr. Jadeau, 24 December 1763, *JP*/13, 317–18. Two days later, Lieutenant Jehu Hay noted that Navarre was helping the British publicize details of the peace to the French and Indians; Franklin B. Hough, ed., *Diary of the Siege of Detroit in the War with Pontiac; also a Narrative*

of the Principal Events of the Siege by Major Robert Rogers; a Plan for Conducting Indian Affairs by Colonel Bradstreet and Other Authentick Documents, Never before Printed (Albany, N.Y., 1860), 39 (cited hereafter as "Hay Diary"). Navarre's covert support for the British was handsomely acknowledged by Gladwin in a letter to Amherst, 8 July 1763, NA/WO/34/49 fols. 196–97. Navarre's principal motives for writing the journal were seemingly to exonerate the majority of the French inhabitants from participation in the war and to expose Pontiac as an enemy of both the French and British. For further analysis of the journal, see Gregory Evans Dowd, War under Heaven: Pontiac, the Indian Nations, and the British Empire (Baltimore, 2002), 6, 97, 281–82.

10. Conference with the Six Nations, Speech of Serrehoana, 15 December 1763, JP/10, 964–65.
11. Ibid., 7.
12. Testimony of Mr. Chapman Abraham, 6–9 August 1763, NA/WO/34/49 fol. 262.
13. Navarre Journal, 15–16.
14. Ibid., 17.
15. Ibid., 6.
16. Conference with the Six Nations, Speech of Serrehoana, 15 December 1763, JP/10, 965–66.
17. Navarre Journal, 18–20.
18. Navarre Journal, 22–24.
19. Ibid., 24–25.
20. Ibid, 26–27. Although Navarre names the informant, there has been endless speculation about the true identity of the individual. For a survey of the possible candidates, see Howard H. Peckham, Pontiac and the Indian Uprising (Princeton, N.J., 1947; reprint, Detroit, 1994), 121–25.
21. Journal of Pontiac's Siege, 7 May 1763, Diary of John Porteous, II 3–4, BHC; and Gladwin to Amherst, 14 May 1763, NA/CO/5/63 fols. 89–90.
22. Porteous Diary, II, 5–6, BHC; and Journal of the Siege of Detroit by Lt. James McDonald, NA/WO/34/49 fol. 2. McDonald may have kept this journal on behalf of Gladwin, obtaining, like Porteous, much of his information about the Indians from the interpreters. He subsequently transcribed part of his journal into a letter to George Croghan, 12 July 1763, JP/10, 736-45.
23. Porteus Diary, II, 3, BHC.
24. Ibid., II, 7–8; and Navarre Journal, 31–32.
25. Navarre Journal, 32–33; and McDonald Journal, 9 May 1763, NA/WO/34/49, fol. 2.
26. Porteous Diary, II, 11–12.
27. McDonald Journal, 9 May 1763, NA/WO/34/49 fol. 2.
28. Deposition of Mr. Clermont, Detroit, 11 May 1764, in Charles Moore, ed., "The Gladwin Manuscripts, together with an Introduction and a Sketch of the Conspiracy of Pontiac," Michigan Pioneer and Historical Society 27:663–64.
29. Quaife, Siege of Detroit in 1763, 230.
30. Navarre Journal, 38–40.
31. Porteous Diary, I, 14; and Navarre Journal, 47.
32. McDonald Journal, 10 May 1763, NA/WO/34/49 fol. 3; and Gladwin to Amherst, 14 May 1763, NA/CO/5/63 fols. 89–90.

33. Evidence of Lieutenant McDougall, 6 August 1763, *NA/WO/34/49* fols. 262–63.
34. Gladwin to Amherst, 14 May 1763, *NA/CO/5/63* fols. 89–90.
35. McDonald Journal, 10 May 1763, *NA/WO/34/49* fols. 3–4; and Gladwin to Amherst, 14 May 1763, *NA/CO/5/63* fols. 89–90.
36. Brian Leigh Dunnigan, *Frontier Metropolis: Picturing Early Detroit, 1701–1838* (Detroit, Mich., 2001), 52–57.
37. Navarre Journal, 46.
38. Porteous Diary; and II, 17. McDonald Journal, 11 May 1763, *NA/WO/34/49* fol.5
39. Navarre Journal, 60–62.
40. McDonald Journal, 11 May 1763, *NA/WO/34/49* fols. 4-5, Porteous Diary, II, 18; Navarre Journal, 60-67; and Gladwin to Amherst, 14 May 1763, *NA/CO/5/63* fols. 89–90. There are some discrepancies about the sequence of these events, since McDonald records the attack as occurring on the 11th rather than 12 May 1763, the date given by other sources.
41. Navarre Journal, 66–67, 76. Gladwin affected to be more optimistic, writing to Amherst on 14 May 1763, "We are in high spirits and have provisions and ammunition enough to serve us till a relief arrives," *NA/CO/5/63*, fol. 90.
42. Speech of Serrehoana, Genesee Speaker, 15 December 1763 *JP/10*, 965–66. Kanawagus (or Conewago) had been used before as a meeting place between the western nations and the Seneca; Johnson to General James Abercromby, 17 February 1758, *JP/9*, 874–75.
43. For a history of the Iroquois League, see William N. Fenton, *The Great Law and the Longhouse: A Political History of the Iroquois Confederacy* (Norman, Okla., 1998); Daniel K. Richter, *The Ordeal of the Longhouse: The Peoples of the Iroquois League in the Era of Colonization* (Chapel Hill, N.C., 1992); and Daniel K. Richter and James H. Merrell, eds., *Beyond the Covenant Chain: The Iroquois and Their Neighbors in Indian North America, 1600–1800* (Syracuse, N.Y., 1987).
44. Information of Dekanandi, Seneca Chief, 6 October 1763, *JP/10*, 891–92. Johnson described Dekanandi as "a great friend of mine." Dekanandi claimed to have received his information from Seneca warriors returning after a raid against the Cherokee.
45. Navarre Journal, 86–89.
46. Copy of an embassy sent to the Illinois by the Indians at Detroit, May 1763, *NA/WO/34/49* fol. 270. There is another copy of this document in the Gage Papers, *WCL/GP/15*. Both are not specifically dated. Lieutenant James McDonald asserts in his journal that the emissaries departed on 12 May 1763, *NA/WO/34/49* fol. 4. Navarre states in his Journal, 86-88, that they left on the 18 May, but acknowledges that the plan had been "pondered on for some time."
47. Letter of the Inhabitants of Detroit to the Commanding Officers at the Illinois, May 1763, *NA/WO/34/49* fol. 268; and Gage Papers, *WCL/GP/15*.
48. For details of this mission, see the third section of chapter 5.
49. Porteous Dairy, II, 18; and Navarre Journal, 73–75.
50. Porteous, Diary, II, 18–19; and Gladwin to Amherst, 14 May 1763, *CO/5/63* fols. 89–90.
51. Navarre Journal, 70–72.
52. Ibid., 76–79.
53. Ibid., 84–85.

54. Gladwin to Amherst, 28 May 1763, *NA/WO/34/49* fol. 182.

55. Navarre Journal, 94–101.

56. Navarre Journal, 100.

57. Evidence of Ensign Paullie, 6 July 1763, *JP*/10, 730–32.

58. Court of Enquiry, 8 August 1763, *NA/WO/34/49* fol. 236; and Navarre Journal, 104–5.

59. Wilkins to Amherst, 15 June 1763, *NA/WO/34/22* fol. 128–29; and Court of Enquiry into the Conduct of Mr. Newman, Master of the Huron Schooner, 8 August 1763, *NA/WO/34/49* fol. 236.

60. Lt. Culyer's Account of His Defeat, 6 June 1763, *NA/WO/34/22* fols. 120–21.

61. Navarre Journal, 113–14; and McDonald Journal, 29 May 1763, *NA/WO/34/49* fol. 5.

62. Ibid., 31 May 1763; and Peckham, Pontiac, 158.

63. Navarre Journal, 91.

64. Ibid., 121.

65. Ibid., 129.

66. Ibid., 121. Lieutenant Jehu Hay suggests that the flotilla only departed about 9 June rather than 1 June 1763; Hay Diary, 36.

67. See chapter 5, section three for the details of these operations.

68. Navarre Journal, 140–41. See the second section of chapter 5 for the capture of Michilimackinac. It is not certain who Kinonchamek's father was, since Navarre could have been referring either to Menehwehna, "the great chief of the village of Michilimackinac," or the Grand Saulteur "the Great Chippewa Chief" from Grand Island, Lake Superior. For further information on the identity of the northern Ojibwa chiefs, see chapter 5, note 65. For the Grand Saulteur's possible links with Grand Isle, and hence name, see Journal of Daniel Claus, 16 September 1770, *JP*/7, 949

69. Navarre Journal, 142.

70. Hay Diary, 33. Hay presumably got this information indirectly through the interpreters.

71. Navarre Journal, 142.

72. Navarre Journal, 142–46. Kinonchamek's claim that the Ojibwa had respected their prisoners was disingenuous, since a number of the garrison were killed in cold blood. Those who survived did so mainly due to the intervention of the neighboring Ottawa. See the second section of chapter 5.

73. Navarre Journal, 144–45. Navarre refers to the Shawnee as "the Erie" at this point. This is certainly a slip of the pen, since the Erie had disappeared as a distinct group during the seventeenth-century Beaver Wars; Bruce Trigger ed., *The North East*, vol. 15 of *The Handbook of North American Indians,* 20 vols., ed. William C. Sturtevant (Washington, D.C., 1978), 412–17.

74. Gage to Amherst, 19 September 1763, *NA/WO/34/5* fol. 314. Gage obtained this information from the Ottawa who accompanied the Michilimackinac survivors to Montreal. See the second section of chapter 5.

75. Navarre Journal, 150–52; and Wilkins to Amherst, 15 June 1763, *NA/WO/34/22* fol. 128.

76. Navarre Journal, 154–55.

77. Hay Diary, 35.

78. Ibid., 36. Navarre mistakenly suggests that the first warriors from Presque Isle returned on 22 June, the same day that the fort surrendered; Navarre Journal, 149–50. But he also notes the return of other warriors on 29 June 1763; Navarre Journal,156.

79. Navarre Journal, 158–59; and McDonald Journal, 2 July 1762, *NA/WO/34/49* fol. 6.

80. Hay Diary, 34.

81. Ibid., 34.

82. Navarre Journal, 160–62.

83. Ibid., 162–64.

84. Declaration of Mr. Jadeau to Gladwin, 24 December 1763, *JP/13*, 318; Navarre Journal, 164–65; and McDonald Journal, 3 July 1763, *NA/WO/34/49* fols. 6–7. Jadeau was another covert supporter of the British, being subsequently described by Captain James Montresor as "a faithful inhabitant below the river"; J. C. Webster, ed., "Journal of John Montresor's Expedition to Detroit in 1763," *Proceedings and Transactions of the Royal Society of Canada*, series III, 22:25.

85. Evidence of Lieutenant McDougall, 6–9 August 1763, *NA/WO/34/49* fols. 263. McDougall was lodging in Cuillerier's house until his escape the following day.

86. Testimony of Private John McConnie, 20 December 1763, *GP/WCL/15*.

87. Testimony of Private John Packs, 12 October 1763, in Moore, "Gladwin Manuscripts," 653.

88. Hay Diary, 39.

89. Navarre Journal, 166–67.

90. Hay Diary, 39; Navarre Journal, 171–75; and Gladwin to Amherst, 8 July 1763, *NA/WO/34/49* fols. 196–99.

91. Hay Diary, 40–41. Hay was told this by the interpreter La Butte.

92. Ibid.; and C. C. Trowbridge, "Witness Accounts of the Siege of Detroit," *Michigan Pioneer and Historical Society* 8 (Lansing, 1886): 348.

93. Quaife, *Siege of Detroit in 1763*, 248–50.

94. Testimony of Mr. Rutherford, 6 August 1763, *NA/WO/34/49* fol. 262.

95. Declaration of Mr. Jadeau, 24 December 1763, *JP/13*, 318–19.

96. Navarre Diary, 177–78; and Hay Diary, 41.

97. Testimony of Private John Severings, 4 October 1763, *WLC/AP/2*; Testimony of Private James Connor, 4 October 1763, *WLC/AP/2*; and Testimony of Private John Packs, 12 October 1763, in Moore, "Gladwin Manuscripts," 653.

98. Navarre Journal, 181–84; and Hopkins to Amherst, 11 July 1763, *NA/WO/34/49* fol. 217.

99. Navarre Journal, 189–90; Hay Diary, 49; and Hopkins to Amherst, 22 July 1763, *NA/WO/34/49* fol. 218.

100. Navarre Journal, 190–91.

101. Ibid., 193–96.

102. Ibid., 138–39.

103. Hay Diary, 41–43; ibid., 178–79; and Gladwin to Amherst, 8 July 1763, *NA/WO/34/49* fols. 196–99.

104. Hay Diary, 44; and Navarre Journal, 181.

105. Hay Diary, 45–46.

106. Navarre Journal, 188.

107. Ibid., 192.

108. McDonald Journal, 25 July 1763, *NA/WO/34/49* fol. 7.
109. Navarre Journal, 196–98.

Chapter 5

1. "William Trent's Journal at Fort Pitt, 1763," 30 May 1763, ed. A. T. Volwiler, *MVHR* 11:394 (cited hereafter as Trent Journal). The arrival of this envoy was confirmed subsequently by four Shawnee to Thomas McKee, *MVHR* 16 June 1763, Ibid., *MVHR* 11:399.
2. Intelligence from Seneca Chief Dekanandi, 6 October 1763, *JP*/10, 891–92.
3. Ibid., 891–92.
4. Trent Journal, 27 May 1763, *MVHR* 11:393–94. McKee's mother was a Shawnee.
5. Kenny Journal, 27 May 1763, *PMHB* 27:197–98.
6. Ecuyer to Bouquet, 29 May 1763, *BP*/6, 193.
7. Ibid.
8. Ecuyer: Speech to the Indians, 29 May 1763, *BP*/6, 196–97.
9. Ecuyer to Bouquet, 30 May 1763, *BP*/6, 195–96.
10. Intelligence Brought to Fort Pitt by Mr Calhoun, 1 June 1763, *BP*/6, 197. There is another copy of this document in the Johnson Papers: see *JP*/10, 685–88.
11. Intelligence from Calhoun, *BP*/6, 198–99.
12. A Narrative of the Captivity of John McCullough Esquire, printed in Archibald Loudon, ed., *A Selection of Some of the Most Interesting Narratives of Outrages Committed by the Indians in Their Wars with the White People,* 2 vols. (Carlisle, 1808–1811; reprint, Lewisburg, 1996), 1:278–80.
13. Ecuyer to Bouquet, 2 June 1763, *BP*/6, 202–3.
14. Ourry to Bouquet, 31 May 1763, *BL*/Add Mss 21649 fol. 132.
15. Ourry to Bouquet, 3 June 1763, *BP*/6, 204–5.
16. Ibid., 7 June 1763, *BL*/Add Mss 21649 fol. 150.
17. Interrogation of John Hudson, 10 June 1763, *BP*/6, 214–16. For the links between the Sandusky Wyandot and the Ohio nations, see "An Account of the Remarkable Occurrences in the Life and Travels of Colonel James Smith during His Captivity with the Indians," in Loudon, *Selection of Some of the Most Interesting Narratives,* 1:119–205.
18. Blane to Bouquet, 4 June 1763, *BP*/6, 206–7.
19. Blane to Bouquet, 28 June 1763, *BP*/6, 268–69.
20. Croghan to Johnson, 2 July 1763, *JP*/10, 728.
21. Trent Journal, 16 June 1763, *MVHR* 11:399.
22. Ecuyer to Bouquet, 16 June 1763, *BP*/6, 231–33.
23. Trent Journal, 17 June 1763, *MVHR* 11:399.
24. Ecuyer to Bouquet, 26 June 1763, *BP*/6, 259–60. For the movements of the Mingo at this time, see below.
25. McKee: Conference with the Delaware, 24 June 1763, *BP*/6, 261–62.
26. Ibid.
27. Trent Journal, 24 June 1763, *MVHR* 11:400. Trent subsequently sought reimbursement for the blankets and silk handkerchief, "which were taken from people in the hospital." The expense for replacing the items was subsequently presented to Bouquet on behalf of Levy, Trent and Company: Account against the Crown, 13 August 1763, *BL*/Add Mss 21654 fols. 218–19. Historians are divided regarding whether the blankets were effective, since smallpox was already widespread.

For a recent investigation of the subject, see Elizabeth Fenn, "Biological Warfare in Eighteenth Century North America: Beyond Jeffery Amherst," *Journal of American History* 86:1552–80.

28. Trent Journal, 26 June 1763, *MVHR*, 11:401–2.

29. Indian Conference, 16 April 1763, *BP*/6, 183.

30. Stuart to Bouquet, 2 July 1763, *BL*/Add Mss 21649 fols. 212–14. The lack of weapons supports Michael Bellesiles's argument that Americans during the colonial period had relatively few firearms; see his *Arming America: The Origins of a National Gun Culture* (New York, 2000).

31. Hamilton to Pennsylvania Assembly, 4 July 1763, *PCR* 9:31–33.

32. Hamilton to Bouquet, 6 July 1763, *BP*/6, 298–99.

33. Ourry to Bouquet, 2 July 1763, *BP*/6, 286–87.

34. Ourry to Bouquet, 10 July 1763, *BL*/Add Mss 21642 fol. 452.

35. Major James Livingston to Bouquet, 16 July 1763, *BP*/6, 317–18.

36. John B. Linn and William H. Egle, eds., "Journal Kept at Fort Augusta by Lieutenant Samuel Hunter," 29 July 1763, *PA*, second series, vol. 7, 439.

37. Extract of a Letter from Carlisle, 12 July 1763, *Pennsylvania Gazette* for 21 July 1763, no. 1804; and "Narrative of Robert Robison," in Loudon, *Selection of Some of the Most Interesting Narratives,* 2:166–70.

38. McCullough Captivity Narrative, in Loudon, *Selection of Some of the Most Interesting Narratives,* 1:280–81.

39. St. Clair to Amherst, 19 July 1763, *NA*/WO/34/59 fol. 87. See also Bouquet to Hamilton, 13 July 1763, *BP*/6, 307–8.

40. Fauquier to Amherst, 2 August 1763, *NA*/CO/5/63 fol. 261. See also Washington to Robert Stewart, 13 August 1763, account book 1, Washington Papers, Library of Congress.

41. Trent Journal, 3 July 1763, *MVHR*, 11:403–4.

42. Ibid., 4 July 1763, 404–5.

43. Ibid., 21 July, 406.

44. Indian Speeches at Fort Pitt, 26 July 1763, *BP*/6, 333–35.

45. Captain Ecuyer's Reply to the Indians, 27 July 1763, *BP*/6, 336–37.

46. Smith Captivity Narrative, in Loudon, *Selection of Some of the Most Interesting Narratives,* 1:119–205.

47. Bouquet to Gladwin, 28 August 1763, *BL*/Add Mss 21649 fol. 313.

48. Trent Journal, 28 July to 1 August 1763, *MVHR*, 11:408–9.

49. Bouquet to Amherst, 11 August 1763, *BP*/6, 361–62.

50. Trent Journal, 1 August 1763, *MVHR*, 11:409.

51. Ibid., 2 August 1763, 410; Ecuyer to Bouquet, 5 August 1763, *BP*/6, 341–42.

52. Ecuyer to Bouquet, 5 August 1763, *BP*/6, 341–42.

53. Leslie to Gladwin, 16 September 1762, *NA*/WO/34/49 fol. 116.

54. Joseph Tassé, "Memoir of Charles Langlade," *Wisconsin Historical Collections* 7 (Madison, 1876): 153.

55. Alexander Henry, *Travels and Adventures in Canada and the Indian Territories between the Years 1760 and 1776* (New York, 1809; facsimile reprint, Ann Arbor, 1966), 73–75.

56. Claus to Johnson, 6 August 1763, *JP*/10, 777–78.

57. Henry, *Travels*, 114. There is some dispute as to who led the attack. Menehwehna is the leader named by Henry, *Travels*, 99. Later legend ascribes it to Matchekewis; see Lyman Copeland Draper, "Note on Matchekewis, Captor of Mackinaw," *Report and Collection of the State Historical Society of Wisconsin* 7 (Madison, 1876–): 188. Henry's attribution is probably correct, since he met both chiefs in memorable circumstances and was unlikely to have been confused about their identity; see *Travels*, 99–103, 114, 164–65.

58. Henry, *Travels*, 77–78; and Ethrington to Gladwin, 12 June 1763, *NA/WO/34/49* fols. 207–8.

59. Henry, *Travels*, 78–80; and Ethrington to Gladwin, 12 June 1763, *NA/WO/34/49* fols. 207–8.

60. Tassé, "Memoir of Charles Langlade," 156–57.

61. Speech by an Ottawa Chief [from L'Arbre Croche], 9 August 1763, *JP*/10, 779–82.

62. Henry, *Travels*, 97; and Indian Conference, August 1763, *JP*/10, 779–86.

63. Speech by an Ottawa Chief from L'Arbre Croche, 9 August 1763, *JP*/10, 779–80.

64. Henry, *Travels*, 103–4.

65. Historians have often confused the Grand Saulteur with Minavavana and Menehwehna, despite evidence to the contrary in Henry's *Travels*. Although the *Travels* were written many years after the event, Henry had earlier learned the Ojibwa language to assist his trading activities (*Travels*, 60), and was meticulous in his subsequent spelling of Indian names, not least those of Minavavana (*Travels*, 41–46) and Menehwehna (*Travels*, 100, 102, and 114), both of whom he met.

66. Norman Gelb, ed., *Jonathan Carver's Travels through America, 1766–1768: An Eighteenth Century Explorer's Account of Uncharted America* (New York, 1993), 93.

67. Henry, *Travels*, 103–4.

68. Louis B. Porlier, "Capture of Mackinaw, 1763: A Menomonee Tradition," *Report and Collections of the Wisconsin State Historical Society* 8 (Madison, 1879): 229–30.

69. Henry, *Travels*, 107–9.

70. See the third section of chapter 4.

71. Indian Conference, 11 August 1763, *JP*/10, 786. Gage believed the idea for a trade route via the Ottawa River was concocted to benefit the French merchants.

72. Lieutenant James Gorrell Journal, *Collections of the State Historical Society of Wisconsin* 1 (Madison, 1855): 38–40.

73. Ibid., 42–45.

74. Ibid., 45–47; and Ethrington to Gladwin, 18 July 1763, *NA/WO/34/49* fol. 235.

75. Testimony of Ensign Schlosser, 6 July 1763, *JP*/10, 731.

76. Richard Winston to the English Merchants at Detroit, 19 June 1763, *NA/WO/34/49* fol. 209.

77. Declaration of Caesar Cormick, Samuel Fleming and James Sterling, 11 June 1763, *NA/WO/34/39* fol. 364. One of the merchants was sent to Fort Chartres; the fate of the other is unknown.

78. Navarre Journal, 137–38.

79. Declaration of Caesar Cormick, Samuel Fleming and James Sterling, 11 June 1763, *NA/WO/34/39* fol. 364.

80. Testimony of Private James Burns, 6 July 1763, *JP*/10, 731–32.

81. Testimony of John McCoy, 21 Feb 1764, in Charles Moore, ed., "The Gladwin Manuscripts," *Michigan Pioneer and Historical Society* 27 (Lansing, 1897): 660–61.
82. Lieutenant Jenkins to Gladwin, 1 June 1763, *NA/WO/34/49* fol. 204.
83. Indian Conference, 26 May 1763, *JP/10*, 679–80.
84. Johnson to Amherst, 6 June 1763, *NYCD/7*, 522–24. Johnson did not keep a record of his actual speech to the Six Nations, 27 May 1763, *JP/10*, 682.
85. De Couagne to Johnson, 6 June 1763, *JP/4*, 137–38.
86. Journal of an Indian Congress, 15 December 1763, *JP/10*, 965.
87. Indian Intelligence, Johnson Journal, 11 July 1763, *JP/10*, 770.
88. Indian Intelligence, 11 July 1763, *JP/10*, 769–70.
89. Indian Intelligence, Chief Gawehe, 9 July 1763, *JP/10*, 768–69. Gawehe was an Oneida chief.
90. Ibid. The presence of the Mingo at the capture of Venango was confirmed by another informant, Soghsonowana, a Mohawk chief, who told Johnson that the attack "was done by a party of Chenussio who live near the said place"; Johnson Journal, 11 July 1763, *JP/10*, 769. It would be surprising in these circumstances if Kiashuta were not present, given his part in the plan of 1761 and his later role during the 1764 campaign. See David Dixon, *Never Come to Peace Again: Pontiac's Uprising and the Fate of the British Empire in North America* (Norman, OK, 2005), 147, 237–40.
91. Intelligence from Soghsonowana, 11 July 1763, *JP/10*, 769.
92. Trent Journal, 26 June 1763, *MVHR* 11:401. Trent got his information about Le Boeuf from Price after his escape to Fort Pitt early on 26 July 1763. See also Price to Bouquet, 26 June 1763, *BP/6*, 266–67.
93. The presence of the Ottawa, Ojibwa, Wyandot, and Seneca was confirmed by one of the garrison who escaped to Fort Pitt; Trent Journal, 26 June 1763, *MVHR* 11:402.
94. Ecuyer to Bouquet, 16 June 1763, *BP/6*, 231.
95. Court of Enquiry, 9 July 1763, *NA/WO/34/49*, fols. 212–13; and Christie to Bouquet, 10 July 1763, Detroit, *BP/6*, 301–3.
96. Court of Enquiry, 9 July 1763, *NA/WO/34/49* fols. 213–14; and Christie to Bouquet, 10 July 1763, *BP/6*, 301–3.
97. Amherst to Major Duncan, 16 July 1763, *NA/WO/34/20* fols. 145–46.
98. Court of Enquiry, 9 July 1763, *NA/WO/34/49* fol. 214.
99. Bouquet to Ecuyer, 4 July 1763, *BP/6*, 293–94.
100. Bouquet to the Commanding Officer (Presque Isle), 28 August 1763, *BL/Add Mss 21653* fol. 213. Bouquet did not know that the post still had to be reestablished by the garrison at Niagara.
101. List of the Killed at the Upper Posts, Captain George La Hunte to Gage, 2 July 1763, *WCL/GP/9*.

Chapter 6

1. Welbore Ellis to Amherst, 12 February 1763, Kentish Record Office, U/1350/O/43/5B; and Amherst to Ellis, 26 April 1763, *WCL/AP/1*. For the details of the new peacetime military establishment in North America, see John Shy, *Toward Lexington: The Role of the British Army in the Coming of the American Revolution* (Princeton, 1965).

2. There has been no recent biography of Amherst. The best remains J. C. Long, *Lord Jeffery Amherst: A Soldier of the King* (New York, 1933).
3. Ecuyer to Bouquet, 29 May 1763, *BP/6*, 193.
4. Ecuyer to Bouquet, 30 May 1763, *BP/6*, 195–96.
5. Amherst to Bouquet, 6 June 1763, *BP/6*, 209–10.
6. Amherst to Ligonier, 11 June 1763, Kentish Record Office, U/1350/O/35/54.
7. Amherst to Johnson, 12 June 163, *NA/WO/34/38* fol. 231.
8. Amherst to Bouquet, 12 June 1763, *BP/6*, 220–21.
9. Amherst Journal, 12 June 1763, Kentish Record Office, U/1350/O/15/11.
10. Disposition of His Majesty's Troops Serving in North America, December 1762, *NA/WO/34/74* fol. 181.
11. Amherst to Dalyell, 16 June 1763, *NA/WO/34/38* fol. 218; and Amherst to Gladwin, 16 June 1763, *NA/WO/34/49* fol. 327.
12. Amherst to Loring, 17 June 1763, *NA/WO/34/65* fol. 225.
13. Amherst to Northern Governors, 17 June 1763, *NA/WO/34/36* fol. 219. Most of the provincials still in service were from New York.
14. Bouquet to Amherst, 16 June 1763, *BP/6*, 225–26.
15. Amherst to Bouquet, 19 June 1763, *BP/6*, 239–41.
16. Amherst to Bouquet, 23 June 1763, *NA/WO/34/41* fol. 103.
17. Bouquet to Amherst, 25 June 1763, *BP/6*, 255–56.
18. Johnson to Amherst, 19 June 1763, *NYCD/7*, 524–25.
19. Bouquet to Amherst, 25 June 1763, *BP/6*, 255–56.
20. Amherst to Bouquet, 29 June 1763, *BP/6*, 277.
21. Amherst to Johnson, 28 July 1763, *NA/WO/34/38* fol. 248.
22. Johnson to Amherst, 1 July 1763, *NYCD/7*, 530–31; and Amherst to Johnson, 16 July 1763, *NA/CO/5/63* fol. 181.
23. Amherst to Hamilton, 25 June 1763, *NA/WO/34/32* fol. 112.
24. Hamilton to Amherst, 11 July 1763, *NA/WO/34/33*, fol. 185; and Hamilton to Bouquet, 12 July 1763, *BP/6*, 305–7.
25. Amherst to Johnson, 16 July 1763, *JP/4*, 173.
26. Dalyell to Amherst, 20 June 1763, *NA/WO/34/39* fol. 343.
27. Amherst to Gladwin, 2 July 1763, *NA/WO/34/54* fols. 84–85.
28. Dalyell to Amherst, 3 July 1763, *NA/WO/34/39* fol. 354.
29. Amherst to Duncan, 16 July 1763, *NA/WO/34/20* fols. 145–46.
30. Wilkins to Dalyell, 3 July 1763, *NA/WO/34/39* fol. 354.
31. Dalyell to Amherst, 15 July 1763, *NA/WO/34/39* fol. 383.
32. A letter from Detroit, 8 August 1763, printed in Armand Francis Lucier, ed., *Pontiac's Conspiracy and Other Indian Affairs: Notices Abstracted from Colonial Newspapers* (Bowie, MD, 2000), 61. The author of this letter has not been identified, but the style is reminiscent of Robert Rogers, who joined the expedition as a volunteer. See below.
33. Gladwin to Amherst, 26 July 1763, *NA/WO/34/49* fol. 222.
34. Hopkins to Amherst, 28 July 1763, *NA/WO/34/49* fol. 225.
35. Navarre Journal, 199–201.

36. Timothy J. Todish, ed., *The Annotated and Illustrated Journals of Major Robert Rogers* (Fleischmanns, N.Y., 2002), 134, 145–47. According to Caleb Stark, the later revolutionary commander, this was a regular practice to give British officers the experience of frontier conditions; Force Transcripts, Reel 43, Sprague Collection, Library of Congress.
37. Account of the Action of 31 July 1763, [forwarded by Major Alexander Duncan from Fort Ontario, Oswego], *JP*/10, 762. The author of this document is unknown but may have been Captain James Grant of the 80th regiment, since the focus is on his company after he took command. The original is in the Amherst Papers, *NA/WO/34/49* fols. 239-41. There is a similar account by Lieutenant James McDonald in a letter to Captain Horatio Gates, 8 August 1763, Michigan Collection, *WCL*.
38. Account of the Action, 31 July 1763, *JP*/10, 763.
39. Evidence of Manning Fisher, 8 September 1763, *WCL/AP/2*.
40. Milo Milton Quaife, ed., *The Siege of Detroit in 1763: The Journal of Pontiac's Conspiracy and John Rutherford's Narrative of a Captivity* (Chicago, 1961), 263.
41. Navarre Journal, 204–5; and Mrs. Meloche's Account, in C. C. Trowbridge, ed., "Witness Accounts of the Siege of Detroit, 1763," *MPHC* 8 (Lansing, Mich., 1886): 340–44.
42. McDonald to Gates, 8 August 1763, Michigan Collection, *WCL*.
43. Account of the Action, 31 July 1763, *JP*/10, 762–63; and McDonald to Gates, 8 August 1763, Michigan Collection, *WCL*.
44. Account of the Action, 31 July 1763, *JP*/10, 764–65; and Letter from Detroit, 8 August 1763, in Lucier, *Notices Abstracted from Colonial Newspapers*, 61–64.
45. McDonald to Gates, 8 August 1763, Michigan Collection, *WCL*. Account of the Action, *JP*/10, 765–66.
46. Quaife, *Rutherford's Narrative*, 263–64.
47. Sterling to John Sterling, 7 August 1763, Sterling Letter Book, *WCL*.
48. Letter from Detroit, 8 August 1763, Lucier, *Notices Abstracted from the Colonial Newspapers*, 64.
49. Gladwin to Gage, 9 January 1764, *WLC/GP/12*.
50. Captain William Dunbar to Gage, 15 September 1763, *WCL/GP/9*.
51. Amherst to Gladwin, 9 September 1763, *NA/WO/34/49* fol. 343.
52. Gladwin to Amherst, 8 August 1763, *NA/WO/34/49* fol. 230.
53. Gladwin to Amherst, 11 August 1763, *NA/WO/34/49* fol. 243.
54. Gladwin to Amherst, 26 July 1763, *NA/WO/34/49* fol. 222.
55. Statutes at Large, 29 George II, chapter 5.
56. Foreign subjects were forbidden any office under the terms of the 1701 Act of Settlement.
57. There is no modern biography of Bouquet. His papers have been extensively published; see Donald H. Kent, Louis M. Waddell, and Autumn L. Leonard, eds., *The Papers of Henry Bouquet*, 6 vols. (Harrisburg, PA, 1951–1994).
58. Amherst to Bouquet, 2 July 1763, *BP*/6, 283.
59. Bouquet to Amherst, 29 June 1763, *BP*/6, 270–71; and Bouquet to Amherst, 3 July 1763, *BP*/6, 288–89.
60. Amherst to Bouquet, 7 July 1763, *BP*/6, 299–301.
61. Bouquet to Amherst, 13 July 1763, *NA/WO/34/40* fol. 305; and ibid., Add Mss 21634 fol. 321.

62. Amherst to Bouquet, 16 July 1763, *BP*/6, 315.

63. See the first section of chapter 5.

64. For a wider discussion of the topic, see Elizabeth A. Fenn, "Biological Warfare in Eighteenth Century North America: Beyond Jeffery Amherst," *Journal of American History* 86:1552–80; and Mathew C. Ward, "The Microbes of War: The British Army and Epidemic Disease among the Ohio Indians, 1758–1765," in *The Sixty Years War for the Great Lakes, 1754–1814,* ed. David Curtis Skaggs and Larry L. Nelson (East Lansing, MI, 2001), 65–78.

65. Bouquet to Ourry, 4 July 1763, *BP*/6, 296–98.

66. Bouquet to Hamilton, 8 July 1763, *BL*/Add Mss 21649 fol. 238.

67. Hamilton to Bouquet, 12 July 1763, *BP*/6, 306–7.

68. Bouquet to Amherst, 13 July 1763, *NA*/*WO*/34/40 fols. 304–5.

69. Amherst to Bouquet, 16 July 1763, *BP*/6, 313–14.

70. Amherst to Hamilton, 16 July 1763, *BP*/6, 315; and Amherst to Robertson, 17 July 1763, *NA*/*WO*/34/59 fol. 287.

71. Robertson to Bouquet, 19 July 1763, *BP*/6, 322.

72. Bouquet to Amherst, 26 July 1763, *BP*/6, 325–26.

73. Bouquet to Amherst, 5 August 1763, *BP*/6, 338.

74. Ibid., 338–39.

75. Bouquet to Amherst, 5 August 1763, *BP*/6, 339.

76. Cyrus Cort, *Colonel Henry Bouquet and His Campaigns of 1763 and 1764* (Lancaster, PA, 1883), 40. Cort obtained this information about Kickyuscung from family hearsay based on an account by his great great grandfather, who had witnessed the battle.

77. Bouquet to Amherst, 6 August 1763, *BP*/6, 342–44.

78. Amherst to Gladwin, 28 August 1763, *NA*/*WO*/34/49 fol. 335.

79. Journal of Indian Affairs, 2 March 1765, *JP*/11, 618. Johnson, however, claimed to have had similar estimates from adopted whites who fought with the Indians at Bushy Run; Review of the Trade and Affairs of the Indians in the Northern District of America, September 1767, *NYCD*/7, 962. See Dixon, *Never Come to Peace Again,* 310 n. 24.

80. Bouquet to Amherst, 11 August 1763, *BP*/6, 361–62.

81. Bouquet to Hamilton, 11 August 1763, *BL*/Add Mss 21649 fol. 295.

Chapter 7

1. Strength of the Regiments from the Havana, 29 July 1763, *NA*/*CO*/5/63 fol. 226.

2. Amherst to Gage, 1 August 1763, *NA*/*WO*/34/7 fol. 152; and Amherst to Wilkins, 3 August 1763, *NA*/*WO*/34/23 fol. 129.

3. Amherst to Gladwin, 10 August 1763, *NA*/*WO*/34/49 fol. 331.

4. Amherst to Gardiner, 10 August 1763, *NA*/*WO*/34/54 fol. 87.

5. Amherst to Gladwin, 10 August 1763, *NA*/*WO*/34/49 fol. 331.

6. Bouquet to Amherst, 26 August 1763, *NA*/*WO*/34/40 fol. 330.

7. Bouquet to Amherst, 27 August 1763, *NA*/*WO*/34/40 fol. 332.

8. Amherst to Gladwin, 28 August 1763, *NA*/*WO*/34/49 fol. 335.

9. Amherst to Bouquet, 31 August 1763, *BP*/6, 377–79.

10. Amherst to Fauquier, 29 August 1763, in George Reese, ed., *The Official Papers of Francis Fauquier, Lieutenant Governor of Virginia, 1758–1768,* 3 vols. (Charlottesville, VA, 1980–1983), 2:1004.

11. Amherst to Stephen, 31 August 1763, *BP*/6, 380–81.
12. Fauquier to Amherst, 18 September 1763, in Reese, *Official Papers of Francis Fauquier,* 2:1031.
13. Amherst to Bouquet, *BP*/6, 394–96.
14. Bouquet to Amherst, 7 September 1763, *NA*/*WO*/34/40 fol. 343.
15. Amherst to Fauquier, 29 August 1763, in Reese, *Official Papers of Francis Fauquier,* 2:1004.
16. Amherst to Gladwin, 9 September 1763, *NA*/*WO*/34/97 fols. 343–46.
17. Amherst to Wilkins, 3 September 1763, *NA*/*WO*/34/23 fol. 136.
18. See below.
19. Wilkins to Gage, 25 June 1763, *WCL*/*GP*/9.
20. Wilkins to Amherst, 26 July 1763, *NA*/*WO*/34/22 fol. 140.
21. Pierre Pouchot, *Memoirs on the Late War in North America between France and England,* ed. Brian Leigh Dunnigan, trans. Michael Cardy (Youngstown, N.Y., 1994), 418–19.
22. Present State of the Garrison at Niagara, 9 August 1763, *NA*/*WO*/34/22 fol. 148.
23. For details about Niagara, see Brian Leigh Dunnigan, *A History and Guide to Old Fort Niagara* (Youngstown, N.Y., 1985).
24. Wilkins to Amherst, 26 August 1763, *NA*/*WO*/34/22 fol. 161.
25. Montresor to Wilkins, 29 August 1763, *NA*/*WO*/34/22 fol. 161.
26. Court of Enquiry into the Conduct of an Indian Named Andrew, 1 September 1763, *BP*/6, 386.
27. J. C. Webster, ed., "Journal of John Montresor's Expedition to Detroit in 1763," *Transactions of the Royal Society of Canada,* series III, 22:14–16.
28. Ibid., 16–18.
29. Colin Andrews to Johnson, 9 September 1763, *JP*/10, 812.
30. Montresor to Captain Thomas Basset (Engineers), 2 November 1763, *BL* Add Mss 21649 fol. 434. By this time, Montresor had acquired some familiarity with the Detroit nations; see the third section of this chapter.
31. Indian Conference, 18–20 July 1763, *JP*/10, 746–53.
32. Journal of Indian Congress, 4–7 September 1763, *JP*/10, 829–30.
33. Ibid., 830–31.
34. Moncrieffe to Amherst, 4 October 1763 *NA*/*WO*/34/95 fol. 187.
35. Bouquet to Amherst, 7 September 1763, *BP*/6, 385.
36. Wilkins to Amherst, 10 September 1763, *NA*/*WO*/34/22 fol. 170; and Return of the Troops, 9 September 1763, *WCL*/*AP*/2.
37. Wilkins to Amherst, 17 September 1763, *NA*/*WO*/34/22 fols. 183–84.
38. A Letter from Niagara, 16 September 1763, in Armand Francis Lucier, *Pontiac's Conspiracy and Other Indian Affairs: Notices Abstracted from Colonial Newspapers, 1763–1765* (Bowie, MD, 2000), 82–83.
39. Information from Chief Dekanandi, 6 October 1763, *JP*/10, 892–93. Dekanandi was from Canadasaga and was probably motivated by a desire to exculpate his village from the affair. It has not proved possible to identify further the warriors named by him as leading the attack.
40. Ibid. See also Johnson to Amherst, 6 October 1763, *JP*/10, 867–69.

41. Action at the Carrying Place, 14 September 1763, *NA/WO/34/22* 176; Wilkins to Amherst, 17 September 1763, *NA/WO/34/22* fols. 183–84; and extracts of letters from Niagara, 16–17 September 1763, printed in Lucier, *Pontiac's Conspiracy,* 79–83.

42. Bradstreet to Gage, 30 March 1764, *WCL/GP/16.*

43. James E. Seaver, ed., *A Narrative of the Life of Mrs Mary Jemison* (Canandaigua, N.Y., 1824), 51–53.

44. Amherst Journal, 30 September 176, Kentish Record Office, U/1350/O.15/11.

45. Amherst to Moncrieffe, 1 October 1763, *NA/WO/34/97* fol. 138.

46. Amherst to Browning, 10 October 1763, *NA/WO/34/23* fol. 154.

47. Journal of Indian Affairs, 8 October 1763, *JP/10,* 893–95.

48. Information from Dekanandi, 6 October 1763, *JP/10,* 891.

49. Bradstreet to Amherst, 6 October 1763, *NA/WO/34/37* fols. 377–78.

50. Amherst to Bradstreet, 12 October 1763, *NA/WO/34/56* fol. 322.

51. Amherst to Wilkins, 1 October 1763, *NA/WO/34/23* fol. 148.

52. Amherst to Gladwin, 6 October 1763, *NA/WO/34/49* fol. 354.

53. Gladwin to Johnson, 7 October 1763, *JP/10,* 873.

54. Moncrieffe to Johnson, 4 October 1763, *JP/4,* 212–13.

55. Browning to Johnson, 22 October 1763, *JP/10,* 906.

56. Ibid. Silver Heels, a Seneca chief, subsequently denied that his nation had been involved in the incident; Journal of Indian Affairs, 12 December 1763, *JP/10,* 962. The assailants may have been Ojibwa from the northern shore of Lake Erie and Lake Ontario, since three weeks earlier Johnson had accused them of being in league with the Seneca; Johnson to Amherst, 30 September 1763, *JP/4,* 210.

57. Wilkins to Amherst, 27 November 1763, *WCL/AP/7.*

58. Moncrieffe to Gladwin, 12 November 1763, *WCL/AP/7;* and Wilkins to Amherst, 27 November 1763, *WCL/AP/7* .

59. Browning to Amherst, 10 November 1763, *WLC/AP/7.*

60. De Couagne to Johnson, 11 November 1763, *JP/10,* 921–22.

61. Gladwin to Amherst, 11 August 1763, *NA/WO/34/49* fol. 243. Gladwin does not identify the "Grand Saulteur" as leading the new arrivals or that they were from Lake Superior. However, Captain Thomas Hopkins had written to Amherst a few days earlier that "the enemy expect great reinforcements from Lake Superior"; 28 July 1763, *WO/34/49* fol. 225. The Grand Saulteur himself was subsequently identified as being present by a French inhabitant; Deposition of Monsieur La Ville, 14 November 1763, *WCL/GP/9.*

62. See the second section of chapter 5. Strictly speaking the term "Saulteur" referred to the Ojibwa from Sault St. Marie and the villages around Lake Superior. However it was often used to describe all Ojibwa.

63. Evidence of Andrew, the Messenger, 1 September 1763, *BP/6,* 386–87.

64. Gladwin to Amherst, 7 October 1763, *NA/WO/34/49* fols. 253–54.

65. Hay Journal, 67. Hay believed the Mohawks intended treachery; Amherst thought so, too. However, Gladwin exonerated them; Gladwin to Amherst, 7 October 1763, *NA/WO/34/49* fol. 255.

66. Relation of the Gallant Defence by the Crew of the Schooner on Lake Erie, September 1763, *NA/CO/5/63* fol. 388; and Gladwin to Amherst, 9 September 1763, *NA/WO/34/49* fol. 246.

67. Sterling Letter Book, 8 September 1763, *WCL*; and John Stoughton to Johnson, 16 September 1763, *JP*/10, 814.
68. Relation of Some Events at Detroit, 4 September 1763, *BL*/Add Mss 21655 fols. 221–22.
69. Gladwin to Amherst, 9 September 1763, *NA/WO*/34/49 fol. 246.
70. Hay Diary, 70–71.
71. Deposition of Monsieur La Ville, 14 November 1763, *WCL/GP*/9. La Ville had left Detroit for Montreal with a pass on 4 October 1764.
72. Relation of Some Events at Detroit, 2 October 1763, *BL*/Add Mss 21655 fols. 221–22; Hay to Bouquet, 5 October 1763, Add Mss 21,649 fol. 381; and Gladwin to Amherst, 7 October 1763, *NA/WO*/34/49 fol. 253.
73. Montresor Journal, *Royal Canada Society* 22:22.
74. Deposition of Monsieur La Ville, 14 November 1763, *WCL/GP*/9.
75. Rogers to Johnson, 7 October 1763, *JP*/10, 872; and Loring to Johnson, 9 November 1763, *PHS*, Gratz Collection, case 4, box 7.
76. Montresor Journal, *Royal Canada Society* 22:22.
77. De Villiers to D'Abbadie, 1 December 1763, in Clarence Walworth Alvord and Clarence Edwin Carter, eds., *The Critical Period, 1763–1765, Collections of the Illinois State Historical Library,* vol. 10 (Springfield, 1915), 49–57.
78. Rogers to Johnson, 7 October 1763, *JP*/10, 872.
79. Montresor Journal, *Royal Canada Society* 22:22.
80. Ibid., 22–23.
81. Gladwin to Amherst, 7 October 1763, *NA/WO*/34/49 fols. 253–54.
82. Montresor Journal, *Royal Canada Society* 22:23; and Gladwin to Amherst, 1 November 1763, *BP*/6, 446–48.
83. Montresor Journal, *Royal Canada Society* 22:23–24.
84. Ibid., 24–25.
85. Neyon de Villiers to the Indian Nations, 27 September 1763, *JP*/10, 819–21.
86. De Villiers to the Inhabitants of Detroit, 27 September 1763, *JP*/10, 822–23.
87. Pontiac to Gladwin, 30 October 1763, *BP*/6, 448–49.
88. Gladwin to Pontiac, 30 October 1763, *BP*/6, 448–49.
89. Montresor Journal, *Royal Canada Society* 22:26.
90. Gladwin to Amherst, 1 November 1763, *BP*/6, 446–48.
91. Gladwin to Johnson, 11 May 1764, *JP*/11, 192.
92. Johnson to Colden, 30 December 1763, *JP*/4, 281–82.
93. Gage to Halifax, 7 January 1763, in *The Correspondence of General Thomas Gage with the Secretaries of State, 1763–1775,* ed. Clarence E. Carter, 2 vols. (New Haven, Conn., 1931–1933), 1:9–11.
94. Montresor Journal, *Royal Canada Society* 22:26.
95. Egremont to Amherst, 13 August 1763, *WCL/AP*/1.
96. Amherst to Egremont, 13 October 1763, *NA/CO*/5/63 fols. 361–66.
97. Amherst to Gage, 11 October 1763, *NA/WO*/34/7, fol. 178; and Amherst to Gage, 17 November 1763, *NA/WO*/34/7 fol. 184.
98. Amherst to the Army in America, 17 November 1763, *BL*/Add Mss 21656 fols. 20–21.
99. Amherst Journal, 17 November–29 December 1763, Kentish Record Office, U/1350/O/15/12.
100. Amherst to Eyre, 15 January 1764, *NA/WO*/34/100 fol. 177.

101. Basset to Bouquet, 10 December 1763, *BL*/Add Mss 21649 fols. 497–98.
102. Croghan to Johnson, 24 February 1764, *JP*/4, 339–40.
103. Loring to Johnson, 9 November 1763, *JP*/10, 920.
104. Eyre to Johnson, 7 January 1764, *PHS*, Gratz Collection, case 4, box 7.
105. Croghan to Johnson, 28 September 1763, *JP*/10, 825–27.
106. Gladwin to Bouquet, 1 November 1763, *BP*/6, 445.

Chapter 8

1. *Dictionary of American Biography*. His wife's name was Margaret Kemble.
2. Extract of a letter from Schenectady, 2 July 1756, Hardwicke Papers, *BL*/Add Mss 35909 fols. 260–62.
3. Gage to Loudoun, 22 December 1757, Loudoun Papers, box 112, fol. 5066, Huntington Library.
4. Gage to Halifax, 7 January 1764, in Clarence E. Carter, ed., *The Correspondence of General Thomas Gage with the Secretaries of State, 1763–1775* (cited hereafter as Gage Correspondence), 2 vols. (New Haven, Conn., 1931–1933), 1:10–11.
5. Gage to Johnson, 26 December 1763, *JP*/4, 280.
6. Egremont to the Board of Trade, 5 May 1763, *NA/CO/5/65*, fols. 43–51; and Board of Trade to Egremont, 8 June 1763, *NA/CO/5/65* fols. 59–78.
7. A Royal Proclamation, 7 October 1763, *JP*/10, 977–84.
8. Gage to Halifax, 9 December 1763, in *Gage Correspondence*, 1:2.
9. Ibid., 23 December 1763, 6–7.
10. Ibid., 9 December 1763, 2–3.
11. Armstrong to Bouquet, 26 August 1763, *BP*/6, 370.
12. Jonas Seely to Hamilton, 10 September 1763, *PCR* 9:43–44; and *Pennsylvania Gazette*, 15 September 1763.
13. Seely to Hamilton, 11 September 1763, *PCR* 9:44.
14. Petition of the Inhabitants of the Great Cove, 17 September 1763, Pennsylvania Archives, 8th series, VI, 5437–8. For Smith's account of his role, see Archibald Loudon, ed., *A Selection of the Some of the Most Interesting Narratives of Outrages Committed by the Indians in Their Wars with the White People*, 2 vols. (Carlisle, PA, 1808, reprint, Lewisburg, PA, 2001), 1:205–6.
15. Minutes of the Council, 20 September 1763, *PA*, 8th series, VI, 5440.
16. Hamilton to the Assembly, 15 October 1763, *PA*, 4th series, III, 216–18.
17. Pennsylvania Assembly to Hamilton, 22 October 1763, *PCR* 9:64–66.
18. Loudon, *Selection of the Some of the Most Interesting Narratives*, 2:174.
19. "Journal Kept at Fort Augusta by Lieutenant Samuel Hunter," 27 August 1763, *PA*, 2nd series, VII (Harrisburg, 1895), 469; and Loudon, *Selection of Some of the Most Interesting Narratives,* 2:174–77, 2:191–92.
20. *Pennsylvania Gazette,* 27 October 1763; and *Fort Augusta Journal,* 11–12 October 1763, *PA*, 2nd series, VII, 474.
21. *Fort Augusta Journal,* 17 October 1763, *PA*, 2nd series, VII, 475.
22. Extract of Letter from Captain William Ingles to the President of the Virginia Council [John Blair], *Pennsylvania Gazette*, 17 November 1763.
23. Lewis to Blair, 3 October 1763, in Armand Francis Lucier, *Pontiac's Conspiracy and Other Indian Affairs: Notices Abstracted from Colonial Newspapers, 1763–1765* (Bowie, MD, 2000), 86.

24. Blair to Gage, 22 October 1763, *JP*/10, 908–9; and Extract of a Letter from Colonel Andrew Lewis to the President of the Virginia Council, 10 October 1763, *Pennsylvania Gazette,* 17 November 1763.
25. Conference with Six Nations, 24 March 1764, *JP*/11, 134–38.
26. Johnson to Gage, 23 December 1763, *JP*/10, 975.
27. Hamilton to James Burd and Thomas McKee, 2 June 1763, *PCR* 9:29–30; and Pennsylvania Gazette, no. 1798, 9 June 1763.
28. Jane T. Merritt, *At the Crossroads: Indians and Empires on a Mid-Atlantic Frontier, 1700–1763* (Chapel Hill, N.C., 2003), 275–77.
29. Ibid., 261.
30. *Pennsylvania Gazette,* no. 1820, 10 November 1763.
31. Extract of a Letter from Paxton, 23 October 1763, *Pennsylvania Gazette,* no. 1818, 27 October 1763.
32. Elder to Hamilton, 25 October 1763, Susquehanna Company Papers, 2:277–78.
33. *Pennsylvania Gazette,* no. 1823, 1 December 1763. Bull subsequently confessed his involvement in this incident; Marsh to Johnson, 2 April 1764, *JP*/11, 119–20.
34. Indian Conference, 1 December 1763, *PCR* 9:77–79.
35. The Remonstrance of the Paxton Boys, 13 February 1764, *PCR* 9:138–42.
36. Elder to John Penn, 16 December 1763, *PA*, 1st series, IV, 148–49.
37. Edward Shippen to John Penn, 14 December 1763, *PCR* 9:89–90.
38. Proclamation by John Penn, 22 December 1763, *PCR* 9:95–96.
39. Edward Shippen to Governor John Penn, 27 December 1763, *PCR* 9:100–1.
40. Sheriff John Hay to John Penn, 27 December 1763, *PCR* 9:102–3.
41. Armstrong to Penn, 28 December 1763, *PA*, 1st series, IV, 152–53.
42. John Penn to Gage, 31 December 1763, *PCR* 9:104–5.
43. Journal of Indian Affairs, 20 January 1763, *JP*/11, 31.
44. Johnson to Penn, 9 February 1764, *JP*/4, 323.
45. Petition of Whitehall, Heidelberg etc., 9 January 1764, *PA*, 8th series, VII, 5508–9.
46. Petition of David Scott, 11 January 1764, *PA*, 8th series, VII, 5509–11.
47. Peters to Monckton, 19 January 1764, in *Aspinwall Papers, Collections of the Massachusetts Historical Society,* 4th series, vol. 10 (Boston, 1871), 508–11.
48. Penn to Colden, 5 January 1764, in 1761–1764, vol. 6 of *The Letters and Papers of Cadwallader Colden,* 7 vols., New York Historical Society Publications, nos. 50–56 (New York, 1917–1923), 274–75.
49. Colden to Penn, 10 January 1764, *PCR* 9:120–21.
50. Penn to the Assembly, 3 February 1764, *PA*, 8th series, VII, 5536–7.
51. Minutes of the Pennsylvania Council, 4 February 1764, *PCR* 9:132–33.
52. Remonstrance of the Frontier Inhabitants by Mathew Smith and James Gibson, 13 February 1764, *PCR* 9:138–42. See also Declaration of the Injured Frontier Inhabitants, 17 February 1764, *PCR* 9:142–45.
53. Quoted in Richard Middleton, *Colonial America: A History, 1565–1776* (Oxford, 2002), 457.
54. Penn to Johnson, 17 February 1763, *JP*/4, 327–28.
55. Amherst to Browning, 10 October 1763, *NA/WO/34/23* fol. 154.
56. Browning to Amherst, 28 November 1763, *WCL/AP/7.*
57. Johnson to Gage, 23 November 1763, *JP*/4, 251–53.
58. Johnson to Gage, 23 December 1763, *JP*/10, 973–76.

59. Johnson to Gage, 30 December 1763, *JP*/10, 990–91.
60. Gage to Johnson, 12 December 1763, *JP*/10, 953–54.
61. Gage to Murray, 12 February 1764, *WCL/GP*/14.
62. Johnson to Colden, 12 January 1764, *JP*/4, 287–90; and Johnson to Gage, 3 February 1764, *JP*/11, 36.
63. Gage to Johnson, 23 January 176, *JP*/4, 302–3.
64. Instructions to Henry [Andrew] Montour, 9 February 1764, *JP*/11, 51–52.
65. James H. Merrell, *Into the American Woods: Negotiators on the Pennsylvania Frontier* (New York, 1999), 54–55, 76–77.
66. Johnson to Claus, 10 February 1764, *JP*/11 52–53.
67. Johnson to Montour, 21 February 1764, *JP*/4, 336–37; and Gage to Johnson, 13 February 1764, *JP*/4, 325–26.
68. Montour to Johnson, 28 February 1764, *JP*/4, 344–45; and Johnson to Bradstreet, 2 March 1764, *JP*/4, 349.
69. Johnson to Colden, 16 March 1764, *JP*/4, 364–66.
70. Johnson to Gage, 16 March 1764, *JP*/4, 368–69.
71. Marsh to Johnson, 2 April 1764, *JP*/11, 119–20. The interrogation of Bull is a good example of the ludicrous suspicions held about the Quakers because of their strange dress and unorthodox religion.
72. Johnson to Gage, 16 March 1764, *JP*/4, 369, 372.
73. Johnson to the Stockbridge Indians, 17 February 1764, *JP*/11, 68.
74. Montour to Johnson, 2 March 1764, *JP*/11, 87–88.
75. Johnson to Gage, 6 April 1764, *JP*/4, 389–90.
76. Johnson to Gage, 16 April 1764, *JP*/11, 131–32.
77. Johnson to Gage, 16 March 1764, *JP*/4, 371.
78. Journal of an Indian Congress, 2–5 December 1763, *JP*/10, 945.
79. Six Nations Conference, 15 December 1763, *JP*/10, 964–66.
80. Ibid., 16 December 1763, *JP*/10, 966–67.
81. Six Nations Conference, 17 December 1763, *JP*/10, 968–69.
82. Johnson to Gage, 23 December 1763, *JP*/10, 973–74.
83. Gage to Johnson, 12 January 1764, *JP*/4, 291–92.
84. Johnson to Gage, 27 January 1764, *JP*/4, 308–9.
85. Colden to Halifax, 13 February 1764, *NYCD*/7, 609–10.
86. Journal of Indian Affairs, 5–6 March 1764, *JP*/11, 105–6; and ibid., 19 March, 111.
87. Six Nations Conference, 24 March 1764, *JP*/11, 135–49.
88. Ibid., 30 March 1764, 146–50.
89. Ibid., 1 April 1764, 151. The articles are listed under the entry for 2 April 1764, 154–55.
90. Ibid., 2 April 1764, 151–52.
91. Ibid., 3 April 1764, 156–57.
92. Ibid., 158.
93. Ibid., 14 April 1764, 159.
94. Montour to Johnson, 7 April 1764, *JP*/4, 393; and Journal of Indian Affairs, 25 April 1764, *JP*/11, 180–81.
95. Journal of Indian Affairs, 30 April 1764, *JP*/11, 183–85.

Chapter 9

1. Gage to Halifax, 23 December 1763, in Clarence E. Carter, ed., *The Correspondence of General Thomas Gage with the Secretaries of State, 1763–1775,* 2 vols. (New Haven, Conn., 1931–1933) 1:4–7.

2. Chevalier to Gladwin, 24 November 1763, *WCL/GP*/15; and Franklin B. Hough, ed., *Diary of the Siege of Detroit in the War with Pontiac; also A Narrative of the Principal Events of the Siege by Major Robert Rogers; a Plan for Conducting Indian Affairs by Colonel Bradstreet and Other Authentick Documents, Never before Printed* (cited hereafter as Hay Diary) (Albany, N.Y., 1860), 87.

3. De Villiers to D'Abbadie, 1 December 1763, in Clarence Walworth Alvord and Clarence Edwin Carter, eds., *The Critical Period, 1763–1765,* Illinois State Historical Library Collections, vol. 10 (Springfield, 1915), 49–57.

4. Ibid.

5. Indian Intelligence, 10 June 1764, *JP*/11, 228; and *Hay Diary,* 95.

6. Gladwin to Amherst, 3 December 1763, *WCL/AP*/7.

7. Deposition of Mathias Warren, 30 March 1764, *BL*/Add Mss 21650 fol. 116.

8. Re-examination of Hicks, 19 April 1764, *BP*/6, 523–25.

9. Ibid., 525-6.

10. *Conference with Six Nations,* 2 April 1764, *JP*/11, 152; and Journal of Indian Affairs, 25 May 1764, *JP*/11, 206. According to Hicks, his original instructions on returning from Fort Pitt were "to tell his story to the King Beaver," indicating that Tamaqua was leading the pro-war faction among the western Delaware at this point. Re-examination of Hicks, 19 April 1764, *BP*/6, 523.

11. Re-examination of Hicks, 20 April 1764, *BP*/6, 524–26. The Delaware threat was greeted with mirth by the Six Nations, Indian Conference, 2 April 1764, *JP*/11, 152.

12. Johnson to Gage, 16 April 1764, *JP*/11, 132.

13. Journal of Indian Affairs, 22 May 1764, *JP*/11, 206.

14. Indian Intelligence, 10 June 1764, *JP*/11, 228–29.

15. St. Ange to D'Abbadie, 9 September 1764, *NYCD*/10, 1157–8.

16. Speech of the Shawnee, 24 June 1764, in Charles Moore, ed., "The Gladwin Manuscripts," *MPHC* 27 (Lansing, 1979): 671–72; and ibid., Speech of the Mingo, 672.

17. Information given to Gladwin, 21 March 1764, *WCL/GP*/15.

18. Alexander Henry, *Travels and Adventures in Canada and the Indian Territories between the Years 1760 and 1776* (New York, 1809; facsimile reprint, Ann Arbor, MI, 1966), 157.

19. The identity of the Ojibwa with Pontiac is not known. They could have been Lake Superior "Saulteurs" or Ojibwa from Saginaw Bay, since Wasson's presence there was later confirmed by the army of Bradstreet; journal of James Montresor, 23 August 1764, *The Montresor Journals* (cited hereafter as *Montresor Journal*), Collections of the New York Historical Society for 1881 (New York, 1882), 283.

20. Indian Intelligence, Detroit, 4 June 1764, *JP*/11, 218.

21. De Villiers to D'Abbadie, 1 December 1763, in Alvord and Carter, *The Critical Period,* 49–57.

22. Indian Intelligence, Detroit, 4 June 1764, *JP*/11, 218.

23. At a Council with Neyon de Villiers, 15 and 17 April 1764, contained in Major Farmar to General Gage, 21 December 1764, *WCL/GP*/28.

24. Ibid.

25. Indian Intelligence, 9 June 1764, *JP*/11, 226–27.

26. De Villiers to D'Abbadie, 20 April 1764, in Alvord and Carter, *The Critical Period*, 242–43.

27. Cummon Shields to Bradstreet, 31 July 1764, *PHS*, Gratz Collection, case 4, box 5.

28. Gage to Halifax, 14 April 1764, in Clarence E. Carter, ed., *The Correspondence of General Thomas Gage with the Secretaries of State, 1763–1775*, 2 vols. (New Haven, Conn., 1931–1933), 1:25–26.

29. Indian Intelligence, 4 June, *JP*/11, 218–19.

30. St. Ange to D'Abbadie, 15 July 1764, in Alvord and Carter, *The Critical Period*, 289–91.

31. Ibid., 12 August 1764, in Alvord and Carter, *The Critical Period*, 292–97.

32. St. Ange to D'Abbadie, 15 July 1764, in Alvord and Carter, *The Critical Period*, 289–91.

33. Henry, Travels and Adventures, 157.

34. Bouquet to Gage. 27 December 1763, *BP*/6, 486–87.

35. Amherst to Gage, 27 October 1763, *NA*/*WO*/34/7 fol. 181.

36. Gage to Halifax, 10 March 1764, in Carter, Gage Correspondence, 1:17–18.

37. Murray to Gage, 5 March 1764, *WCL*/*GP*/15.

38. Gage to Murray, 12 February 1764, *WCL*/*GP*/14.

39. Gage to Fauquier, 28 February 1764, *WCL*/*GP*/14.

40. John Penn to Gage, 24 March 1764, *WCL*/*GP*/15.

41. Gage to Johnson, 22 April 1764, *JP*/4, 401–2.

42. The most recent biography of Bradstreet is that by William G. Godfrey, *The Pursuit of Profit and Preferment in Colonial North America: John Bradstreet's Quest* (Waterloo, ON, 1982).

43. Instructions for Colonel Bradstreet, 2 April 1764, *WCL*/*GP*/16.

44. Bouquet to Gage, 2 May 1764, *BP*/6, 533.

45. Gage to Halifax, 12 May 1764, in Carter, *Gage Correspondence*, 1:28.

46. Bradstreet to Gage, 6 April 1764, *WCL*/*GP*/16.

47. Gage to Johnson, 25 April 1764, *JP*/4, 408–9.

48. Johnson to Bradstreet, 5 May 1764, *JP*/4, 416.

49. Bradstreet to Gage, 7 May 1764, *WCL*/*GP*/18.

50. Bradstreet to Charles Gould, 7 May 1764, National Library of Wales, Tredegar Mss, 128/124.

51. Browning to Gage, 31 January 1764, *WCL*/*GP*/13.

52. Bradstreet to Gage, 26 March 1764, *WCL*/*GP*/16; and Gage to Browning, 29 March 1764, *WCL*/*GP*/16.

53. Browning to Gage, 30 April 1764, *WCL*/*GP*/17.

54. Bradstreet to Johnson, 10 June 1764, *PHS*, Gratz Collection, case 4, box 6.

55. Heads for Colonel Bradstreet's Inspection, 12 June 1764, *JP*/11, 231–33.

56. Indian Conference, 10 May 1764, *JP*/11, 178–80.

57. Gladwin to Johnson, 11 May 1764, *JP*/11, 191–92.

58. Gladwin to Gage, 7 June 1764, *WCL*/*GP*/19.

59. Gladwin to Bradstreet, 18 June 1764, *PHS*, Gratz Collection, case 4, box 29.

60. *Hay Diary*, 100.

61. Gladwin to Bradstreet, 12 July 1764, *WCL*/Michigan Collection.

62. Henry, *Travels*, 157. However, the Lake Superior Ojibwa only completed their negotiations in June 1765, when Cadotte brought a flotilla of eighty canoes to Michilimackinac; Howard to Johnson, 24 June 1765, *JP*/11, 804–6. See the third section of chapter 11.
63. *Hay Diary*, 103.
64. Ibid., 104.
65. Gage to Johnson, 2 July 1764, *JP*/11, 249–50.
66. Gage to Gladwin, 23 April 1764, *WCL/GP*/17.
67. Bradstreet to Gage, 12 July 1764, *WCL/GP*/21.
68. Conference with the Indians, 13 July 1764, *JP*/11, 267–70.
69. Ibid., 14–15 July 1764, *JP*/11, 270–72.
70. Ibid., 17 July 1764, *JP*/11, 278–80.
71. Conference with the Huron of Detroit, 17 July 1764, *JP*/11, 281–83.
72. Conference with the Ottawa etc, 19 July 1764, *JP*/11, 283–88.
73. Conference with the Indians, 23 July 1764, *JP*/11, 290.
74. Ibid., 24 July 1764, 291–92.
75. Ibid., 25 July 1764, 293–94.
76. Bradstreet to Gage, 20 November 1764, *WCL/GP*/27. See also Bradstreet to Gage, 29 September 1764, *WCL/GP*/25; and "Testimony of Thomas King," 3 October 1764, *JP*/11, 369–72.
77. Indian Congress, 25 July 1764, *JP*/11, 295.
78. Ibid., 26 July 1764, 295–97.
79. Ibid., 29 July 1764, 308–9.
80. Ibid., 31 July 1764, 309–11.
81. Ibid., 3 August 1763. 313–17.
82. Ibid., 318–20.
83. Treaty of Peace, 6 August 1764, *NYCD*/7, 652–53.
84. Johnson to Gage, 5 August 1764, *JP*/11, 324–27.
85. Gage to Johnson, 15 August 1764, *JP*/4, 508–10.
86. Johnson to Gage, 1 September 1764, *JP*/4, 518–20.
87. Gage to Bradstreet, 16 July 1764, *WCL/GP*/21.
88. Bradstreet to Gage, 5 August 1764, *WCL/GP*/22.
89. Bradstreet to Gould, 6 August 1764, National Library of Wales, Tredegar Mss, 128/126.
90. Edward Ward to Johnson, 2 May 1764, *JP*/11, 170–71. Ward was Croghan's half brother.
91. Treaty of Peace, 12 August 1764, *BP*/6, 603–4.
92. Speech of the Shawnee, 24 June 1764, in Charles Moore, ed., "The Gladwin Manuscripts," *MPHC* 27 (Lansing, 1979), 671–72; and ibid, Speech of the Six Nations [Mingo], 672. For the British response, see the second section of chapter 10.
93. Treaty of Peace, 12 August 1764, *BP*/6, 603–6.
94. Ibid., 607.
95. Bradstreet to Bouquet, 14 August 1764, *BP*/6, 603.
96. *Montresor Journal*, 22 August 1764, 283.
97. Ibid., 23 August 1764, 283.
98. Ibid., 25 August 1764, 284.
99. Gage to Bradstreet, 2 July 1764, *WCL/GP*/21.

100. Bradstreet to Gage, 28 August 1764, *WCL/GP/23*; and Bradstreet to Morris, 28 August 1764, *WCL/GP/23*.
101. St. Ange to D'Abbadie, 15 July 1764, in Carter, *The Critical Period*, 289–91.
102. *Montresor Journal*, 26 August 1764, 284.
103. Journal of Captain Thomas Morris, in Reuben Thwaites, ed., *Early Western Travels, 1748–1846* (New York, 1966), 301–2. This version was published by Morris many years after the event in *Miscellanies in Prose and Verse* (London, 1791). It contains additional material not in the original manuscript, including the circumstances of Godfroy's pardon. Morris's original journal, which he sent to Bradstreet, has been published by Howard H. Peckham, ed., "The Journal of Captain Thomas Morris, 1764," *Old Fort News* 6:1–11 (cited hereafter as Peckham, *Morris Journal*).
104. Bradstreet to St. Ange, 26 August 1764, *NYCD/10*, 1158–9.
105. *Montresor Journal*, 27–31 August 1764, 285–86; and Bradstreet to Captain William Howard, 1 September 1764, *WCL/GP/24*.
106. *Montresor Journal*, 31 August 1764, 286–87.
107. Morris to Bradstreet, 31 August 1764, *WCL/GP/24*.
108. Peckham, *Morris Journal*, 27 August 1764, 5.
109. Morris to Bradstreet, 31 August 1764, *WCL/GP/24*.
110. Peckham, *Morris Journal*, 5.
111. Morris added the information about St. Vincent's being a half-breed and former drummer to his later version of the journal; Thwaites, *Early Western Travels*, 304.
112. Testimony of Thomas King, 3 October 1764, *JP/11*, 369–70.
113. Peckham, *Morris Journal*, 5–6.
114. Morris to Mante, 31 August 1764, *WCL/GP/24*.
115. *Montresor Journal*, 31 August 1764, 286.
116. Ibid., 2 September 1764, 287.
117. Ibid., 5 September 1764, 288–89.
118. *Congress with Western Nations*, 7 September 1764, *JP/4*, 526–28.
119. Ibid., 528–33. Bradstreet contravened British policy in using the word "subject" since this would have made the Indians equal to the king's other subjects. See below.
120. *Montresor Journal*, 13 September 1764, 291.
121. Morris to Bradstreet, 31 August 1764, *WCL/GP/24*.
122. Morris to Bradstreet, 2 September 1764, *WCL/GP/24*.
123. Peckham, *Morris Journal*, 7–8; and testimony of Thomas King, 3 October 1764, *JP/11*, 370.
124. Peckham, *Morris Journal*, 7.
125. Ibid.; and testimony of Thomas King, 3 October 1764, *JP/11*, 370–72.
126. Peckham, *Morris Journal*, 9–11.
127. Journal of Indian Affairs, 30 December 1764, *JP/11*, 515.
128. St. Ange to D'Abbadie, 9 November 1764, in Alvord and Carter, *The Critical Period*, 354–56.
129. *Montresor Journal*, 16 September 1764, 293.
130. Ibid., 17 September 1764, 293–94.
131. Ibid., 19 September 1764, 294.
132. Ibid., 20 September 1764, 295.

133. Ibid., 22 September 1764, 296–97.
134. Ibid., 24 September 1764, 297–98.
135. Ibid., 25 September 1764, 298–99.
136. Bouquet to Gage, 27 August 1764, *BP*/6, 621.
137. Gage to Bradstreet, 2 September 1764, *BP*/6, 637–38.
138. Bradstreet to Gage, 29 September 1764, *WCL*/*GP*/25.
139. *Montresor Journal*, 28 September 1764, 301.
140. Ibid., 29 September 1764, 302; and Court of Enquiry, 29 September 1764, *WCL*/*GP*/25.
141. *Montresor Journal*, 5 October 1764, 304.
142. Proceedings with the Five Nations, 5 October 1764, *JP*/11, 373–74.
143. Bradstreet to Gage, 5 October 1764, *WCL*/*GP*/25.
144. *Montresor Journal*, 11 October 1764, 306.
145. Ibid., 12 October 1764, 307.
146. Ibid., 14 October 1764, 308–9.
147. Ibid., 5–6 October 1764, 304–5.
148. Ibid., 18 October 1764.
149. Bradstreet to Bouquet, 17 October 1764, *BP*/6, 667–68.
150. Bradstreet to St. Ange, 17 October 1764, *NA*/*CO*/5/83.
151. Bradstreet to Gage, 4 November 1764, *WCL*/*GP*/26. For the details of their mission, see Court of Enquiry Held by Order of Colonel Campbell, 21 February 1765, *WCL*/*GP*/31.
152. Bradstreet to Gage, 4 November 1764, *WCL*/*GP*/26.
153. *Montresor Journal*, 19 October–4 November 1764, 312–18.
154. Bradstreet to Gage, 4 November 1764, *WCL*/*GP*/26; and Bradstreet to Gould, 4 November 1764, *NLW*/*Tredegar*/128/130.
155. Thomas Mante, *The History of the Late War in North America and the Islands of the West Indies: Including the Campaigns of MDCCLXIII and MDCCLXIV* (London, 1772), 531–32.
156. Gage to Bradstreet, 20 November 1764, *WCL*/*GP*/27.
157. Johnson to Gage, 31 October 1764, *JP*/11, 394–96.
158. Johnson to Gage 20 November 1764, *JP*/11, 471–74.
159. Indian Proceedings, 2–8 December 1764, *JP*/11, 500–4.
160. Indian Proceedings, 16 December 1764, *JP*/11, 506–8.

Chapter 10

1. Gage to Bouquet, 26 January 1764, *BL*/Add Mss 21638 fol. 277.
2. Gage to Bouquet, 4 April 1764, *BP*/6, 506–8.
3. Bouquet to Gage, 20 May 1764, *BP*/6, 542–44.
4. Ibid., 2 May 1764, *BP*/6, 532–33.
5. Gage to Bouquet, 14 May 1764, *BP*/6, 538–40.
6. Bouquet to Gage, 27 May 1764, *BP*/6, 547–49. For the failure of the Loftus mission, see the first part of chapter 11.
7. Bouquet to Gage, 31 May 1764, *BP*/6, 549–51.
8. Ibid.
9. Gage to Bouquet, 5 June 1764, *BP*/6, 556–57.
10. Bouquet to Gage, 21 June 1764, *BP*/6, 575–77.
11. Bouquet to Reid, 15 June 1764, *BP*/6, 570–71.

12. Bouquet to George Broderick, 24 June 1764, *BL*/Add Mss 21653 fol. 305.

13. Bouquet to Gage, 21 June 1764, *BP*/6, 575–78.

14. Bouquet to Gage, 3 July 1764, *WCL/GP*/21; and Bouquet to Colonel Adam Stephen, 5 July 1764, *BL*/Add Mss 21650 fol. 317.

15. Pennsylvania Proclamation, 7 July 1764, *PCR* 9:190–92.

16. Bouquet to Governor John Penn, 4 June 1764, *BP*/6, 555.

17. Bouquet to Mr. John Harris, 19 July 1764, *BP*/6, 594–95.

18. Bouquet to Stephen, 5 July 1764, *BL*/Add Mss 21650 fol. 317.

19. Thomas Rutherford to Bouquet, 2 August 1764, *WCL/GP*/22. See also Harry M. Ward, *Major General Adam Stephen, and the Cause of American Liberty* (Charlottesville, VA, 1989), 86–91.

20. Lewis to Bouquet, 26 July 1764, *BL*/Add Mss 21650 fol. 369.

21. Mathew C. Ward, *Breaking the Backcountry: The Seven Years War in Virginia and Pennsylvania, 1754–1765* (Pittsburgh, 2003), 171–72.

22. Captain Grant to Bouquet, 25 June 1764, *BL*/Add Mss 21650 fol. 291.

23. Indian Intelligence, 10 June 1764, *JP*/11, 228.

24. Extract of a Letter from Fort Cumberland, 5 June 1764, *Pennsylvania Gazette,* no. 1851, 14 June 1764.

25. Armstrong to Governor Penn, 6 June 1764, *PA*, 1st series, IV, 175–76.

26. Livingston to Bouquet, 24 June 1764, *BL*/Add Mss 21650 fol. 283.

27. A Narrative of the Captivity of John McCullough, in Archibald Loudon, ed., *A Selection of the Some of the Most Interesting Outrages Committed by the Indians in Their Wars with the White People,* 2 vols. (New York, 1808; reprint, 1971), 1:283.

28. News from Carlisle, *Pennsylvania Gazette,* no. 1859, 9 August 1764.

29. McCullough Captivity Narrative, in Loudon, *Indian Outrages,* 1:283.

30. Bouquet to Livingston, 11 June 1764, *BP*/6, 568–69.

31. Bouquet to Reid, 15 August 1764, *BL*/Add Mss 21656 fols. 31–32.

32. Dispositions for the March from Ligonier, 15 September 1764, *BL*/Add Mss 21653 fol. 316.

33. Reid to Bouquet, 17 September 1764, *BL*/Add Mss 21650 fol. 504.

34. Reid to Bouquet, 16 September 1764, *WCL/GP*/24.

35. Reid to Bouquet, 18 September 1764, *BL*/Add Mss 21650 fol. 505.

36. Speech of Colonel Bouquet, 20 September 1764, *BP*/6, 649–50.

37. A List of Names That Shot Best at the Target, 21–22 September 1764, *BL*/Add Mss 21653 fol. 320.

38. Bouquet to Gage, 26 September 1764, *BP*/6, 646–48.

39. Speech of the Onondaga and Oneida Chiefs, 2 October 1764, *BP*/6, 653–54.

40. Bouquet's Answer to the Onondaga and Oneida Chiefs, 2 October 1764, *BP*/6, 655–57.

41. Orders to the Army, 2 October 1764, *BL*/Add Mss 21653 fol. 322.

42. William Smith, *An Historical Account of the Expedition against the Ohio Indians in the Year 1764 under the Command of Henry Bouquet* (London, 1765; reprint, Ann Arbor, 1966), 8. Smith, a Philadelphian minister by profession, wrote this account with the assistance of Bouquet, who allowed him access to his papers; see Dictionary of American Biography.

43. Bouquet to Gage, 21 October 1764, *BP*/6, 676.

44. Loudon, *Indian Narratives,* 1:284–85.

45. Delaware Reply to Bouquet, 14 October 1764, *BP*/6, 660–61. This was very likely the prophet Neolin, a view supported by Gregory Evans Dowd, *War under Heaven: Pontiac, the Indian Nations and the British Empire* (Baltimore, 2002), 164.
46. Bouquet to the Delaware, 15 October 1764, *BP*/6, 661–62.
47. Smith, *Expedition against the Ohio Indians,* 13.
48. Ohio Indian Conference, 16 October 1764, *BP*/6, 665–66.
49. Ohio Indian Conference, 17 October 1764, *BP*/6, 669–70.
50. Bouquet's Speech to Ohio Indians, 20 October 1764, *BP*/6, 671–74.
51. Bouquet to Gage, 21 October 1764, *BP*/6, 675–77.
52. Bouquet to Gage, 15 November, *BP*/6, 703.
53. Gage to Bouquet, 21 October 1764, *BP*/6, 680.
54. Smith, *Expedition against the Ohio Indians,* 18.
55. Bouquet to the Shawnee, 27 October 1764, *BP*/6, 681.
56. Bouquet Address to Big Wolf, 31 October 1764, *BP*/6, 681–82.
57. Minutes of Bouquet's Conference, 1 November 1764, *BP*/6, 682–83.
58. Bradstreet to Bouquet, 17 October 1764, *BP*/6, 667.
59. Indian Proceedings, 4 November 1764, *JP*/11, 450.
60. Indian Proceedings, 5 November 1764, *JP*/11, 450.
61. Smith, *Expedition against the Ohio Indians,* 26–29.
62. Indian Proceedings, 7 November 1764, *JP*/11, 451.
63. Red Hawk to Bouquet, 8 November 1764, *JP*/11, 451–52.
64. Indian Conference, 9 November 1764, *JP*/11, 452–54.
65. Indian Conference, 9 November 1764, *JP*/11, 454–56.
66. Indian Conference, 10 November 1764, *JP*/11, 456–58; and ibid., *BP*/6, 690–92. Bouquet had no power to do this on his own authority, and there is no evidence that the soldier was handed over.
67. Indian Conference (Private), 11 November 1764, *JP*/11, 458–60; and ibid, *BP*/6, 692–93.
68. Indian Congress, 9–11 May 1765, *JP*/11, 723. See also Michael N. McConnell, *A Country Between: The Upper Ohio and Its Peoples, 1724–1774* (Lincoln, NE, 1992), 203.
69. Indian Conference, 12 November 1764, *JP*/11, 461–63; and ibid., *BP*/6, 694–96.
70. Speech to the Shawnee, 13 November 1764, *BP*/6, 698–99.
71. Conference with the Shawnee, 14 November 1764, *BP*/6, 700–1.
72. M. de St. Ange to M. D'Abbadie, 9 September 1764, *NYCD*/10:1157–8.
73. Johnson to Gage, 3 April 1765, *JP*/11, 664.
74. Intelligence from Kiashuta, 9 May 1765, *WLC*/*GP*/36.
75. Intelligence from Killbuck, 2 March 1765, *JP*/11, 618.
76. Indian Conference, 14 November 1764, *BP*/6, 700–3.
77. Bouquet to Gage, 15 November 1764, *BP*/6, 703–5.
78. Bouquet to Captain Hay, 18 November 1764, *BL*/Add Mss 21651 fol. 60.
79. Orders for the Suspension of Arms, 29 November 1764, *BP*/6, 710.
80. Bouquet to Gage, 30 November 1764, *BP*/6, 711.
81. *Pennsylvania Gazette,* no. 1873, 15 November 1764.
82. Bouquet to Johnson, 3 December 1764, *JP*/4, 608–9.
83. Bouquet to Governor Sharpe, 20 December 1764, *BP*/6, 738–39.
84. Benevissica to Captain Murray, 8 January 1765, *BP*/6, 761–62.

85. Bouquet to Gage, 30 November 1764, *BP*/6, 711–15; and Bouquet to Johnson, 30 November 1764, *BP*/6, 716.
86. Smith, *Expedition against the Ohio Indians*, 29.
87. Gage to Bouquet, 7 December 1764, *WCL*/*GP*/28.
88. Gage to Halifax, 13 December 1764, in Clarence E. Carter, ed, *The Correspondence of General Thomas Gage with the Secretaries of State, 1763–1775*, 2 vols. (New Haven, CT, 1931–1933), 1:44–47.
89. "Reflections on the War with the Savages of North America," in Smith, *Expedition against the Ohio Indians*, 47–65. Although Smith had access to Bouquet's papers, there is no extant copy of this document. One possible explanation is that Bouquet dictated these thoughts to Smith.
90. Conference with Six Nations and Delaware Indians, 8 May 1765, *NYCD*/7:733. However, Long Coat lost his position as chief of the Eastern Delaware; ibid., 737 10 May 1765.
91. Journal of Indian Affairs, 27–30 May 1765, *JP*/11, 768.
92. Treaty of Peace with the Delaware, 8 May 1765, *NYCD*/7:738–41.
93. Indian Congress at Fort Pitt, 10 May 1765, *JP*/11, 731.
94. Ibid., 9 May, *JP*/11, 725.
95. Conference with the Ohio Nations, 13 July 1765, *NYCD*/7:754–55.

Chapter 11

1. Loftus to Gage, 9 April 1764, in Clarence Walworth Alvord and Clarence Edwin Carter, eds., *The Critical Period, 1763–1765*, Illinois State Historical Library, Collections, vol. 10 (Springfield, 1915), 237–39. See also Loftus to Gage, 17 August 1764, Mobile, *WCL*/*GP*/23.
2. Captain Desmazellieres to D'Abbadie, 14 March 1764, in Alvord and Carter, *The Critical Period*, 234–36.
3. D'Abbadie: Memoir on Major Loftus's Attempt to Ascend the River [undated], in Alvord and Carter, *The Critical Period*, 225–32.
4. Gage to Johnson, 28 May 1764, *JP*/4, 432–34.
5. Farmar to D'Abbadie, 12 June 1764, in Alvord and Carter, *The Critical Period*, 264–65.
6. D'Abbadie to Farmar, 22 June 1764, in Alvord and Carter, *The Critical Period*, 265–66.
7. Address of D'Abbadie to the Tunica Indians, 14 July 1764, in Alvord and Carter, *The Critical Period*, 285–86.
8. Pitman to the French Voyageurs, 12 August 1764, in Alvord and Carter, *The Critical Period*, 297–98.
9. D'Abbadie to Gage, 16 August 1764, in Alvord and Carter, *The Critical Period*, 300–3.
10. D'Abbadie to de Villiers, 30 January 1764, in Alvord and Carter, *The Critical Period*, 233–34.
11. D'Abbadie to minister of marine, 10 September 1764, in Alvord and Carter, *The Critical Period*, 308–12. British suspicions were that D'Abbadie had an interest in the Mississippi River trade.
12. D'Abbadie Journal, 5 September 1764, in Alvord and Carter, *The Critical Period*, 197; and Gage to Stuart, 13 May 1765, New York, *WCL*/*GP*/36.
13. St. Ange to D'Abbadie, 2 October 1764, *NYCD*/10, 1159.

14. St. Ange to D'Abbadie, 9 November 1764, in Alvord and Carter, *The Critical Period,* 354–56.
15. D'Abbadie to minister of marine, 30 September 1764, in Alvord and Carter, *The Critical Period,* 315–20.
16. St. Ange to Aubry, 9 November 1764, in Alvord and Carter, *The Critical Period,* 355–59.
17. St. Ange to D'Abbadie, 9 November 1764, in Alvord and Carter, *The Critical Period,* 354–56.
18. Gage to Halifax, 9 November 1764, in Carter, *Gage Correspondence,* 1, 42.
19. Aubry to minister of marine, 25 February 1765, in Alvord and Carter, *The Critical Period,* 455-61.
20. Aubry to minister of marine, 4 February 1765, in Alvord and Carter, *The Critical Period,* 428–32.
21. Ibid., 12 February 1765, 433–36.
22. Farmar to secretary at war, 24 November 1764, in Alvord and Carter, *The Critical Period,* 364.
23. D'Abbadie Journal, 11 December 1764, in Alvord and Carter, *The Critical Period,* 200.
24. Ibid., 17 December 1764, 203.
25. D'Abbadie to minister of marine, 29 January 1765, in Alvord and Carter, *The Critical Period,* 423–26.
26. Ross to Farmar, 25 May 1765, *WCL/GP/37.*
27. Statement by Hugh Crawford, 22 July 1765, in Alvord and Carter, *The Critical Period,* 483–84.
28. Ross to Farmar, 21 February 1765, in Alvord and Carter, *The Critical Period,* 442–43.
29. St. Ange to D'Abbadie, 21 February l765, in Alvord and Carter, *The Critical Period,* 439–42. For the identity of Minawouanon, See below, note 32.
30. St. Ange to Gage, 7 April 1765, *WCL/GP/37*; and St. Ange to D'Abbadie, 7 April 1765, in Alvord and Carter, *The Critical Period,* 469–70.
31. Council Held at Illinois, 7 April 1765, *WCL/GP/37.*
32. St. Ange to D'Abbadie, 7 April 1765, in Alvord, *The Critical Period,* 469–70. Minawouanon may have been the Indian name of the Grand Saulteur, since the Ojibwa chief subsequently admitted to Croghan that he had gone to the Illinois to oppose the British.
33. St. Ange to Gage, 7 April 1765, *WCL/GP/37*; and Ross to Farmar, 25 May 1765, in Alvord, *The Critical Period,* 481–83.
34. Ross to Farmar, 25 May 1765, in Alvord and Carter, *The Critical Period,* 481–83.
35. Croghan to Gage, 2 March 1765, *WCL/GP/31.*
36. Court of Enquiry, 16 March 1765, *WCL/GP/35.*
37. Colonel John Campbell to Johnson, 21 May 1765, *JP/11,* 745.
38. Captain Howard to Johnson, 17 May 1765, *JP/11,* 739–40.
39. Croghan to Johnson, 12 July 1765, *JP/11,* 838. Croghan got this information from a Wea chief.
40. Campbell to Gage, 28 April 1765, *WCL/GP/35.*
41. Court of Enquiry, 6 April 1765, *JP/4,* 673–76. The story about de Villiers was mere rumor and was untrue.

42. Johnson to Gage, 18 December 1764, *JP/4*, 625–26.
43. Gage to Bouquet, 20 December 1764, *BP/6*, 733–34.
44. Gage to Bouquet, 24 December 1764, *BL*/Add Mss 21638 fol. 402.
45. Gage to Bouquet, 30 December 1764, *BL*/Add Mss 21638 fol. 404.
46. Proclamation to the Inhabitants of the Illinois, 30 December 1764, in Alvord and Carter, *The Critical Period,* 395–96.
47. Gage to Johnson, 31 December 1764, *JP/11*, 515–17.
48. Gage to Campbell, 18 January 1765, *WCL/GP/30*.
49. Croghan to Johnson, 18 February 1765, *JP/11*, 576–77.
50. Croghan to Gage, 2 March 1765, *WCL/GP/31*.
51. Croghan Journal, 2 March 1765, *PCR* 9:250–51.
52. Nathaniel McCullough to Croghan, 12 March 1765, *JP/11*, 635–36. See also David Dixon, *Never Come to Peace Again: Pontiac's Uprising and the Fate of the British Empire in North America* (Norman, OK, 2005), 253–59.
53. Croghan to Gage, 12 May 1765, *WCL/GP/36*. For Croghan's conflict of interest, see Nicholas B. Wainwright, George Croghan, *Wilderness Diplomat* (Chapel Hill, NC, 1959), 211–18.
54. Croghan Journal, 20–21 March 1765, *PCR*, 10:251.
55. Croghan to Fraser, 21 March 1765, *PHS*, Cadwalader Collection, series IV, box 5; and Croghan to Gage, 22 March 1765, *WCL/GP/32*.
56. Fraser to Gage, 27 April 1765, *WCL/GP/137*.
57. Ibid.
58. Ibid.
59. Harangue Made to the Illinois Nation and Chief Pontiac by Monsieur St. Ange, 18 April 1765, *WCL/GP/36*.
60. Fraser to Gage, 27 April 1765, *WCL/GP/137*.
61. Ibid.
62. St. Ange to [a British Officer], 28 April 1765, *WCL/GP/137*. The recipient of this letter is not clear. It could have been Gage or Bouquet, but more likely was Colonel John Campbell at Detroit, the nearest senior British officer in the region.
63. Fraser to Gage, 27 April 1765, *WCL/GP/137*.
64. Postscript, St. Ange to [British officer], 28 April 1765, *WCL/GP/137*. Surprisingly, there is no reference to the Grand Saulteur during these and subsequent events at Fort Chartres. He may have decided to return home via Lake Michigan on finding that Pontiac had changed his mind about continuing the war.
65. Ibid.
66. Fraser to Gage, 15 May 1765, *WCL/GP/36*.
67. Conference between D'Abbadie and the Shawnee Led by Charlot Kaské, 24 February 1765, in Alvord and Carter, *The Critical Period,* 10:444–54. D'Abbadie's journal shows the date to have been 20 December 1764.
68. Fraser to Gage, 15 May 1765, *WCL/GP/36*.
69. Fraser to Gage, 18 May 1765, *WCL/GP/36*.
70. Ibid.
71. Fraser to Gage, 26 May 1765, *WCL/GP/36*.
72. Ibid.
73. Fraser to Gage, 17 June 1765, in Alvord and Carter, *The Critical Period,* 516–19.
74. Instructions to Mr. Sinnott, enclosed with Stuart to Gage, 19 March 1765, *WCL/GP/32*.

75. Sinnott to Farmar, 3 June 1765, *WCL/GP/*38.

76. Sinnott to Croghan, 14 June 1765, *JP/*11, 788–89.

77. Croghan to Johnson, 17 August 1765, *JP/*11, 900.

78. Stuart to Johnson, 30 March 1766, *JP/*12, 54.

79. Croghan Journal, 1 April 1765, Council Minutes, *PCR* 9:252.

80. Croghan Journal, 29–30 April 1765, Council Minutes, *PCR* 9:254–55. Neolin is not named by Croghan, but it is unlikely that the three Delaware clans would have brought someone else.

81. Croghan Journal, 15 May 1765. There are two versions of the journal starting on 15 May 1765, one in the Hutchins Papers in the Pennsylvania Historical Society, and the other in the Public Record Office, London. The Hutchins version has more detail about the countryside and may have been written as a private prospectus for land settlement. The more official version, submitted to the Board of Trade, contains most of the material on the political and diplomatic aspects of the mission. Both are printed in Theodore C. Pease, ed., *Anglo-French Boundary Disputes in the West, 1749–1763,* Collections of the Illinois State Historical Library, French Series, 2 (Springfield, 1936), 23–52.

82. Croghan Official Journal, 23–28 May 1765, Pease, *Anglo-French Boundary Disputes,* 2:39.

83. Croghan to Captain William Murray, 12 July 1765, *JP/*11, 841–43.

84. Croghan to Johnson, 12 July 1765, *JP/*11, 837–38.

85. Croghan to Johnson, 12 July 1765, Pease, *JP/*11, 839; and Croghan Official Journal, 11–12 July 1765, *Anglo-French Boundary Disputes,* 2:41.

86. Conference with the Kickapoo etc, 13 July 1765, *JP/*11, 847–50.

87. Croghan to Johnson, 12 July 1765, *JP/*11, 838.

88. Croghan Official Journal, 18 July 1765, *Anglo-French Boundary Disputes,* 2:42.

89. Croghan Private Journal, 1 August 1765, Pease, *Anglo-French Boundary Disputes,* 2:36.

90. Croghan Official Journal, 23–24 August 1765, Pease, *Anglo-French Boundary Disputes,* 2:43–44. For the Wabash view about the sovereignty of their lands, see below, and ibid., 30 August 1765.

91. Ibid., 27 August 1765, 2:44–45.

92. Ibid., 28 August 1765, 2:46–47.

93. Ibid., 30 August 1765, 2:47–48.

94. Ibid., 2–4 September 1765, 2: 48.

95. Howard H. Peckham, *Pontiac and the Indian Uprising* (Princeton, N.J., 1947; reprint, Detroit, 1994), 286.

96. Howard to Johnson, 24 June 1765, *JP/*11, 805–6.

97. Croghan Official Journal, 12 September 1765, Pease, *Anglo-French Boundary Disputes,* 2:49.

98. Ibid., 14 September 1765, 2:49–50.

99. Ibid., 15 September 1765, 2:50.

100. Ibid., 25 September 1765, 2:50–52.

101. Campbell to Gage, 11 September 1765, *WCL/GP/*41.

102. Croghan to Johnson, October/November 1765, *NYCD/*7:787–88.

103. Ibid.

104. Stirling to Gage, 18 October 1765, in Clarence Walworth Alvord and Clarence Edwin Carter, eds., *The New Regime, 1765–1767,* Illinois State Historical Library, Collections, vol. 11 (Springfield, 1916), 107–11. Stirling does not mention Kaské by name but identifies him as "the Shawnee chief who Lieutenant Fraser mentioned in his letter to have come to the Illinois with a talk from Monsieur Aubry."
105. Ibid.

Conclusions

1. Croghan to Board of Trade, January 1764, *NYCD*/7, 603.
2. The British ministry had been rocked by a series of riots in the West Country following an attempt to tax cider.
3. New England was an exception with regard to its own frontiers because of its homogeneous population.
4. Gage to Bradstreet, 6 May 1764, *WCL/GP*/18.
5. Croghan to the Board of Trade, January 1764, *NYCD*/7, 602–7.
6. Richard Middleton, "Pontiac: Local Warrior or Pan Indian Leader?" *The Michigan Historical Review* 32 (2006): 1–32. One writer who suggests that historians have gone too far in their downgrading of Pontiac is Gregory Evans Dowd, *War under Heaven: Pontiac, the Indian Nations, and the British Empire* (Baltimore, 2002), 9.
7. Proceedings at a Congress with Pontiac and the Chiefs of the Ottawa, Potawatomi, Huron and Chippewa, 23–31 July 1766, *NYCD*/7, 854–67.
8. Richard White, *The Middle Ground: Indians, Empires, and Republics in the Great Lakes Region, 1650–1815* (Cambridge, 1991), 349–50.
9. David Dixon, *Never Come to Peace Again: Pontiac's Uprising and the Fate of the British Empire in North America* (Norman, OK, 2005). See also Colin G. Calloway, *The Scratch of a Penn: 1763 and the Transformation of North America (Pivotal Moments in American History* (New York, 2006), 59.
10. Gage to Johnson, 23 March 1766, *JP*/5, 94.
11. Hillsborough to Gage, 15 April 1768, in Clarence E. Carter, ed., *The Correspondence of General Thomas Gage with the Secretaries of State, 1763–1775,* 2 vols. (New Haven, CT, 1931–1933), 2:61–66.
12. Report of the Lords of Trade, 7 March 1768, *NYCD*/8, 19–31.
13. Johnson to Gage, 20 May 1767, in *Documentary History of the State of New York,* 2:853–55; and Johnson to Shelburne, 26 October 1767, *JP*/5, 762–64.
14. Benjamin Roberts to Johnson, 23 June 1766, *JP*/5, 279–80.
15. Howard H. Peckham, *Pontiac and the Indian Uprising* (Detroit, 1994), 297–308.
16. Edward Cole to Johnson, 13 June 1769, *JP*/7, 15–16. For a discussion of Pontiac's death, see Gregory Evans Dowd, *War under Heaven: Pontiac, the Indian Nations, and the British Empire* (Baltimore, 2002), 250, 260–62.
17. Norman Gelb, ed., *Jonathan Carver's Travels through America, 1766–1768: An Eighteenth Century Explorer's Account of Uncharted America* (New York, 1993), 95.
18. Gage to Johnson, 9 November 1767, *JP*/12, 376–78.
19. Croghan to Johnson, 18 September 1769, *JP*/7, 182–83.
20. Michael McConnell, A *Country Between: The Upper Ohio and Its Peoples, 1724–1774* (Lincoln, NE, 1992, 226–28.
21. Gage to Hillsborough, 18 August 1770, in Carter, *Correspondence of General Thomas Gage,* 1:264–65.
22. Ibid., 12 November 1770, 281–82; and White, *Middle Ground,* 363–64.
23. McConnell, *A Country Between,* 270–79.

Select Bibliography

Manuscript Sources

American Antiquarian Society, Worcester, Massachusetts
   Bradstreet Papers, 1742–1782: Orderly Book Collection

American Philosophical Society, Philadelphia
   Indian and Military Affairs of Pennsylvania, 1737–1775

British Library, London
   Bouquet Papers

Burton Historical Collection, Detroit Public Library
   John Porteous Papers, Diaries, and Journals
   Robert Navarre Journal

Canadian National Archives, Ottawa
   Archives Nationales, Paris, Archives des Colonies, Series C11A (microfilm copy)
   Northcliffe Collection, Papers of Robert Monckton
   Indian Affairs Records: Minutes and Journals, 1755–1790
   Superintendent of Indian Affairs (Johnson Papers)

Historical Society of Pennsylvania, Philadelphia
   Cadwalader Collection, George Croghan Papers
   Gratz Collection, Indian Commissioners Papers, French and Indian Wars
   Journal of Christian Frederick Post, 1760

Kent County Record Office/Centre for Kentish Studies, Maidstone, Kent
   Amherst Papers

Library Company of Philadelphia
   Pennsylvania Gazette

Library of Congress, Washington, D.C.
   Force Transcripts, French and Indian Wars

National Library of Wales, Aberystwyth, Dyfed, Wales

Tredegar Park Manuscripts (Bradstreet Papers)

Newberry Library, Chicago

Ayer Manuscripts
Papers relating to the Indian Wars of 1763 and 1764

Nottingham University Library

Galway Collection, Correspondence of Robert Monckton

National Archives (Formerly the Public Record Office [PRO]), London

Amherst Papers
Colonial Office Papers

William L. Clements Library, Ann Arbor, Michigan

Amherst Papers
Gage Papers, American Series
Henry Bouquet Orderly Books
James Stirling Letter Book
Lt. Jehu Hay, Diary

Printed Primary

Alvord, Clarence Walworth, and Clarence Edwin Carter, eds., *The Critical Period, 1763–1765*, Collections of the Illinois State Historical Library, vol. 10 (Springfield, 1915).

Alvord, Clarence Walworth, and Clarence Edwin Carter, eds., *The New Regime, 1765–1767*, Collections of the Illinois State Historical Library, vol. 11 (Springfield, 1916).

American Antiquarian Society, *Manuscript Records of the French and Indian War*, edited by Charles Harvey Lincoln (Worcester, Mass., 1909).

Amherst, Jeffery, *Amherst and the Conquest of Canada: Selected Papers from the Correspondence of Major General Jeffery Amherst while Commander in Chief in North America, from September 1758 to December 1760*, edited by Richard Middleton for the Army Records Society (Sutton, England, 2002).

Amherst, Jeffery, *The Journal of Jeffery Amherst, Recording the Military Career of General Amherst in America from 1758–1763*, edited by J. C. Webster (Toronto, 1931).

Booth, Russell H., Jr., *The Tuscarawas Valley in Indian Days, 1750–1797: Original Journals and Old Maps* (Cambridge, Ohio, 1994).

Bouquet, Henry, *The Orderly Book of Colonel Henry Bouquet's Expedition against the Ohio Indians, 1764*, edited by Edward G. Williams (Pittsburgh, Pa., 1960).

Bouquet, Henry, *The Papers of Henry Bouquet*, 6 vols., edited by Donald H. Kent, Louis Waddell, and Autumn L. Leonard (Harrisburg, Pa., 1951–1994).

Boyd, Julian P., ed., *The Susquehanna Company Papers* vol. 2 *1756–1767*, (Ithaca, N.Y., 1962).

Carroon, Robert G., ed., *Broadswords and Bayonets: The Journals of the Expedition under the Command of Captain Thomas Stirling, Royal Highland Regiment (The Black Watch) to occupy Fort Chartres...* (Springfield, Ill., 1984).

Carver, Jonathan, *Jonathan Carver's Travels through America, 1766–1768: An Eighteenth Century Explorer's Account of Uncharted America*, edited by Norman Gelb (New York, 1993).

Colden, Cadwallader, *The Letters and Papers of Cadwallader Colden*, 7 vols., *Collections of the New York Historical Society for 1917–1923*, vols. 50–56 (New York, 1918–1923).

Collections of the Massachusetts Historical Society, 4th series, 9–10, *Aspinwall Papers* (Boston, 1871).

Croghan, George, *George Croghan, A Selection of His Letters and Journals, 1750–1765*, in *Early Western Travels, 1748–1846*, edited by Reuben Thwaites (New York, 1966).

Dunbar, John R., ed., *The Paxton Papers* (The Hague, 1957).

Fauquier, Francis, *Official Papers of Francis Fauquier, Lieutenant Governor of Virginia, 1758–1768*, 3 vols., edited by George Reese (Charlottesville, Va., 1980–1983).

Gage, Thomas, *The Correspondence of General Thomas Gage with the Secretaries of State, 1763–1775*, 2 vols., edited by Clarence E. Carter (New Haven, Conn., 1931–1933).

Gladwin, Henry, "The Gladwin Papers, together with an Introduction and a Sketch of the Conspiracy of Pontiac," edited by Charles Moore, *Michigan Pioneer and Historical Society* 27 (Lansing, 1897): 606–78.

Gorrell, James, "Lieutenant James Gorrell's Journal," edited by Lyman Copeland Draper, *Collections of the State Historical Society of Wisconsin* 1 (Madison, 1903): 24–48.

Hazard, Samuel, ed., *Documents Commencing 1756*, Pennsylvania Archives, first series, 3 (Philadelphia, 1852–1854).

Hazard, Samuel, ed., *Documents Commencing 1760*, Pennsylvania Archives, first series, 4 (Philadelphia, 1852–1854).

Heckewelder, John, *Narrative of the Mission of the United Brethren among the Delaware and Mohegan Indians, from Its Commencement in the Year 1740 to the Close of the Year 1808* (Philadelphia, 1820; reprint, New York, 1971).

Henry, Alexander, *Travels and Adventures in Canada and the Indian Territories between the Years 1760 and 1776* (New York, 1809; facsimile reprint, Ann Arbor, Mich., 1966).

Charles F. Hoban, ed., *Votes of the Assembly*, VI, *1756–1764*, Pennsylvania Archives, eighth series (Harrisburg, 1935).

Hough, Franklin B., *Diary of the Siege of Detroit in the War with Pontiac; also a Narrative of the Principal Events of the Siege by Major Robert Rogers; a Plan for Conducting Indian Affairs by Colonel Bradstreet and Other Authentick Documents, Never before Printed* (Albany, N.Y., 1860).

Hunter, Lieutenant Samuel, "Journal kept at Fort Augusta, 1763," Pennsylvania Archives, 2nd series, vol. 7 (Harrisburg, 1878), 459–84.

Johnson, William, *Calendar of Sir William Johnson Manuscripts*, edited by Richard E. Day (Albany, N.Y., 1909).

Johnson, William, *The Papers of Sir William Johnson*, 14 vols., edited by James Sullivan (Albany, N.Y., 1921–1965).

Jordan, John W., ed., "The Journal of James Kenny, 1761–1763," *Pennsylvania Magazine of History and Biography* 37 (1913): 1–47, 152–202.

Langlade, Charles, Sieur de, "Langlade Papers, 1737–1800," *Report and Collections of the State Historical Society of Wisconsin* 8 (Madison, 1879): 213-25.

Linn, John B., and William Egle, eds., *Papers relating to the French Occupation in Western Pennsylvania, 1631–1764*, Pennsylvania Archives, second series, 6 (Harrisburg, 1895).

Linn, John B., and William Egle, eds., *Papers relating to Provincial Affairs, 1682–1763*, Pennsylvania Archives, second series, 7 (Harrisburg, 1895).

Loudon, Archibald, ed., *A Selection of the Some of the Most Interesting Narratives of Outrages Committed by the Indians in Their Wars with the White People*, 2 vols. (Carlisle, Pa., 1808, reprint, Lewisburg, Pa., 2001).

Lucier, Armand Francis, *Pontiac's Conspiracy and Other Indian Affairs: Notices Abstracted from Colonial Newspapers, 1763–1765* (Bowie, Md., 2000).

McCulloch, Ian, and Timothy Todish, eds., *Through So Many Dangers: The Memoirs and Adventures of Robert Kirk, Late of the Royal Highland Regiment* (Limerick, Ireland, 1775; reprint, New York, 2004).

Montresor, John, "Journal of John Montresor's Expedition to Detroit in 1763," edited by J. C. Webster, *Transactions of the Royal Society of Canada*, series 3, 22: section 2, 1-32 .

Montresor, John, *The Montresor Journals*, edited by D. G. Scull, Collections of the New York Historical Society for 1881 (New York, 1882).

Navarre, Robert, *see* Milo Milton Quaife.

New York, *Documentary History of the State of New York*, 4 vols., edited by Edmund B. O'Callaghan (Albany, 1849–1851).

New York, *Documents relating to the Colonial History of the State of New York*, 15 vols., edited by Edmund B. O'Callaghan (Albany, 1853–1887).

Ohio Company, *The Ohio Company Papers, 1753–1817*, edited by Kenneth P. Bailey (Arcata, Calif., 1947).

Pease, Theodore C., ed., *Anglo-French Boundary Disputes in the West, 1749–1763*, Collections of the Illinois State Historical Library, French series, 2 (Springfield, 1936).

Pennsylvania Colonial Records, *Minutes of the Provincial Council of Pennsylvania*, vols. 8–9 (Harrisburg, 1852).

Peyser, Joseph L., *Letters from New France: The Upper Country, 1686–1783* (Urbana, Ill., 1992).

Pouchot, Pierre, *Memoirs on the Late War in North America between France and England*, edited by Brian Leigh Dunnigan, translated by Michael Cardy (Youngstown, N.Y., 1994).

Quaife, Milo Milton, ed., *The Siege of Detroit in 1763: The Journal of Pontiac's Conspiracy and John Rutherford's Narrative of a Captivity* (Chicago, 1961).

Reed, George E., ed., *Papers of the Governors, III, 1759–1785*, Pennsylvania Archives, fourth series (Harrisburg, 1900).

Rogers, Robert, *Journals of Major Robert Rogers, Containing an Account of the Several Excursions He Made under the Generals Who Commanded upon the Continent of North America during the Late War* (London, 1765).

Rogers, Robert, "Journal of Robert Rogers... 1760–1761," edited by Victor Paltsits, *Bulletin of the New York Public Library* (April 1933): 261-76.

Seaver, James E., *A Narrative of the Life of Mrs Mary Jemison* (Canandaigua, N.Y., 1824; reprint, New York, 1982).

Smith, William, *An Historical Account of the Expedition against the Ohio Indians in the Year 1764 under the Command of Henry Bouquet* (London, 1765; reprint, Ann Arbor, Mich., 1966).

Thomson, Charles, *An Enquiry into the Causes of the Alienation of the Delaware and Shawanese Indians from the British Interest* (London, 1759).

Thwaites, Reuben G., ed., *Early Western Journals, 1748-1765* (1904; reprint, Lewisburg, Pa., 1998).

Thwaites, Reuben G., ed., *Early Western Travels, 1748-1846*, vol. 1 (New York, 1966).

Thwaites, Reuben G., ed., "The French Regime in Wisconsin, 1748-1760" and "The British Regime in Wisconsin, 1760-1800", *Collections of the State Historical Society of Wisconsin* (18 Madison, 1908): 1-222, 223-467 .

Trent, William, "Journal at Fort Pitt, 1763," edited by A. T. Volwiler, *Mississippi Historical Review* 11:390-413.

Trowbridge, C. C., ed., "Witness Accounts of the Siege of Detroit, 1763," *Michigan Pioneer and Historical Society* 8 (Lansing, 1886): 340-64.

Wainwright, Nicholas B., ed., "George Croghan's Journal, 1759-1763," *Pennsylvania Magazine of History and Biography* 62 (1947): 411.

Printed Secondary

Acquila, Richard, *The Iroquois Restoration: Iroquois Diplomacy on the Colonial Frontier, 1701-1754* (Detroit, 1983).

Alden, John Richard, *General Gage in America: Being Principally a History of His Role in the American Revolution* (Baton Rouge, LA, 1948).

Alden, John Richard, *John Stuart and the Southern Colonial Frontier: Study in Indian Relations: War, Trade and Land Problems in the Southern Wilderness, 1754-1775* (Ann Arbor, MI, 1944).

Anderson, Fred, *Crucible of War: The Seven Years' War and the Fate of Empire in British North America, 1754-1766* (New York, 2000).

Anderson, Niles, *Battle of Bushy Run*, Pennsylvania Historical and Museum Commission (Harrisburg, 1966).

Axtell, James, "The White Indians of Colonial America," *William and Mary Quarterly* 32 (1975): 55-88.

Bellesiles, Michael A., *Arming America: The Origins of a National Gun Culture* (New York, 2000).

Boissonault, C. M., "Les Canadiens et la Revolte de Pontiac," *La Revue de l'Université de Laval* 2 (1948): 784-87.

Brasseaux, Carl A., and Michael J. Le Blanc, "Franco-Indian Diplomacy in the Mississippi Valley, 1754-1763: Prelude to Pontiac's Uprising?" *Journal de la Société des Américanists* 68 (1982): 59-71.

Brumwell, Stephen, *Redcoats: The British Soldier and War in the Americas, 1755-1763* (Cambridge, 2002).

Brumwell, Stephen, "'A Service Truly Critical': The British Army and Warfare with the North American Indians, 1755-1764," *War in History* 5 (April 1998): 146-75.

Calloway, Colin G., *The Scratch of a Penn: 1763 and the Transformation of North America (Pivotal Moments in American History* (New York, 2006).

Cappon, Lester, *Atlas of Early American History: The Revolutionary Era, 1760–1790* (Princeton, NJ, 1976).

Cave, Alfred, "The Delaware Prophet, Neolin: A Reappraisal," *Ethnohistory* 46 (1999): 265–90.

Cort, Cyrus, *Colonel Henry Bouquet and His Campaigns of 1763 and 1764* (Lancaster, PA, 1883).

Cuneo, John R., *Robert Rogers of the Rangers* (New York, 1959).

Daudelin, Don, "Numbers and Tactics at Bushy Run," *Western Pennsylvania Historical Magazine* 68 (1985): 153–79.

Desrosiers, Leo-Paul, *Iroquois*, 4 vols. (Sillery, PQ, 1998–1999).

Diedrich, Marck, *Ojibwa Chiefs: Portraits of Anishinaabe Leadership* (Rochester, MN, 1999).

Dixon, David, *Never Come to Peace Again: Pontiac's Uprising and the Fate of the British Empire in North America* (Norman, OK, 2005).

Dowd, Gregory Evans, "The French King Wakes Up: Pontiac's War in Rumour and History," *Ethnohistory* 37 (1990): 254–78.

Dowd, Gregory Evans, *A Spirited Resistance: The North American Indian Struggle for Unity, 1745–1815* (Baltimore, 1992).

Dowd, Gregory Evans, *War under Heaven: Pontiac, the Indian Nations, and the British Empire* (Baltimore, 2002).

Dunn, Walter S., *Frontier Profit and Loss: The British Army and the Fur Traders, 1760–1764* (Westport, CT, 1998).

Dunnigan, Brian, *Siege, 1759: The Campaign against Niagara* (Youngstown, N.Y., 1996).

Dunnigan, Brian Leigh, *Frontier Metropolis: Picturing Early Detroit, 1701–1838* (Detroit, 2001).

Eccles, W. J., *The French in North America, 1500–1783* (East Lansing, MI, 1998).

Eid, Leroy V., "'A Kind of Running Fight': Indian Battlefield Tactics in the Late Eighteenth Century," *Western Pennsylvania History Magazine* 71 (1988): 147–71.

Fenn, Elizabeth, "Biological Warfare in Eighteenth Century North America: Beyond Jeffery Amherst," *Journal of American History* 86 (200): 1552–80.

Fenton, William N., *The Great Law and the Longhouse: A Political History of the Iroquois Confederacy* (Norman, OK, 1998).

Ferling, J. E., *A Wilderness of Miseries: War and Warriors in Early America* (Westport, CT, 1980).

Flexner, James Thomas, *Mohawk Baronet: A Biography of Sir William Johnson* (New York, 1959).

Fregault, Guy, *Canada: The War of the Conquest* (Toronto, 1969).

Garraty, John A, and Carnes, Mark C., eds., *American National Biography*, 24 vols (New York, 1999)

Gipson, Lawrence Henry, *History of the British Empire before the American Revolution*, 15 vols. (New York, 1936–1970).

Godfrey, William G., *John Bradstreet's Quest: The Pursuit of Profit and Preferment in Colonial North America* (Waterloo, ON, 1982).

Hale, Nathaniel C., *Pontiac's War: The Great Indian Uprising against the English in 1763* (Wynnewood, PA, 1973).

Hamilton, Milton W., "Myths and Legends of Sir William Johnson," *New York History* 34 (1953): 15.

Hamilton, Milton W., *Sir William Johnson, Colonial American, 1715–1763* (Port Washington, NY, 1976).

Harburn, Todd E., "A Most Unfortunate Officer: Lieutenant John Jamet of the 60th Royal American Regiment," *Michigan History* 72 (1988): 44–48.

Harburn, Todd E., *In Defence of the Red Ensign at Michilimackinac, 1763* (Okemos, MI, 2000).

Heckewelder, John, *History, Manners, and Customs of the Indian Nations Who Once Inhabited Pennsylvania* (Philadelphia, 1819).

Hinderaker, Eric, *Elusive Empires: Constructing Colonialism in the Ohio Valley, 1673–1800* (Cambridge, 1997).

Houlding, J. A., *Fit for Service: The Training of the British Army, 1715–1795* (Oxford, 1971).

Hunter, Charles E., "The Delaware Nativist Revival of the Mid-Eighteenth Century," *Ethnohistory* 18 (1971): 39–49.

Jacobs, Wilbur R., *Dispossessing the American Indian: Indians and Whites on the Colonial Frontier* (New York, 1972).

Jacobs, Wilbur R., *The Fatal Confrontation: Historical Studies of American Indians, Environment and Historians* (Albuquerque, 1996).

Jacobs, Wilbur R., *The Paxton Riots and the Frontier Theory* (Chicago, 1967).

Jacobs, Wilbur R., *Wilderness Politics and Indian Gifts: The Northern Colonial Frontier, 1748–1763* (Lincoln, NE, 1950).

Jennings, Francis, *The Ambiguous Iroquois Empire: The Covenant Chain of Indian Tribes with English Colonies from Its Beginnings to the Lancaster Treaty of 1744* (New York, 1984).

Jennings, Francis, *Empire of Fortune: Crowns, Colonies and Tribes in the Seven Years War in America* (New York, 1988).

Jennings, Francis, "Francis Parkman: A Brahmin among Untouchables," *William and Mary Quarterly* 42 (1985): 305–28.

Kellogg, Louise Phelps, *The British Regime in Wisconsin and the North West* (Madison, 1935).

Kellogg, Louise Phelps, *The French Regime in Wisconsin and the North West* (Madison, 1925).

Kelsey, Harry, "The Amherst Plan: A Factor in the Pontiac Uprising," *Ontario History* 65 (1973): 149–58.

Kelsey, Isobel Thompson, *Joseph Brant, 1743–1807: Man of Two Worlds* (Syracuse, NY, 1984).

Knollenburg, Bernard, "General Amherst and Germ Warfare," *Mississippi Valley Historical Review* 41 (1954): 489–94. See also Donald Kent's rejoinder, 762–63.

Knollenburg, Bernard, *Origin of the American Revolution, 1759–1766* (New York, 1960).

Leach, Douglas Edward, *Arms for Empire: A Military History of the British Colonies in North America, 1607–1763* (New York, 1973).

Long, J. C., *Lord Jeffery Amherst: A Soldier of the King* (New York, 1933).

Malone, Dumas, ed., *Dictionary of American Biography*, 20 vols (New York, 1935)

Mancall, Peter C., *Deadly Medicine: Indians and Alcohol in Early America* (Ithaca, NY, 1995).

Mante, Thomas, *The History of the Late War in North America and the Islands of the West Indies: Including the Campaigns of MDCCLXIII and MDCCLXIV* (London, 1772).

Marshall, Peter, "Colonial Protest and Imperial Retrenchment: Indian Policy, 1764–68," *Journal of American Studies* 5 (1971): 1–17.

McConnell, Michael N., *A Country Between: The Upper Ohio and Its Peoples, 1724–1774* (Lincoln, NE, 1992).

McDonnell, Michael A., "Charles-Michel Mouet de Langlade: Warrior, Soldier, and Intercultural 'Window' on the Sixty Years' War for the Great Lakes," in *The Sixty Years War for the Great Lakes, 1754–1814*, edited by David Curtis Skaggs and Larry L. Nelson (East Lansing, MI, 2001), 79–103.

McLeod, D. Peter, *The Canadian Iroquois and the Seven Years' War* (Toronto, 1996).

McLeod, D. Peter, "Microbes and Muskets: Smallpox and the Participation of the Amerindian Allies of New France in the Seven Years' War," *Ethnohistory* 39 (1992): 42–64.

Merrell, James H., *Into the American Woods: Negotiators on the Pennsylvania Frontier* (New York, 1999).

Merrell, James H., "'I desire all that I have said…may be taken down aright': Revisiting Teedyuscung's 1756 Treaty Council Speeches," *William and Mary Quarterly* 53 (2006): 777-826

Merritt, Jane T., *At the Crossroads: Indians and Empires on a Mid-Atlantic Frontier, 1700–1763* (Chapel Hill, NC, 2003).

Middleton, Richard, *The Bells of Victory: The Pitt Newcastle Administration and the Conduct of the Seven Years War, 1757–1762* (Cambridge, 1985).

Middleton, Richard, *Colonial America: A History, 1563–1776* (Cambridge, 2002).

Middleton, Richard, "Pontiac: Local Warrior or Pan-Indian-Leader?" *Michigan Historical Review* 32 (2006): 1–32.

Mullin, Michael J., "Sir William Johnson's Reliance on the Six Nations at the Conclusion of the Anglo-Indian War of 1763–1765," *American Indian Culture and Research* 17 (1993): 69–90.

Nammack, Georgiana C., *Fraud, Politics, and the Dispossession of the Indians: The Iroquois Land Frontier in the Colonial Period* (Norman, OK, 1969).

Nester, William R., *The First Global War: Britain, France and the Fate of North America, 1756–1775* (Westport, CT, 2000).

Nester, William R., *"Haughty Conquerors": Amherst and the Great Indian Uprising of 1763* (Westport, CT, 2000).

Pargellis, Stanley M., "Braddock's Defeat," *American Historical Review* 41 (1936): 253–69.

Parkman, Francis, *The Conspiracy of Pontiac and the Indian War after the Conquest of Canada* (Boston, 1851; reprint, Lincoln, NE, 1994).

Parmenter, Jon William, "Pontiac's War: Forging New Links in the Anglo-Iroquois Covenant Chain, 1758–1766," *Ethnohistory* 44 (1997): 614–54.

Parmenter, Jon, "After the Mourning Wars: The Iroquois as Allies in Colonial North American Campaigns, 1676–1760," *William and Mary Quarterly* 54 (2007): 39–82.

Peckham, Howard H., *Pontiac and the Indian Uprising* (Princeton, NJ, 1947; reprint, Detroit, 1994).

Peckham, Howard H., ed., "Lieutenant Jehu Hay's Diary, 1763," in *Narratives of Colonial America, 1704–1765* (Chicago, 1971).

Porlier, Louis B., "The Capture of Mackinaw, 1763: A Menomonee Tradition," in *Report and Collections of the State Historical Society of Wisconsin*, vol. 8 (Madison, 1876), 227–29.

Quaife, Milo Milton, ed., *Alexander Henry's Travels and Adventures in the Years 1760–1776* (Chicago, 1921).

Richter, Daniel K., *The Ordeal of the Longhouse: The Peoples of the Iroquois League in the Era of European Colonization* (Chapel Hill, NC, 1992).

Richter, Daniel K., "War and Culture: The Iroquois Experience," *William and Mary Quarterly* 40 (1983): 209–22.

Richter, Daniel K., "Whose Indian History?" *William and Mary Quarterly* 50 (1993): 379–93.

Richter, Daniel K., and James H. Merrell, eds., *Beyond the Covenant Chain: The Iroquois and Their Neighbors in Indian North America, 1600–1800* (Syracuse, NY, 1987).

Riddell, William R., "The Last Indian Council of the French at Detroit," *Proceedings and Transactions of the Royal Society of Canada*, third series, 25 (1931): 165–68.

Rogers, Robert, *A Concise Account of North America* (London, 1765; reprint, Ann Arbor, MI, 1966).

Russell, Peter E., "Redcoats in the Wilderness: British Officers and Irregular Warfare in Europe and America, 1740–1760," *William and Mary Quarterly* 35 (1978): 629–52.

Sawaya, Jean-Pierre, ed., *La Fédération des Sept Feux de la vallée du Saint-Laurent, XVIIe au XIXe siècle* (Quebec, 1998).

Severance, Frank H., *An Old Frontier of France: The Niagara Region and Adjacent Lakes under French Control*, 2 vols. (New York, 1917).

Severance, Frank H., "The Story of Joncaire: His Life and Times on the Niagara," *Buffalo Historical Society Publications* 9 (Buffalo, 1906): 83–219.

Shy, John, *Toward Lexington: The Role of the British Army in the Coming of the American Revolution* (Princeton, NJ, 1965).

Sipe, C. Hale, *Fort Ligonier and Its Times: A History of the First English Fort West of the Allegheny Mountains* (Harrisburg, PA, 1932).

Sipe, C. Hale, *The Indian Chiefs of Pennsylvania* (Butler, Pa., 1927; reprint, Lewisburg, PA, 1994).

Sipe, C. Hale, *The Indian Wars of Pennsylvania* (Harrisburg, Pa., 1929; reprint, Bowie, MD, 2000).

Skaggs, David Curtis, and Larry L. Nelson, eds., *The Sixty Years War for the Great Lakes, 1754–1814* (East Lansing, MI, 2001).

Sosin, Jack M., *Whitehall and the Wilderness: The Middle West in British Colonial Policy, 1760–1775* (Lincoln, NE, 1961).

Stagg, Jack, *Anglo-Indian Relations to 1763 and an Analysis of the Royal Proclamation of 7 October 1763* (Ottawa, 1981).

Starkey, Armstrong, *European–Native American Warfare, 1675–1815* (London, 1998).

Steele, Ian K., *Betrayals: Fort William Henry and the "Massacre"* (New York, 1990).

Steele, Ian K., *Warpaths: Invasions of North America* (Oxford, 1994).

Stotz, Charles Morse, *Outposts of the War for Empire: The French and English in Western Pennsylvania: Their Armies, Their Forts, Their People, 1749–1764* (Pittsburgh, PA, 1985).

Tanner, Helen Hornbeck, *The Settling of North America: The Atlas of Great Migrations* (New York, 1995).

Tanner, Helen Hornbeck, Adele Hast, and Jacqueline Peterson, *Atlas of Great Lakes Indian History* (Norman, OK, 1986).

Tassé, Joseph, "Memoir of Charles Langlade," *Collections of the State Historical Society of Wisconsin* 7 (Madison, 1876): 123–87.

Thompson, Charles, *An Enquiry into the Causes of Alienation of the Delaware and Shawnee Indians from the British Interest, and into the Measures Taken for Recovering Their Friendship* (1759; reprint, St. Clair Shores, MI, 1970).

Titus, J., *The Old Dominion at War: Society, Politics and Warfare in Late Colonial Virginia* (Columbia, SC, 1991).

Trigger, Bruce, *Natives and Newcomers: Canada's "Heroic Age" Reconsidered* (Montreal, 1985).

Trigger, Bruce, ed., *The North East*, vol. 15 of *The Handbook of North American Indians* (Washington, D.C., 1978).

Waddell, Louis M., *The French and Indian War in Pennsylvania, 1753–1763: Fortification and Struggle during the War for Empire* (Harrisburg, PA, 1996).

Wainwright, Nicholas B., *George Croghan, Wilderness Diplomat* (Chapel Hill, NC, 1959).

Wallace, Anthony F. C., *The Death and Rebirth of the Seneca* (New York, 1969).

Wallace, Anthony F. C., *Teedyuscung, King of the Delawares* (Syracuse, NY, 1990).

Wallace, Paul A., *Indians in Pennsylvania* (Harrisburg, PA, 1961).

Ward, Mathew C., *Breaking the Backcountry: The Seven Years War in Virginia and Pennsylvania, 1754–1765* (Pittsburgh, PA, 2003).

Ward, Mathew C., "'Fighting the Old Women'; Indian Strategy in the Virginia and Pennsylvania Frontier, 1754–1758," *Virginia Magazine of History and Biography* 102 (1995): 297–320.

Ward, Mathew C., "The Microbes of War: The British Army and Epidemic Disease among the Ohio Indians, 1758–1765," in *The Sixty Years War for the Great Lakes, 1754–1814*, edited by David Curtis Skaggs and Larry L. Nelson (East Lansing, MI, 2001), 63–78.

Westlager, C. A., *The Delaware Indians: A History* (New Brunswick, NJ, 1972).

White, Richard, *The Middle Ground: Indians, Empires, and Republics in the Great Lakes Region, 1650–1815* (Cambridge, 1991).

Williams, Edward G., *Bouquet's March to the Ohio: The Forbes Road* (Pittsburgh, PA, 1975).

Index

DATE DUE

2/1/12			
8/3/15 ILL			

Demco, Inc. 38-293